THE RÓM F

C000141803

*birds* of
ONTARIO

JANICE M. HUGHES

RÓM

M&S

First published in 2001 by the Royal Ontario Museum and McClelland & Stewart Ltd.

Project Director: Glen Ellis
Senior Consultants: Dr. Ross James (ROM), Mark Peck (ROM), Dr. James Rising (University of Toronto)
Editors: Andrea Gallagher, Alexander Schultz, Donna Williams
Designer (Interior): Virginia Morin
Designer (Cover): Tara Winterhalt
Production Managers: Victoria Black, Krystyna Ross
Photo Researchers: Dora Nudelman, Pamela Vega

Author's dedication: For Ron and Eliana

**National Library of Canada Cataloguing in Publication**

Hughes, Janice Maryan
  The ROM field guide to birds of Ontario

Includes bibliographical references and index.
ISBN 0-7710-7650-9

1. Birds – Ontario – Identification.
I. Royal Ontario Museum.    II. Title.

QL685.5.O5H83 2001      598'.09713      C2001-930237-1

The Royal Ontario Museum is an agency of the Ontario Ministry of Tourism, Culture, and Recreation.

Royal Ontario Museum
100 Queen's Park
Toronto, Ontario
M5S 2C6
www.rom.on.ca

McClelland & Stewart Ltd.
*The Canadian Publishers*
481 University Avenue
Toronto, Ontario
M5G 2E9
www.mcclelland.com

2  3  4  5    07  06  05  04  03

# CONTENTS

# BIRDS IN ONTARIO

The magic of birds—the haunting call of the loon across a woodland lake, the simple devotion of nesting cardinals, the miraculous global journeys of terns—inspired legendary ornithologist Roger Tory Peterson to assert that birds are the affirmation of life. For landbound creatures such as ourselves, they symbolize freedom. The whimsy of their songs has filled our souls with joy and wonder. Captivated by the beauty of their forms, we have celebrated their images in our art and icons through the ages.

Ontarians are fortunate to have such geographic and biological diversity within their political boundaries. More than a million square kilometres (386,000 square miles) in area, Ontario stretches from the St. Lawrence Lowlands in the east to the gateway of the prairie provinces in the west, a distance of 1600 kilometres (1000 miles), and approximately the same distance from the Carolinian forests of the southern counties to the northern tundra coastline.

Yet the extent of the province is insufficient to explain fully the birdlife that populates it. One of the joys of birding in Ontario is the sheer diversity of recorded species. Many birds associated with more southerly latitudes are visitors here—Glossy Ibis, Scissor-tailed Flycatcher, and Mississippi Kite among them. Another, the purple-and-indigo Little Blue Heron, ranges from Pelee Island to Ottawa, and as far north as Thunder Bay. Others still, such as King Rail, Prothonotary Warbler, and Yellow-breasted Chat, breed here.

This rich birding habitat is the result of several factors. Ontario is in effect blessed with two inland seas—one fresh (the Great Lakes), the other salt (Hudson and James bays). The moderating influence of the Great Lakes ensures a diverse population of wintering birds along the region's shorelines. An early spring is promised by the latitude that the lower peninsula shares with northern California. As warm weather settles into the southern counties, winter is just beginning to give way in the far north. Forests and bogs once again spring to life with the insect blooms that annually entice the northern breeders to leave their tropical winter homes. The season of long days and short nights passes quickly, however, and with the first hint of autumn, shorebirds, seabirds, and waterfowl gather in sheltered bays along the northern coastline. As they move south, they are joined by flushes of migrants from lower latitudes. Some will linger in the relative warmth as they pass through southern Ontario; others will continue their journey to their wintering grounds.

Although we acclaim the biodiversity on our doorstep, we cannot allow ourselves to become complacent. Even now, our province has been so modified by its human inhabitants that many bird species cling tenuously to their ancestral breeding grounds. The twentieth century saw two, perhaps three, breeding species lost. We must remain sensitive, not only to the birdlife that surrounds us, but also to other species that share their habitats. They are inextricably connected to all of us. Our children must hear for themselves the dawn song of the Purple Martin, the flute of the Wood Thrush, the bugling call of the Trumpeter Swan, and know that these treasures will be here tomorrow.

# BIRD IDENTIFICATION

Bird identification presents many challenges, particularly to the novice. Closely related species frequently exhibit few superficial differences. Other species demonstrate numerous idiosyncrasies of plumage, distribution, and song. When presented with an identification dilemma, however, one must remember that birds are multi-faceted creatures. Although some species can be identified accurately by a single characteristic, many require the observer to diagnose the "essence" of the bird that results from the union of visual, auditory, and behavioural cues. Experienced birders often know intuitively the identity of a specie from a single glance or song phrase. This results from their holistic approach to bird identification. Presented below are several birding techniques that should be considered in combination when necessary.

## BIRDING BY SIGHT

### Size

Size can be a valuable clue when identifying birds, but estimating the dimensions of a bird without a point of reference can be difficult. Try committing to memory the visual size of a few well-known species, suc as American Robin, House Sparrow, Mallard, or Rock Dove. When an unfamiliar bird is observed, judge if it is "larger than a sparrow" or "smaller than a robin." In this way, a measurable size range can be assigned to the unknown species, which can be compared to the approximate sizes of candidate species in this field guide. With practice estimating the size of a bird at a distance will become more routine.

### Shape

Many birds have distinctively shaped wings, bills, and bodies, as well as necks, legs, and tails of differing lengths. Some avian families can be identified by profile alone. Cuckoos (Family *Cuculidae*) are slim and long-tailed; falcons (Family *Falconidae*) have pointed, swept-back wings. The stocky, short-tailed, black bird is a European Starling, not a Common Grackle. Even inexperienced birders will recognize the shape of an owl. Furthermore, within some bird groups, including shorebirds (Order *Charadriiformes*), shape characters in combination can be helpfu in identifying individual genera or species. For example, avocets (*Recurvirostra*) have long, upturned bills. Knowing the shapes of birds will direct you to the appropriate section of the field guide every time.

### Plumage

Many birders rely on plumage colour and pattern for bird identification. Fortunately, many birds have highly distinctive plumage. Northern Cardinal, American Robin, and Blue Jay are not easily confused with other species. Little brown birds can be more troublesome, although even these can usually be distinguished by less obvious differences, suc as wing bars, facial stripes, and tail-patches. Certain species groups, including *Empidonax* flycatchers and fall *Dendroica* warblers, are notoriously difficult to identify, and may even perplex some experts. When these species are encountered, it may be more rewarding to forgo the struggle and merely enjoy the experience.

Remember that any one species can display a number of different plumages based on season, age, gender, and geographic location. Know in advance what you should expect to see.

## Behaviour

Avian body language provides many clues to proper identification. Some species exhibit such distinctive locomotory or foraging behaviour that this alone may be sufficient to identify them. For example, a perch-diving Belted Kingfisher is unmistakable, even from a great distance.

When observing birds, note their style of flight. Is it fluttery, undulating, or direct? Are the wingbeats rapid or slow? If the bird glides between wingbeats, notice how the wings are held. Does the bird hop or run along the ground? Observe any wing-flicking or tail-pumping. These subtle behaviours can greatly assist in sorting out many little brown, green, or grey birds.

Feeding behaviour, both how and where it occurs, can also be highly informative. Is the bird feeding on the ground or in the canopy? Is it spiralling up or climbing down the tree trunk? Similarly plumaged migratory shorebirds can often be identified by observing how they peck, probe, or drill while foraging.

## BIRDING BY EAR

Many birds, including rails, cuckoos, nightjars, and wood-warblers, are heard more often than they are seen. In addition, there are times when failing light or great observational distances will prevent identification by sight. These circumstances provide opportunities for birding by ear. Learn the birds' calls and you will discover an entirely different dimension to bird observation.

Bird calls are typically transliterated by an onomatopoeic description—a series of words that sound like the call itself. They can be comical, such as the Olive-sided Flycatcher's *"Quick! Three beers!"* or utilitarian, like the *churr* of the Yellow-bellied Sapsucker. These descriptions permit the call to be represented in text and, consequently, more easily learned. Not everyone hears the same words in each bird's call. If any of the descriptions in this field guide fail to "sing," do not hesitate to invent your own. Frequently, personalized renditions are more easily committed to memory.

High-quality recordings of bird songs and calls are readily available on both tape and CD. Regional collections are particularly helpful.

## BIRDING BY HABITAT

Bird identification can often be simplified by knowing what species may occur in a particular location. While this is not always a straightforward process, one can often narrow the choices in a problematic identification by considering the habitat in which the bird was observed. For example, a small, brown songbird with a conical bill, streaked back, and reddish feathering on its head, throat, and breast could be a Purple Finch or a House Finch. If observed in a coniferous forest, it is likely a Purple Finch. House Finches are found more typically in towns and agricultural areas. Remember, however, that a few general categories, such as wetlands, mixed forest, or lakes, cannot fully describe the many components that comprise a species' habitat preferences. Furthermore, some species' preferences may change from one geographic region to another or between seasons. Birding by habitat is just another tool to assist in correct identification. Listed below are general descriptions of several Ontario habitats.

### Carolinian Forest

The Carolinian Forest stretches from southwest Huron County, in Ontario's southern peninsula, east along the north shore of Lake Ontario to Kingston. This primarily deciduous habitat is an extension of the broad-leaved forest type that occurs in the eastern United States. Maples, beeches, oaks, and basswood dominate the forest canopy. Black walnut, sassafras, and tulip trees are typical. Unfortunately, the Carolinian Forest has been heavily modified by human activities and only a few isolated tracts remain. The region's southerly latitude, however, and its proximity to the moderating effects of the lower Great Lakes produce relatively mild winters, early springs, and hot summers. Hence, it supports many bird species that rarely occur elsewhere in the province, such as Red-bellied Woodpecker, Carolina Wren, and Hooded Warbler. In addition, the peninsula's shape has a funnel-like effect on weary migrants, granting the north shore of Lake Erie some of the best birding sites in Canada.

### Great Lakes—St. Lawrence Forest

Most Ontarians are familiar with the maples, oaks, birches, and pines of the Great Lakes–St. Lawrence Forest. Spanning the province in two distinct sections from Timiskaming to Wawa and from Thunder Bay to Kenora, this mixed forest is predominantly deciduous in the south but yields to spruce and other conifers in more northerly areas. Agricultural development and deforestation have reduced much of the continuous tract of forest into small, isolated woodlots. This has had a devastating impact on forest birds, such as Wood Thrush and Cerulean Warbler, which once thrived in the virgin landscape.

## Boreal Forest

The Boreal Forest, the largest forested area in Ontario, occurs north of the Great Lakes–St. Lawrence Forest and spans 1200 kilometres (720 miles) from Lake Abitibi west to the Manitoba border. This is the land of 400,000 lakes. The deciduous trees here are aspen and birch, and the coniferous stands are dominated by spruce. The Boreal Forest is the summer home of many thrushes, sparrows, and wood-warblers that pass through southern Ontario during migration. It is also permanent home to many boreal specialists, including Spruce Grouse, Three-toed and Black-backed woodpeckers, Gray Jay, and Boreal Chickadee. Natural regeneration following the harvesting of northern forests has reduced the prevalence of spruce and pine in favour of deciduous species. This has caused the replacement of many boreal birds by other species, such as Alder Flycatcher, Red-eyed Vireo, and White-throated Sparrow, which prefer successional habitats.

## Hudson Bay Lowland Forest

Typified by flat topography, fens and bogs, black spruce and tamarack, the Hudson Bay Lowland Forest and its breeding birds are not well known. Primarily accessible only by air, this extensive forest region traverses northern Ontario between the Boreal Forest and Tundra zones. Poorly drained habitats attract many wetland and waterfowl species, while the denser forests of spruce, aspen, and birch that line riverbanks favour birds found typically in more southern forests. Greater Yellowlegs, American Bittern, and Northern Harrier are relatively common in the Hudson Bay Lowland Forest region, but adventurous birders often travel here in search of the rare Sandhill Crane.

## Tundra

A thin strip of tundra stretches along Hudson Bay to northwestern James Bay. Contrary to popular thought, tundra is not a barren wasteland underlain by continuous permafrost. This hauntingly beautiful habitat includes lichen- and heath-covered uplands, grassy fens, ponds, lakes, and beaches. Furthermore, the landscape is dotted with dwarf willows and birches, and patches of stunted spruce. Many bird species thrive in these surroundings, particularly during the summer's brief respite from ice and snow. Tundra breeders include Pacific Loon, Snow Goose, Greater Scaup, Willow Ptarmigan, Semipalmated Sandpiper, American Pipit, American Tree Sparrow, and Lapland Longspur.

## Wetlands

Wetland habitats are rich in bird life. Typical marshlands of cattails and open shallow water are summer home to many diverse species, including Pied-billed Grebe, Virginia Rail, Marsh Wren, Swamp Sparrow, and Red-winged Blackbird. Alder and willow trees, which often surround the marsh, provide hunting perches for Northern Harrier and Belted

Kingfisher. In addition, wetlands are an ideal location to observe waterfowl and shorebirds during migration. Unfortunately, wetlands are frequently drained for agricultural, residential, or recreational development. Only a small fraction of Ontario's wetland habitat remains intact.

## Great Lakes

Ontario is endowed with some of the largest freshwater lakes in the world, with over 3800 kilometres (2280 miles) of shoreline within its borders. Nesting on beaches, rocky ledges, and offshore islands are colonies of cormorants, herons, gulls, and terns. For migrating landbirds these huge bodies of water often act as barriers, but for many species of waterfowl and shorebirds, the beaches, mudflats, and marshes surrounding the Great Lakes are important stopover points on their journey.

## Urban Areas

As Ontario's urban areas expanded, the avian species most sensitive to habitat disturbance disappeared. As a result, common downtown birds include three tolerant yet troublesome species introduced from the Old World—Rock Dove, House Sparrow, and European Starling. People who live or work in the downtown core, and who are able to overlook the prejudice sometimes attached to these urban denizens, may find something interesting happening outside their windows, particularly during breeding season. In addition, the parks, ravines, and harbours of Ontario cities often contain a wealth of avian diversity. Rarer species are occasionally observed in urban green spaces during migration.

## Suburban Areas

A well-treed suburb offers many of the qualities of open woodland—edge habitat, shrubby understorey, and open areas for feeding. Consequently, suburban areas are often inhabited by open woodland birds, including Mourning Dove, Brown-headed Cowbird, American Robin, Northern Cardinal, and American Goldfinch. During migration, mature suburbs provide a temporary refuge for many other species, particularly in areas adjacent to a water source or green space. In addition, backyard feeding stations often attract nomadic winter wanderers, such as Evening Grosbeak and Common Redpoll.

## Farmlands

When Ontario was first settled, much of the province was covered by forest. The subsequent conversion of a treed landscape to an agricultural patchwork caused considerable declines in forest-bird populations. Although barren to some species, pastures and meadows are a haven for open-country birds, such as American Kestrel, Killdeer, Upland Sandpiper, and Eastern Meadowlark, which once occupied fewer aturally occurring fields and grasslands. Agricultural land, however, offers its own form of succession as some farms become neglected, abandoned, then overgrown. These new second-growth forests are preferred by a third complement of bird species, including Chestnut-ided Warbler.

## BIRDING BY SEASON

### Spring Migration

Successful birding is often just a matter of timing. In the south, returning migrants are first observed in February, with the greatest influx occurring from late March to mid-May. The first arrivals may be more than a month later in the north; by late April, however, migration is well underway. Most landbird migration occurs at night, and major movements are often associated with warmer weather systems. During colder weather, migrants may extend their foraging stopovers. They are generally less selective in their habitat choice than during breeding season, and are often concentrated along shorelines, and in wet fields, groves, and sheltered backyards and ravines.

### Breeding Season

Early breeders, such as owls and some jays, may begin nesting in February or March. Most other species do not begin breeding until April or May in the south, and somewhat later in northern habitats. By late June, however, nesting activities are in progress all over the province. A few species, including crossbills and doves, may be in breeding condition throughout the year, but most others do not nest after August.

Providing nest boxes will entice some species to breed in your backyard. Usually only those species that typically nest in cavities, such as Black-capped Chickadee, Eastern Bluebird, and House Wren, will use a nest box. Cavity nesters are frequently very particular about the size, shape, and placement of their homes. Check your library or bookstore for the appropriate nest-box type and the species' habitat preferences in order to attract the birds of your choice.

### Fall Migration

Some species, particularly shorebirds and swallows, actually begin their fall migration in the second half of summer. By the end of August, many flycatchers, warblers, and thrushes are also moving southward. Nevertheless, fall migration peaks in September with major flights of hawks and falcons observed along the northern shorelines of the Great Lakes. October brings heavy movements of ducks and geese. Far fewer migrants can be observed in November, but among them are more northern breeders, such as American Tree Sparrow, Snow Bunting, winter finches, and some diving ducks. By early December, fall migration has dwindled to a few straggling hawks and waterfowl.

Remember that many migrating birds will already be sporting their winter plumages, and that flocks frequently contain young birds in immature plumage differing in appearance from the adults.

## Winter

Considerably fewer people watch birds in winter than at other times of the year, but bird identification in winter is often easier because there are far fewer resident species. Winter birds often forage nomadically in flocks of varying size. They tend to congregate in areas where there is an abundance of food and good sheltering spots, such as in coniferous trees. Consequently, many different kinds of birds can be attracted to feeders in winter. Some rarer species, such as Red-bellied Woodpecker and Tufted Titmouse, may be observed more frequently in winter because they visit feeders regularly.

Offer different styles of feeders and a variety of food types to attract the greatest number of species. In addition, a heated water source is irresistible to many birds. Consider landscaping with trees and shrubs that retain their berries or seeds after the leaves have fallen in autumn, such as mountain ash, dogwood, and cotoneaster. Contrary to popular myth, feeding birds does not create dependence on artificial food sources, nor does it cause them to forget their foraging skills. Most human-modified habitats, such as urban and suburban areas, are relatively impoverished landscapes. In some measure, feeding birds replaces resources that were available naturally in the habitat before human settlement. Libraries and bookstores can provide more information on feeding birds throughout the year.

# USING THIS BOOK

## THE SPECIES ACCOUNTS

Experienced birders know that even the most casual observer may see a bird that makes the record books. For this reason, this guide includes all 473 officially recorded Ontario birds according to the Ontario Bird Records Committee (OBRC). There are 347 full species accounts, each including size, plumage, vocalizations, behaviour, habitat preferences, and status descriptions. Very abundant to extremely rare species are included. Among these are 288 species that have bred in the province. Where plumages differ between genders, the breeding male is described first, the exception to this convention being the phalaropes, in which the breeding female's much more striking plumage takes precedence. In all cases, subsequent plumage and age classes (e.g., breeding female, immatures, juveniles) are in **bold text** to facilitate access. An arrow (▶) indicates information that can be used to distinguish the species from others of similar appearance. Abbreviated descriptions of accidental species—frequently single sightings, usually far outside their normal range—as well as extirpated and extinct species follow the full species accounts. Information about the photography appears on page 18.

## TAXONOMY

Biologists classify all living things into increasingly inclusive hierarchical ranks collectively called *taxa* (singular: *taxon*). The basic unit of classification is the *species*. Although the definition of "species" is a continual source of controversy among biologists, most will agree that members of a species breed with each other but rarely, if ever, breed with members of another species. Closely related species are combined in a *genus* (plural: *genera*). Most amateur birders are more familiar with common names for birds. Common names are unreliable, however, because they tend to change geographically and over time; for example, Yellow-billed and Black-billed cuckoos are often both called "Raincrow." To avoid such confusion, scientists assign all types of animals and plants a universal Latin name, with the genus listed first and the species second. This scientific name is always italicized or underlined, and only the genus is capitalized. Yellow-billed Cuckoo (*Coccyzus americanus*) and Black-billed Cuckoo (*Coccyzus erythropthalmus*) are two species in the same genus. Genera are grouped into *families,* and families, in turn, are grouped into *orders.* The level above "order" is *class.* There are about 27 orders in the class *Aves,* which includes all birds.

Unfortunately, taxonomy can be somewhat ephemeral. As new scientific evidence reveals more of the evolutionary relationships within and among bird species, both specific and generic names can change. Latin names in older publications may be considerably different from more recent sources. This field guide uses the classification of the *American Ornithologists' Union Check-list of North American Birds* (1998) and the 42nd Supplement to it (2000), the up-to-date authorities on the taxonomy and distribution of all birds recorded in North America.

Furthermore, the order of species accounts in this guide follows the sequence of the AOU *Check-list.* Although some guides choose to list their species accounts alphabetically or by habitat type, such an approach actually sacrifices valuable information. Standard taxonomic sequences are arranged with what is perceived as the most primitive species near the beginning following through to the most derived specie toward the end. Most ornithologists agree that loons (Order *Gaviiformes*) are among the more primitive avian orders and that songbirds (Order *Passeriformes*) are the most derived. In addition, many identification challenges involve one or more closely related species with similar plumage. In a guide that is organized taxonomically, such a this one, closely related species are likely to be on adjacent pages and can therefore be checked in rapid succession.

## STATUS

Bird species are ranked customarily according to their abundance or rarity. This categorization can assist the observer in cases of problematic identification. Common birds are usually, although not always, seen more often than rarer species. The following categories are used in this guide.

**abundant**—present in great numbers in a given area.

**very common**—present in large numbers, but less so than an abundant species.

**common**—usually present in a given area.

**uncommon**—seen infrequently in a given area, although larger number of individuals may be present in some local populations.

**rare**—present in very low density.

**very rare**—usually occurring only five to twenty times in the provinc in a given season; often susceptible to extirpation.

**extremely rare**—usually occurring five or fewer times in the province in a given season; particularly vulnerable to extirpation.

**casual**—not occurring annually, but demonstrating some pattern of occurrence over decades.

**accidental**—reported only a few times in the province; well out of their normal range.

**vagrant**—a bird that has strayed off its usual migratory route.

**irruptive**—erratic and sporadic in occurrence; may be common in a given area one year, but absent the next.

The Ontario Ministry of Natural Resources uses the following categories to rank the severity of imperilment of jeopardized bird species.

**vulnerable**—of special concern in Ontario but not yet threatened or endangered.

**threatened**—at risk of becoming endangered.

**endangered**—at risk of becoming extirpated or extinct.

**extirpated**— no longer existing in the wild in Ontario but occurring elsewhere.

**extinct**—no longer existing.

## DISTRIBUTION MAPS

Each full species account is accompanied by a colour distribution map, which represents the overall distribution of the species in Ontario in a typical year. The range maps have been prepared with utmost care; however, birds do not necessarily occur in the same area each year. Observers can therefore expect occasionally to see a bird outside its typical distribution, particularly during migration. Likewise, birds may not always be present in all areas indicated on the range map. Most species occur only in specific habitat types within their overall geographic distribution. Furthermore, bird ranges continually expand and contract according to environmental and habitat changes. Remember to use distribution maps as a tool. If you are convinced that you have seen a bird well outside its usual range, contact your local ornithological or naturalists' society for more information. Your observation may be of value to others.

Summer or breeding distribution

Winter distribution

Year-round distribution

Approximate distribution of stopover sites during migration

Approximate distribution of casual reports

Limit of non-breeding birds in summer

Limit of winter dispersal

? Possible breeding area

# FURTHER INFORMATION ON ONTARIO BIRD:

## BOOKS

American Ornithologists' Union. 1998. *The A.O.U. Check-list of North American Birds,* 7th ed. American Ornithologists' Union, Washington, D.C. (42nd Supplement—*Auk* 117:847–858).

Austen, M. J. W., M. D. Cadman, and R. D. James. 1994. *Ontario Birds at Risk: Status and Conservation Needs.* Federation of Ontario Naturalists, Don Mills, ON.

Cadman, M. D., P. F. J. Eagles, and F. M. Helleiner, eds. 1987. *Atlas of the Breeding Birds of Ontario.* University of Waterloo Press, Waterloo, ON.

Dunn, J. 1997. *Field Guide to the Warblers of North America.* Houghton Mifflin Company, Boston, MA.

Farrand, J., Jr., ed. 1983. *The National Audubon Society Master Guide to Birding,* 3 vols. Alfred A. Knopf, New York, NY.

Goodwin, C. E. 1995. *A Bird-Finding Guide to Ontario.* University of Toronto Press, Toronto, ON.

James, R. D. 1991. *An Annotated Checklist of the Birds of Ontario.* Royal Ontario Museum, Toronto, ON.

Kaufman, K. 1990. *A Field Guide to Advanced Birding.* Houghton Mifflin Company, Boston, MA.

National Geographic Society. 1999. *Field Guide to the Birds of North America.* National Geographical Society, Washington, D.C.

Peck, G. K., and R. D. James. 1983. *Breeding Birds of Ontario: Nidiology and Distribution,* vol. 1: *Nonpasserines.* Royal Ontario Museum, Toronto, ON.

Peck, G. K., and R. D. James. 1987. *Breeding Birds of Ontario: Nidiology and Distribution,* vol. 2: *Passerines.* Royal Ontario Museum, Toronto, ON.

Poole, A., and F. Gill, eds. 1992–2001. *The Birds of North America: Life Histories for the 21st Century.* The Birds of North America, Inc., Philadelphia, PA.

Pyle, P. 1997. *Identification Guide to North American Birds.* Slate Creek Press, Bolinas, CA.

Sibley, D. A. 2000. *The Sibley Guide to Birds.* Alfred A. Knopf, New York, NY.

Stokes, D. W. 1979. *A Guide to Bird Behavior,* vol. 1. Little, Brown and Company, Boston, MA.

Stokes, D. W., and L. Q. Stokes. 1983. *A Guide to Bird Behavior,* vol. 2. Little, Brown and Company, Boston, MA.

Stokes, D. W., and L. Q. Stokes. 1989. *A Guide to Bird Behavior,* vol. 3. Little, Brown and Company, Boston, MA.

Stokes, D. W., and L. Q. Stokes. 1996. *Field Guide to Birds: Eastern Region.* Little, Brown and Company, Boston, MA.

## INTERNET SOURCES

Many ornithological and naturalist societies maintain Web sites and welcome new members at all levels of birding expertise. The list below provides access to many additional sites through links. Addresses are current at time of publication.

Bird Studies Canada
  http://www.bsc-eoc.org/

Canadian Wildlife Service
  http://www.on.ec.gc.ca/wildlife/

Federation of Ontario Naturalists
  http://www.ontarionature.org/

Hamilton Naturalists' Club
  http://www.freenet.hamilton.on.ca/link/hamnature/

Kingston Field Naturalists
  http://psyc.queensu.ca/~davids/kfn.html

Kitchener-Waterloo Field Naturalists
  http://www.sentex.net/~tntcomm/kwfn/

McIlwraith Field Naturalists
  http://info.london.on.ca/environment/mfn

Muskoka Field Naturalists
  http://www.geocities.com/RainForest/Vines/7334/

Norfolk Field Naturalists
  http://www.kwic.com/~nfn/

Ontario Field Ornithologists
  http://www.interlog.com/~ofo/home.html

Ottawa Field Naturalists
  http://www.achilles.net/ofnc

Pembroke Area Field Naturalists
  http://www.renc.igs.net/~cmichener/pafn.index.html

Penokean Hills Field Naturalists
  http://www.penokeanhills.ottawaweb.com/

Peterborough Field Naturalists
  http://www3.sympatico.ca/jbyoung/pfnhome.htm

Royal Ontario Museum
  http://www.rom.on.ca/biodiversity/cbcb/

Thunder Bay Field Naturalists
  http://tbfn.baynet.net/

Toronto Field Naturalists
  http://www.sources.com/tfn/

Woodstock Field Naturalists' Club
  http://www.execulink.com/~wfnc/

# SPECIES ACCOUNTS

**A Note About the Illustrations**

The photographs have been carefully selected to facilitate identification through characteristic plumage. Unless otherwise captioned, they depict the summer (breeding) male. There are exceptions. Female plumage is not always muted or drab, and some of the images reveal the female's equally or more bold and colourful patterning (e.g., phalaropes, Pileated Woodpecker, and Belted Kingfisher). In some species, the winter (non-breeding) bird is more likely to be observed in Ontario (e.g., Rock Ptarmigan, Purple Sandpiper, Mew Gull). In others (e.g., Ivory Gull), immatures may be more numerous and therefore more observable. In Ontario, the migrant Northern Gannet is almost always observed in flight and is represented thus. Birds often exhibit transitional plumage. The European Starling illustrated combines elaborately spotted winter plumage and a summer (yellow) bill. When observing in the field, always keep in mind that plumage may vary in colour depending on lighting conditions.

# GAVIIFORMES
## Loons

Loons are large swimming birds found only in the Northern Hemisphere. They are best distinguished from other waterbirds by their heavy, dagger-like bills and hunch-backed flight profiles. Their superlative diving ability is conferred by the placement of webbed feet far back on their bodies. This anatomical design makes them exceedingly awkward on land, however, and they generally come ashore only to nest. Three species of loons breed in Ontario; one species is accidental (Yellow-billed Loon, see p. 382).

# RED-THROATED LOON *Gavia stellata*

L 61.0–68.5 cm / 24–27" Wt 1.6–2.0 kg / 3.5–4.4 lb

Loons typically require a long stretch of open water for takeoff. However, the Red-throated Loon's ability to take flight quickly, with little effort from a standing position, allows it to choose smaller lakes and ponds for nest sites.

**APPEARANCE:** Breeding adults have grey head with black-and-white striped nape and hind-neck. Slender, slightly upturned, black bill. Brick-red throat-patch and eyes. Mantle dark brown flecked with white. Underparts white. **Winter adults** have greyish upperparts with extensive white spotting on back. Cheeks, sides of neck, and underparts whitish. Bill grey. **Immatures** resemble winter adults but browner with more extensive brown streaking on head. Throat may be tinged with red.

SUMMER

WINTER

► No contrasting white patches on upperparts as in other loons in breeding plumage. Pacific Loon has purplish patch on throat and white checkers on back. Common and Yellow-billed loons have dark head with white necklace. Pacific, Common, and Yellow-billed loons in winter plumage lack white speckling on back. Immature Red-throated Loon distinguished by paler plumage overall, greyish brown on sides of neck, and thin, upturned bill.

**VOICE:** In flight utters Mallard-like *gah-gah-gah-gah*. Also gives various quacks, wails, and shrieks during breeding season.

**HABITAT AND BEHAVIOUR:** Small tundra lakes and ponds, and ocean. Larger lakes over winter. Flies with drooping neck. Wingbeats faster than other loons. Holds bill tilted slightly upward when swimming. Dives deeply to capture prey.

**STATUS:** Rare breeder. Rare migrant. Extremely rare winter resident.

# PACIFIC LOON *Gavia pacifica*
. 60–72 cm / 23.5–28.5" Wt 1.2–2.5 kg / 2.6–5.5 lb

The breeding distribution of the Pacific Loon in Ontario is limited to regions of tundra and muskeg north of the treeline. Its nests can be observed from a great distance across this open habitat.

**APPEARANCE:** Breeding adults have silver grey crown and nape. Eyes red. Black bill held horizontally. Black back checkered with white. Iridescent purple throat bordered by white stripes. Underparts white. Breast striped with black at sides. **Winter adults** grey above. Well-defined, whitish cheek and throat. Grey bill. Greyish brown chinstrap. Underparts white. **Immatures** resemble winter adults, but crown and nape may be slightly lighter than back, and chinstrap may be faint.

▶ Grey head and dark throat distinctive in breeding plumage. Common and Yellow-billed loons larger and lack sharp contrast between black and white on neck in winter plumage; pale collar may be present in winter; head and feet appear larger in flight. Red-throated Loon swims with bill tilted upward; back heavily spotted in winter plumage.

**VOICE:** Various quacking, growling, yelping, and croaking calls.

**HABITAT AND BEHAVIOUR:** Tundra lakes and ocean. Large freshwater lakes in migration. Breeding birds perform spectacular distraction display of splashing, diving, and yelping when disturbed at nest.

**STATUS:** Locally common breeder. Extremely rare spring and fall migrant.

# COMMON LOON *Gavia immer*

L 71–89 cm / 28–35" Wt 3–6 kg / 6.6–13.2 lb

Our provincial bird gives a yodelling cry reminiscent of northern wilderness. Central to Native Canadian mythology, in Chippewa legend the Common Loon is credited with creating the world.

**APPEARANCE:** Breeding adults have black head and neck. Eyes red. Heavy, black, dagger-like bill. Vertical white stripes on neck resemble necklace. Back, scapulars, and wing coverts checkered black and white. Wings black. Rump, sides, and flanks black with small white spots. Tail black. Breast, belly, and wing linings white. **Winter adults** and **immatures** blackish above and white below. Bill whitish with blue tinge. Pale collar may be present. Immatures have more prominent barring on back.

► Yellow-billed Loon distinguished in all plumages by uptilted, yellow bill; upperparts browner in winter. Breeding Red-throated Loon smaller with red throat, grey head, upturned bill, and less striking markings on back; winter plumage has more extensive white on face and neck. Pacific Loon in breeding plumage has pale grey crown and neck; distinguished in winter by small size, thin bill, and sharp vertical division between light and dark on neck.

**VOICE:** Loud, distinctive yodel that carries over long distances. Also utters short hoot and prolonged, wailing *oo-oo-oo* that resembles wolf howl.

**HABITAT AND BEHAVIOUR:** Lakes surrounded by forest and rocky shorelines. Flight strong with shallow, rapid wingbeats. Takes off from water only. Walks awkwardly on land. Floats low in water. Dives well; foot-propelled underwater swimming.

**STATUS:** Fairly common breeder. Common migrant. Rare winter resident.

# PODICIPEDIFORMES
## Grebes

Grebes are small to medium-sized diving birds with long, slender necks and short tails. In flight, their drooping necks and laboured wingbeats are diagnostic. Grebes rarely come on land; even their nests are usually floating or loosely attached platforms built with decaying vegetation. Incubating grebes use similar material to conceal their eggs when the nest is left unattended. Four grebe species breed in Ontario. One species occurs as an accidental (Western Grebe, see p. 382).

# ✓ PIED-BILLED GREBE *Podilymbus podiceps*

L 30.5–38.0 cm / 12–15" Wt 295–545 g / 10.5–19.5 oz

The Pied-billed Grebe dives when foraging or to escape predators. It alters buoyancy by expelling air from between its feathers or from air sacs in its body. This allows the bird to crash-dive, leap-dive, or merely sink out of sight.

**APPEARANCE:** Short, laterally compressed, bluish white bill has black ring during summer. Breeding adults have dark brownish upperparts; crown somewhat darker. Eyes brown with narrow, white eye-ring. Black throat-patch outlined with white. Breast yellowish brown with irregular dark spots. Sides of neck and flanks greyish buff. Wings and very short tail, dark brown. Belly and undertail coverts white. **Winter adults** somewhat warmer brown on sides of neck and flanks. Throat white. Lacks black ring on bill. **Juveniles** resemble winter adults but with variable dark brown and white striping on head and sides of neck.

► Other grebes have thinner, longer bills and white wing-patches visible in flight.

**VOICE:** Territorial call a long, cuckoo-like *kuk-kuk-cow-cow-cow-cowp-cowp-cowp* that accelerates toward the end. Submerges breast and neck while calling. Alarm call a single, short *kwah*. Also utters rapid, staccato *ek-ek-ek*.

**HABITAT AND BEHAVIOUR:** Ponds, lakes, and marshes. Flight strong but not manoeuvrable. Takes off from water with long running start. Usually escapes predators by diving. Swims with alternate strokes of feet. Awkward on land. Runs with head drawn back.

**STATUS:** Uncommon breeder. Fairly common migrant. Rare winter resident.

# HORNED GREBE *Podiceps auritus*

30.5–38.0 cm / 12–15" Wt 350–475 g / 12.5–17.0 oz

Horned Grebes nest on a floating mat of vegetation in shallow water. A small pond may be home to only a single breeding pair; however, larger wetlands can support several family groups.

**APPEARANCE:** Breeding adults have black head with golden ear tufts that do not extend below eye-line. Red eyes. Short, straight black bill. Hind-neck and back black. Foreneck, breast, and flanks rufous. Belly white. **Winter adults** have black crown, hind-neck, and back. Cheeks, throat, and underparts white. Whitish spot in front of eye. Large white patch on trailing edge of wing in all plumages. **Immatures** resemble winter adults but sides of head and throat striped with dull brown.

▶ Eared Grebe has upturned bill; neck black in breeding plumage; golden ear tufts extend below eye-line; wintering birds have greyish neck and cheeks. Red-necked Grebe has heavy, dagger-like, yellowish bill and dark eyes; breeding adults have prominent white cheeks and throat; no ear tufts; distinguished in winter by longer and heavier dusky white neck, yellow bill, and white chin extending to white crescent behind face.

**VOICE:** Loud croaking, trilling, and squeaking notes given on breeding grounds. Generally silent remainder of year.

**HABITAT AND BEHAVIOUR:** Wetlands, lakes, and ponds. Dives gracefully and quickly with closed wings. Infrequently walks on land. Carries young on back while swimming.

**STATUS:** Very rare breeder. Locally common migrant.

## RED-NECKED GREBE *Podiceps grisegena*

L 43–56 cm / 17–22" Wt 900–1500 g / 2.0–3.3 lb

Like other grebes, the Red-necked Grebe adopts a characteristic flight posture with its head and neck drooped low and feet trailing behind. The small, narrow wings must beat rapidly to keep the bird aloft.

**APPEARANCE:**
Breeding adults have black forehead, crown, nape, and back. Distinctive whitish cheeks and rusty red neck and breast. Eyes dark brown. Long, pointed, yellowish bill. Dark brownish black wings with prominent white patches, visible in flight, on leading and trailing edges. Belly pale grey. Sides and flanks

greyish. **Winter adults** have black cap, greyish ear coverts, and white throat-patch extending to crescent behind face. Whitish upper throat. Pale grey foreneck blending to darker grey hindneck. Breast dingy grey. Otherwise, resembles breeding plumage. **Immatures** resemble winter adults but dingier. White crescent on head faint or absent. Foreneck may be washed with pale chestnut. Eyes yellowish.
　　► Wintering Eared and Horned grebes smaller with red eyes and shorter bills. Horned and Western grebes have white forenecks. Loons much larger with proportionately shorter necks.

**VOICE:** Distinctive loud braying call uttered on breeding grounds. Also gives various wailing, squeaking, hissing, and honking calls. Generally silent in winter.

**HABITAT AND BEHAVIOUR:** Lakes and ponds. Flight weak. Rarely flies except during migration. Does not occur on land. Strong swimmer and diver.

**STATUS:** Rare to uncommon breeder. Common migrant. Rare winter resident.

# EARED GREBE *Podiceps nigricollis*

L 30–35 cm / 11.8–13.8" Wt 295–505 g / 10.5–18.0 oz

Like other members of its family, the Eared Grebe begins incubation with the first egg laid, which results in chicks hatching asynchronously. Consequently, parents take turns carrying young on their backs until the chicks are all old enough to swim and forage for themselves.

**APPEARANCE:** Breeding adults have black head, throat, neck, breast, and back. Blackish crest contrasts with bright red eyes and golden ear tufts. Sharp, slightly upturned, black bill. Wings brownish black with white speculum in all plumages. Sides, flanks, and rump chestnut. Belly white. **Winter adults** have blackish head, hindneck,

and mantle. Eyes red. Whitish patch behind ear. Chin, throat, belly, and rump white. Foreneck, sides, and flanks greyish. **Immatures** similar to winter adults except with brownish wash on back and neck. Eyes brownish orange. **First-year** bird somewhat darker with orangish red eyes.

▶ Horned Grebe in summer has reddish neck and breast; ear tufts more defined but do not extend below eye-line; prominent white cheeks, lores, throat, and breast in winter. Red-necked Grebe in winter much larger with longer neck, dark eyes, and dull yellow bill.

**VOICE:** Utters repeated *poo-eechk*. Female call higher pitched and shorter. Also gives various trilling, chittering, and soft whirring calls. Alarm a series of sharp *kowee* notes.

**HABITAT AND BEHAVIOUR:** Lakes and ponds. Flies with head and neck held low and feet trailing behind. Skitters across water when disturbed. Swims and dives well using alternating foot strokes.

**STATUS:** Extremely rare breeder. Rare migrant.

# PROCELLARIIFORMES
## Shearwaters, Petrels, and Storm-Petrels

Members of this order are collectively known as "tubenoses" because of their tube-like external nostrils and heavy, plated bills. Shearwaters and petrels (Procellariidae) are gull-like birds of the open sea that fly expertly with alternating rapid wingbeats and stiff-winged glides. Storm-petrels (Hydrobatidae) are small, blackish birds with long wings and short tails. They are almost swallow-like in flight as they flit about near the water's surface. The Northern Fulmar is the only procellariiform to occur with some regularity in Ontario. Six species are accidental (Black-capped Petrel, Greater Shearwater, Audubon's Shearwater, Wilson's Storm-Petrel, Leach's Storm-Petrel, and Band-rumped Storm-Petrel, see pp. 382–83).

# NORTHERN FULMAR *Fulmarus glacialis*

L 45–50 cm / 17.7–19.7"  Wt 505–800 g / 1.1–1.8 lb

This gull-like petrel has nostrils enclosed in a tube positioned atop a plated, hooked bill. Primarily a pelagic species, the Northern Fulmar is reported occasionally in northern Ontario.

**APPEARANCE:**
Thick, yellowish, "tube-nosed" bill. Thick neck, bulging forehead, and short tail. **Light morph** has white head and underparts. Dark patch in front of dark brown eyes. Mantle grey grading to black at tip of wings. Base of primaries whitish. Rump and tail

somewhat paler grey. **Dark morph** uniformly dark grey. Light wing-patch may be absent in some individuals. **Intermediate morph** may have grey head, white or grey breast, and dark upperparts. Adults and **immatures** inseparable.

▶ Plumage gull-like at a distance, but gulls have longer necks and slimmer bills that lack nostril tubes. Gulls more agile in flight. Shearwaters more slender with thinner bills and narrower wings.

**VOICE:** Cackling or braying *aaark aaww-aaark-aaww-aaark.* Also hoarse, grunting *ek-ek-ek-ek-ek.*

**HABITAT AND BEHAVIOUR:** Open ocean. Breeds colonially on cliffs. Flight stiff-winged alternating with glides usually close to water's surface. Highly buoyant swimmer. Rarely dives. Shuffling gait on land.

**STATUS:** Very rare fall and winter visitor along Hudson's Bay.

## PELECANIFORMES
### Pelicans and Allies

This diverse panglobal order comprises six avian families that share the "totipalmate" foot, in which all four toes are connected by webs. Pelecaniforms occur in coastal or marine habitats, and are adapted for catching and eating fish by plunge-diving, dipping, or pursuing under water. Many species have long bills and leathery throat pouches that may be large, like that of the American White Pelican, or small, like that of the Double-crested Cormorant. Seven species representing five pelecaniform families occur in Ontario. Four species are accidental (Brown Pelican, Great Cormorant, Anhinga, and Magnificent Frigatebird, see pp. 382–83).

# NORTHERN GANNET *Morus bassanus*
89–98 cm / 35.0–38.5" Wt 2.5–3.5 kg / 5.5–7.7 lb

The Northern Gannet is a rare visitor to southern Ontario. Dark-plumaged juvenile birds are most commonly observed, particularly along Lake Ontario in late fall.

**APPEARANCE:** Adults white with broad, black wing tips. Yellowish wash on head. Yellowish eyes surrounded with black. Long, stout, grey bill. Black legs and feet. **Juveniles** dark grey to black with pale speckling above and grey below. **First-year** birds have increasingly paler head and underparts. Mantle and upper wings begin to lighten during second year. **Third-year** birds resemble adults but with dark tail and secondaries. Young birds in transition may appear splotchy.

ADULT

► Distinguished from gulls by much larger size, longer neck and bill, and pointed tail. In flight, appears pointed at both ends.

IMMATURE

**VOICE:** Utters low, barking *arrah* at nesting colony.

**HABITAT AND BEHAVIOUR:** Offshore. Breeds on cliffs. Plunge-dives for prey headfirst with spear-like bill pointed toward surface of water from heights of 30 m (100'). Dives to depths of 12–15 m (39–49'). Bill and wings used extensively in elaborate agonistic and courtship displays.

**STATUS:** Rare fall and winter visitor in Great Lakes.

31

# AMERICAN WHITE PELICAN F
*Pelecanus erythrorhynchos*
L 127–165 cm / 50–65" Wt 5.5–12.0 kg / 12.1–26.4 lb

The White Pelican is gregarious in all seasons. This species frequently forages cooperatively by herding fish into shallow water where they are more easily caught. Flocks form long lines or V-formations in flight that rise and fall with a wave-like effect.

**APPEARANCE:** Large, predominantly white bird with 3-m (9.5') wingspan. Primaries and secondary feathers black. Long, heavy, yellowish orange bill has large gular pouch that becomes greatly distended when full. Bill develops raised orange "fin" on upper mandible during breeding season. **Immatures** similar but with somewhat duskier plumage and grey bill.

▶ Distinguished from other large white aquatic birds, such as swans, geese, and egrets, by very long, yellowish orange bill with gular pouch.

**VOICE:** Usually silent except for frequent, low grunts.

**HABITAT AND BEHAVIOUR:** Remote islands in freshwater lakes. Flight graceful, with alternate flapping and gliding. May fly close to water, or soar on thermal updrafts on sunny days. Head retracted in flight like herons. Swims buoyantly. Feeds by submerging neck and scooping up fish in bill. Unlike Brown Pelican, never plunge-dives from the wing for food.

**STATUS:** Rare to locally common breeder. Endangered in Ontario through human violation of nesting colonies.

# DOUBLE-CRESTED CORMORANT ✓
*Phalacrocorax auritus*

70–90 cm / 27.5–35.4" Wt 1.2–2.5 kg / 2.6–5.5 lb

Low buoyancy and wettable plumage allows the Double-crested Cormorant to remain submerged for up to 70 seconds at depths of 8–12 m (26–39'). Cormorants dry their feathers by standing on an open perch and facing into the wind with their wings outstretched.

**APPEARANCE:** Black with iridescent green and purple above. Gular pouch orange. Indistinct, blackish crests above eye present during courtship. Hooked bill black. Eyes bluish green in spring. Gape bright blue in breeding birds. **Juveniles** brownish above with variable amounts of white on foreneck, breast, and sides. Gular pouch and

lower mandible yellow. Eyes brown. **First-year** birds intermediate between juvenile and adult.

▶ Gangly, long-necked, and long-tailed profile distinctive in all plumages. Accidental Great Cormorant larger with white on chin and sides of face; also white on crown, nape, neck, and flanks in spring and summer; immatures blackish brown above with light brown throat and breast and white belly.

**VOICE:** Usually silent. Utters few guttural grunts before takeoff, *t-t-t-t,* and in flight, *urg-urg-urg.* Male gives *ok-ok-ok-ok* and *arr-r-r-r-t-t* during courtship. Threat call repeated *eh-hr.*

**HABITAT AND BEHAVIOUR:** Lakes. Flies with regular wingbeats usually close to water surface. Flocks may fly in shallow Vs. Stands with neck in S-shape and bill tilted upward. Awkward on land. Swims readily on surface. Dives with leaping entry. Foot-propelled under water.

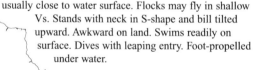

**STATUS:** Uncommon to locally common breeder. Very rare winter resident.

33

# CICONIIFORMES
## Herons, Ibises, Storks, and Vultures

The order Ciconiiformes comprises primarily long-necked, long-legged wading birds found in a variety of wetland habitats. Although structurally similar, they can be categorized by bill shape and flight profile. Herons, bitterns, and egrets (Ardeidae) have spear-like bills. In flight, they fold their necks into an S-shape. In contrast, ibises (Threskiornithidae) have slender decurved bills and hold their necks extended when flying. Ontario has only a single species of stork (Ciconiidae). The Wood Stork has a heavy, decurved bill and flies (like ibises) with neck outstretched. The exception among ciconiiforms are the vultures (Cathartidae), recent additions to the order based on DNA evidence. These large, black scavengers are best known for their soaring ability. Seventeen ciconiiform species occur in Ontario, including nine breeding birds and three accidentals (White Ibis, White-faced Ibis, and Wood Stork, see pp. 383–84).

# AMERICAN BITTERN *Botaurus lentiginosus*
60–85 cm / 24.0–33.5" Wt 365–505 g / 13–18 oz

When disturbed, this generally shy and retiring heron assumes a reed-like stance with its bill and neck pointed upward. It may even sway in unison with the cattails when a breeze blows through the surrounding vegetation.

**APPEARANCE:** Upperparts brown, finely specked with black. White stripe above eye. Long, black patch extends down side of neck from below eye. Throat white. Underparts buffy and heavily streaked with brown and white. Dark brown wing ends contrast sharply with paler body plumage. Iris yellow. Bill broad at base; dull yellow, but blackish on top. Legs yellow or green. **Juveniles** lack black neck stripe.
   ▶ Juvenile night-herons have darker, less contrasting, mottled plumage and paler wing ends; they lack black neck-patch and are less hurried in flight.

**VOICE:** Most frequent sound a loud *pump-er-lunk* that can be heard for 1 km (0.6 mile) or more.

**HABITAT AND BEHAVIOUR:** Wetlands with cattails, sedges, bogs, alder or willow thickets, and pastures. Most active early in morning and in evening. Flight hurried and stiff; beats wings rapidly when taking off. Neck usually retracted. Walks along ground deliberately, lifting feet slowly, toes outspread. Runs quickly with wings folded in pursuit of prey. Unlike other herons, bitterns rarely perch in trees.

**STATUS:** Rare to fairly common breeder.

# LEAST BITTERN *Ixobrychus exilis*

L 28–35 cm / 11–14" Wt 70–85 g / 2.5–3.0 oz

The Least Bittern is the smallest member of the heron family. It seldom flies, but prefers to clamber secretively through reeds and marsh grasses.

**APPEARANCE:** Male has black crown and back. Back of neck and wings chestnut. Wings have large, conspicuous, pale buff patches. Underparts buff. Thin, yellow bill. Legs green on front, yellow behind. **Female** similar to male, but with chestnut crown and back. Neck and chest streaked with dark brown. **Juveniles** paler and browner than female.

▶ Distinguished from American Bittern and other herons by bright, contrasting plumage and small size. Very rare Cory's Least Bittern much darker with chestnut, not buff, plumage.

**VOICE:** Series of three to five soft, low coos that resemble call of Black-billed Cuckoo: *coo-coo-coo.* Most frequently heard at dawn, sometimes at night. Call often only indication of presence. Also utters *gack-gack* from nest. Alarm call a loud, shrieking *quoh.*

**HABITAT AND BEHAVIOUR:** Freshwater marshes; also marshy areas or ditches, creeks, rivers, and lakes. Flies weakly with legs dangling when flushed. Prefers to move deliberately through vegetation by grasping stalks with toes. If threatened, may "freeze" with bill pointed upward and eyes directed forward.

**STATUS:** Rare to uncommon breeder. Vulnerable in Canada because of destruction and pollution of wetland habitat.

# GREAT BLUE HERON *Ardea herodias*

110–130 cm / 43–51" Wt 2.0–2.5 kg / 4.4–5.5 lb

The Great Blue Heron is most frequently observed standing motionless in shallow water waiting for small fish and amphibians to move into striking range. The heron catches prey in its bill with a rapid forward thrust of its neck and head.

**APPEARANCE:** Very large. Head white with wide, black stripe above eye extending to nape, and black plumes projecting back. Neck grey, streaked with white and black ventrally. Elongated grey feathers at base of neck and on back. Body bluish grey with black sides and rusty thighs that are usually obscured by folded wings. Flight feathers darker grey. Long, dagger-like, yellow bill. **Immatures** similar but paler with black crown and no plumes.

► Distinguished from other herons by large size. Sandhill Crane more uniformly grey with shorter, dark bill; flies with neck fully extended.

**VOICE:** Usually silent. Occasionally utters deep, harsh, croaking *rawnk*. Also gives *go-go-go* clucks that are answered by other herons in vicinity. Male makes loud bill snap as part of courtship display.

**HABITAT AND BEHAVIOUR:** Wet and dry woodlands near water, sparsely treed islands, marshes, riverbanks, and ponds. Flies with deep, slow wingbeats, neck retracted into S-shape, and legs extended well beyond tail. Walks erect with long strides, toes spread as foot placed on ground. Wades in water, often up to belly. Perches in trees.

**STATUS:** Common breeder.

# GREAT EGRET *Ardea alba*

L 94–104 cm / 37.0–40.5" Wt 800–950 g / 1.8–2.1 lb

This stately, white wading bird usually breeds colonially in groups of five to thirty-five nests. However, there are several reports of isolated Great Egret pairs nesting within Great Blue Heron colonies.

**APPEARANCE:** Large, long-necked, white heron with orangish yellow bill and black legs and feet. Greenish bare skin at lores. Long, lacy white plumes on throat and rump. **Winter adults** and **immatures** have yellowish lores and bill, and lack long plumes.

▶ Snowy Egret smaller with black bill and yellow feet. Much smaller Cattle Egret has yellowish to reddish legs and buffy plumes on crown, back, and foreneck during breeding season. Immature Little Blue Heron smaller with bluish bill and dull greenish legs. Extremely rare accidental Whooping Crane larger with red chin and crown, black mask, and black primaries.

**VOICE:** Utters hoarse croak. Also gives loud, low-pitched *cuk cuk cuk*

**HABITAT AND BEHAVIOUR:** Marshes, riverbanks, and lakeshores. Flies with neck retracted and legs extending beyond tail. Feeds by stalking slowly in shallow water or standing motionless in forward-leaning posture, waiting for prey to reveal itself by movement. Extends neck and grabs prey with bill.

**STATUS:** Rare to locally common breeder. Rare wanderer.

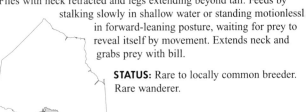

# SNOWY EGRET *Egretta thula* F

56–66 cm / 22–26" Wt 280–365 g / 10–13 oz

During the late 1880s, Snowy Egret breeding plumes were valued at $32 per ounce—twice the value of gold at that time—as decoration for women's hats. Uncontrolled hunting between 1880 and 1910 caused many local extirpations.

**APPEARANCE:** White in all plumages. Slender black bill. Yellow, unfeathered lores become red during breeding. Yellow eyes. Prominent white plumes on head, back, and breast during breeding season. Legs black. Feet bright yellow. **Immatures** resemble adults but have greenish yellow feet and full yellow stripe on back of legs. Base of lower mandible greyish.

▶ Great and Cattle Egrets have yellow bills. Breeding plumes of Cattle Egret buff, not white. Immature Little Blue Heron has dark lores, bluish dark-tipped bill, greenish yellow legs and feet, and dark primary tips.

**VOICE:** Rarely vocal except at breeding sites. Utters high-pitched *aargaarg* when flushed while foraging. Sometimes gives low-pitched *rg arg* during agonistic encounter. Male produces low, gurgling *wah-wahwah* during courtship.

**HABITAT AND BEHAVIOUR:** Marshes, swamps, and flooded fields. Flight buoyant with deep wingbeats. Glides only when landing. Walks upright with wings held close to body and neck slightly arched. Forages frantically for small fish and crustaceans by running, hopping, paddling with feet, hovering, and wing-flicking.

**STATUS:** Extremely rare breeder. Rare wanderer.

# LITTLE BLUE HERON *Egretta caerulea*

L 56–74 cm / 22–29" Wt 310–370 g / 11.1–13.2 oz

Like other herons, the Little Blue Heron stalks its prey silently and methodically while wading in shallow water. It is most readily observed foraging in early morning and late afternoon.

**APPEARANCE:** Breeding adults have reddish purple head and neck. Grey bill with black tip. Grey lores. Slate-blue to indigo back, wings, and underparts. Black legs and feet. **Non-breeding adults** have dark purple head and neck, and dull green legs. **Immatures** white with blue-grey lores; dusky, tipped primaries; and yellowish olive feet and legs. Individuals moulting from immature to adult plumage are spotted with blue and white.

▶ Tricolored Heron distinguished by dark greyish blue head and hind-neck, and contrasting white foreneck, rump, and belly. Great Blue Heron much larger with whitish head, paler grey back, and long, yellow bill. Immature Snowy Egret distinguished from immature Little Blue Heron by yellow lores, entirely dark bill, bright yellow feet, and lack of dusky primary tips. Adult Snowy Egret has black legs and bright yellow feet. Cattle Egret has short, yellow bill.

**VOICE:** Males give repeated harsh *arrh arrh arrh* during breeding season. Adults give strident croak or rough *gerr gerr gerr gerger* when disturbed.

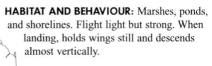

**HABITAT AND BEHAVIOUR:** Marshes, ponds, and shorelines. Flight light but strong. When landing, holds wings still and descends almost vertically.

**STATUS:** Rare to occasional visitor March to December.

# TRICOLORED HERON *Egretta tricolor* F

61-71 cm / 24-28" Wt 320-420 g / 11.4-15.0 oz

The Tricolored Heron, formerly known as the Louisiana Heron, breeds primarily along the Atlantic coast south of New Jersey. Most individuals winter in Mexico and Central America; however, some stragglers have been observed inland on the Great Lakes.

**APPEARANCE:** Breeding adults slate-grey above with brownish grey plumes on back and rump. White plumes on crown. Male has purple eyes during courtship; red in female. Bill turquoise with black tip. White stripe extends from bill to breast. Neck and breast have purplish plumes. Underparts white. Legs pinkish. **Non-breeding adults** similar but somewhat duller. Head plumes purplish. Eyes pinkish brown. Neck plumes shorter. Legs greyish yellow. Head and neck of **immatures** chestnut and white. Mantle brownish olive washed with chestnut. Lower back, rump, and underparts white. Tail dark grey. Chestnut streaking on breast.

► Distinguished from other herons by predominantly dark upper-parts contrasting with white underparts. Great Blue Heron much larger with pale head and neck. Green Heron and night-herons differ in plumage and generally assume hunched posture.

**VOICE:** Noisy species with limited repertoire. Utters aggressive *aaah* and groaning *culh-culh*. Male snaps mandibles.

**HABITAT AND BEHAVIOUR:** Marshes, swamps, and shores. Flies with head retracted and steady wingbeats. Flocks rarely fly in formation. Walks and runs well, but forages slowly.

**STATUS:** Rare spring to fall visitor.

# CATTLE EGRET *Bubulcus ibis*

L 48.5–53.5 cm / 19–21" Wt 295–450 g / 10.5–16.1 oz

The Cattle Egret is a recent immigrant from the Old World, being first recorded in South America in the 1880s. However, its unprecedented northward range expansion brought breeding birds to Florida by 1953 and Ontario by 1968.

**APPEARANCE:**
Breeding adults white with orangish buff plumes on crown, breast, and lower back. Short, stout bill. Eyes, bill, and legs turn bright red at peak of breeding cycle. Lores purplish pink. **Non-breeding adults** entirely white. Bill, lores, and eyes yellow. Yellowish green legs. **Immatures** resemble non-breeding adults but sometimes have greenish to black legs.

▶ Buffy plumes diagnostic. Snowy Egret has long black bill and white plumes. Great Egret much larger with longer bill, neck, and legs. Immature Little Blue Heron has bluish bill and olive-green legs.

**VOICE:** Most common call loud, high-pitched *rick-rack.* Threat call a harsh *raa* or drawn-out *kraah.* Male gives muffled *thonk.* Both sexes utter variable chattering calls.

**HABITAT AND BEHAVIOUR:** Farms, marshes, parks, roadsides, and garbage dumps. Wingbeats shallow and rapid. Neck retracted during flight. Walks with swaying, goose-like gait. Typically seen in grassy fields foraging among livestock.

**STATUS:** Rare breeder. Rare wanderer.

# GREEN HERON *Butorides virescens* ✓ +F

41–46 cm / 16–18" Wt 210–240 g / 7.5–8.5 oz

The Green Heron frequently baits for fish with a variety of lures, including crusts of bread, feathers, and earthworms freshly dug for this purpose. Capture rate is highest using live bait, and less experienced juvenile birds rarely achieve the success of adults.

**APPEARANCE:**
Head, neck, and breast rich maroon. Glossy greenish black cap with shaggy greenish black erectile crest. Bill blackish above, yellowish green below. Whitish malar stripe bordered above by blackish streak. Back covered with

greyish plumes with greenish sheen. Wings and tail greenish black, faintly edged in buff. White streak down throat to grey underparts. Legs orangish yellow. **Female** similar, but somewhat duller and lighter. **Immatures** browner, with indistinctly spotted upperparts and heavily streaked underparts. Wing coverts have buffy edging. Bill orange with dark tip. Legs yellowish green.

▶ Little Blue Heron larger, lacks orangish yellow legs and rich maroon on foreparts. American Bittern also larger with browner plumage and prominent black neck stripes. Much smaller Least Bittern best distinguished by large, buff wing-patches.

**VOICE:** Loud, repeated *skouwp* given in flight and during alarm. Gives less emphatic *keeyou* at night or in flight. Other calls include hostile *raaah-raaah* and rapid *ku-ku-ku-ku-ku-ku*.

**HABITAT AND BEHAVIOUR:** Woodland pools and swampy thickets. Flies with slow, steady wingbeats, usually with head retracted and legs extended beyond body. Scans for prey from crouched position on overhanging branches or in shallow water.

**STATUS:** Rare to locally common breeder.

√ 2 immature

# BLACK-CROWNED NIGHT-HERON ✓f
## Nycticorax nycticorax
L 58–66 cm / 22.8–26.0" Wt 840–1000 g / 1.9–2.2 lb

As its name suggests, this stocky, short-legged heron is most active at night. When perched in a tree or standing on a rocky shore, the Black-crowned Night-Heron has a characteristic hunched posture.

**APPEARANCE:** Glossy greenish black cap, scapulars, and upper back. Long white plumes on back of head. Stout black bill. Eyes red. Wings, tail, and rump grey. Underparts white to pale grey. Legs yellowish green except pinkish when breeding. **Juveniles** dark greyish brown profusely spotted with whitish buff on upperparts. Chin and throat whitish; otherwise, underparts heavily streaked with whitish buff and brown. Eyes yellowish orange. Bill black with yellow sides. **First-year** birds predominantly brown but with obvious darker upperparts and lighter underparts as in adults.

► Juveniles confused with American Bittern, which has blackish wings and lacks whitish spots on upperparts. Adult Yellow-crowned Night-Heron grey with bold white and black facial markings; juvenile greyer with finer pale spotting on upperparts, and black bill. Feet and lower legs project beyond tail in flight.

**VOICE:** Gives loud *kwawk* most frequently at dusk or night and when flushed from roost. Guttural *oc-oc-goc!* given at nest.

**HABITAT AND BEHAVIOUR:** Marshes and shores. Flies with deep wingbeats on arched wings. Holds neck curled and toes extended beyond tail. Walks slowly and deliberately with neck lowered when foraging. Roosts in trees.

**STATUS:** Locally common breeder

# YELLOW-CROWNED NIGHT-HERON F
*Nyctanassa violacea*
55–70 cm / 21.6–27.6" Wt 600–800 g / 1.3–1.8 lb

This small, stocky heron is somewhat more active during the day than the Black-crowned Night-Heron. Unlike its congener, the Yellow-crowned Night-Heron may nest close to human habitation.

**APPEARANCE:** Head glossy black with white crown and cheek-patch. Whitish crown plumes. Yellowish forehead. Eyes red. Neck and body bluish grey. Feathers of back and wing coverts have black centres with grey edges. Similarly coloured scapular plumes extend beyond tail. Legs yellowish green; pink to scarlet during courtship. **Juveniles** slate-brown with fine, buffy spots on mantle, back, and wing coverts. Eyes yellowish orange. Underparts whitish with brown streaks.

► Black-crowned Night-Heron has black crown on white head, black back, and whitish underparts. Juvenile Black-crowned Night-Heron has longer legs, larger spots on browner upperparts, and somewhat heavier streaking below. In flight, entire foot of Yellow-crowned Night-Heron extends beyond tail.

**VOICE:** Loud *kwawk* heard throughout day and night; somewhat higher pitched than that of Black-crowned Night-Heron. Utters guttural, aggressive *ahhh ahhh*. Other calls include *whoop, huh,* and *yup yup*. Also claps bill.

**HABITAT AND BEHAVIOUR:** Marshes, streams, and forest wetlands. Flies with head retracted. Wingbeats slower than those of Black-crowned Night-Heron. Walks slowly and deliberately with head fully or partially retracted while foraging. Otherwise, walks erect like day herons. Rarely goes into deep water.

**STATUS:** Rare visitor from April to October.

## GLOSSY IBIS *Plegadis falcinellus*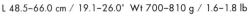

L 48.5–66.0 cm / 19.1–26.0" Wt 700–810 g / 1.6–1.8 lb

From a distance, the Glossy Ibis looks like a cross between a large, dark curlew and a heron. The Glossy Ibis and White-faced Ibis were once considered the same species.

**APPEARANCE:**
Breeding adults rich chestnut with metallic purple gloss on head, neck, shoulders, and underparts. Greyish facial skin narrowly bordered above and below with white. Brown eyes. Crown, back, wings, and tail iridescent green. Legs greyish brown.

**Winter adults** have brown-and-white streaked head an neck, and dark green body. Face greyish and bordered below by fine blue line. **Immatures** resemble winter adults.

▶ Accidental White-faced Ibis very similar; distinguished in breeding plumage by conspicuous white border around maroon facial skin and red eyes; legs reddish; non-breeding adults separated best by eye colour. Immature Glossy and White-faced ibises nearly identical. Curlews much smaller and paler.

**VOICE:** Utters repeated guttural *ka-onk* and low *kruk kruk.*

**HABITAT AND BEHAVIOUR:** Marshes and swamps. Flies with rapid, almost duck-like, wingbeats. Alternates flapping with long glides. Neck and legs held extended but somewhat drooped.

**STATUS:** Rare visitor April to October.

# BLACK VULTURE *Coragyps atratus* F
58–68 cm / 23–27" Wt 1.6–2.2 kg / 3.5–4.8 lb

Unlike the Turkey Vulture, the Black Vulture lacks an acute sense of smell. However, it exploits Turkey Vultures' food-procuring abilities by following them in their search for food and then aggressively displacing them from the carcass.

**APPEARANCE:** Entirely black except for whitish underside of primaries, which are visible in flight. Unfeathered, wrinkled head dark grey. Bill greyish. Tail short and square. In flight, grey legs extend beyond tail. **Immatures** resemble adults.
► Turkey Vulture larger with reddish head and feet, and longer wings and tail; feet much shorter than tail when in flight; lacks white wing-patch. Immature Turkey Vulture has grey head but has longer tail and lacks white wing patch. In flight, Golden Eagle has much longer wings with dark primaries, and longer, broader tail.

**VOICE:** Lacks syrinx and associated musculature. Vocalizations limited to grunting *guff guff guff,* drawn-out hiss, and "yapping" sound. Wings produce whistle during sharp descents.

**HABITAT AND BEHAVIOUR:** Open areas. Laboured, flapping flight used mainly between roosting sites. Usually soars while foraging. Soars in tight circles with wings held horizontally, not V-shaped like Turkey Vulture. Also does not wobble in flight like Turkey Vulture. Runs and hops on ground, sometimes with wings held half open.

**STATUS:** Rare but increasingly frequent visitor, usually from May to October.

# TURKEY VULTURE *Cathartes aura* ⚥

L 65–80 cm / 26–32" Wt 1.8–2.0 kg / 4.0–4.4 lb

Studies have demonstrated that the Turkey Vulture locates its food by smell. Natural gas companies have exploited this keen olfactory sense by introducing an attractive odorant into pipelines and identifying leaks by monitoring the locations of vultures circling overhead.

**APPEARANCE:** Plumage entirely blackish brown. Underside of flight feathers, which appear silver grey in flight, contrast with black underwing coverts. Small, unfeathered head; bare skin red. Short, weakly hooked, whitish bill with perforate nares. Legs dull orange. **Immatures** similar to adults, but bare skin on head greyish; bill black.

► Black Vulture stouter with shorter wings and tail; black head somewhat larger than that of Turkey Vulture; white patches at base of primaries visible in flight; Black Vultures fly closer together, and with rapid, shallow wingbeats. Eagles have larger, feathered heads with strongly hooked bills; fly with wings held horizontally.

**VOICE:** Inability to produce bird-like sounds due to lack of syrinx and associated muscles. Gives low-pitched nasal whine in flight. Also utters short, low, guttural hisses.

**HABITAT AND BEHAVIOUR:** Nests in caves, cliffs, and hardwood forests. Forages over mixed farmland, open woodland, and swamps. Flapping flight deep and laborious. Soars singly or in loose groups. Holds wings in a shallow dihedral with outer primaries separated. Tilts side to side in flight.

**STATUS:** Common breeder.

# ANSERIFORMES
## Ducks, Geese, and Swans

The order Anseriformes includes typical waterfowl, characterized generally by webbed feet, boat-shaped bodies, and variably flattened bills. The breeding plumage of male and female ducks can differ substantially. However, after breeding, most male ducks moult rapidly into a dull eclipse-plumage phase in which they are often difficult to distinguish from females. In contrast, goose and swan species differ little between the genders and across the seasons. Most anseriform species are highly migratory. Some fly in diagnostic "V" or line formations. Forty-three waterfowl species have been recorded in Ontario. Thirty-one species breed in the province. Five species are accidental (Black-bellied Whistling-Duck, Fulvous Whistling-Duck, Garganey, Tufted Duck, and Smew, see p. 384).

# GREATER WHITE-FRONTED GOOSE
*Anser albifrons*

L 66.0–86.5 cm / 26–34" Wt 2.4–2.8 kg / 5.3–6.2 lb

The Greater White-fronted Goose makes long migrations from Alaska and the Canadian Arctic south across the boreal forest to the American Great Plains. Although they occur with other goose species, they tend to maintain family groups rather than disperse within the large flock.

**APPEARANCE:** Generally greyish brown with variable blackish bars on lower breast and belly. Pink bill surrounded by prominent white patch. Rump and undertail coverts white. Legs and feet orange. Some individuals more greyish or brownish than others. **Immatures** similar but lack white bill patch and dark bars on belly. Upperparts somewhat darker than underparts.
► Immature blue-phase Snow Goose distinguished by dark bill

and feet, and pale bluish grey wing coverts best seen in flight.

**VOICE:** High-pitched, melodious, laughing call: *kah-lah-a-luk.* Alarm calls a loud mew or *gig-gog.* Also gives characteristic honk.

**HABITAT AND BEHAVIOUR:** Breeds on tundra meadows and bogs. Wetlands, lakes, ponds, and agricultural areas during migration and winter. Flies in single or multiple lines and V-formation. Slip-slides to lose altitude before landing. Rises quickly from water or land. Strong walker and runner. Lies prone after short run. Goslings freeze in presence of predator.

**STATUS:** Rare spring and fall visitor. Extremely rare summer and winter visitor.

# SNOW GOOSE *Chen caerulescens*
71–84 cm / 28–33" Wt 3.0–4.5 kg / 6.5–10.0 lb

Snow Geese occur in both white and "blue" colour morphs in Ontario. In addition, their facial plumage is frequently stained rusty red from feeding on vegetation in iron-rich water.

**APPEARANCE: White-morph adults** white with black wing tips. Pink bill has blackish "grinning" patch. Legs and feet pink. **Immatures** sooty grey on crown, hindneck, and mantle. Black wing tips. Underparts whitish. Greyish bill, legs, and feet. **Blue-morph adults** have white head and upper neck. Body dark bluish grey with whitish tail coverts and varying amounts of white on belly. Wings pearl grey with black primaries. **Immatures** brownish grey, somewhat lighter below. White chin spot. Wing coverts grey. Bill, feet, and legs grey.

► Ross's Goose smaller with shorter bill and neck; flies with faster wingbeats. Adult White-fronted Goose has dark head and neck; immatures have pinkish bill outlined with white and orange legs. Swans much larger with white wing tips.

**VOICE:** Very vocal. Loud, resonant, shrill *houk-houk* given in flight.

**HABITAT AND BEHAVIOUR:** Tundra ponds and lakes, and coastal marshes. Wetlands, lakes, and fields during migration. Migrating flocks fly in wavy, undulating lines. Often seen feeding on waste grain in agricultural fields en route to wintering grounds.

**STATUS:** Common breeder and locally common migrant. Rare winter resident.

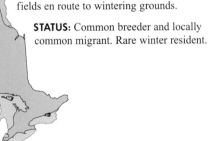

# ROSS'S GOOSE *Chen rossii*

L 58–63 cm / 22.8–24.8" Wt 1.0–1.7 kg / 2.2–3.7 lb

The Ross's Goose was first recorded breeding in Ontario in 1975. Identification of this rare species is made difficult by its similarity to the common Snow Goose and is compounded by the existence of hybrids.

**APPEARANCE:** Small white goose with short neck. Pink bill has bluish grey caruncles near base. Black primaries. Feet and legs pink. **Immatures** like adults, but may have pale grey wash on head, back, and flanks. Extremely rare **blue morph** has bluish grey body and white face and belly.

▶ Snow Goose is larger with longer bill that has dark "smile" patch on sides; usually lacks reddish ferrous stain observed on foreparts of some Snow Geese. Immature Snow Goose darker grey.

**VOICE:** High-pitched squawk given on breeding grounds. Flight calls repeated *keek keek keek* or grunting *hawh hawh*. Female utters low, soft *kuk-kuk-kuk* to goslings. Calls higher pitched and less melodious than those of Snow Goose.

**HABITAT AND BEHAVIOUR:** Low arctic tundra. Powerful, rapid wingbeats. Flight highly manoeuvrable; resembles twisting and turning of shorebirds. Rises rapidly from water surface. On rare occasions, dives to escape predators.

**STATUS:** Rare breeder. Rare to uncommon spring and fall migrant.

# CANADA GOOSE *Branta canadensis* ✓

58–109 cm / 22.8–43.0" Wt 2.3–7.5 kg / 5.0–16.5 lb

The Canada Goose was extirpated from the Great Lakes during the early years of human settlement. However, a highly successful reintroduction program in the mid-twentieth century established a large feral breeding population throughout southern Ontario. Unlike northern populations, southern geese are largely non-migratory.

**APPEARANCE:**
Head and neck black with large, white cheek-patch that extends from throat to behind eye. Back and wings dark greyish brown. Breast and sides pale grey, darkening toward flanks. Belly and undertail coverts white. Broad white chevron across base  of black tail visible in flight. Bill black. **Female** and **immatures** similar. Considerable variation in size and coloration possible. Birds breeding in southern Ontario are among largest. Some migrants much smaller with darker breasts and shorter necks. Others have white ring around base of neck.

▶ Brant has black upper breast and lacks white chinstrap. Greater White-fronted Goose has brown neck and head, white around base of bill, but lacks white chinstrap.

**VOICE:** Deep, musical *ka-ronk* uttered repeatedly during takeoff and in flight. Smaller migrants give higher-pitched *unc* note.

**HABITAT AND BEHAVIOUR:** Tundra and open muskeg in north; marshes, ponds, lakes, and large streams in the south. Commonly seen grazing in urban parks and golf courses. Noisy flocks travel in distinctive V-formation.

**STATUS:** Uncommon to locally common breeder. Common spring and fall migrant. Rare to common winter resident.

# BRANT *Branta bernicla*

L 55–65 cm / 22–26" Wt 1.2–1.6 kg / 2.6–3.5 lb

Although the Brant is known primarily as an Ontario migrant, there are a few isolated records of this small, stocky goose nesting in the province well south of its typical arctic breeding distribution.

**APPEARANCE:**
Head, neck, and upper breast black. Irregular white collar. Bill black. Otherwise, upper-parts brownish olive. Sides of rump and upper-tail coverts white, forming conspicuous V-shape visible from above. Tail black. Lower breast, belly, sides, and

flanks lighter brownish olive barred broadly with light grey. Undertail coverts white. **Immatures** have brownish head and neck with indistinct white collar. Mantle and wing feathers broadly tipped with white. Tail brownish grey with white tips on outer feathers.

▶ Canada Goose has white chin-patch, paler breast, and somewhat darker sides and flanks. Greater White-fronted Goose browner, particularly on head and neck; adults have conspicuous white patch surrounding base of pink bill; sides, flanks, and belly variably barred dark brownish grey.

**VOICE:** Guttural *cronk.* Utters *cut cut cut cronk* in flight. Alarm call short *cruk* or deep, growling *gurr.*

**HABITAT AND BEHAVIOUR:** Estuaries and tundra in summer. Open sea, lakes, and rivers during migration. Flight rapid. Takes flight in response to disturbance or predators. Walks while grazing. Upends to feed on sea grasses. Occasionally dives to avoid predators.

**STATUS:** Rare to locally common spring and fall migrant. Rare winter resident.

# MUTE SWAN *Cygnus olor*

L 130–150 cm / 51–59" Wt 8–11 kg / 17.6–24.2 lb

The beautiful Mute Swan that adorns our parks and ponds is native to Eurasia. However, fossils resembling this species have been found in several North American Pleistocene deposits.

**APPEARANCE:**

Adult plumage entirely white. However, head and neck may be stained green or reddish from foraging in algae-rich or iron-containing ponds. Bill reddish orange with black terminal nail and fleshy black knob at base. Knob larger in male. Bare, black skin on lores extends to eye. Legs and feet dark grey or pinkish. **Immatures** greyish brown, becoming whiter in second year. Bill bluish grey and lacks knob.

► Swimming posture diagnostic. Adults of both larger Trumpeter Swan and smaller Tundra Swan have black bills that lack knobs. Tundra Swan also has yellow lore spot; immatures have pinkish bills with black tips. Both species hold neck erect when swimming.

**VOICE:** Variable grunts, snorts, bugles, whistles, and hisses. Wings make rhythmic, swooshing sound in flight, audible to 2 km (1.2 miles).

**HABITAT AND BEHAVIOUR:** Urban parks, cattail marshes, and ponds. Flies low with head and neck outstretched. Wingbeats deep and powerful. Swims with long neck curved gracefully and head tipped down. Wings often raised and fluffed; tail elevated. Aggressively chases native waterfowl from wetlands.

**STATUS:** Introduced. Uncommon to common year-round resident.

# TRUMPETER SWAN *Cygnus buccinator*

L 149.5–183.0 cm / 58.5–72" Wt 10–12 kg / 22.0–26.4 lb

The Trumpeter Swan was extirpated from Ontario during the 1880s. However, since the 1980s, efforts to restore the species have had some success. Reintroduction programs typically use captive birds to foster Trumpeter cygnets to independence.

**APPEARANCE:** Large, entirely white swan. Head and neck may be stained from iron-rich waters in which it forages. Profile of head and bill long and flat. Black bill lacks yellow; lower mandible has reddish edge. Wide black area at base of bill appears to encompass eye rather than isolate it. Feet black. **Immatures** dusky with pinkish, black-tipped bill.
▶ Smaller Tundra Swan has yellow spot at base of bill, more rounded head, and shorter bill profile. Mute Swan has orange bill with prominent black knob at base.

**VOICE:** Typical call a series of loud, low-pitched trumpeting notes, *koo-koh,* with emphasis on second syllable. Also hisses and gurgles.

**HABITAT AND BEHAVIOUR:** Freshwater marshes, ponds, and lakes. Runs on surface of water while flapping during takeoff. Short-distance flights tend to be low. Walks awkwardly on land because of short legs and posterior centre of gravity. Older cygnets and moulting adults may dive and swim under water to escape predators.

**STATUS:** Rare reintroduced breeder. Rare migrant.

# UNDRA SWAN *Cygnus columbianus*
120–148 cm / 47–58" Wt 4–9 kg / 8.8–19.8 lb

Breeding Tundra Swans were extirpated from Ontario in the nineteenth century by overhunting. Recovery began following protective legislation in 1916, and this species has since established a limited breeding distribution near Hudson Bay.

**APPEARANCE:** White with black bill and black legs and feet. Small, oblong, yellow spot in front of eye diagnostic, but difficult to see at distance. Black base of bill ends just at front of eye. Crown and forehead have rounded profile. Head and neck held erect. **Immatures** have dusky plumage and pink bill with black tip.

► Trumpeter Swan larger and lacks yellow on bill; also, base of bill sufficiently broad to encompass eye; profile of crown and forehead long and flat. Mute Swan has orange bill with black knob. Snow and Ross's geese smaller, with pink bills and black on wings.

**VOICE:** Suggestive of Canada Goose, higher pitched and less harsh than Trumpeter Swan. Utters series of mellow notes, *hoo-ho-hoo,* in flight. Hisses associated with threat display in agonistic interactions.

**HABITAT AND BEHAVIOUR:** Tundra lakes and ponds in coastal areas. Migrates in V-formation, but may also form long strings on local flights. Takes off from land or water with running steps. Slides with feet forward when landing on water.

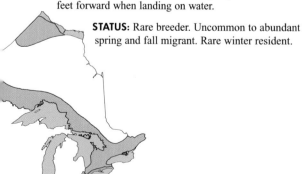

**STATUS:** Rare breeder. Uncommon to abundant spring and fall migrant. Rare winter resident.

## WOOD DUCK *Aix sponsa*

L 47–54 cm / 18.5–21.3" Wt 605–700 g / 1.3–1.6 lb

The Wood Duck is Canada's only perching duck. It occurs in swampy and wooded areas where it nests in natural cavities, old woodpecker holes, and artificial nest boxes.

♂        ♀

**APPEARANCE:** Breeding male has bold iridescent green, purple, and white facial pattern. Eyes red. Long green-and-purple crest has two white streaks. Red bill has yellow base and black tip. White throat and U-shaped cheek-patch. Neck and breast burgundy. Breast stippled with white and bordered at sides by black-and-white stripe. Wings and tail blackish with iridescent sheen. Flanks gold-bordered with pointed tawny and black feathers. **Female** much duller than breeding male. Grey crest and head with elliptical white eye-patch. Eyes dark brown. Bill grey. Chin and throat white. Upperparts olive-green with bronze to violet sheen. Breast and sides brownish with broad tan streaks. **Eclipse male** resembles female, but retains red eye and white pattern on side of face. Bill yellowish. **Immatures** resemble female but have streaked brown bellies. Immature male identified by U-shaped cheek-patch.
▶ Distinctive in all plumages.

**VOICE:** Female gives loud *oo-eek oo-eek.* Other calls include rapid, piercing *ter-wee* and *tetetetetet.* Male gives prolonged, whistling *jeeb* that rises in pitch, then ends abruptly. Also gives multi-syllabic *jib-jib-jib-jib.*

**HABITAT AND BEHAVIOUR:** Wooded swamplands, rivers, and ponds. Flies with fast wingbeats. Rapid takeoff from water. Manoeuvres well through dense vegetation. Walks quickly with more erect posture than dabbling ducks. Commonly perches and walks along branches, particularly when searching for nest sites.

**STATUS:** Uncommon to very common breeder.

# GADWALL *Anas strepera* ✓

48.5–56.0 cm / 19–22" Wt 725–1000 g / 1.6–2.2 lb

Breeding Gadwalls were first observed in Ontario during the 1950s. They have since become much more widespread, and may outnumber Mallards in some localized nesting areas.

**APPEARANCE:** Breeding male has mottled sandy brown head and neck. Bill dark grey. Body mottled grey with elongated, rusty scapulars. Wings greyish brown with chestnut patch mid-wing, and white speculum bordered on outside by black. Rump and uppertail coverts black. Tail greyish brown. Lower belly and undertail coverts whitish. Feet and legs yellowish orange. **Female** mottled brown, somewhat paler on face, neck, and underparts. Narrow orange bill has longitudinal, dark grey ridge and lateral grey spots. Belly whitish. Indistinct brownish eye-line. Wings brownish olive with greyish white speculum. Tail greyish brown edged in buff. **Eclipse male** and **immatures** similar to female. Immature male may have a few adult feathers on breast and back.

♂

♀

► Male distinguished by greyish body ending in black stern. In flight, white speculum is distinctive. Female resembles many other dabbling ducks. Best separated by characteristic bill coloration, white speculum, and steep forehead in profile.

**VOICE:** Male utters deep, reedy *raeb raeb*. Female quacks; higher pitched and more nasal than Mallard.

**HABITAT AND BEHAVIOUR:** Lakes, ponds, and marshes. Takes off vertically from water. Wingbeats somewhat faster than Mallard's. Runs and walks holding body horizontally. Seldom dives for food.

**STATUS:** Uncommon to common breeder. Rare to common winter resident.

48

# EURASIAN WIGEON *Anas penelope*

L 42–52 cm / 16.5–20.5" Wt 545–910 g / 1.2–2.0 lb

The Eurasian Wigeon is native to the northern palaeoarctic region. Although this species is not known to nest in Ontario, regular spring sightings suggest an isolated breeding population somewhere in the province.

♂

**APPEARANCE:** Bill greyish blue with black tip. Dusky wing linings in all plumages. Breeding male has russet red head with buff forehead and crown. Breast pinkish. Back and sides grey. Black stern. Dark wings have large white patch on wing coverts. Green speculum. White belly. **Female** warm brown with russet tinge to head and breast. Whitish wing-patch and dull green speculum. Belly white. **Eclipse male** resembles female but has more reddish head. **Immature** male similar to breeding male but duller and browner overall.

▶ Breeding male American Wigeon has greyish brown head with white crown and green, crescent-shaped patch behind eyes. Female American Wigeon distinguished by white wing linings and somewhat warmer brown plumage. Male Redhead has black breast and lacks pale crown-patch.

**VOICE:** Male gives shrill two-note whistle: *whee-oo.* Female utters low quack and purring notes.

**HABITAT AND BEHAVIOUR:** Wetlands, small lakes, and ponds. Dabbles for food. Walks well and often grazes on shore. Most often observed in mixed flocks with American Wigeons, Mallards, and Northern Pintails.

**STATUS:** Rare spring and fall migrant.

# AMERICAN WIGEON *Anas americana* F
47–58 cm / 18.5–22.8" Wt 755–1300 g / 1.7–2.9 lb

This duck is called the Baldpate because of its distinctive white crown. It is also distinguished from its congeners by several bill adaptations that facilitate grazing on emergent and agricultural plants.

**APPEARANCE:** Grey bill has black tip. Breeding male has white forehead and crown. Broad, green patch extends from eye to nape. Remainder of head and upper neck buffy white, heavily speckled with black. Back, breast, and sides pinkish brown. Wings greyish black with large white patch on forewing. Green speculum. Tail coverts black. Creamy head and upper neck of **female** speckled with brown. Back greyish brown barred with buff. Rump black edged with white. Wings and tail blackish brown. Forewing has poorly defined whitish patch. Speculum greenish black. Breast and sides brown. Belly white. **Eclipse male** similar but with white wing-patch and brighter sides and flanks. **Immatures** similar to female. Mainly white wing linings in all plumages.

♂

♀

► Eurasian Wigeons have dusky wing linings; male has russet head with buff crown; lacks green patch; female has browner head and neck. Female Gadwall has mottled orange bill and pale chin. Female Mallard has orange bill, blue speculum, and mottled brown belly.

**VOICE:** Male gives tri-syllabic, high-pitched whistle, *whew-whew-whew.* Also long, drawn-out *pheeooo pheeooo.* Female infrequently utters low quack.

**HABITAT AND BEHAVIOUR:** Shallow wetlands, sloughs, ponds, and small lakes. Flight rapid with deep wingbeats. Takes off from water surface. Spends much of its time on land.

**STATUS:** Rare to locally common breeder. Uncommon to abundant spring and fall migrant.

713 (sully 363)

# AMERICAN BLACK DUCK *Anas rubripes*

L 51.0–63.5 cm / 20–25" Wt 1.0–1.4 kg / 2.2–3.1 lb

The American Black Duck has been called the Black Mallard because it resembles the female of that species. These species often occur together in mixed flocks in which male Mallards may actively pursue unmated female Black Ducks. Hybrids are generally infertile.

**APPEARANCE:** Sooty brown with somewhat lighter head and neck. Purple speculum bordered with black. White wing linings contrast with dark underside plumage in flight. Feet and legs reddish (brighter in male). Male has yellow bill. **Female** has greenish bill mottled with black. **Immatures** similar but with olive-green bill.

▶ Male Mallard distinctive in breeding plumage. Female and eclipse-male Mallards lighter brown with pale belly and whitish tail. Speculum bordered with black and white. Gadwall has black stern and prominent black-and-white wing-patch. American Black Duck darker than other drakes in eclipse. Female Scoters have white on head and lack "puddle duck" bill shape.

♂

♀

**VOICE:** Talkative while feeding. Male utters weak, low croak. Female gives loud, resonant Mallard-like quack.

**HABITAT AND BEHAVIOUR:** Marshes, ponds, rivers, and lakes. Flight swift and high on quick wingbeats. Swims buoyantly; takes off rapidly from water. More wary and watchful than Mallard. Frequently feeds at night and rests in rafts well offshore during daylight.

**STATUS:** Uncommon to common breeder. Rare to locally common winter resident.

# MALLARD *Anas platyrhynchos* ✓+F

51–71 cm / 20–28" Wt 1.1–1.4 kg / 2.4–3.1 lb

The Mallard is the ancestor of most domestic duck varieties. Although today's barnyard ducks bear little resemblance to the elegant wild form, their genealogy is revealed by a trait most share with Mallard drakes —recurved tail feathers.

**APPEARANCE:** Breeding male has green head and neck. Thin white necklace. Yellowish bill. Chestnut breast. Back and underparts grey. Rump and tail coverts black. Recurved black central tail feathers; outer tail feathers white. **Female** mottled brown, somewhat lighter on face and belly. Dark eye-line. Bill dull orange spotted with black. Both sexes have dark blue speculum bordered by white and black, white wing linings, and orange legs and feet. **Eclipse male** and **immatures** resemble females but have dull olive bills.

♂

♀

► Male Northern Shoveler distinguished by long, spoon-shaped bill, white breast, and rufous sides and belly. Male Common and Red-breasted mergansers have red spike-like bill. American Black Duck resembles female Mallard but much darker brown with purplish speculum bordered by black. Other female dabbling ducks lack blue speculum bordered with white.

**VOICE:** Male gives low, reedy *kwek-kwek-kwek-kwek*. Female utters boisterous, loud *quack quack quack* like barnyard duck.

**HABITAT AND BEHAVIOUR:** Marshes, ponds, and lakes. Flight swift on quick wingbeats. Takes off from water with strong vertical spring. Forages by upending in shallow water.

**STATUS:** Common year-round resident near open water.

# BLUE-WINGED TEAL *Anas discors*

L 38.0–40.5 cm / 15–16" Wt 335–390 g / 12–14 oz

Blue-winged Teals fly quickly in small to moderate-sized flocks. When landing, they often circle the marsh or pond cautiously several times before finally settling on the water's surface.

**APPEARANCE:**
Breeding male has bluish grey head and neck with white, crescent-shaped patch near base of bill. Long black bill. Breast, sides, and underparts tan spotted with dark brown. Black stern bordered in front by white flank patch. **Female** greyish brown mottled with

♀          ♂

darker brown, somewhat lighter on face and neck. Buffy white patch near base of bill, dark line through eye, and prominent, incomplete eye ring. Bill dark grey. Wings of both sexes have large powder-blue patch on forewing and green speculum. **Immatures** and **eclipse male** resemble female.

▶ Male distinctive in breeding plumage. Female more easily distinguished from other brown female ducks primarily by size and blue forewing-patch. Female Green-winged Teal has black-and-green speculum and lacks blue wing-patch. Rare Cinnamon Teal richer brown with somewhat larger bill. Northern Shoveler has large, spoon-shaped bill.

**VOICE:** Usually silent. Male gives soft, lisping *keck-keck-keck*. Female rarely utters quiet *quack*.

**HABITAT AND BEHAVIOUR:** Ponds and marshes. Flight very fast. Usually feeds at surface of water or just below. Rarely tips up. Sometimes forages on bank.

**STATUS:** Common breeder. Rare winter resident.

# CINNAMON TEAL *Anas cyanoptera*

38–43 cm / 15–17" Wt 280–420 g / 10–15 oz

Breeding of the Cinnamon Teal was not reported in Ontario until 1983. Nests may be difficult to observe because they are built among dense foliage and often concealed under dead vegetation.

**APPEARANCE:** Breeding male has bright cinnamon head, breast, neck, and belly. Eyes red. Bill black. Back and scapulars brown edged with tawny and cinnamon. Outer wings brown. Large, light blue patch on inner wings best observed in flight. Speculum iridescent green. Rump and tail brown. **Female** mottled brown above and below. Face buffy brown streaked with tawny brown; chin and throat unmarked. Indistinct brown eye-line. Bill slate-blue to dark grey. Wings brown with large, light blue patch. Speculum dull green. **Eclipse male** similar to female but with red eyes; bright, iridescent green speculum, and white at base of tail. **Immatures** resemble female; male acquires red eyes by age three months.

♂

♀

▶ Breeding male distinctive. Female, immatures, and male in eclipse easily confused with female Blue-winged Teal. However, latter has more distinct eye-line, steeper forehead, and shorter bill; male Blue-winged Teal lacks red eye.

**VOICE:** Usually silent. Male gives rattling, low-pitched *karr karr karr* during courtship. Female utters soft *rrrr* and weak *gack-gack-ga-ga*.

**HABITAT AND BEHAVIOUR:** Marshes and ponds. Takes off with leap from surface of water. Rapid, continuous wingbeats. Agile in flight and on land. Rarely dives for food.

**STATUS:** Very rare breeder. Rare migrant.

# NORTHERN SHOVELER *Anas clypeata* ⌐

L 45.5–51.0 cm / 18–20" Wt 545–800 g / 1.2–1.8 lb

The Northern Shoveler uses its distinctive bill for straining small aquatic crustaceans. It feeds in shallow marshes and ponds with its head extended and bill skimming the water's surface.

**APPEARANCE:** Large, spatulate bill. Breeding male has dark green head and neck. Yellow eyes. Bill black. Back black bordered with white and blue scapulars. Wings blackish with large blue patch on inner wing best observed in flight. Glossy green speculum bordered above by white stripe. Rump black with green sheen. Black tail has white outer feathers. Breast and rear flanks white. Sides and belly rusty red.

♂

**Female, eclipse male,** and **immatures** generally drab mottled brown. Dusky upperparts have buff-edged feathers. Face and throat somewhat paler. Bill brownish with orangish edges. Wings dark brown with large, bluish grey wing-patch and green speculum. Underparts mottled

♀

buffy brown with whitish wing linings. Most eclipse males have brownish olive bills and white crescent on face like Blue-winged Teal.

▶ Bill distinctive in all plumages.

**VOICE:** In spring, male gives wheezy *thic*. Loud, nasal *paaay* and rapid *took* calls often combined: *paaay took-took took-took*. Female gives feeble *quack, gaek,* and quiet, trilling calls: *bub bub bub bub bububububub*.

**HABITAT AND BEHAVIOUR:** Nests in short grassy areas typically near water. Flies with distinctive "humped" posture with long bill angled downward. Walks well on land.

**STATUS:** Rare breeder. Uncommon to common spring and fall migrant.

# ORTHERN PINTAIL *Anas acuta* F

5–75 cm / 21.5–29.5" Wt 740–1050 g / 1.7–2.3 lb

is elegant duck is distinguished in flight by its long, narrow wings,
inted tail, and slim silhouette. Flocks may number several thousand
dividuals during migration.

**PPEARANCE:** Adult male in
eeding plumage has chocolate-
own head with white point
tending up from white neck,
east, and belly. Bill bluish
ck. Elongated black feathers
scapulars edged in tan or
ite. Grey back and sides
parated by elliptical black
tch. Wings grey with green
eculum. Flanks white. Upper
l and undertail coverts black.
il grey with very long, black
ntral feathers. **Female** mottled
nnamon brown above and
low, with somewhat lighter
wn head and breast. Bill
ish grey. Belly white.
eculum dull brown or bronze.
inted, brownish tail has long,
ckish central feathers.
**matures** and **eclipse male**
semble female except for
etallic greenish bronze speculum on adult male.

♂

♀

► Male distinctive in breeding plumage. Female, male in eclipse,
d immatures distinguished from other brownish ducks by long neck,
inted tail, and greenish bronze to brown speculum.

**ICE:** Male gives wheezy, whistling *whee*. Also high-pitched, piping
*eegee* followed by loud, trilled whistle. Female utters harsh quack:
*kuk-kuk-kuk-kuk kuk-kuk-kuk-kuk.*

**HABITAT AND BEHAVIOUR:** Shallow marshes,
tundra, meadows, ponds, and lakes. Flight
graceful and acrobatic. Flies quickly and
may drop rapidly to lower altitudes. Swims
high in water with tail pointed upward.
Sometimes dives for food. Fairly agile
on land.

**STATUS:** Rare to locally common
breeder. Common spring and
fall migrant.

67

# GREEN-WINGED TEAL *Anas crecca*

L 30.5–40.5 cm / 12–16" Wt 280–425 g / 10–15 oz

Our smallest puddle duck flies in moderately large flocks that twist and turn in unison. Males and females sometimes travel in separate flocks during fall migration.

**APPEARANCE:** Breeding male has cinnamon head with iridescent green crescent sweeping back from eye. Bill blackish. Back, inner wing, and tail grey. Outer wing feathers brownish olive. Speculum green bordered by buff and white. Breast pinkish with small black spots. Vertical white stripe in front of folded wing visible when swimming. Sides grey. Undertail coverts black with triangular yellow patch on sides. **Female** mottled brown. Sides of head and throat lighter than crown. Dark brown eye-line. Back, wings, and tail somewhat darker than underparts. Speculum green bordered by buff and white. **Eclipse male** and **immatures** resemble female, but black speckles on bluish bill distinguish female.

♂

♀

▶ Male in breeding plumage distinctive. Female distinguished from most dabbling ducks by small size. May be confused with female Blue-winged Teal and Cinnamon Teal, which can be distinguished by light blue wing-patches, somewhat steeper crown, and yellowish, not greyish, legs.

**VOICE:** Male gives clear whistle and rapid chittering call associated with displays. Female utters repeated, crisp quacks.

**HABITAT AND BEHAVIOUR:** Marshes, bogs and beaver ponds. Flight rapid, agile, and buoyant. Occasionally leaves water to loaf on rocks or overhanging branches. Dives only to escape predators.

**STATUS:** Uncommon breeder. Uncommon to common spring and fall migrant. Rare winter resident.

# ANVASBACK *Aythya valisineria*
48.5–56.0 cm / 19–22" Wt 1.1–1.4 kg / 2.5–3.1 lb

he Canvasback is a western breeder that rarely nests in Ontario. It is
ore commonly seen as a migrant as it passes through the province en
ute to the Atlantic coast.

**PPEARANCE:** Long bill;
oping head profile. Male
s chestnut head with red
es. Bill, breast, and stern
ack. Back, inner wing, and
derparts whitish. **Female**
s pale brown head and
ck, somewhat darker breast.
distinct buffy eye-line. Bill
ack. Eyes dark brown. Back
d sides pale brownish grey.
ings and tail brown.
matures and eclipse male
semble female. Speculum
distinct in all plumages.

♂

▶ Redhead has rounded,
her than sloped, head
ofile; male has shorter,
uish bill with black tip;
ck greyish; female best
stinguished by head and
l shape, and tawnier colour.
aups and Ring-necked
cks have darker heads
d backs and show
hter specula.

♀

**DICE:** Generally silent except during courtship. Male occasionally
es low cooing or croaking call. Female utters soft, purring quack.

**HABITAT AND BEHAVIOUR:** Marshes, ponds, and lakes.
Flight very fast. Rapid wingbeats appear as
flickering of white. Small flocks fly in lines or
V-formation. Running start required for takeoff.
Walks awkwardly on legs set far back on
body. Deep divers; usually observed in
deepest part of wetlands.

**STATUS:** Locally common to abundant
spring and fall migrant and winter
resident. Rare breeder.

69

# REDHEAD *Aythya americana*

L 45.5–56.0 cm / 18–22" Wt 900–1300 g / 2.0–2.9 lb

The Redhead occasionally lays its eggs in other ducks' nests, such as Blue-winged Teal, Gadwall, Lesser Scaup, and Ring-necked Duck. The most obvious evidence of this behaviour is the bright yellow Redhead chicks swimming among the broods of other species.

**APPEARANCE:** Male has rounded red head. Blue bill has white ring bordering black tip. Breast and stern black. Back and sides grey. Belly white. Wings dark grey with pale grey secondaries visible in flight. **Female** has tawny brown head and body. Crown darker. Paler at base of bill and chin. Dark greyish blue bill has black tip. Dark brown wings have pale grey secondaries. Belly whitish. **Immatures** and **eclipse male** resemble female. In flight, all plumages have grey stripe on trailing edge of wing.

▶ Canvasback has long bill and sloping forehead; both sexes have paler backs. Female Ring-necked Duck dark brown with obvious white eye-ring and white ring on bill; peaked crown. Female scaups darker brown with prominent white patch at base of bill.

♂

♀

**VOICE:** Male gives deep, cat-like *me-ow* in spring. Female utters very quiet *que-eek*.

**HABITAT AND BEHAVIOUR:** Lakes, large marshes and ponds, bays, and rivers. Flies fast and low over water with rapid wingbeats. Migrates in pairs or small, tight wedge-shaped flocks. Feeds primarily by diving; occasionally dabbles.

**STATUS:** Rare breeder. Fairly common to common spring and fall migrant. Uncommon winter resident.

# ING-NECKED DUCK *Aythya collaris*

39–45 cm / 15.4–17.7" Wt 505–850 g / 1.1–1.9 lb

ior to the 1930s, the distribution of the Ring-necked Duck in Ontario
as limited to the northwestern districts. Despite mortality due to
unting and environmental degradation, its range and abundance
creased during the 1980s and 1990s.

**PPEARANCE:** Dark grey
ll has white ring near black
. Peaked crown. Breeding
ale blackish above with
ossy purple sheen on head.
yes yellow. White feathers
rround bill. White vertical
ripe separates contrasting
ack breast and light grey
des. Tail black. **Female** dark
eyish brown above.

♂

nspicuous white eye-ring and
e-line. Eyes brown. Chin and
se of bill whitish. Wings dark
own with pale grey
condaries. Breast and flanks
rm brown. Belly whitish.
:lipse male browner than
eeding male. Olive sides.
nmatures duller than
rresponding adult plumages.
ll blackish with indistinct
ish ring.

♀

▶ Male Tufted Duck has crown plumes and lacks white at base of
ll; female has yellow eyes; lacks conspicuous white eye-ring and eye-
ie. Female Redhead warmer brown with rounded head profile. Male
eater and Lesser scaups paler grey above with rounded heads; lack
iged bill; female has yellow eyes and white patch at base of bill.

**VOICE:** Male gives short, whistling cough. Female
utters high-pitched growl: *burr.* Alarm call
short, soft *cut-cut-cut.*

**HABITAT AND BEHAVIOUR:** Wetlands,
sedge meadows, and fens. Flocks fly in
compact wedges. Runs on water during
takeoff. Leaves water only when nesting
or loafing. Dives with forward and
upward leap.

**STATUS:** Rare to common breeder.
Common spring migrant. Uncommon
fall migrant.

71

# GREATER SCAUP *Aythya marila*

L 38–51 cm / 15–20" Wt 820–1350 g / 1.8–3.0 lb

The scaups, also known as "bluebills," are difficult to distinguish und
suboptimal conditions. Fortunately, they can usually be distinguished
summer by differences in habitat and geographic distribution.

♂                                                    ♀

**APPEARANCE:** Breeding male has rounded, blackish head glossed wi
green. Eyes bright yellow. Pale blue bill has dark tip. Mantle pale gre
Wings dark grey with long white wing stripe visible in flight. Breast
and hindparts blackish. Belly, flanks, and sides white. **Female** dark
brown. Pale blue bill has large white patch of feathers at base. Some
have crescent-shaped, white cheek-patch. Eyes dark yellow. Greyish
brown breast, sides, and flanks. Belly white. **Immatures** similar but
lack white bill patch. **Eclipse male** similar to female but retains
bright eyes.

▶ Lesser Scaup has peaked head; male has purplish head, darker
upperparts, and greyish flanks; female darker greyish brown, particula
on head; white wing stripe shorter in both sexes. Male Ring-necked
Duck has peaked head with ringed bill, black mantle, and darker sides
bordered by vertical white patch; female has white eye-ring and eye-lir
Tufted Duck crested with darker mantle. Female Redhead
has dark eyes and lacks white bill patch.

**VOICE:** Male gives soft purring, cooing, and
whistling notes. Female utters harsh growling
*kerr.* Flocks call *scaup* when alarmed.

**HABITAT AND BEHAVIOUR:** Forested
ponds, tundra, lakes, and ocean bays. Fligh
rapid and agile. Often present in large raft
in winter. Dives well.

**STATUS:** Rare to uncommon
breeder. Abundant spring and fall
migrant. Common winter resident.

# LESSER SCAUP *Aythya affinis*

38–45 cm / 15–18" Wt 650–1200 g / 1.4–2.6 lb

The Lesser Scaup is among the last ducks to migrate south in the fall. Greater and Lesser scaups may occur together during migration; however, they rarely intermix.

**APPEARANCE:** Breeding male has peaked black head with purplish sheen. Bill pale blue with black tip. Eyes bright yellow. Mantle medium grey. Wings greyish with short, white wing stripe. Breast and hindparts black. Flanks pale greyish. **Female** has peaked brown head with small white patch at base of bill. Dull yellow eyes. Upperparts dark greyish brown. Breast and flanks greyish brown. Dark brown wings have short white stripe. **Eclipse male** similar with brighter eyes. **Immatures** resemble female but lack white patch near bill.

▶ Male Greater Scaup has rounded, greenish black head; mantle and flanks lighter; white wing stripe longer; female lighter brown overall, particularly head, with larger white bill-patch. Ring-necked Duck has ringed bill, black back, and vertical white patch in front of folded wing; female has white eye-ring and eye-line. Tufted Duck crested with white sides. Female Redhead has dark eyes and lacks white bill patch.

**VOICE:** Male gives soft *whee-oo* and whistling *whew.* Female utters low *arrr.* Alarm call loud *scaup.*

**HABITAT AND BEHAVIOUR:** Marshy ponds, lakes, and bays. Flight fast and manoeuvrable. Glides only when landing. Walks well. Excellent diver.

**STATUS:** Rare to uncommon breeder. Common spring and fall migrant. Rare to uncommon winter resident.

# KING EIDER *Somateria spectabilis*

L 53–60 cm / 20.9–23.6" Wt 1.2–2.0 kg / 2.6–4.4 lb

This boldly patterned duck breeds rarely near Hudson Bay. It is more readily observed on the Great Lakes during migration or in winter.

**APPEARANCE:** Breeding male has grey crown, greenish cheeks, and bright orange bill-shield outlined with black. Bill reddish orange. Neck, breast, and upper back white. Body black with white patches on rump. Elongated black scapulars appear as triangular "sails" over closed wings. Black wings have large white patches on forewing. **Female** deep reddish brown mottled and barred with black. Greenish grey bill. Crescent-shaped, blackish markings on feathers of sides and flanks. **Eclipse male** similar but with blackish wings. White wing spot visible at rest or in flight. Bill-shield small and dark. **Immature** male variable dull brownish or blackish with lighter breast and bright yellowish orange bill.

♂

♀

▶ Plumage of adult male distinctive. Female King Eider generally more rufous than female Common Eider and has crescent-shaped markings on sides.

**VOICE:** Male gives soft, dove-like *croo croo croooo* and threatening *kwack*. Female utters low growling and grunting notes.

**HABITAT AND BEHAVIOUR:** Dry tundra. Large freshwater lakes during migration and in winter. Rapid, manoeuvrable, and buoyant flight. Flies in long, undulating lines. Walks or runs with agility. Holds wings open slightly while running. Very strong swimmer. Deep-diving duck; dives may last up to 100 seconds.

**STATUS:** Rare breeder. Uncommon spring and fall migrant. Rare winter visitor. Resident off north coast (Hudson Bay).

# OMMON EIDER *Somateria mollissima*

58.5–68.5 cm / 23–27" Wt 1.5–2.0 kg / 3.4–4.4 lb

♂

♀

he elegant Common Eider was first reported breeding in Ontario
1960. Its nesting distribution may be underestimated because of its
reference for offshore islands and river-delta islets.

**PPEARANCE:** Long, sloping
rehead characteristic in all
umages. Adult male has black
own. Bill yellowish green with
ontal shield extending up
rehead. Head, breast, and
pperparts white. Nape and ear
verts have greenish tinge.
lanks black except for white
ot in front of tail. Outer wing,
il, and belly black. Black-and-
hite plumage distinctive
flight. **Female** varies from
ch brown to greyish brown.
reast, flanks, and back
irred with dark brown. Bill
ey. **Eclipse male** dark
own with white feathering
back. **Immature** male has
rk brown body with white
reast developing over
rst winter.

▶ Male distinctive.
male and immature King Eiders
ive steeper forehead and crescent-shaped brown marks on flanks;
old bill parallel to water. Male scoters dark overall; female lacks
ertical barring. Other black-and-white (male) or brown (female) ducks
ck the characteristic sloping facial profile.

**VOICE:** Male gives hollow, moaning *he-ho-ha-ho* and soft
cooing. Female utters Mallard-like *wak-wak-wak-wak-
wak* and grating *kor-r-r.*

**HABITAT AND BEHAVIOUR:** Rocky coasts,
tundra, and large lakes. Flight slow and
steady with occasional short glides. Flocks
fly in long lines low over water.

**STATUS:** Rare breeder. Locally common
winter resident off north coast
(Hudson Bay).

ANSERIFORMES: Anatidae / Ducks, Geese, and Swans

# HARLEQUIN DUCK *Histrionicus histrionicus*

L 35.5–48.5 / 14–19" Wt 550–675 g / 1.2–1.5 lb

The Harlequin Duck breeds along clear, fast-flowing rivers and streams. Highly buoyant, it is able to maintain position in both rough surface conditions and strong underwater currents.

**APPEARANCE:** Breeding male slate-blue with unmistakable white bands and collars bordered with black lines. Large white crescent at base of bill and white spots on sides of head. Chestnut stripe on crown. Elongated scapulars form conspicuous white stripes. Mantle greyish blue grading to black at rump. Bluish speculum and white wing-patch visible in flight. Belly blue. Flanks chestnut. Undertail coverts black. **Female** dark greyish brown. Two or three round white spots on side of head. Speculum bluish. Chin and foreneck paler brown. Breast and belly white with brown bars. Sides and flanks brown. **Eclipse male** similar to female but richer chocolate-brown above and below. **Immatures** in fall resemble female. Young males acquire breeding plumage during winter.

♂

♀

▶ Male distinctive. Female Bufflehead has white breast, single white mark behind eye, and white wing-patch visible in flight. Female scoters larger with larger bills and less well defined facial spots.

**VOICE:** Utters mouse-like squeak. Male gives low whistle with descending trill. Female utters coarse *ek-ek-ek.*

**HABITAT AND BEHAVIOUR:** Large lakes and rivers. Rocky shorelines in winter. Flies low over water. Rapid wingbeats. More frequently on land than most sea ducks. Uses wings when hopping onto rocks. Swims well in surf and rough water. Strong diver.

**STATUS:** Rare from September to April.

# URF SCOTER *Melanitta perspicillata* F

44–48 cm / 17–19" Wt 900–1100 g / 2.0–2.4 lb

ne Surf Scoter is the only scoter with its breeding range restricted to
orth America. In Ontario, they are observed most frequently on ponds
ıd lakes with well-treed shorelines on the Hudson Bay Lowlands.

**PPEARANCE:** Breeding male
ıack with white patches on
rehead and nape. Large, multi-
ıloured bill (appears orange)
ıs circular black feathering at
ıse. Adult **female** blackish
rown. Two indistinct white
ıeek-patches. Nape may have
ıhitish patch. Bill blackish.
**:clipse male** sooty brown with
ıhite patch on nape. Bill muted
ı colour. All plumages have
ırk wings in flight. **Immatures**
ınerally paler and browner than
ı male. Breast and belly whitish.
ıvo distinct facial patches;
ıpe-patch absent. **First-winter**
ıale** blacker with developing
ıhite nape.

♂

♀

▶ Breeding male White-
inged and Black scoters have
ıfferent bills and lack white
ıead-patches. Facial patches
ımewhat paler than White-
inged Scoter, but Black Scoter
ıas noticeably lighter cheeks. White-winged Scoter has conspicuous
ıhite speculum. Black Scoter has two-toned underwing.

**OICE:** Generally silent. Occasionally utters low whistles, gurgles, and
guttural croaks. Female sometimes gives crow-like *crahh*.

**HABITAT AND BEHAVIOUR:** Muskeg ponds
and lakes. Large lakes and rivers in migration.
Rarely flies in lines like other scoters. Often
flies low over water. Holds wings extended
up over back when landing on water.
Occasionally flaps wings while swimming.
Jumps forward with partially open wings
to dive.

**STATUS:** Rare breeder. Common
spring and fall migrant.

77

# WHITE-WINGED SCOTER *Melanitta fusca*

L 49–56 cm / 19.5–22.0" Wt 1.0–1.6 kg / 2.2–3.5 lb

In Europe, the rich black plumage of this "bay duck" has earned it the name Velvet Scoter. It is rarely seen in Ontario because of its low density, secretive nature, and preference for inaccessible nesting sites.

**APPEARANCE:** Adult male black. Small white patch around light eye. Bill orange with black knob at base. Diagnostic large, white speculum best seen in flight. **Female** and **immatures** sooty brown with white speculum. Two light patches on face are more obvious in immatures. Bill dark grey. Eyes dark brown. **Second-year male** looks like adult male but somewhat duller.

♂

► Largest scoter. Others lack white speculum. Adult male Surf Scoter has white patches on crown and nape, and bill patterned with orange, black, and white; female and immatures more difficult to distinguish. Pale spot in front of eye more oval in Surf Scoter, and feathering does not extend toward bill. Adult male Black Scoter has bright orangish yellow knob on bill; female and immatures have light cheeks that contrast with dark crown.

♀

**VOICE:** Low, bell-like whistle. Also low, repeated *gutta gutta gutta*. Wings whistle in flight.

**HABITAT AND BEHAVIOUR:** Lakes, muskeg ponds, and rivers. Frequently nests on islands. Takes flight by running along water surface. Flight fast and direct. Flocks fly in stringy formation. Dives for food.

**STATUS:** Rare breeder. Common spring and fall migrant. Rare to locally common winter visitor.

# BLACK SCOTER *Melanitta nigra*
L 17–21 cm / 43.0–53.5" Wt 950–1100 g / 2.1–2.4 lb

The Black Scoter migrates through Ontario en route to wintering grounds on the Atlantic and Gulf of Mexico coasts. Relatively few individuals winter on the Great Lakes.

**APPEARANCE:** Adult male entirely black. Black bill has conspicuous orange knob at base. Adult **female** dark brown with pale cheeks and foreneck that contrast strongly with darker crown. **Immatures** resemble female but with somewhat lighter upperparts and white-and-brown mottling on breast and belly. Young males acquire some black feathering and yellowish colour on bill during first winter. Black Scoter in flight has silvery underside of flight feathers contrasting with dark wing linings.

♂

► Male Surf Scoter has white patches on head, and orange, white, and black bill. Male White-winged Scoter has white patch beneath eye and white speculum. Female Surf and White-winged scoters have two pale spots on sides of head; bill somewhat broader at base.

♀

Winter Ruddy Duck distinguished from female Black Scoter by pale flanks, paler cheeks crossed by dark stripe, and preference for shallow-water habitats.

**VOICE:** Male utters plaintive, musical whistle, *cour-cour-cour-lou-cour-lou,* and rattling *tuka-tuka-tuka-tuk.* Female gives *pe-e-e-e-e-e-ut* when flushed and reedy *toooo-it toooo-it* in flight.

**HABITAT AND BEHAVIOUR:** Open sea coasts and large lakes. Flies in lines close to water surface. Swims in small groups while feeding. Holds bill parallel to water. Dives in shallow water.

**STATUS:** Common summer resident off north coast. Common migrant. Uncommon winter resident.

GB

# LONG-TAILED DUCK *Clangula hyemalis*

L 40.5–59.0 cm / 16–23" Wt 685–770 g / 1.5–1.7 lb

Male and female Long-tailed Ducks, formerly known as Oldsquaws, have distinct summer and winter plumages. Only males possess the characteristic tail feathers that give this species its common name.

**APPEARANCE:** Breeding male has dark brown head with large white eye-patch. Neck, breast, and upperparts dark brown. Elongated scapulars edged with buff. Very long, dark central tail feathers. Underparts white. **Winter male** has white head with dark patches. Black bill has pinkish orange band. Breast, wings, and back dark brown. Neck and belly white. Elongated scapulars pearl-grey. Tail as in breeding plumage. Breeding **female** greyish brown. Head pale brown with darker brown cheek-patch. White patch around and behind eye. Back feathers edged with buff. Underparts white. **Winter female** has white head with narrow brown crown and cheek stripes. Both sexes have plain dark brown wings in flight. **Immatures** resemble female but darker.

♂

♀

▶ Male Northern Pintail has white breast, grey sides and back; lacks pale facial patch. Female Harlequin Duck smaller and darker with two or three facial spots.

**VOICE:** Breeding flocks babble continuously. Male gives musical *poorh-porrdle-ooh* during courtship.

**HABITAT AND BEHAVIOUR:** Breeds in tundra pools and lakes. Ocean and large lakes in winter. Flight swift and careening. Generally stays in deeper water.

**STATUS:** Rare breeder. Fairly common migrant in May and October. Locally common winter resident.

# BUFFLEHEAD *Bucephala albeola*

L 32–40 cm / 12.6–15.7" Wt 325–450 g / 11.6–16.1 oz

This small diving duck, also known as the "Butterball," uses old Northern Flicker holes for nesting; populations may be limited by the availability of cavities.

**APPEARANCE:** Black head of breeding male glossed with green and purple, with large white patch from ear coverts to nape. Back, rump, and wings black. Large white wing-patch on inner wing visible in flight. Tail dark grey. Underparts and sides white. Bill bluish grey. **Female** has dark greyish brown head and neck. Oval white cheek-patch beneath eye. Upperparts, including wings, dark brown. White speculum. Breast and belly whitish; otherwise underparts greyish. Bill greyish. **Eclipse male** resembles female but has larger white wing- and face-patches. **Immatures** also resemble female. Immature male has somewhat darker back and paler underparts.

♂

♀

► Male distinguished from Common and Barrow's goldeneyes by large white head patch and dark eyes. Female goldeneyes generally greyer above with yellowish eyes; also, lack white ear patch.

**VOICE:** Male gives loud, squeaky whistle and low, guttural growl. Female utters hoarse, quacking *ec-ec-ec-ec*. Calls young with low, buzzy *cuc-cuc-cuc*.

**HABITAT AND BEHAVIOUR:** Freshwater ponds of boreal forest and aspen parkland. Flies with rapid wingbeats. Rarely on land. Buoyant swimmers. Dives well; foot propelled under water.

**STATUS:** Rare to uncommon breeder. Common migrant and winter resident.

# COMMON GOLDENEYE *Bucephala clangula*
L 40.5–51.0 cm / 16–20"  Wt 740–950 g / 1.7–2.1 lb

In flight, the wings of the Common Goldeneye make a distinctive whistling sound for which it has earned the vernacular name "Whistler."

**APPEARANCE:** Breeding male has blackish green head with large white spot between eye and bill. Eyes yellow. Bill black. White neck. Upperparts generally black, but wings have large white patch that extends almost to front of wing. Underparts white. Breeding **female** has chocolate-brown head and white neck. Eyes yellow. Bill has yellow tip; all black in winter. Upperparts grey. Wings have white patch like male. Breast, flanks, and belly white. **Eclipse male** and **immatures** similar to female; however, head of eclipse male somewhat blackish with faint white spot. **First-year male** has white crescent on cheek.

♂

▶ Barrow's Goldeneye male has glossy purple head with crescent-shaped white patch; less white on sides, with smaller white wing-patch; female has darker body than Common Goldeneye, and more yellow on bill. Male Bufflehead smaller with large, white, puffy patch at back of head; female browner with oval white patch behind eye. Common Merganser slimmer with long, thin, orange bills. Scaups have dark breasts.

♀

**VOICE:** Usually silent. Rarely gives soft coos and whistles. Female utters harsh, croaking *gack*.

**HABITAT AND BEHAVIOUR:** Wetlands, lakes, and rivers bordered by mature forest. Flies in small groups; flight fast with rapid wingbeats. Dives easily without exaggerated leap or plunge. Uses feet for propulsion under water.

**STATUS:** Common breeder. Common migrant and winter resident.

# BARROW'S GOLDENEYE *Bucephala islandica*

40.5–51.0 cm / 16–20" Wt 680–1130 g / 1.5–2.5 lb

Native to the Rocky Mountains, Alaska, and Labrador, the Barrow's Goldeneye is a rare pleasure for southern Ontario birders in winter. Individuals are usually observed among flocks of Common Goldeneyes.

**APPEARANCE:** Breeding male has puffy, oval-shaped, purplish head with white, crescent-shaped cheek-patch. Eyes yellow. Bill black. Back black with row of spots formed by white scapulars. White wing-patch visible in flight and when swimming. Tail black. Neck, breast, and underparts white. **Female** and **immatures** have dark brown head with puffy nape. Eyes yellow. Female has yellow or orange bill tipped with black (greyish in winter). Body dark greyish brown, somewhat lighter on sides and flanks. White wing-patch crossed by dark bar. Neck and belly white. **First-year male** similar to female but with pale crescent on cheeks and whiter breast and underparts.

♂

♀

► Breeding male Common Goldeneye has greenish head with round white facial patch, more white on sides, and larger white wing-patch; female has lighter brown, more oval-shaped head; bill less yellow.

**VOICE:** Usually silent. Male utters mewing notes during courtship. Female gives hoarse quacks.

**HABITAT AND BEHAVIOUR:** Wooded or open lakes and ponds. Lakes and rivers during winter. Wings whistle while in flight. Pops up like a cork following foraging dive.

**STATUS:** Rare winter visitor.

# HOODED MERGANSER *Lophodytes cucullatus*

L 40–48 cm / 16–19" Wt 545–700 g / 1.2–1.6 lb

This striking duck performs elaborate courtship displays that include bobbing, crest-raising, wing-flapping, and ritualized preening.

**APPEARANCE:** Adult male has black head with white, fan-shaped crest that can be raised or lowered. Neck and back black. Wings also black with long white and black tertiaries. White breast separated from bright rusty flanks by two vertical black stripes. Tail blackish brown. Thin serrated bill black. Eyes yellow. **Female** has grey head with bushy rufous crest. Chin and upper throat white. Back, wings, and tail dark brown. Wing has small white speculum, most visible in flight. Flanks brownish grey; breast somewhat lighter. Dark bill orange only near base. Eyes brown. **Eclipse male** similar to female with heavier mottling on head and neck. **Immature** male resembles female but has white head-patch and lack distinctive shaggy crest.

♂

♀

▶ Mergansers distinguished from other ducks by thin bill and crested head. Male markedly different from other mergansers. Female distinguished by overall darker plumage, dark bill, and smaller size.

**VOICE:** Usually silent. Male utters rolling, croaking *craaa-crrrooooo* during courtship display. Female responds with hoarse *gack*. Also gives rough *croo-croo-crook* in flight.

**HABITAT AND BEHAVIOUR:** Secluded wetland ponds and rivers. Runs across water during takeoff. Rapid, continuous wingbeats. Only glides when landing.

**STATUS:** Uncommon breeder. Common spring and fall migrant.

# COMMON MERGANSER *Mergus merganser*

L 56.0–68.5 cm / 22–27" Wt 1.2–1.7. kg / 2.6–3.7 lb

Common Mergansers generally fly in pairs and small flocks along a broad front. They can be recognized on the wing by their flat head, belly, and legs, often likened to a "lawn dart" in flight.

**APPEARANCE:** Breeding male has black head with greenish sheen. Eyes brown. Bill red. Neck and upper mantle white. Back and scapulars black bordered by longitudinal white patch. Wings have greyish brown primaries and white secondaries. Large white wing-patch. Rump and tail grey. Underparts white tinged with salmon except belly, which is sometimes mottled grey. Flanks pale grey. **Female** has reddish brown head with shaggy crest and red bill. Chin white. Upperparts bluish grey. Wings greyish brown with white speculum. Lower neck grey. Otherwise, underparts white, sometimes tinged with salmon. Sides and flanks greyish. **Eclipse male** similar to female but with rounder head profile and larger white wing-patch. **Immatures** resemble female.

♂

♀

► Male Red-breasted Merganser has shaggy crest, red eyes, and streaked breast; female browner with red eyes; lacks white throat-patch and sharp demarcation between head and neck. Female Hooded Merganser darker brown with blackish back.

**VOICE:** Male gives twanging *uig-a* and *kragagagagagaga* during courtship. Female utters harsh *gruk gruk gruk* and high-pitched, rapid *cro cro cro*.

**HABITAT AND BEHAVIOUR:** Lakes and rivers bordered by mature forest. Flight fast with fairly steep takeoff. Rarely observed on land; walks awkwardly. Dives well.

**STATUS:** Rare to common breeder. Common migrant and winter resident.

85

# RED-BREASTED MERGANSER *Mergus serrator*

L 48.5–66.0 cm / 19–26" Wt 850–1300 g / 1.9–2.9 lb

The serrated bills of mergansers are adapted for catching small fish, such as minnows, herring, and sticklebacks. They feed from the surface by submerging their heads, or may dive to depths of 2–9 m (6.5–29.0').

**APPEARANCE:** Breeding male has glossy, greenish black head with shaggy crest. Red eyes. Thin, red bill. Conspicuous white collar. Elongated scapulars and back blackish. Wings blackish grey with broad white stripe across inner wing. Rump and tail grey. Central breast reddish brown streaked with black. Sides of breast black and white. Sides and flanks pale grey. Remaining underparts white. **Female** greyish brown above with cinnamon head that blends into whitish foreneck and greyish breast. Shaggy crest. Red eyes. **Immatures** resemble female.

♂

▶ Male Common Merganser distinguished by whitish breast, dark eyes, and lack of crest. Female has prominent white chin-patch and sharp separation between head and breast. Female Hooded Merganser has dark eyes and bill, and blackish back.

♀

**VOICE:** Male utters cat-like *yeow-yeow* during displays. Female gives raspy, croaking *krrrr-krrrr*. Alarm call a deep *grack*.

**HABITAT AND BEHAVIOUR:** Lakes and rivers, often with rocky shorelines. Flight strong and fast; up to 130 km/h (78 mph). Runs along surface to take off. Walks awkwardly on land. Swims and dives well.

**STATUS:** Uncommon breeder. Uncommon to locally abundant migrant. Uncommon winter resident.

# RUDDY DUCK *Oxyura jamaicensis* ⌐

L 38–41 cm / 15–16" Wt 500–600 g / 1.1–1.3 lb

Ruddy Ducks use their distinctive long tails as rudders when swimming under water. Young "Stiff-tails" can dive in search of food at their first contact with water, whereas most other duck species require several weeks of surface feeding before diving is mastered.

**APPEARANCE:** Stocky and short-necked with long, stiff tail. Breeding male has black cap and nape, white cheeks, and large, bright blue bill. Body rufous with white belly and undertail coverts. Blackish tail often held cocked up. **Female** has dark brown cap, nape, and mantle. Pale brown cheeks crossed by dark brown line. Bill blackish brown. Tail dark brown. Underparts, sides, and flanks mottled greyish brown. **Winter male** similar to female but with bright white cheeks and greyish bill. **Immatures** resemble female.
► Only Ontario diving duck with stiff tail. Male Cinnamon Teal lacks blue bill and white cheeks.

**VOICE:** Silent most of year. Male gives low, nasal, sputtering *chick-ik-ik-ik-k-k-kwrrr* during courtship.

♂

♀

**HABITAT AND BEHAVIOUR:** Marshes, ponds, and lakes. Rapid, buzzy flight on whirring wingbeats. Lethargic; flies rarely. Patters across surface of water for some distance to become airborne. Cannot walk on land. Agile and powerful swimmer and diver. Sinks silently beneath surface to escape disturbances.

**STATUS:** Rare breeder. Uncommon spring and fall migrant.

# FALCONIFORMES
## Hawks, Eagles, and Falcons

The diurnal birds of prey range in size from the diminutive American Kestrel, averaging at approximately 115 grams (4 ounces), to the stately Bald Eagle, averaging at about 4.5 kilograms (10.5 pounds). All are effective predators equipped with sharp, hooked bills and powerful talons. Most species are sexually monomorphic in plumage, but females are generally larger than males. Species identification is often confounded by the existence of highly variable plumage colour morphs in some raptors, particularly hawks of the genus *Buteo*.

This order is represented by twenty-one species in Ontario, four of which are accidental (Swallow-tailed Kite, Ferruginous Hawk, Crested Caracara, and Prairie Falcon, see p. 385).

# OSPREY *Pandion haliaetus*

, 56.0–63.5 cm / 22–25" Wt 1.4–1.8 kg / 3.1–4.0 lb

Ospreys build a large, conspicuous nest high in a tree near the water's edge. Where suitable natural sites are not available, this species will use utility poles, channel markers, and artificial nest platforms. A mated pair will renovate and reuse nests over successive breeding seasons.

**APPEARANCE:** Head white with brownish crown and broad, dark brown eye-line. Upperparts dark brown. Long, narrow wings appear bent at wrist. Tail banded with dark brown and white. Underparts white. Variable buff to brown speckling on foreneck (more on **female**). Wing linings whitish with prominent dark brown patch at wrist. **Immatures** have buff edging on back feathers and somewhat more heavily streaked underparts.

► Subadult Bald Eagle similar but much larger with dark head and much less white on undersides; wings lack obvious crook at wrist in flight and dark brown wrist-patches.

**VOICE:** Utters melodious series of whistles: *chewk-chewk-chewk*. Also gives loud *kip kip kiweek kiweek* when alarmed.

**HABITAT AND BEHAVIOUR:** Lakes and rivers. Powerful flapping strokes alternate with glides. Forages for fish by hovering above water at considerable height, then plunging feet-first. Occasionally dives beneath surface. Carries fish with head pointed forward for optimal aerodynamics. Sharp spines on soles of feet prevent slippery prey from escaping.

**STATUS:** Uncommon to fairly common breeder.

## MISSISSIPPI KITE *Ictinia mississippiensis*
L 35–40 cm / 13.8–15.7" Wt 250–320 g / 9.0–11.5 oz

Both an elegant and acrobatic flyer, the Mississippi Kite captures and consumes its prey—mostly large insects, such as grasshoppers, cicadas, and dragonflies—on the wing. These birds are known to fly before advancing brush fires to snatch retreating insects.

**APPEARANCE:** Falcon-shaped in flight. Pale grey head and underparts. Eyes red. Back darker grey. Grey wings long and pointed with shorter first primary. Whitish secondaries contrast with blackish primaries on open wing. Folded wings same length as tail when perched. Black tail has square, or slightly notched, tip. Feet brownish yellow. **Juveniles** blackish brown above. Whitish underparts heavily streaked with brown. Black tail crossed by several pale bars. **First-year** birds resemble adults but retain barring on tail and lack white wing-patch.

▶ Peregrine Falcon similar in soaring silhouette but lacks all-black tail and whitish patch on secondaries. Female Merlin and immature Peregrine Falcon distinguished from immature Mississippi Kite by bold facial patterning and barring on undersides of wings.

**VOICE:** Clear, thin two-note whistle: *kee-ee.*

**HABITAT AND BEHAVIOUR:** Wooded streams and groves of tall trees in open country. Flight leisurely and buoyant with alternate periods of deep flapping and gliding. Migrant flocks frequently fly at great heights after gaining altitude by soaring on ascending thermals.

**STATUS:** Rare spring visitor.

# BALD EAGLE *Haliaeetus leucocephalus*  ✓+F

75–110 cm / 29.5–43.3" Wt 4.0–5.5 kg / 8.8–12.1 lb

Bald Eagle populations have suffered greatly in southern counties from illegal shooting, habitat destruction, and pesticide use. Fortunately, their distribution remains relatively continuous across the boreal forest region of northern Ontario.

**APPEARANCE:** Very large with wing spread up to 2.5 m (8'). White head and tail. Dark brown body. Massive yellow beak and feet. **Juveniles** dark overall with some blotchy white feathering on underside of wings and tail. Bill brownish grey. **Second-** and **third-year** birds have variable white feathering on head, body, and tail.

▶ Adult Golden Eagle brown overall. Immature Golden Eagle distinguished from immature Bald Eagle by orderly pattern of white feathering on underside of wing near wrist and base of tail. Osprey distinguished from subadult Bald Eagles by much smaller size, proportionately longer wings, dark bill and feet, whiter body, and dark wrist-patches on underside of wings.

**VOICE:** Harsh, squeaky, cackling *kleek-iki-kik-kik.* Also various guttural grunts, *kak kak kak kak,* and metallic chittering.

**HABITAT AND BEHAVIOUR:** Large lakes and rivers. Flies with slow, powerful wingbeats; soars with wings held flat. Descends in rapid dive on half-closed wings in pursuit of fish or other prey. Commonly perches for long periods on dead branches overlooking water.

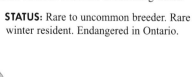

**STATUS:** Rare to uncommon breeder. Rare winter resident. Endangered in Ontario.

## NORTHERN HARRIER *Circus cyaneus* ⊦

L 40.5–61.0 cm / 16–24" Wt 350–550 g / 12.5–19.6 oz

The Northern Harrier holds its wings in a shallow dihedral as it glides low over marshes and meadows in search of prey. This majestic species is declining in Ontario because of loss of its preferred habitat.

**APPEARANCE:**
Owl-like facial ruff and white rump diagnostic in all plumages. Head, back, and wings of adult male grey. Eyes yellow. Wings have black tips. Long, grey tail has six to eight greyish brown bands. Underparts pale grey to white spotted with

cinnamon. Adult **female** resembles adult male but brownish rather than grey, with heavier brown streaking on breast and flanks. **Immatures** similar to adult female but more reddish brown above and below. Breast, belly, and wing linings cinnamon. Eyes brown.

▶ Red-tailed and Rough-legged hawks larger, with broader wings and shorter tail. Red-tailed Hawk lacks white rump. Rough-legged Hawk has dark wrist-patches on underside of wings.

**VOICE:** Utters rapid, high-pitched *ke ke ke ke ke* at nest. Female calls male with shrill, descending scream: *eeyah eeyah.*

**HABITAT AND BEHAVIOUR:** Marshes, wet meadows, bogs, and fields. Flight slow and low over ground with strong flaps and buoyant glides. Occasionally soars. Male performs elaborate "stalling" U-shaped courtship flight. Rarely walks or hops on ground.

**STATUS:** Uncommon to common breeder. Rare winter resident.

# SHARP-SHINNED HAWK *Accipiter striatus* ✓+F

26–36 cm / 10.2–14.2" Wt 95–130 g / 3.4–4.6 oz

The Sharp-shinned Hawk has declined steadily in southern Ontario since the mid-twentieth century owing to destruction of preferred nesting habitat, pesticide use, and shooting. It has remained on the Audubon Blue List as a "species of concern" since 1972.

**APPEARANCE:** Small, short-winged, long-tailed hawk. Upper-parts bluish grey. Eyes reddish. Underparts white barred with cinnamon. Flight feathers barred with white and dark grey below. Folded tail square or slightly notched. Undertail coverts white. **Immatures** brown above with variable white spots on mantle. Eyes yellow. Underparts cream-coloured with brown streaks on breast and brown bars on flanks. Head scarcely extends beyond wing line in flight.

► Cooper's Hawk and Northern Goshawk larger with proportionately slower rate of wing-flapping; in flight, head well ahead of leading edge of wings. Cooper's Hawk similar in coloration but has rounded tail with white tip and broader dark subterminal band. Northern Goshawk greyish below with prominent white eyebrow. Merlin flies more quickly on pointed wings; also has contrasty facial pattern and buff underparts streaked with brown.

**VOICE:** Utters intense, shrill, repetitive *kik-kik-kik-kik-kik* during breeding season.

**HABITAT AND BEHAVIOUR:** Woodlands and thickets. Flight buoyant with alternating periods of flapping and gliding. Short, rounded wings and long tail allow for manoeuvrability through dense foliage at high speed. Attracted to bird feeders in winter by finches and sparrows on which to prey.

**STATUS:** Rare to uncommon breeder. Common spring and fall migrant. Rare winter resident.

# COOPER'S HAWK *Accipiter cooperii*

L 37–47 cm / 14–19" Wt 280–450 g / 10–16 oz

Female Cooper's Hawks are markedly larger and heavier than males. Size dimorphism in raptors allows a mated pair to exploit a greater size-range of prey items.

**APPEARANCE:** Adult male has dark bluish grey mantle, wings, and tail. Crown somewhat darker. Ear coverts and foreneck washed with cinnamon. Eyes orange or red. Underparts white with profuse cinnamon barring. Underside of tail pale grey with four blackish transverse bars and white terminal band. Legs yellow. **Female** somewhat browner above with less reddish barring on underparts. **Immatures** dark brown above with variable white spots on mantle. Eyes yellow. Underparts white to pale buff, heavily streaked with dark brown or cinnamon. Underside of tail crossed by five to six narrow dark brown bars. Undertail coverts white.

▶ Sharp-shinned Hawk similar but much smaller with square or slightly notched tail (not rounded); proportionately longer wings and smaller head visible in flight. Immature Northern Goshawk larger, darker, and more heavily streaked than immature Cooper's Hawk; undertail coverts streaked.

**VOICE:** Male gives rapid *kik kik kik* that resembles call of Northern Flicker. Female primarily utters extended *whaaa* note.

**HABITAT AND BEHAVIOUR:** Deciduous and mixed forest, sometimes near human habitation. Rapid wingbeats alternate with brief glides. Highly manoeuvrable when attacking prey. Flies near ground when hunting or approaching nest.

**STATUS:** Rare to uncommon breeder. Fairly common spring and fall migrant. Rare winter resident.

# NORTHERN GOSHAWK *Accipiter gentilis*
50–65 cm / 20–26" Wt 700–1200 g / 1.5–2.6 lb

The highly agile Northern Goshawk pursues its prey at astonishing speeds through dense forest and across clearings. Occasionally, it stalks its quarry on foot.

**APPEARANCE:** Rounded wings and long tail. Upperparts dark bluish grey. Crown and cheeks blackish. Broad white eyebrows. Eyes red. Wings dark grey. Grey tail crossed by five to six wavy darker bands; narrow white tip. Breast whitish with grey barring; heaviest in female. Undertail coverts white. Underwings have dark flight feathers contrasting with whitish underwing coverts barred with dark grey. Upperparts of **immatures** dark brown with buff-and-cinnamon streaks. Brown head has less-distinct buff eyebrow. Eyes yellow. Wings and tail dark brown. Underparts

buffy white with thick brown streaking. Undertail coverts also streaked.
  ▶ Sharp-shinned and Cooper's hawks much smaller with rufous bars on underparts and more contrasting tail pattern; lack conspicuous black-and-white face pattern; immatures have white undertail coverts and straight tail bands. Male Northern Harrier has plain grey face, yellow eyes, white rump, and more uniform coloration. Grey morph Gyrfalcon has pointed wings with pale flight feathers contrasting with darker wing linings; lacks broad white eyebrow and dark cheeks.

**VOICE:** Numerous, rapid *kak kak kak kak* notes. Also single *chuuk*.

**HABITAT AND BEHAVIOUR:** Forest. Flies with several rapid flaps followed by glide. Wingbeats slower and deeper than smaller *Accipiter* hawks.

**STATUS:** Rare to uncommon year-round resident.

# RED-SHOULDERED HAWK *Buteo lineatus* ⨍

L 43–61 cm / 17–24" Wt 560–700 g / 1.3–1.6 lb

This hawk procures most of its food—small mammals, frogs, and snakes—by still-hunting from perches. Hunting perches range in heig from 2 to 4 m (6.5–13.0') and include poles, fences, haystacks, and trees.

**APPEARANCE:** Upperparts brown with extensive black-and-white checkering, particularly on wings. Crescent-shaped white patch near base of primaries visible on spread wing from below. Shoulders rusty red. Upper-tail coverts white-tipped. Black tail has four to seven narrow white bands. Under-parts barred with rusty red. Wings "two-toned" from below with rufous underwing coverts contrasting with black-and-white wing lining. **Immatures** brownish above with little rufous. Underparts buff, heavily streaked with dark brown. Wing linings pale with dark tips.

► Broad-winged Hawk more uniformly brown above, has shorter wings with white wing linings bordered with black and broad white tail bands. Immature Broad-winged Hawk paler below with fine streaks. Red-tailed Hawk has bright red tail, bright white breast, and underparts streaked with dark brown.

**VOICE:** Most common call, *kee-aah,* has accent on first syllable and drawn-out second syllable with downwar inflection. Usually given five to twelve times. Also *kip* call.

**HABITAT AND BEHAVIOUR:** Moist deciduous and mixed woodlands; prefers mature forests. Soars with wings held flat and tail outspread. Flaps occasionally while soaring.

**STATUS:** Uncommon breeder and migrant. Rare winter resident. Vulnerable in Ontario from clearing of mature forests.

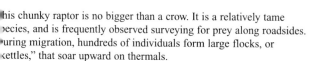

# BROAD-WINGED HAWK *Buteo platypterus*

34–43 cm / 13–17" Wt 325–450 g / 11.5–16.0 oz

This chunky raptor is no bigger than a crow. It is a relatively tame species, and is frequently observed surveying for prey along roadsides. During migration, hundreds of individuals form large flocks, or "kettles," that soar upward on thermals.

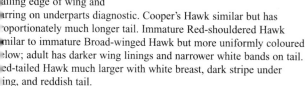

**APPEARANCE:** Dark brown to greyish brown above. Uppertail coverts tipped with white. Dark tail has white band near base, broad white median band, and narrow pale terminal band. Chin and throat white. Breast and belly whitish with heavy reddish brown barring becoming finer on belly. Wing linings pale with dark trailing edge. **Immatures** similar to adults, but underparts streaked longitudinally with brown. Tail buffy with many dark brown bands. Undersurface of wing has dusky trailing edge.

▶ Narrow, dark trailing edge of wing and barring on underparts diagnostic. Cooper's Hawk similar but has proportionately much longer tail. Immature Red-shouldered Hawk similar to immature Broad-winged Hawk but more uniformly coloured below; adult has darker wing linings and narrower white bands on tail. Red-tailed Hawk much larger with white breast, dark stripe under wing, and reddish tail.

**VOICE:** Most frequently heard call a high-pitched, shrill *pe-heeeeeeeeee.*

**HABITAT AND BEHAVIOUR:** Deciduous or mixed forest. Flies with combination of flapping and soaring. Soars in circles above forest during breeding season.

**STATUS:** Common breeder. Uncommon spring migrant. Abundant fall migrant.

**FALCONIFORMES: Accipitridae / Hawks, Kites, and Eagles**

# ✓SWAINSON'S HAWK *Buteo swainsoni*＋F

L 49–56 cm / 19–22" Wt 760–1200 g / 1.7–2.7 lb

Long wings with distinctly pointed tips give the Swainson's Hawk an in-flight profile that differs from other *Buteo* hawks. While soaring, this rare migrant holds its wings in a shallow dihedral position.

**APPEARANCE:**
**Light-phase adult** dark greyish brown above with light brown feather edging. Tail greyish with narrow dark bands and white tip. Subterminal band widest. Chin and forehead white. Rufous throat and upper breast form "bib." Otherwise, underparts whitish

with few rufous streaks. Underwing pattern shows dark flight feathers contrasting with pale wing coverts. **Dark morph** blackish brown with white throat and forehead. Undertail coverts whitish barred with black. Wing linings dark brown. **Light-phase immatures** and **first-year** birds blackish brown above with pale streaking. Face and forehead white. dark brown eye-line and malar streak. Buff below with variable spotting. Tail brown with blackish bands and white tip. Undertail coverts whitish. Dark phase more heavily marked with brown on underparts; sometimes spotted rufous.

▶ Broad-winged Hawk has white wing linings and broadly banded tail. Adult Red-tailed Hawk larger with reddish tail and dark patch on underwing; immatures have bright white upper breast. Dark phase Red-tailed, Ferruginous, and Rough-legged hawks have whitish flight feathers and lack pale undertail coverts. Perched Prairie Falcon distinguished by dark patch behind eye and short wings.

**VOICE:** Adults scream a shrill, plaintive *kreeeee* that fades off at the end. Female's call shorter and lower pitched. Repeated *pi-tick pi-tick* given during territorial disputes.

**HABITAT AND BEHAVIOUR:** Grasslands and sparse shrub lands. Flight strong, buoyant, and graceful. Hovers when foragings. Runs quickly on ground in pursuit of insects; catches prey with beak or talons.

**STATUS:** Rare spring and fall migrant

# ED-TAILED HAWK *Buteo jamaicensis*
8–61 cm / 19–24" Wt 1.0–1.3 kg / 2.2–2.8 lb

e Red-tailed Hawk is probably the best known raptor in North
merica. Unlike many other birds of prey, this open-country species
s thrived with the conversion of virgin forest to agricultural land.

**PEARANCE:** Head and
perparts brown with
riable white-and-rufous
ottling on mantle. Head
d nape lighter brown. Tail
ck-red with narrow black
oterminal band and narrow
iite tip. Underparts cream-
oured. Sides of breast
eaked with black and
namon. Broad band of
k brown barring and
eaking across belly. Wing
ings whitish with brown
agial stripe and wrist
ch. Flight feathers
rrowly barred with dark
wn. **Immatures** resemble
ilts but lack rufous tinge
upperparts. Tail greyish
wn with several narrow
k brown bands.

▶ Broad-winged Hawk has broad white bands on tail and lacks
k brown streaking on belly. Rough-legged Hawk has large, dark
ist-patch visible in flight; tail white at base with broad dark terminal
id. Red-shouldered Hawk has reddish shoulders, wing linings, and
ierparts. Swainson's Hawk has brown bib; dark flight feathers
itrast with pale wing linings from below.

**VOICE:** Loud, descending scream: *keeer-r-r.*

**HABITAT AND BEHAVIOUR:** Open country,
fields, and mixed forests. Soars gracefully on
broad wings. Perches conspicuously on tree
limbs, fence posts, and utility poles.

**STATUS:** Common to abundant
year-round resident.

# ROUGH-LEGGED HAWK *Buteo lagopus*

L 50–60 cm / 19.5–23.5" Wt 1.0–1.3 kg / 2.2–2.9 lb

The reproductive success of Rough-legged Hawks is dependent on the availability of lemmings and voles as prey. In prosperous years, a pair may raise as many as seven chicks; in poor years, nests often fail entirely.

**APPEARANCE: Light-phase adult** greyish brown above tinged with rufous, and has white or buff feather edges. Head and breast creamy buff streaked with brown. Upper tail coverts white, barred with dark brown. Tail white at base with wide, dark brown subterminal band and white tip. Belly dark brown, sometimes sparsely spotted with white and buff. Wing linings whitish with dark brown spotting and blackish patch at wrist. **Dark-phase adult** has dark head, underparts, and wing linings. **Immatures** have somewhat paler heads, darker bellies, and single broad, dark tail band. Legs heavily feathered to toes in all plumages.

▶ Dark wrist-patches and white at base of tail diagnostic from below. Also, other *Buteo* hawks rarely hover. Northern Harrier lacks dark belly and has longer, thinner tail that lacks broad, dark subterminal band.

**VOICE:** Screeching, catlike alarm call, *kee-we-uk,* descen◼ to last note.

**HABITAT AND BEHAVIOUR:** Tundra. Open fields and marshes in winter. Hovers while hunting by flapping upwind to maintain position.

**STATUS:** Extremely rare breeder. Rare to uncommon visitor from September to Ma◼

# GOLDEN EAGLE *Aquila chrysaetos* ⁴ᴮ

84.0–101.5 cm / 33–40" Wt 4.1–5.5 kg / 9–12 lb

he Golden Eagle was once perceived as a threat to livestock and
onsequently was targeted in shooting, trapping, and poisoning
ampaigns. It is now protected in Ontario under the *Endangered
pecies Act*.

**APPEARANCE:**
ery large hawk
ving spread 2.2 m;
) with long,
ctangular wings
d heavy, dark
ll. Uniformly
rk brown. Crown
d nape edged
ith golden buff.
rown eyes. Dark
own tail faintly
anded with
reyish white.
egs feathered.

eet yellow. **Immatures** similar but somewhat darker. White patch at
ase of primaries visible from below. Tail white at base. **Second-** and
**ird-year** birds have decreasing amounts of white.

▶ Adult Bald Eagle has white head and tail; immatures and
ibadults have irregular white patches on wings and tail. Dark-phase
ough-legged Hawk much smaller with pale flight feathers and white
base of tail. Turkey Vulture has naked red head, and greyish flight
athers contrasting with dark wing linings. Black Vulture has short,
quare tail and whitish primaries.

**OICE:** Generally silent except when breeding. Courting birds utter
elodious, yelping cry: *weeo-hyo-hyo.*

**ABITAT AND BEHAVIOUR:** Open country; frequently near mountains
and lakeshores. Soars on flat wings with occasional
wingbeats. Swoops from soaring flight to snatch
prey. Often eats carrion.

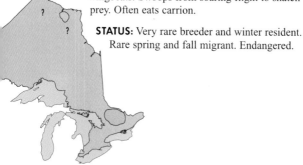

**STATUS:** Very rare breeder and winter resident.
Rare spring and fall migrant. Endangered.

# AMERICAN KESTREL *Falco sparverius*

L 22.5–30.5 cm / 8.8–12.0"  Wt 100–130 g / 3.6–4.6 oz

The "twinkling wings" of a foraging American Kestrel as it hovers ove fields and open country are a familiar sight throughout Ontario. Durin the breeding period, the male provides virtually all the food required b the female and growing offspring.

**APPEARANCE:** Small falcon with long, pointed wings. Adult male rufous above with narrow black barring. Crown slate-blue with central rufous patch. White throat and cheeks crossed by two vertical black stripes. Black spot on nape. Wings slate-blue. Tail rufous with broad, dark band near tip. Pale buff to cinnamon below with variable black spotting heaviest on flanks. Adult **female** larger with rufous upperparts (including wings) barred with black. Facial pattern like male but duller. Buffy underparts spotted and streaked with rufous and brown. **Immatures** resemble adults of respective genders but somewhat more heavily marked above and below.

▶ Other falcons larger, rarely hover, and lack predominant rufou coloration. Sharp-shinned Hawk has short, rounded wings and lacks strong facial markings; does not hover.

**VOICE:** Shrill, repeated, high-pitched *killy-killy-killy.*

**HABITAT AND BEHAVIOUR:** Open fields, riparian woodlands, and grasslands. Frequently swoops from hovering position while foraging. Perches with erect posture on fences, posts, and power lines. Nests in tree cavities.

**STATUS:** Common breeder. Irregular winter resident.

# MERLIN *Falco columbarius* F

24–30 cm / 9.5–11.8" Wt 160–240 g / 5.7–8.6 oz

The Merlin feeds largely on small to medium-sized birds, which it generally captures in mid-air. It is capable of spectacular aerial manoeuvres when chasing prey on the wing.

**APPEARANCE:**
small falcon. Adult male has slate-grey upperparts, with dark grey crown finely streaked with black. Face white or tan with dark brown streaks. Tan stripe above eye. Pointed wings black above with uniform, well-defined white spots visible in flight. Black tail has two

to five highly contrasting, narrow light bands. Underparts tan or buff with heavy brown streaking. Rufous wash on legs and sides of breast. Tawny striped wing lining and banded pattern on underside of tail visible in flight. Adult **female** and **immatures** similar to male but are dark brown above and have grey to buff tail patterns. Female much larger than male.

▶ Larger Peregrine Falcon has more striking facial pattern and flies with slower wingbeats. Smaller American Kestrel rufous in coloration.

**VOICE:** Most common call a harsh, high-pitched *ki-ki-ki-ki-ki;* varies in intensity, duration, and speed according to purpose.

**HABITAT AND BEHAVIOUR:** Semi-open areas of coniferous and mixed forests well suited for hunting. Flight fast with deep and powerful wingbeats. Resembles pigeon in flight, hence vernacular name "Pigeon Hawk." Occasionally soars. Hunts birds using shallow swoops that continue until successful.

**STATUS:** Rare to uncommon breeder. Rare migrant. Rare winter resident.

# GYRFALCON *Falco rusticolus*

L 48–61 cm / 19–24" Wt 1.1–2.1 kg / 2.4–4.6 lb

This large falcon is Canada's most northern diurnal raptor. It occurs only as a winter visitor in Ontario.

**APPEARANCE:** Plumage highly variable. Most common **grey phase** has whitish upperparts heavily streaked with greyish brown to medium grey. Breast and belly white to pale brown, moderately streaked and spotted to heavily streaked and barred with dark brown or dark grey. Wing feathers whitish, barred with brown or grey. Tail dark brown or grey with narrow dusky bars. Bill grey with yellow cere, often with dark tip. Eyes dark. **White phase** largely white with dark brown mottling on upperparts. **Dark phase** dark brownish black with buffy feather edging. Generally, **immatures** more heavily marked with streaks, not bars, on underparts.

▶ Relatively broad and less-pointed wings and long tail resemble those of *Accipiter* hawks. Northern Goshawk distinguished by blackish crown and cheek, and prominent white stripe over eye; underparts may be more finely patterned. Smaller Peregrine Falcon has dark hood with broad, black sideburns, and narrow, pointed wings.

**VOICE:** Harmonic, guttural *kak kak kak*. Also sharp, stuttering *chu-chu-chu-chu*. Calls harsher and louder than Peregrine Falcon.

**HABITAT AND BEHAVIOUR:** Open, flat areas; coasts, reservoirs, and farmland. Wingbeats slower, deeper, and more powerful than other falcons. Captures prey by pouncing, chasing, or hovering.

**STATUS:** Very rare winter visitor.

# PEREGRINE FALCON *Falco peregrinus* F

38–53 cm / 15–21" Wt 500–615 g / 1.1–1.4 lb

Ontario's Peregrine Falcon population faces extirpation due to the use of persistent, bio-accumulating pesticides, such as DDT, which cause infertile and thin-shelled eggs. Although banned in North America in 1972, DDT is still used in parts of Latin America where this falcon winters.

**APPEARANCE:**

Slate-grey above. Blackish head and malar stripe resemble dark helmet. Orbital ring and cere yellow. Chin and underparts buff, spotted and barred with black on lower breast and belly. Pointed wings and long, narrow tail have light and dark barring visible from below. Feathered thighs whitish barred with black. Feet yellow. **Immatures** similar to adult but brownish rather than slate-grey. Feathers on upperparts edged with buff. Dark brown streaking heavier below. Orbital ring, cere, and feet greyish.

▶ Merlin smaller and darker, and lacks "helmeted" head. Gyrfalcon larger with longer wings and tail; less contrasting above and below; lacks prominent facial markings. Accidental Prairie Falcon brownish with dark wing linings.

**VOICE:** Alarm call a loud, harsh *hak hak hak hak*. Also gives repeated *e-chew* at nest.

**HABITAT AND BEHAVIOUR:** Open country, cliffs, valleys, and city skyscrapers. When foraging, folds wings and dives headfirst at speeds in excess of 360 km/h (216 mph). Strikes avian prey with feet in mid-air.

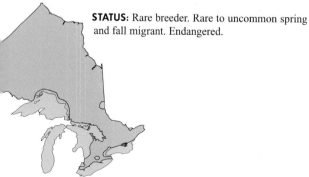

**STATUS:** Rare breeder. Rare to uncommon spring and fall migrant. Endangered.

# GALLIFORMES
## Fowl-like Birds

Strong legs, stout bills, and rounded wings characterize these primarily terrestrial birds. Although they rarely fly, most galliforms are capable of short, strong flights that are often initiated with explosive takeoffs. Some species perform elaborate courtship displays. Most galliforms are rather cryptically coloured, with females being somewhat more so than males. The ptarmigans exhibit marked seasonal differences in plumage with predominantly white feathering adopted in winter to enhance concealment in snowy habitats. Ten gallinaceous species have been reported in Ontario; one of them no longer occurs in the province (Greater Prairie-Chicken, see p. 399).

# GRAY PARTRIDGE *Perdix perdix*

q B

28–35 cm / 11–14" Wt 365–420 g / 13–15 oz

The Gray Partridge was introduced as a game bird to North America in the early 1900s. It is most easily observed during fall and winter when coveys, numbering twenty or more individuals, forage on the ground in open agricultural land.

**APPEARANCE:** Round, cocky bird. Breast and upper back grey. Face and throat orangish brown, generally brighter and more extensive in male. Dark brown patch on white belly often horseshoe-shaped; small or absent in female. Reddish brown bars on flanks. Wings short and round; heavily mottled with grey and brown. Short, chestnut tail best observed in flight. Bill pale blue. **Immatures** pale brown with dark brown streaks and spots. Dusky brown bill.

► Distinguished from Northern Bobwhite by larger size, orangish brown foreparts, and generally greyer appearance.

**VOICE:** Most frequently heard at dawn and dusk. Rapidly repeated *kuta-kut-kut-kut* usually accompanied with tail-flicking. In spring, gives coarse *keee-uk*, with first note higher and resembling sound of rusty gate. Also utters rapid cackle when flushed.

**HABITAT AND BEHAVIOUR:** Agricultural fields and grasslands, and roadsides. Winters in crop stubble and wooded cover. Walks and runs rapidly on ground. Flies short distances (usually about 100 m; 328'), low to ground; rapid wingbeats alternate with glides. Explosive takeoffs. Roosts in tight groups in deep snow in winter.

**STATUS:** Uncommon year-round resident. Introduced.

# RING-NECKED PHEASANT *Phasianus colchicus*

Male: L 76–90 cm / 30.0–35.5" Female: L 51–66 cm / 20–26"
Wt 1.1–2.0 kg / 2.5–4.4 lb

This Asian native was introduced to Ontario in the late 1800s for the benefit of local hunters. Ill-equipped to handle cold Canadian winters, Ring-necked Pheasant populations persist only in low-snowfall areas in the south.

**APPEARANCE:** Male has iridescent green head with small, elongated crest. Red wattles on face surround yellow eyes. Incomplete white necklace. Body bronze and gold with areas of green iridescence. Feathers of back have white spots. Flanks spotted with black. Greyish green shoulder and rump patches visible in flight. Long, pointed golden tail barred with black. **Female** buffy mottled with brown and black. Somewhat lighter below with few markings on breast and belly. Pointed tail much shorter than that of male. **Immatures** resemble female.

♂

♀

▶ Male unmistakable. Sharp-tailed Grouse resembles female pheasant but smaller with much shorter tail with white outer feathers and is more heavily marked below. Other grouse smaller with short tails.

**VOICE:** Male utters loud, raspy *caw-cawk,* accompanied by muffled wing flutter and stamping feet. Both sexes give croaking alarm calls.

**HABITAT AND BEHAVIOUR:** Farmland, brushy fields, and marsh edges. Flight strong over short distances with noisy, almost vertical, takeoff. Runs quickly; often holds tail cocked up.

**STATUS:** Uncommon year-round resident. Introduced.

# JFFED GROUSE *Bonasa umbellus*
8–49 cm / 15–19" Wt 450–600 g / 1.0–1.3 lb

ffed Grouse populations fluctuate over cycles of nine or ten years.
though declines were once thought to be due to periodic outbreaks
disease, recent studies have demonstrated that lower populations
y be linked to densities of predators, such as the Northern Goshawk.

**PEARANCE:**
dy mottled
yish brown or
ous brown
ove. Small
ctile crest on
d. Black
thers on sides of
er neck (longer
male) fluffed out
ing courtship.
derside buffy,
vily barred with
wn or grey.
nks greyish
red with

ckish brown. Fan-shaped greyish or brownish tail has many dark
nsverse bars and blackish brown subterminal band. **Immatures**
emble female.

► Sharp-tailed Grouse browner and lacks fan-shaped tail and
ck feathers on neck. Spruce Grouse darker; squarish tail has rusty
. Willow Ptarmigan in summer has white wings and legs.

**ICE:** Male produces hollow drumming sound with wings. Usually
en in morning and at night and repeated at four-minute intervals.
male occasionally gives various clucking and hissing calls,
rticularly near chicks.

**ABITAT AND BEHAVIOUR:** Understorey of deciduous and
mixed woodlands. During courtship display, male fans
tail, extends neck ruff, and droops wings. Similar
posture given by female when defending brood.
Often runs to escape danger. Flushes
explosively. Feeds in treetops at dawn or
dusk during winter.

**STATUS:** Common year-round resident.

# SPRUCE GROUSE *Falcipennis canadensis*

L 38–50 cm / 15–20" Wt 350–430 g / 12.5–15.4 oz

This species has been called the "fool hen" because it allows observer to approach within a few feet before it retreats. The Spruce Grouse is noted for its elaborate courtship displays.

**APPEARANCE:** Male upperparts grey, barred with blackish grey. Barring on wings olive-brown. Upper breast and throat black; lower breast and belly also black, but feathers tipped variously with white. Tail dark brown with broad rufous terminal band. Comb of red skin above eye. **Female** dark rusty brown, thickly barred with cinnamon and black. Breast, flanks, and uppertail coverts tipped with white. Tail short and dark with buff or rusty tip. **Immatures** resemble female.

♂

♀

▶ Male distinguished from Sharp-tailed Grouse and Ruffed Grouse by black breast; female can be distinguished by tail. Ruffed Grouse has long, square tail with broad, dark band at tip. Tail of Sharp-tailed Grouse short and pointed.

**VOICE:** Male occasionally utters guttural *krrrrk krrrrk krr krrk krrk,* said to be lowest-pitched vocal sound of any North American bird. Territorial female gives chicken-like call that increases in volume with first few syllables, then decreases: *prrp prrrp prrp prrp prrp prrp prp prp prp.*

**HABITAT AND BEHAVIOUR:** Coniferous and mixed woodlands, particularly with ground cover of blueberry, grasses, and honeysuckle. Largely terrestrial. Flies rapidly and with great dexterity.

**STATUS:** Common year-round resident

# WILLOW PTARMIGAN *Lagopus lagopus*
35.0–43.5 cm / 13.8–17.1" Wt 500–800 g / 1.1–1.8 lb

During courtship, the male Willow Ptarmigan performs a series of intricate displays that include tail-fanning, strutting and waltzing, and head-wagging. If a female attempts to leave the display area, the male will vigorously chase her back into his territory.

**APPEARANCE:** Breeding male has bright rusty brown head and neck. Body white. Tail black. **Autumn male** has rufous brown upperparts barred and spotted with black. Belly and wings white. **Breeding** and **autumn female** warm brown with yellow barring on underparts. White wings that may be concealed when at rest. **Winter adults** entirely white with black tail feathers. Feet and legs covered with whitish feathers throughout year. Both sexes have red combs above eyes; largest in male during breeding. **Immatures** resemble adults except for blackish outer primaries.

▶ Rock Ptarmigan smaller overall with smaller bill; summer plumage more greyish brown; distinguished by black eye-stripe in winter.

♂ SUMMER

♀ SUMMER

**VOICE:** Breeding male gives loud, staccato *go-back go-back* at end of display flight. Differs from rattling call of Rock Ptarmigan. Female utters low clucking and purring call.

**HABITAT AND BEHAVIOUR:** Coastal tundra. Flight strong with rapid wingbeats interspersed frequently with glides. Rarely flies during breeding season. Generally walks. Feathered feet act as snowshoes in winter.

**STATUS:** Rare to abundant year-round resident.

# ROCK PTARMIGAN *Lagopus mutus*

L 32–40 cm / 12.6–15.7" Wt 475–625 g / 1.1–1.4 lb

During the long arctic winter, many Rock Ptarmigans leave their hostile tundra habitats and withdraw to more hospitable scrubby or forested areas in northern Ontario, Quebec, and the Prairie provinces.

**APPEARANCE:** Male in summer has blackish brown upperparts and breast, finely barred with brownish grey and olive. White feathers scattered throughout. Belly, wings, and legs white. Tail feathers black with white tips. Scarlet comb above eye. **Summer female** largely greyish brown with broad bars of buff and black. Legs, wings, and part of belly white. Tail black with white tips. Both sexes predominantly white in

WINTER

**winter.** Male, and occasionally female, has black lores and eye-lines. Tail black with white tips. Feet and legs feathered with white. **Immatures** brownish black heavily barred with yellow and olive. Feathers of upperparts conspicuously tipped with white.

▶ Foreparts of male Willow Ptarmigan rufous in summer; female browner. In winter, Willow Ptarmigan distinguished by lack of black lores and eye-line.

**VOICE:** Male gives loud, guttural *ah-aah-ah-aaaah* during display flight. Also utters drawn-out *ooww-aaaaa* followed by cackling *a-a-a-a*. Both sexes give various low-pitched clucking, rattling, and chucking notes.

**HABITAT AND BEHAVIOUR:** Arctic or alpine tundra. Sometimes boreal forest and shrubby margins of lakes and rivers in winter. Flies infrequently; usually only when flushed by a predator or during display flights. Runs or walks quickly with regular gait; moves more slowly when foraging.

**STATUS:** Rare to common winter visitor. Very rare in summer.

# SHARP-TAILED GROUSE *Tympanuchus phasianellus*
38–50 cm / 15–20" Wt 600–1000 g / 1.3–2.2 lb

The Sharp-tailed Grouse was an important food source for Native North American societies. Accordingly, its elaborate and highly animated courtship displays have been incorporated into many ceremonial dances.

**APPEARANCE:** Head, neck, back, and wings heavily barred with brown, black, and buff. Crescent-shaped yellowish comb over eyes. Conspicuous white spots on wings. Brownish tail has long, pointed central feathers and shorter, white outer feathers. Underparts white; breast and belly feathers have V-shaped brown edges. Male inflates pinkish purple sacs on neck during courtship. **Female** has lighter, more barred crown. **Immatures** resemble adults but somewhat greyer overall, including underparts.
► White spots on wing and scaly underparts diagnostic. Ruffed Grouse and Spruce Grouse have long, square tails.

**VOICE:** Male gives dove-like *hoo hoo*. Both sexes utter clucking *whucker-whucker-whucker* when taking flight. Also produce various cackling and gobbling calls. Male stomps feet and rattles upturned tail during display.

**HABITAT AND BEHAVIOUR:** Muskeg and open bogs with scattered shrubs and trees. Flights generally short but capable of long, fast flight. Rapid wingbeats separated by several seconds of gliding. Walks on ground. Perches in bushes and trees. Walks well in snow.

**STATUS:** Uncommon to common year-round resident.

# WILD TURKEY *Meleagris gallopavo*
L 90–120 cm / 36–48" Wt 4–8 kg / 8.8–17.6 lb

The Wild Turkey was extirpated in Ontario during the early 1900s as a result of the loss of hardwood habitat and overhunting. It was returned to southern Ontario in 1984 through the introduction of wild-caught birds from the United States.

**APPEARANCE:** Very large gallinaceous bird. Bare blue head; neck with pink wattles and caruncles. Neck and snood of adult male scarlet in spring. Body iridescent bronzy brown; feathers generally tipped with dark brown in male and rust or white in **female**. Tail rusty brown, finely barred with dark brown, has narrow, black subterminal band and rusty tip. Bill orangish yellow. Male much larger than female.

**Immatures** resemble female.

▶ Combination of very large body, small head, and long legs diagnostic in all plumages.

**VOICE:** Various clucking, cackling, and yelping calls. Male gives gobbling call that resembles that of domestic turkey. Also gives *put-put* alarm call. Both give *keow-keow* flocking call. Female clucks to young.

**HABITAT AND BEHAVIOUR:** Open, mature deciduous forest; wooded swamps, fields, and woodlots. Male usually runs to avoid danger, but female may fly. Neck often outstretched level with back when running. Roosts in trees. Male erects tail like fan during courtship.

**STATUS:** Rare to locally common year-round resident.

# NORTHERN BOBWHITE *Colinus virginianus*
21–26 cm / 8.5–10.5" Wt 140–170 g / 5–6 oz

During the night, bobwhite coveys roost on the ground in a circle with their tails pointing inward and bills pointed outward. This position conserves body heat and provides greater vigilance for predators.

**APPEARANCE:**
Adult male has small, erectile head crest on dark chestnut crown; conspicuous white forehead, eyebrow, and throat. Black stripe extends from back of eye to neck. Otherwise, upperparts brown, finely barred with tan and black. Wings brown patterned with buff, black, and  grey. Short bluish grey tail. Throat and neck streaked with black and white. Breast, sides, and flanks white, narrowly barred with black and streaked with chestnut. **Female** resembles male except has buff eyebrow and throat, and less boldly marked plumage. **Immatures** similar to adult female but can be separated by buffy white flecks on upper primary coverts.

▶ Larger Gray Partridge has grey crown, nape, neck, and breast; rusty face and belly-patch. Ruffed Grouse much larger with longer tail; lacks conspicuous facial pattern.

**VOICE:** Clear, whistled *bob-white*. Coveys give *ka-loi-kee?* that is answered by *whoil-kee*.

**HABITAT AND BEHAVIOUR:** Agricultural land, grasslands, brushy open country, and wooded edges. Flies relatively short distances close to ground. Explosive takeoffs. Walks and runs quickly. Coveys forage as a group.

**STATUS:** Extremely rare to rare year-round resident. Endangered in Canada.

# GRUIFORMES
## Rails, Cranes, and Allies

In Ontario, membership of this diverse worldwide order is restricted to two divergent families. Rails and their allies (Rallidae) are aquatic, chicken-like birds with short tails and short, rounded wings. They prefer wetland habitats, which they leave only during migration. Elusive by nature, these birds are best identified by vocalization and habitat preference. In contrast, cranes (Gruidae) are somewhat heron-like in appearance. These tall birds can be observed in open grasslands and fields as well as wetlands. Cranes fly in V-shaped flocks with their necks outstretched, and frequently soar on thermals. In Ontario the order Gruiformes is represented by ten species; three occur as accidentals (Black Rail, Purple Gallinule, and Whooping Crane, see pp. 385–86).

# YELLOW RAIL *Coturnicops noveboracensis*

15–19 cm / 6.0–7.5" Wt 45–65 g / 1.6–2.3 oz

The Yellow Rail has been called the "Clicker" after its distinctive call. Its abundance is frequently underestimated due to its elusive nature and propensity for vocalizing at night.

**APPEARANCE:**
Crown and nape
brownish black,
feathers barred with
white. Lores
blackish brown.
Chin and upper
throat whitish.
Broad tawny stripe
over eye. Otherwise,
upperparts buffy
brown streaked with
dark brown and
black. Feathers of
back, scapulars, and

rump barred and tipped with white. Primaries brown. White secondaries form large patch visible in flight. Tail black with white bands, and edged with brown. Lower throat and breast tawny. Belly white. Bill usually olive-brown in **female** and **winter male** but bright yellow in breeding male. **Immatures** resemble female but somewhat more heavily speckled and barred with white.

▶ Distinguishable from Sora by much smaller size, buffy coloration, and short, quail-like bill. Black Rail much darker. Other rails larger than Yellow Rail with much longer bills.

**VOICE:** Most common call of adult male a rhythmic, five-note clicking usually uttered incessantly after dark: *click-click click-click-click*. Resembles sound of stones tapped together. Female gives wheezes, squeaks, and whines.

**HABITAT AND BEHAVIOUR:** Grassy marshes and wet meadows. Open grain fields in winter. Runs with head stretched forward, often flicking wings for balance. Usually sneaks mouse-like through reeds. If threatened, will freeze or fly off weakly with legs dangling. Swims well but rarely. May dive to escape predators.

**STATUS:** Vulnerable in Ontario. Rare to locally common breeder.

# KING RAIL *Rallus elegans*

L 38–48 cm / 15–19" Wt 300–360 g / 10.7–12.9 oz

The King Rail is Ontario's largest and most colourful rail. Its thinly scattered populations are declining locally because of the drainage of wetland areas and pesticide use.

**APPEARANCE:** Laterally compressed body with long legs and toes. Upper-parts olive-brown with feathers broadly edged with tawny and dark brown. Upper wing coverts bright russet. Light pinkish stripe from base of bill to behind eye. Upper throat white. Breast rufous; flanks dark brown barred with white. Undertail coverts white. Bill longer than head and slightly decurved; orange-yellow with darker tip. Bill light brown in **immatures.**

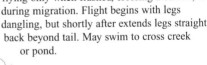

▶ Distinguished from Virginia Rail, Yellow Rail, and Sora by much larger size.

**VOICE:** Low, grunting series of notes (*cheup-cheup-cheup*) that become increasingly softer and more rapidly uttered. Often answered by others. Also harsh, loud *kik-kik-kik* given during day and night. Utters soft *poyeek-poyeek-poyeek* just prior to breeding.

**HABITAT AND BEHAVIOUR:** Freshwater marshes, shrubby swamps, and marshy borders of lakes, ponds, rivers, and creeks. Usually walks or runs, flying only when flushed, crossing a barrier, or during migration. Flight begins with legs dangling, but shortly after extends legs straight back beyond tail. May swim to cross creek or pond.

**STATUS:** Very rare breeder. Endangered in Canada.

# VIRGINIA RAIL *Rallus limicola*
23–27 cm / 9.0–10.5" Wt 65–95 g / 2.3–3.4 oz

Observers rarely see more of this secretive species than its upturned tail as it disappears into dense vegetation. The Virginia Rail is found primarily in freshwater marshes during the breeding season but also inhabits saltwater marshes in winter.

**APPEARANCE:** Laterally compressed body. Upperparts dark brown, feathers edged with rusty brown and olive. Sides of head grey with buffy stripe from bill to above eye. Eyes reddish brown. Long bill reddish brown above to dull orange below. Chin white. Throat and breast bright cinnamon. Flanks and sides dark brown barred with olive and white. Undertail coverts white. **Immatures** have darker plumage, particularly on underparts. Breast and belly marked profusely with dull white in some individuals. Eyes dark brown.

► Plumage similar to King Rail, but Virginia Rail much smaller and has grey cheeks. Other small rails have short bills.

**VOICE:** Metallic *tick-it* heard primarily in spring. Pairs give antiphonal, queting *grunt*. Also utters descending, laughing *wack-wack-wack*.

**HABITAT AND BEHAVIOUR:** Freshwater marshes, pond edges, and sloughs. Rapid wingbeats; often lands with ungraceful drop. Seldom flies except during migration. Walks and runs on ground. Uses long toes to walk on floating vegetation. Tail fanned and erect while walking.

**STATUS:** Uncommon to common breeder.

## SORA *Porzana carolina*

L 20.5–25.5 cm / 8–10" Wt 72–88 g / 2.6–3.1 oz

The Sora, although ungainly in flight when flushed from marsh vegetation, is a strong distance flyer: it winters on the Atlantic Coastal Plain, throughout the Caribbean, and in Bermuda.

**APPEARANCE:**
Crown blackish brown. Face black with short yellow bill. Eyebrow, sides of head, foreneck, and breast grey. Back and scapulars streaked with black, olive-brown, buff, and white. Wings and tail dull brown edged with buff. Sides and flanks blackish,

barred with white and olive-brown. Middle of belly whitish; undertail coverts whitish and visible when tail cocked. **Immatures** similar but buffy brown below with brownish face.

▶ Immature Sora resembles smaller Yellow Rail but latter has white bars running across back, darker undertail coverts, and white wing-patch. Adult Yellow Rail distinguished by buffier plumage that lacks grey on foreparts. Virginia Rail rustier with long, thin bill. Purple Gallinule much more brightly coloured. Other rails much larger with longer bills.

**VOICE:** Descending *whee-hee-hee-hee-hee-hee* that sounds like a horse's whinny. Also gives plaintive *ker-wee* given alone or preceding whinny. Alarm call a sharp *quink-quink-quink*.

**HABITAT AND BEHAVIOUR:** Wetlands, particularly with cattails and sedges. Walks or runs through vegetation. Reluctant to fly; difficult to flush. Flocks fly low with steady beating of wings during migration. Readily swims and dives. Submerges with only bill and eyes above water.

**STATUS:** Uncommon to common breeder.

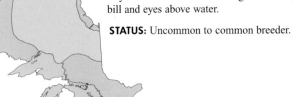

# OMMON MOORHEN *Gallinula chloropus*

30.5–38.0 cm / 12–15" Wt 335–445 g / 12–16 oz

he Common Moorhen, formerly called the Common Gallinule, looks ke a bird built by committee: it has a chicken-like bill, a duck-like ead and body, and a heron-like undercarriage.

**PPEARANCE:** ead, neck, and nderparts black. ill red with rominent red ontal shield and ellow tip. Back nd wings dark rown. White orizontal stripe own sides. Tail lack with white uter feathers. Legs nd feet yellow. **Vinter adults** have rownish facial nield and bill. **mmatures** similar ut paler with reyish foreparts,

hitish throat, white and grey undertail coverts, dull orange bill, and usky legs and feet.

▶ American Coot has white bill and frontal shield, and blackish ack and wings; immatures have greyish bill and legs; lacks white tripe down sides in all plumages. Purple Gallinule has purplish blue oreparts and greenish brown back; immatures distinguished by buffy ead and underparts and brownish green upperparts.

**OICE:** Sharp, repeated *kr-r-ruk kek kek kek kek.* Higher pitched than call of American Coot. Also gives hen-like clucks and various screams and squeaks.

**HABITAT AND BEHAVIOUR:** Marshes and reedy ponds. Flies awkwardly or races into vegetation when flushed. Bobs head back and forth when walking or swimming. Often rafts with American Coots. Feeds in more open areas than other rails.

**STATUS:** Fairly common breeder. Common migrant in spring and fall.

# AMERICAN COOT *Fulica americana*

L 33.0–40.5 cm / 13–16" Wt 475–530 g / 1.1–1.2 lb

The American Coot is sensitive to habitat modification, particularly changes in water levels. Consequently, breeding individuals may not be present every year in the same locations.

**APPEARANCE:**
Black head and neck. White bill has dark red ring near tip. White frontal shield has red swelling near upper edge. Eyes red. Plump, dark blackish grey body. Narrow white border on trailing edge of wing visible in flight. Sides of undertail

coverts white. Legs greenish yellow. Feet have lobed toes. **Immatures** much paler, particularly on head, neck, and underparts. Bill and legs greyish. Lacks frontal shield.

▶ Common Moorhen has red bill and frontal shield, and white streak on sides. Blackish ducks distinguished by bill shape.

**VOICE:** Utters grating *kuk-kuk-kuk-kuk*. Other calls include measured *ka-ha ha-ha* and various other croaks, grunts, and cackles.

**HABITAT AND BEHAVIOUR:** Marshes, ponds, and wetlands with open water. Flies with laboured wingbeats. Big feet trail behind short tail. Patters across water to take flight. Bobs head while swimming. Feeds by dipping head below surface or by diving. Forms large rafts offshore.

**STATUS:** Uncommon breeder. Uncommon to abundant spring and fall migrant. Rare winter resident.

# SANDHILL CRANE *Grus canadensis* F

100–120 cm / 40–48" Wt 3.3–3.8 kg / 7.3–8.4 lb

The Sandhill Crane performs elaborate courtship displays that include leaping and dancing, head pumping, bowing, and duet calling. It was formerly more widespread in Ontario.

**APPEARANCE:** Tall, long-legged bird with long, straight neck. Crown covered with bare red skin. Body and neck generally pale grey; however, in spring, adults rub body with oil, causing variations in plumage colour from drab grey to cinnamon. Added colour lost with moulting in summer. Bill dark green and legs black. **Immatures** reddish brown with brown-feathered crown and pinkish orange bill.

► Whooping Crane predominantly white with black on wings. Great Blue Heron has black-and-white head and much longer, yellowish bill; lacks red crown.

**VOICE:** Rolling, bugling call, *garoooooooooooooooooo,* carries over great distances. Calls most frequently at dusk and dawn. Also, male and female produce synchronized dueting calls. Male gives long, low calls with bill pointed straight up. Female answers with more rapid, shriller notes (*tuck-a-tuck-a-tuck-a*) while holding bill horizontal to ground.

**HABITAT AND BEHAVIOUR:** Low shrub bogs, peaty wetlands, muskeg, fields, and tundra. Flies with neck outstretched. Flight has snapping upstroke and slower downstroke that distinguishes it from other long-legged, long-necked birds. Walks and runs, but does not perch.

**STATUS:** Rare to locally uncommon breeder. Rare to common migrant. Extirpated from southwestern Ontario in 1920s.

123

# CHARADRIIFORMES
## Shorebirds, Gulls, Auks, and Allies

Ontario members of this large, diverse order comprise six anatomically and behaviourally distinct families. Most species occur near shores, wetlands, mudflats, and fields; however, adaptation to numerous divergent niches has resulted in a seemingly endless variety of bill shapes and feeding strategies. Many charadriiforms, particularly among the Scolopacidae, undertake long-distance migrations from deep in the Southern Hemisphere north to the Canadian Arctic. Migrating flocks of mixed species frequently number many thousands of individuals. Ninety-one charadriiform species occur in Ontario as breeders and migrants. Twenty-eight accidental species have been recorded (Mongolian Plover, Snowy Plover, Wilson's Plover, American Oyster catcher, Black-necked Stilt, Spotted Redshank, Wandering Tattler, Eskimo Curlew, Slender-billed Curlew, Long-billed Curlew, Black-tailed Godwit, Little Stint, Sharp-tailed Sandpiper, Heermann's Gull, Slaty-backed Gull, Ross's Gull, Royal Tern, Sandwich Tern, Least Tern, Sooty Tern, White-winged Tern, Black Skimmer, Dovekie, Thick-billed Murre, Razorbill, Long-billed Murrelet, Ancient Murrelet, and Atlantic Puffin, see pp. 386–89).

# BLACK-BELLIED PLOVER *Pluvialis squatarola* ♀
26.5–34.5 cm / 10.4–13.6" Wt 160–190 g / 5.7–6.9 oz

The Black-bellied Plover is frequently observed foraging in mixed shorebird assemblages. Its wary nature and propensity to give alarm serve it well as flock sentinel.

**APPEARANCE:**

Breeding male has marbled silvery-white-and-black-upperparts. Broad white stripe from forehead and eyebrow extends down neck to sides of upper breast. White rump and wing stripe, and black wing-pit patch in all plumages. Tail barred black and white. Face and underparts to belly black. Undertail coverts white. **Female** has somewhat duller dark brown and whitish markings. Winter adults greyish above with whitish spots and feather edges. Dull white eyebrow. Underparts whitish with greyish brown streaking on face and breast. **Immatures** resemble winter adults but with heavier streaking on underparts.

▶ Upperparts (including rump and tail) of breeding American Golden-Plover entirely mottled with golden yellow and blackish brown; undertail coverts black; no black patch under wing; lacks distinct white wing stripe; proportionately shorter bill.

**VOICE:** Male gives whistling *tlee-oo-eeei* with lower middle note. Near female also utters melodious *pljujutipljujut* followed by *tiut-tiut,* trilling *prrlju-juju,* ending with whistling *tiu-li tiu-li.* Call notes include *kleee, too-ree,* and *whee-er-ee.*

**HABITAT AND BEHAVIOUR:** Tundra. Shorelines and flooded fields during migration. Fast, powerful flyer. Runs rather than walks. Rarely forages while wading. Swims short distances.

**STATUS:** Rare to common spring and fall migrant. Rare summer visitor.

# AMERICAN GOLDEN-PLOVER *Pluvialis dominica*

L 24–28 cm / 9.4–11.0"  Wt 165–190 g / 5.9–6.8 oz

Once known collectively as the Lesser Golden-Plover, the American Golden-Plover and its sister species, the Pacific Golden-Plover of Alaska and Siberia, are now considered separate species.

**APPEARANCE:**
Crown, nape, and upperparts (including wings and tail) of breeding adults marbled with golden yellow and blackish brown. Indistinct wing stripe. Broad white stripe from forehead and eyebrow extends down neck to sides of upper breast.

Face, throat, and underparts black. Bill black. **Female** less colourful than male; often has some whitish feathers on face and breast. **Winter adults** retain mottled upperparts. Underparts whitish with dusky brown streaks on sides of head and breast. Conspicuous white eyebrow. Underwing whitish. **Immatures** resemble winter adults but somewhat browner with barred breast and flanks.

▶ Breeding Black-bellied Plover has silvery grey and black upperparts, white shoulders, rump, and undertail coverts, and proportionately larger bill; in winter, shows black wing-pit patch, white wing stripe, and less contrast between crown and eyebrow; immatures have more heavily streaked breast and belly.

**VOICE:** Whistled *queedle* given in flight. Harsher and more abbreviated than call of Black-bellied Plover. Also utters *klee-yeep* when agitated.

**HABITAT AND BEHAVIOUR:** Tundra and rocky slopes. Ploughed fields, pastures, and shorelines during migration. High-speed, sustained flight may exceed 180 km/h (108 mph). Walks, runs, and roosts on ground. Rarely uses elevated perches.

**STATUS:** Extremely rare breeder. Rare to uncommon spring migrant Common fall migrant.

# EMIPALMATED PLOVER *Charadrius semipalmatus* ⊬

17–19 cm / 6.7–7.5" Wt 45–60 g / 1.6–2.1 oz

cubating Semipalmated Plovers typically respond to foxes and avian
edators by running from the nest and calling loudly. However, they
nerally attempt to distract human intruders with an exaggerated
jury-feigning display.

**PPEARANCE:**
reeding male
own above.
orehead and
arrow stripe
ove eye white.
orecrown and
des of head black.
ubby black bill
s orange base.
hite collar
ordered with
ngle black collar.
ings dark brown
ith white stripe.
entral tail feathers

own with white tips. Outer pair white. Underparts white. Legs
ange. **Female** similar but with brownish black markings. **Winter
dults** greyer. Broad white eye-stripe joined to forehead. Bill blackish.
**nmatures** resemble winter adults but somewhat paler. Feathers on
pperparts fringed with brown and buff.

► Accidental Wilson's Plover larger with heavier bill, wider
reast band, and pinkish legs. Piping and Snowy plovers paler above,
pically with incomplete breast bands. Piping Plover has yellowish bill
nd legs. Snowy Plover has blackish bill and legs. Killdeer has two
reast bands.

**OICE:** Call a clear, whistled *chu-wheet* with ascending second
yllable. Flight song a rapid, rough *kee-weep-r-r-r-r-r-r-r* that ends
with descending yelp. Also gives chattering
*chup chup chup.*

**HABITAT AND BEHAVIOUR:** Shorelines and
open sandy areas. Flight fast, powerful, and
acrobatic on long, slender wings. Walks
quickly or runs with head up. Pauses while
scanning for prey. Pats ground with feet to
stir up invertebrates. Rarely wades in
shallow water.

**STATUS:** Common breeder.
Rare to common spring and
fall migrant.

## PIPING PLOVER *Charadrius melodus* ⸕

L 17–18 cm / 6.7–7.1" Wt 43–63 g / 1.5–2.3 oz

The Piping Plover teeters on the verge of extinction throughout its North American range. Decimated by overhunting during the late 1800s, it is now threatened by fluctuating water levels, feral predators, and recreational use of beach habitat.

**APPEARANCE:**
Breeding adults have sandy brown upperparts. Black band on forecrown. White forehead, eye-line, lores, and throat. Bill orange with black tip. Single black collar (sometimes incomplete) bordered above by white band. Wings have brown flight

♀

feathers with white band near base visible in flight. Rump white. Tail whitish with black tips on all but outer feathers. Underparts white. Legs bright orange. **Winter adults** lack black forecrown and collar. Sandy brown patch at sides of breast. Bill entirely black. Legs dull orange. **Immatures** resemble winter adults except somewhat greyer.
▶ Accidental Snowy Plover distinguished by smaller size; thinner, longer black bill; and grey to greyish yellow legs. Semi-palmated Plover much darker above with bolder facial pattern. Wilson's Plover has broader breast band, darker upperparts, longer bill, and greyish to greyish pink legs.

**VOICE:** Male utters plaintive, whistling, persistent *pipe-pipe-pipe-pipe-pipe.* Threat call a low, rattling *bec bec bec.* Drawn-out *woo-up* given in alarm.

**HABITAT AND BEHAVIOUR:** Sandy beaches. Deep, slow wingbeats. Tips body side to side in flight. Walks or runs, rather than flies, to escape predators.

**STATUS:** Extremely rare breeder. Endangered in Ontario and Canada.

# KILLDEER *Charadrius vociferus*

L 23–28 cm / 9–11" Wt 90–98 g / 3.2–3.5 oz

The Killdeer is probably best known for the loud alarm calls and injury-feigning display that it uses to lure potential predators from its nest. This commotion also alerts other birds nesting in the vicinity, who quickly respond with agitation.

**APPEARANCE:**
Largest of ringed plovers. Two black bands on white breast distinctive in adult plumage. Crown and cheeks brown. White forehead bordered above by black line. White eyebrow and collar. Red eye-ring. Long, thin black bill. Upperparts brown. Wings have prominent white

stripe. Rump and uppertail coverts rufous. Black-and-white-tipped tail extends well beyond wing tips. Underparts white. Long, orangish pink legs. **Immatures** resemble adults but somewhat more buffy above.
　▶ Other similar plovers have only one dark breast band in breeding plumage. Downy Killdeer young have only one breast band but can be distinguished by white tips on black wings.

**VOICE:** Loud, insistent *kill-dee kill-dee kill-dee.* Also gives ascending, plaintive *dee-dee-dee* when alarmed.

**HABITAT AND BEHAVIOUR:** Open fields, lawns, beaches, and meadows. Flight swift and erratic. Generally flies low to ground. Walks and runs rapidly, stopping abruptly to scan surroundings. Frequently forages after dusk.

**STATUS:** Common breeder. Rare winter resident.

# AMERICAN AVOCET *Recurvirostra americana*
L 16–20 cm / 40–50" Wt 280–365 g / 10–13 oz

The first record of American Avocets breeding in Ontario occurred in 1980 near Lake of the Woods. Prior to that time, this species was known only as an occasional spring and fall migrant in the southern counties.

**APPEARANCE:**
Thin, black, upturned bill. Breeding adults have cinnamon head and neck; whitish around bill and eye. Middle of back, lower scapulars, rump, tail, and underparts white. Upper scapulars and lateral feathering on back black. At rest, wings and back

appear to have broad black and white stripes. In flight, outer half of wing black, and inner wing crossed diagonally by broad black band. Wing linings white. Legs greyish blue. **Winter adults** and **immatures** have light grey head and neck.

▶ Could be confused with godwits and Willet in distant flight but generally distinguishable by upturned bill and contrasting black and white on back.

**VOICE:** Alarm call a repeated, melodic *plee-eek*. Also utters soft *whuck*.

**HABITAT AND BEHAVIOUR:** Beaches, shallow lakes, and ponds. Head and legs extended in flight. Covers short distances by walking or wading. Shakes feet to remove mud when lifting them from water. Swims well. Forages by turning head rapidly from side to side while moving forward, sweeping bill across surface of mud or water.

**STATUS:** Extremely rare breeder. Rare to uncommon migrant.

# GREATER YELLOWLEGS *Tringa melanoleuca* F

32–38 cm / 12.5–15.0" Wt 150–225 g / 5.4–8.0 oz

The Greater Yellowlegs feeds with a characteristic side-sweeping motion of its bill. It may also catch fish by chasing and lunging, or may probe submerged vegetation for hidden prey.

**APPEARANCE:** bright yellow legs. Breeding adults have upperparts checkered with black, brown, and white. Whitish eye-ring. Wings brown speckled with white. White rump. Tail barred with brown and white. Chin white. Throat and breast whitish, heavily streaked with dark brown. Belly and flanks barred with brown. Mantle greyish brown in **winter** plumage; feathers edged with black and white. Throat and upper breast finely streaked with grey. Belly and undertail coverts white. **Immatures** blackish brown above heavily, marked with small white spots. Throat and upper breast finely streaked with brownish black. Sides often barred with brown.

▶ Distinguished from most other shorebirds by large size, slim body, and long bill, neck, and yellow legs. Lesser Yellowlegs distinguished by smaller size, shorter bill, proportionately longer legs, and *yu-yu* call; belly white in breeding plumage. Immatures have grey breast. Willet has bluish legs and bold black-and-white wing pattern.

**VOICE:** Loud, ringing descending *whew whew whew*. Utters incessant *ty* when disturbed. Repeated yodeling, melodious *too-whee* notes given in spring.

**HABITAT AND BEHAVIOUR:** Bogs and shallow ponds, and shorelines surrounded by vegetation. Flight strong and swift with legs extending beyond tail. Walks with high-stepping gait. Runs with neck extended. Occasionally feeds while swimming.

**STATUS:** Common to very common breeder. Common migrant.

# LESSER YELLOWLEGS *Tringa flavipes* F

L 25–28 cm / 10–11" Wt 70–90 g / 2.5–3.2 oz

The Lesser Yellowlegs walks with a graceful, high-stepping gait. It moves rapidly while foraging with neck held forward to probe muddy substrates, snatch insects from the air, and pluck prey off vegetation.

**APPEARANCE:**
Long, bright yellow legs. Breeding adults have greyish brown upperparts mottled with white and black. Forehead and crown streaked and somewhat darker. White eyebrow and eye-ring. Long, thin, blackish bill. Wings blackish brown edged with white. White rump visible

in flight. Tail narrowly barred with white and dark grey. Underparts whitish with brown streaking on neck and breast. Sides and flanks barred with dark brown. **Winter adults** have more uniformly greyish brown upperparts with pale spots. Underparts white with fine grey streaking on neck and breast. **Immatures** similar but browner above with breast finely streaked with greyish brown.
▶ Greater Yellowlegs much bigger with proportionately longer bi that is thicker at base; distinguished from other shorebirds by slender body, long neck, and long, bright yellow legs. Solitary Sandpiper darker above, including rump, with more conspicuous white eye-ring. Immatures and winter adult Wilson's Phalarope have shorter legs and thinner bills, and lack streaking on foreparts. Stilt Sandpipers have greenish legs, more distinct white eyebrow, and somewhat drooping bi

**VOICE:** High-pitched, double *tew-tew.* Also utters repeated *pill-e wee pill-e wee pill-e wee* and high, clear *queep.* Greater Yellowlegs *whew* cal tri-syllabic and more forceful.

**HABITAT AND BEHAVIOUR:** Marshes, ponds, and shorelines. Flight languid and buoyant. Less strong than that of Greater Yellowlegs. Sometimes lands in deep wate May feed while swimming. Perches on fences and in trees.

**STATUS:** Common breeder. Commo spring and fall migrant.

# OLITARY SANDPIPER *Tringa solitaria*
20–23 cm / 8–9" Wt 40–60 g / 1.4–2.1 oz

though it is most frequently observed foraging in ponds and
eamsides, the Solitary Sandpiper is one of two sandpiper species that
utinely nest in trees. It often uses the abandoned nests of American
obin, Eastern Kingbird, and Gray Jay.

**PPEARANCE:**
perparts of
eeding adults
rk olive-brown,
avily spotted with
ite. Distinctive
rrow, white eye-
g. Greenish
own bill rather
aight and heavy.
derparts white;
reneck and breast
avily streaked
th black. Rump
rk brown. Central
athers of tail dark

own; outer feathers barred with brown and white. Legs green.
entified in flight by dark, unpatterned wings and conspicuous dark
rs on tail. **Winter adults** greyer, and washed with brown on throat
d breast. **Immatures** similar to winter adults but somewhat more
ve and buff.

▶ Lesser Yellowlegs can be distinguished by larger size,
ite rump, yellow legs, and lack of eye-ring. Spotted Sandpiper
aller with white line over eye and heavily spotted underparts in
eeding plumage.

**OICE:** Muted, thin *peet-weet-weet* given frequently in flight. Similar
call of Spotted Sandpiper but higher pitched and sharper.

**HABITAT AND BEHAVIOUR:** Open, wet coniferous
woodlands near wetlands, ponds, and lakes.
Flight somewhat swallow-like from below with
graceful, strong wingbeats. Flies straight up
when flushed. Wades slowly in water up to
belly. Frequently bobs head and teeters body.

**STATUS:** Uncommon breeder. Rare to
uncommon spring and fall migrant.

# WILLET *Catoptrophorus semipalmatus*

L 36–42 cm / 14.2–16.5" Wt 280–450 g / 10–16 oz

This large, stout shorebird breeds along prairie lake margins and Atlantic beaches. Individuals are most frequently observed in Ontario foraging among mixed-species shorebird flocks along the lower Great Lakes shorelines.

**APPEARANCE:**
Breeding adults greyish brown above; somewhat paler below. Upperparts, breast, and flanks finely spotted and barred with black. Long, straight, heavy bill. Wings strongly patterned with black and white, visible in flight. Rump white. Tail white with greyish

brown tip. Long, bluish grey legs. **Winter adults** have drab greyish brown upperparts and breast. Belly whitish. **Immatures** resemble winter adults, but feathers of upperparts have contrasting buff edges.

▶ Black-and-white wing pattern diagnostic in flight. Godwits have very long yellowish or orange bills, with recurving accentuated toward tip. Greater Yellowlegs has yellow legs, more contrasting body plumage, and slightly recurved bill.

**VOICE:** Loud, shrill, rolling *pill-will-willet pill-will-willet.*

**HABITAT AND BEHAVIOUR:** Marshes, wet meadows, and beaches. Flight strong, direct, and somewhat duck-like. Holds wings open for few seconds after landing. Defends young by dive-bombing predators. Walks deliberately while feeding. Sometimes perches in trees or on fences and buildings.

**STATUS:** Rare to uncommon visitor from April to September.

# POTTED SANDPIPER *Actitis macularia* +F

8.0–20.5 cm / 7–8" Wt 34–50 g / 1.2–1.8 oz

e Spotted Sandpiper forages with a characteristic teeter-tottering
it, bobbing its tail up and down with each step. This species
metimes perches in trees and to poles to survey for predators.

**PPEARANCE:**
eeding adults
ve olive-brown
perparts with
rker brown bars.
hite eyebrow and
complete eye-ring.
ackish eye-line.
ll orange with
ck tip. Cheeks
d sides of neck
rrowly streaked
th white and
own. Chin white.
ngs greyish

own; secondaries tipped with white. Diagonal white stripe across
ght feathers visible on open wing. Tail feathers olive-grey, tipped
th white except central pair. Outermost feathers barred with brown
d white. Underparts white with round blackish spots, heaviest on
east and upper belly. Legs and feet pinkish. **Winter adults** lack spots
underparts. Distinctive greyish brown patch at sides of foreneck and
east. Wedge of white visible in front of folded wing. Upperparts
rrowly barred with brown and buff. Bill olive-brown. Legs and feet
ve to yellow. **Immatures** resemble winter birds but with more
nspicuous barring on back.

▶ Large breast spots diagnostic in breeding plumage. Solitary
ndpiper similar in winter but has complete white eye-ring, throat
shed with brown, and conspicuous light dotting on back; lacks pale
ebrow and diagonal white stripes on open wing.

**VOICE:** Alarm call an extended series of similar notes
*tweet-weet-tweet-weet-weet-tweet-weet.* Also
gives metallic *spink spink.*

**HABITAT AND BEHAVIOUR:** Ponds, lakes,
streams, and marshes. Shallow, rapid,
fluttering wingbeats. Deep stroke flight
characteristic of most shorebirds rarely seen.
Sails low over water on stiff wings.

**STATUS:** Common breeder.
Common spring and fall migrant.

135

# UPLAND SANDPIPER *Bartramia longicauda*

L 28–32 cm / 11.0–12.6" Wt 175–220 g / 6.2–7.9 oz

The Upland Sandpiper faced catastrophic declines in population densities from market hunting during the late 1800s. Fortunately, populations rebounded somewhat during the twentieth century and remain stable where suitable grassy habitat persists.

**APPEARANCE:** Very small head and long, thin neck. Upperparts mottled with buff and black, conferring scaly appearance. Large, dark eyes. Short, straight, orangish bill. Wings long and dark in flight. Dark, wedge-shaped tail extends well beyond wing tips. Underparts buff to white. Breast streaked and flanks barred with brown. Wing linings heavily barred with brown and white. Yellowish legs. **Immatures** resemble adults.

► Buff-breasted Sandpiper has shorter neck and larger head; but underparts lack obvious dark markings. Willet has heavier bill, dark legs, and bold black-and-white wing linings. Pectoral Sandpiper has shorter neck and smaller eyes; streaking on underparts ends abruptly; no barring on flanks.

**VOICE:** Utters rolling *quip-ip-ip-ip* when alarmed. Often given at night. Whistles *whip-whee-ee-you* during courtship.

**HABITAT AND BEHAVIOUR:** Grasslands, open meadows and fields. Holds wings open for several seconds after landing to display barred wing linings. Runs in spurts, then stops abruptly. Frequently perches on fence posts.

**STATUS:** Rare to uncommon breeder. Uncommon migrant.

# WHIMBREL *Numenius phaeopus*
38–48 cm / 15–19" Wt 320–475 g / 11.5–17.0 oz

During migration, this medium-sized curlew leaves its northern breeding ground and passes through southern Ontario en route to staging grounds on the Atlantic coast. Thousands of individuals may congregate prior to their non-stop flight to South America.

## APPEARANCE:

Crown has conspicuous buff and dark brown stripes. Chin white. Long, decurved bill dusky brown, paler at base. Otherwise, upperparts greyish brown variably marked with buff. Primaries greyish brown with buff markings. Tail greyish brown barred with brown and tipped with buff. Buffy neck and breast streaked with dark brown. Belly whitish. Wing linings pinkish buff barred with greyish brown. **Immatures** similar with buffier breast and more distinct buff markings on back and scapulars.

► Curlews distinguished from other shorebirds by large size and decurved bill. Long-billed Curlew much warmer brown with longer bill, bright cinnamon wing linings; lacks head stripes. Endangered (or extinct) accidental Eskimo Curlew smaller with less-decurved bill and pale cinnamon wing linings.

**VOICE:** Often repeated, rippling *bibibibibibibibi*. During migration utters rapid, tittering *titti-titti-titti-titti* and soft, whistled *cur-lee*. Calls can be heard at distance.

**HABITAT AND BEHAVIOUR:** Breeds in rolling tundra, wet meadows, and hummocky bogs. Occurs in meadows and beaches during migration. Primarily terrestrial. Walks or runs between bill probes while feeding. Flight moderately fast with long glides.

**STATUS:** Rare breeder. Rare to locally common spring and fall migrant.

# HUDSONIAN GODWIT *Limosa haemastica*

L 35.5–40.5 cm / 14–16" Wt 280–360 g / 10–13 oz

Thousands of Hudsonian Godwits stage on the shores of Hudson and James bays prior to embarking on their non-stop migratory flight to South America. It has been suggested that at least thirty per cent of the North American population of this species gathers on the north coast of Ontario each autumn.

**APPEARANCE:** Breeding adults have streaked grey face and white eyebrow. Very long, tapered slightly upturned bill orangish at base and dark at tip. Upperparts mottled brownish black. Narrow white stripe on wing. White rump; black tail. Underparts chestnut barred with dark brown and white. Black wing linings diagnostic. In flight, bluish grey legs extend well beyond tip of tail. **Winter adults** greyish brown above and on neck and upper breast. Lower breast and belly whitish. Rarely seen **immatures** have brownish black upperparts edged with cinnamon and buffy grey underparts. Bill purplish pink.

▶ Marbled Godwit larger and tawnier with cinnamon wing linings; lacks wing stripe and contrasting tail pattern. Rare Black-tailed Godwit shows white wing linings and pale belly in flight. Greater Yellowlegs and dowitchers shorter with yellowish legs and dark bills.

**VOICE:** Sharp, ascending, and repeated *god-wit* given on breeding grounds.

**HABITAT AND BEHAVIOUR:** Breeds on coastal tundra. Flooded fields, marshes, and lakeshores during migration. Flight powerful and direct. Feeds by probing deep into mud or water with long bill. Often wades into water as deep as its belly. Walks deliberately with hunched posture. Strong swimmer.

**STATUS:** Rare breeder. Rare to uncommon spring and fall migrant.

# MARBLED GODWIT *Limosa fedoa*

42–48 cm / 16.5–18.7" Wt 300–450 g / 10.7–16.1 oz

The Marbled Godwit forages by probing deeply into mud or water with bill. It frequently submerges its face beneath the surface in search of insects and plant tubers.

**APPEARANCE:** Breeding adults tawny buff mottled above and barred below with dark brown and black. Very long, upturned bill orangish pink with black tip. Face paler buff with brownish lores. Wings cinnamon checkered with brown, with dark brown tips and cinnamon linings. Long, bluish black legs. **Winter adults** similar but somewhat plainer with much less barring on underparts. **Immatures** similar to winter adults but lack any barring or streaking on underparts.
► Hudsonian Godwit smaller with prominent chestnut barring on foreneck and underparts; white wing stripe visible in flight. Accidental Black-tailed Godwit has chestnut head, neck, and breast; tail boldly marked with black and white; white wing linings. Whimbrel lacks cinnamon coloration and has decurved bill. Long-billed Curlew larger with very long, decurved bill. Dowitchers and yellowlegs smaller with dark bills and yellowish feet and legs.

**VOICE:** Noisy, duck-like *god-wit god-witi* given on breeding grounds. Also utters barking *rack-a* and loud, harsh *cor-ack.*

**HABITAT AND BEHAVIOUR:** Flooded fields, marshes, mud flats, and shorelines. Flight strong and swift with head slightly retracted and feet trailing behind. Holds bill forward in flight. Walks and runs quickly; occasionally perches on tall objects.

**STATUS:** Rare breeder. Very rare spring and fall migrant.

CHARADRIIFORMES: Scolopacidae / Sandpipers and Phalaropes

# RUDDY TURNSTONE *Arenaria interpres* ⨍

L 20–25 cm / 8.0–9.8" Wt 100–124 g / 3.6–4.4 oz

"Turnstone" aptly describes the foraging behaviour of this pugnacious shorebird. Using its stout, wedged-shaped bill, the Ruddy Turnstone flips aside stones, shells, and shore vegetation in search of small invertebrates.

**APPEARANCE:**
Breeding adults have black-and-white head with streaked crown. Black collar and bib. Back boldly patterned with chestnut and black. Wings in flight show broad bands of rust, black, and white. Tail white with broad, black subterminal band.

Belly white. Legs orangish red. **Winter adults** have mottled and streaked brown head and upperparts. Dark brown bib may be crossed by white line. **Immatures** resemble winter adults but back has scaly appearance.

▶ Other shorebirds lack bold rust, black, and white patterning. Ruddy Turnstones in winter distinguished by characteristic dark bib on white underparts.

**VOICE:** Generally utters a low, harsh, rattling call. Also gives abrupt *cut-a-cut* when alarmed, which resembles call of Short-billed Dowitcher.

**HABITAT AND BEHAVIOUR:** Breeds on coastal tundra. Shorelines of lakes and marshes, and cultivated fields during migration. Flight swift and powerful; usually low to ground in feeding areas. Vigorously defends feeding territories when prey scarce by charging intruder with wings lowered and back hunched. Uses breast to overturn large objects.

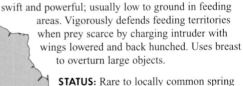

**STATUS:** Rare to locally common spring and fall migrant. Rare winter resident.

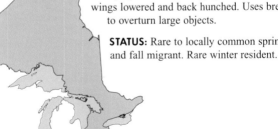

# ED KNOT *Calidris canutus*

25.5–28.0 cm / 10–11" Wt 110–180 g / 4.0–6.5 oz

ens of thousands of Red Knots gather on the shores of Delaware Bay ach spring to feed on horseshoe crab eggs. After leaving this staging rea, they pass through Ontario from late May to early June, then ontinue northward to their arctic breeding grounds.

**PPEARANCE:**
reeding birds have
ark brown
pperparts edged
ith white and
Ifous. Face and
nderparts rich
Ifous. Straight,
ightly tapered bill
Iack. Undertail
overts whitish
Iarked with dark
rown. Pale greyish
Imp, grey tail,

Id white wing linings in all plumages. **Winter adults** have dusky rey upperparts; whitish below with brownish spots on breast and des. **Immatures** resemble winter adults but with scaly appearance mantle.

► Dowitchers have much longer bills. Curlew Sandpiper smaller Id darker with bolder wing pattern and drooped bill. Winter Black-Ellied Plover larger with spotted upperparts and short, stout bill. Uff-breasted Sandpiper paler with thinner, shorter bill.

**OICE:** Soft, musical *ker ek* given in flight. Also utters low, oaky *k-nut.*

**ABITAT AND BEHAVIOUR:** Lakeshores, marshes, and ploughed elds. Flight swift and strong; flies low over feeding areas. Clusters in groups while feeding. Resting birds stand in groups on shoals and dunes, facing into breeze.

**STATUS:** Rare to fairly common spring and fall migrant. Large numbers stage along Hudson and James bays.

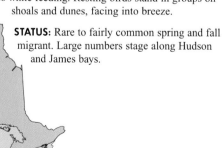

# SANDERLING *Calidris alba* F

L 18–22 cm / 7.1–8.7" Wt 60–85 g / 2.1–3.0 oz

This plump little shorebird resembles a wind-up toy as it chases the retreating surf in search of exposed invertebrates. The Sanderling's probing bill leaves a series of characteristic holes in lines or arcs in the wet sand.

**APPEARANCE:**
Breeding adults have black mantle edged with rufous, fading to white in late summer. Head and upper breast rust-coloured and spotted with black. Black bill straight and slightly tapered. Otherwise, underparts white. Dark wings with white wing stripe

WINTER

and white rump divided by dark median stripe in all plumages. Black legs and feet. Absence of hind toe diagnostic. **Winter adults** pale grey above; eyebrow and underparts white. Dark bend in wing often concealed. **Immatures** resemble adults but have checkered black-and-white upperparts.
► Semipalmated, Western, and Least sandpipers and Dunlin lack rufous breast in breeding plumage. Baird's Sandpiper slimmer with thinner bill; longer wings have no conspicuous stripe. Winter Sanderlings paler than other sandpipers in winter plumage.

**VOICE:** Usually quiet. Short, distinctive *kip* given in flight. Sometimes twitters softly while feeding.

**HABITAT AND BEHAVIOUR:** Tundra in summer. Lakeshores, beaches, and marshes in migration. Often feeds in mixed flocks of other sandpipers and Black-bellied Plovers. Rest in groups on the beach squatting or standing on one leg.

**STATUS:** Common migrant in spring and fall. Rare summer or winter resident.

# SEMIPALMATED SANDPIPER *Calidris pusilla* ⨍

14–17 cm / 5.5–6.5" Wt 21–32 g / 0.75–1.1 oz

These long-distance migrants are most frequently observed south of their subarctic breeding distribution where they gather along lakeshores to feed in large flocks.

**APPEARANCE:**

Upperparts brownish grey with buff-coloured rounded tips on wing coverts. Distinct whitish stripe above eye. Crown brown streaked with rufous and buff. Underparts white with faint brown streaking on breast. In flight, wings show narrow white stripe, and white rump is divided by broad, black median line. Bill black, straight with slightly thickening tip. Legs and toes black. **Winter adults** plain greyish brown above. Underparts whitish; breast washed with grey. **Immatures** similar but have dark brown and chestnut upperparts with buffy edging.

► Distinguished from Least Sandpiper by shorter, stouter bill, greyer upperparts, and blackish legs.

**VOICE:** Most frequently heard call in flight harsh *cherk*. May utter various twittering and chipping notes while foraging.

**HABITAT AND BEHAVIOUR:** Breeds on seacoasts, dry heath-lichen tundra, and wet tussock tundra in subarctic along Hudson Bay and James Bay. Abundant migrant on beaches and mud flats along lakes throughout Ontario. Walks rapidly between pecking and probing attempts while feeding. Rapid flight facilitated by narrow, straight, and pointed wings.

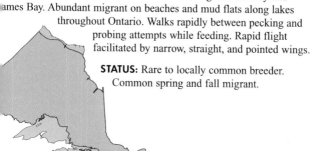

**STATUS:** Rare to locally common breeder. Common spring and fall migrant.

# WESTERN SANDPIPER *Calidris mauri*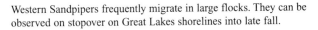

L 14–17 cm / 5.5–6.7" Wt 22–35 g / 0.8–1.3 oz

Western Sandpipers frequently migrate in large flocks. They can be observed on stopover on Great Lakes shorelines into late fall.

**APPEARANCE:**
Dark brown streaked upperparts in breeding adults. Crown, ear coverts, nape, and scapulars have rusty feather edges. Whitish eyebrow and dark brown eye-line. Slightly decurved black bill has fine tip and deep base. Wings brownish with narrow white

WINTER

wing bar. Rump and centre of tail black; outer feathers white. Underparts whitish with streaking across upper breast that extends in a double row of V-shaped marks down flanks. Legs and feet black. **Winter adults** greyish brown above streaked with dark brown. Whitish forehead and eyebrow. Underparts white with fine streaking on breast. **Immatures** resemble winter birds but have bright, rusty-edged scapulars and rufous wash on breast.

▶ Breeding and immature Semipalmated Sandpipers lack rustiness on back and crown. Best distinguished in winter by voice and bill length. Least Sandpiper appears somewhat smaller-headed and with darker mantle edged with chestnut. White-rumped Sandpiper has characteristic white rump visible in flight. Wing tips extend beyond tail when standing.

**VOICE:** Male gives short, rising *tweer-tweer-tweer* followed by descending buzzy trill. Flushed birds give *chir-ir-ip* that is squeakier than Semipalmated Sandpiper's call. High-pitched *cheep* given in flight resembles calls of White-rumped Sandpiper and Dunlin.

**HABITAT AND BEHAVIOUR:** Shores, beaches, and mud flats. Flight fast. Walks or runs during foraging. Rarely forages in belly-deep water. Often stands on one leg.

**STATUS:** Rare spring and fall migrant.

# EAST SANDPIPER *Calidris minutilla*

13–15 cm / 5–6" Wt 19–30 g / 0.7–1.1 oz

s its common name suggests, this is North America's
mallest sandpiper. Less numerous than other similar species,
e Least Sandpiper is often overlooked in population surveys.

**PPEARANCE:**

reeding plumage
as sooty brown
pperparts with
arrow chestnut-
nd-buff edges on
athers. Worn
dges on some
dividuals give
verall brown
ppearance. Fairly
onspicuous white
ripe above eye and
ark patch on lores.
ill black, rather

ng and slightly drooped, with fine tip. Wings brown, with narrow
white stripe formed by white tips on wing coverts. Foreneck and upper
reast pale buff with heavy dark brown streaking. Belly white. Rump
nd tail brownish grey with white sides. **Winter adults** similar but
omewhat dusky grey above. **Immatures** have overall orangish tone
esulting from rufous-fringed upperparts. Also have whitish incomplete
-pattern on sides of back.

▶ Distinguished from other common small sandpipers by overall
arker-brown appearance, shorter bill, smaller size, and shorter,
ellowish legs. Baird's Sandpiper larger, with straighter bill and
ark legs.

**VOICE:** High-pitched, bi-syllabic *kre-eep* given in flight. Also shrill,
apidly repeated, rising *treee.*

**HABITAT AND BEHAVIOUR:** Subarctic bogs and tundra.
Occurs as migrant in muddy lake margins,
ponds, and bogs. Distinguished in flight from
similar sandpipers by shorter, weaker, and more
fluttery wingbeats. Walks slowly, rarely
runs, while feeding; tends to remain within
small area.

**STATUS:** Common breeder. Common spring
and fall migrant.

# WHITE-RUMPED SANDPIPER *Calidris fuscicollis*

L 18.0–20.5 cm / 7–8" Wt 40–60 g / 1.4–2.1 oz

White-rumped Sandpiper flocks frequently defecate in unison upon takeoff. They have also been known to collectively flutter in the face of a predator when agitated.

**APPEARANCE:**
Dark brown mantle of breeding adults has chestnut-and buff-edged feathers. Crown and ear coverts tinged with chestnut. Black bill reddish at base. When folded, brownish wings extend beyond tail. Narrow white wing stripe and white rump visible in flight. Tail brown

WINTER

with dark central feathers. Underparts white with dark brown streaks on neck and upper breast extending to two rows of streaks on flanks. Legs brownish grey. **Winter adults** uniformly brownish grey above with narrow, whitish eyebrow. Foreparts dusky grey with diffuse streaking on foreneck and upper breast. Belly and rump white. **Immatures** resemble breeding adults but somewhat more chestnut above and buffy below. Whitish eyebrow and incomplete V-pattern on back.

▶ Distinguished from similar Semipalmated, Baird's, and Western sandpipers by white rump and double row of streaks on flanks. Curlew and Stilt sandpipers have white rump but are much larger with proportionately longer bills, necks, and legs.

**VOICE:** High-pitched mouse-like *tzeet* given in flight. Call notes include twittering *bzzzzzzzzzz* and squeaky *zip-zip*.

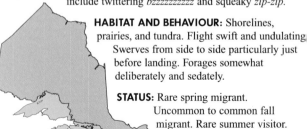

**HABITAT AND BEHAVIOUR:** Shorelines, prairies, and tundra. Flight swift and undulating. Swerves from side to side particularly just before landing. Forages somewhat deliberately and sedately.

**STATUS:** Rare spring migrant. Uncommon to common fall migrant. Rare summer visitor.

# BAIRD'S SANDPIPER *Calidris bairdii*
18–19 cm / 7.1–7.5" Wt 55–65 g / 2.0–2.3 oz

Baird's Sandpiper is superficially similar to the White-rumped Sandpiper. Perhaps the best means to distinguish between these species is to flush them, then observe the rump colour as the birds fly away.

**APPEARANCE:**
Breeding adults brownish with buffy face and pale eyebrow. Buff edges on some blackish feathers of back and scapulars confer splotchy appearance. Wing tips extend beyond tail. Foreneck and upper breast buffy with thin, dark brown streaks. Otherwise, under-

parts unmarked white. Legs black. Pale wing stripe and buffy white rump divided by broad, black median line in all plumages. **Winter adults** greyish brown above. **Immatures** resemble breeding adults but with somewhat scaly, not splotchy, pattern on mantle.

▶ White-rumped Sandpiper distinguished by entirely white rump and breast streaking that extends to flanks. Semipalmated Sandpiper smaller with white face and foreneck in winter plumage; wings do not extend beyond tip of tail. Least Sandpiper has yellow legs. Dark breast of Pectoral Sandpiper ends abruptly at white belly. Sanderling has much more prominent wing stripe visible in flight.

**VOICE:** Utters soft, low *krrrit,* often given twice. Resembles flight call of Pectoral Sandpiper.

**HABITAT AND BEHAVIOUR:** Beaches, wetlands, and mud flats. Typical sandpiper in flight. Often travels in mixed flocks but separates following landing to feed with members of own species.

**STATUS:** Extremely rare spring migrant. Uncommon fall migrant.

# PECTORAL SANDPIPER *Calidris melanotos*

L 20–24 cm / 7.9–9.4" Wt 55–90 g / 2.0–3.2 oz

Unlike most other sandpipers, the male Pectoral Sandpiper is much larger than the female. When alarmed, males increase their size by using air sacs in their neck to erect the overlying feathers.

**APPEARANCE:**
Breeding adults sooty brown above with chestnut-and-buff feather edges. Crown somewhat rusty. Profuse, dark brown streaking on throat and breast ends abruptly (like a bib) at white belly. Flanks and undertail coverts white. Legs yellowish. Slightly decurved, black bill pale at base. Faint

white wing stripe and white rump divided by broad, black median line in all plumages. **Winter adults** similar but duller. **Immatures** resemble adults but with buffy, incomplete V-pattern on sides of back; breast washed with buff; legs and feet yellow.

▶ Combination of well-defined dark bib and yellow legs distinctive. Larger and longer-necked than Least Sandpiper.

**VOICE:** Generally talkative, particularly on breeding grounds. Utters low, guttural *krrick* in flight. Male emits tremulous resonant sound with inflation of neck air sacs.

**HABITAT AND BEHAVIOUR:** Tundra in summer. Shorelines, marshes, and prairie pools in migration. Flight generally strong, swift, and direct, but sometimes erratic and zigzagging when flushed. Freezes and crouches when startled.

**STATUS:** Exceptionally rare breeder. Rare to common spring and fall migrant.

# PURPLE SANDPIPER *Calidris maritima*

20.5–24.0 cm / 8–9.5" Wt 55–80 g / 2.0–3.0 oz

In Ontario, Purple Sandpipers are most commonly observed wearing their dark grey winter colours. This plumage serves them well as they forage along rocky headlands and beaches.

**APPEARANCE:**
Breeding adults have tawny crown. Head, neck, and throat streaked with black. White eyebrow and eye-ring. Dusky ear coverts. Long, thin slightly drooped bill orangish with black tip. Back and scapulars blackish edged with buff and rust. Narrow white

WINTER

bar and white trailing edge of secondaries visible in flight. Breast and flanks streaked with grey. Belly white. Legs orange. **Winter birds** have slate-grey head, neck, and upper breast. Incomplete white eye-ring. Small white spot before eye. Purple sheen sometimes visible on dark grey mantle. Underparts white. Flanks and undertail coverts streaked with brown. **Immatures** have broad buff-and-chestnut edges on wing coverts, greyish brown neck, and streaked breast.

▶ Other sandpipers lack combination of distinctive bicoloured bill and orangish legs. Grey hood diagnostic in winter plumage.

**VOICE:** Flocks twitter like swallows. Utter soft *prrt-prrt* in flight.

**HABITAT AND BEHAVIOUR:** Rocky shorelines, breakwaters, beaches, and piers. Flight swift and usually low over shore. Avoids crashing waves while foraging among crevices for invertebrates and plant material.

**STATUS:** Extremely rare spring migrant. Rare winter visitor.

## DUNLIN *Calidris alpina*

L 16–22 cm / 6.3–8.7" Wt 48–64 g / 1.7–2.3 oz

Dunlins frequently fly wing tip to wing tip in flocks that number a thousand or more individuals. They migrate through southern Ontario en route to wintering grounds on the Gulf of Mexico.

**APPEARANCE:**
Long, decurved black bill and black legs in all plumages. Crown, back, and scapulars of breeding adults chestnut streaked and spotted with black and white. Wings greyish black with white stripe visible in flight. White rump divided by bold black line. Tail

greyish black edged with white. Face and breast whitish, finely streaked with black. Belly white with conspicuous black patch. **Winter adults** greyish brown above. Whitish eyebrow. Neck and breast washed with diffuse brown streaking. Belly white. **Immatures** similar but somewhat brighter with rusty upperparts and buffy edges on scapulars. White belly has brown spots.

▶ Black spot on belly distinctive in breeding plumage. Winter Sanderling much paler than winter Dunlin and has much shorter bill. Winter Purple Sandpiper darker with orangish legs and yellow at base of bill. Western and Least sandpipers smaller and darker in winter. Least Sandpiper has yellow legs. Winter Semipalmated Sandpiper browner overall with less-decurved bill.

**VOICE:** Male gives series of trills that begin with accented *drurr-drurr,* followed by descending hum, ending with *tri-ririri.* When flushed, both sexes utter *krree.* High-pitched *dear-dear-dear* given at nest.

**HABITAT AND BEHAVIOUR:** Coastal tundra. Mudflats, marshes, and lakes during migration. Usually walks when foraging. Sometimes perches on high objects. Occasionally swims.

**STATUS:** Rare to uncommon breeder. Uncommon to abundant spring and fall migrant.

150

# CURLEW SANDPIPER *Calidris ferruginea*

. 18–23 cm / 7.1–9.0" Wt 50–80 g / 1.8–2.9 oz

This striking shorebird is native to northern Eurasia. Most individuals observed in southern Ontario are young birds in full immature plumage or adults undergoing moult from breeding to winter plumages.

**APPEARANCE:**
Long, black, decurved bill with whitish area at base. Breeding adults have rich chestnut underparts. Upperparts sooty brown with chestnut feather edging. Pale eyebrow. Bold white wing stripe, wide white rump, and grey tail in all plumages. Legs black. **Winter**

**adults** greyish brown above with white eyebrow. Underparts white with pale streaking on upper breast. **Immatures** resemble winter adults but with scaly back due to pale feather edges. Breast washed with rich buff.

▶ Breeding plumage and long, downturned bill distinctive. Winter Dunlin distinguished from winter Curlew Sandpiper by dark rump. Immature Stilt Sandpiper has longer, greenish legs; blunt bill; short, narrow wing stripe; and whitish tail. White-rumped Sandpiper smaller with straighter bill; more heavily marked below in winter plumage.

**VOICE:** Soft, whistled *chirrup* given in flight.

**HABITAT AND BEHAVIOUR:** Tidal flats, beaches, and pools. Wet tundra in summer. Flight swift. After landing, holds wings up and open over back to flash white wing linings. Usually forages belly-deep in water. Usually observed singly in North America.

**STATUS:** Rare fall and spring visitor.

## STILT SANDPIPER *Calidris himantopus*

L 18–23 cm / 7–9" Wt 50–70 g / 1.8–2.5 oz

Known to nineteenth-century hunters as the Mongrel, Long-legged Sandpiper, and Frost Snipe, the Stilt Sandpiper was once considered of hybrid origin between dowitchers and yellowlegs.

**APPEARANCE:** Head and neck of breeding adults streaked with brownish black. Whitish eyebrow. Chestnut crown, lores, and ear coverts. Mantle black, edged with white. White tail coverts. Wings and tail brownish. Underparts white with heavy dark brown barring. Legs greyish green. **Winter adults** brownish grey above with indistinct whitish feather edging on wing coverts. Whitish eyebrow; dark grey eye-line. Underparts white with fine grey streaking on throat and foreneck; darker on breast. **Immatures** blackish brown above with buff-edged

feathers. Whitish eyebrow. Foreneck and breast buff, finely streaked with brown. Scapulars and ear coverts tinged with chestnut.

► Heavily barred underparts of breeding adult diagnostic. Lesser Yellowlegs and dowitchers similar in winter. Dowitchers heavier with longer bills and white lower backs. Lesser Yellowlegs larger with bright yellow legs and less distinct eyebrow. Curlew Sandpiper resembles immatures but has finer bill, much shorter, blackish legs, and bold white wing stripe.

**VOICE:** Call harsh, chattering *xxree-xxree-xxree-xxree-ee-haw ee-haw.* Squawking *querp* given in flight. Also utters threatening *kyow-it* at nest.

**HABITAT AND BEHAVIOUR:** Wet sedge-tundra meadows. Flight fast and direct. Walks slowly. Wades belly-deep while foraging; often submerges head. Sometimes rests on one leg. Adults swim well.

**STATUS:** Uncommon breeder. Rare spring migrant. Uncommon fall migrant.

*e Sweten*

# BUFF-BREASTED SANDPIPER
*Tryngites subruficollis*

L 18–20 cm / 7–7.9"  Wt 50–75 g / 1.8–2.7 oz

The Buff-breasted Sandpiper breeds along arctic shorelines. It moves southward through Ontario during fall migration en route to wintering grounds on the pampas of Argentina, Uruguay, and Paraguay.

**APPEARANCE:**
Crown and hind neck speckled with buff and brown. Unpatterned pale buff face with large, dark eyes. Pale eye-ring. Short, straight, dark bill. Upper-parts brown with buff feather edges, giving scaly appearance. Tail dark brown with buffy brown edges. Underparts strongly buff with dark spotting on sides of breast. White underwing contrasts with buff body in flight. No wing stripe. Bright yellow legs. **Immatures** similar but with wider, whitish feather edges on upperparts. Also somewhat paler buff below with whitish belly.

▶ Only shorebird entirely buff below. Upland Sandpiper larger with small head, thin neck, and long tail; also has streaked face and underparts, and barred underwing. Baird's Sandpiper has buff breast that contrasts with white belly; legs black. Immature Ruff much larger with white wing bar and sides of rump.

**VOICE:** Rarely calls. Utters thin *tik-tik-tik*. Also gives low, trilling *pr-r-r-reet* when alarmed. Female utters quiet *chwup* at nest.

**HABITAT AND BEHAVIOUR:** Tundra and short-grass prairie. Flight low and fast with many turns and zigzags. Walks or runs with high-stepping gait between pecks while foraging.

**STATUS:** Extremely rare spring migrant. Rare fall migrant.

## RUFF *Philomachus pugnax*

L 22–31 cm / 8.7–12.2"  Wt 100–160 g / 3.6–5.7 oz

During courtship, male Ruffs erect their ornate neck and ear feathers in concert with elaborate posturing in an attempt to attract females, known as Reeves. Many males display concurrently and females choose the individual they prefer.

**APPEARANCE:**
Breeding male has large, elaborate black, white, or rufous neck ruff. which is often flattened. Appears thick-necked in flight. Plumage variable. Upperparts barred rufous and dark brown. Underparts whitish with heavily marked breast. All plumages

♀

exhibit narrow white wing stripe and oval white rump patches divided by dark median line. Legs yellow, orange, or red. Breeding **female** mottled black and brown above. Underparts white. Feathers of foreneck and breast edged with black and brown. Winter adults greyish brown above. Short, tapered bill orangish with black tip. White patch on face at base of bill. Underparts whitish with scaly greyish brown wash on breast. **Immatures** dark brown above with rufous feather edges on mantle. Underparts white with bright buff foreneck and breast streaked with dark brown at sides.

▶ Yellowlegs slimmer with streaked breast, longer yellow legs, and unstriped wings in flight. Winter Red Knot white-breasted with dark lores, and greyish white rump and tail. Pectoral Sandpiper has streaks terminating abruptly on lower breast.

**VOICE:** Rarely heard flight call a short, whistled *tu-whit.*

**HABITAT AND BEHAVIOUR:** Marshes, flooded fields, and sewage lagoons. Flight rapid and strong with regular wingbeats. Male feigns attacks on competitors during displays.

**STATUS:** Rare visitor from April to September.

# SHORT-BILLED DOWITCHER *Limnodromus griseus* F

28–30 cm / 11.0–11.8" Wt 110–120 g / 4.0–4.3 oz

Dowitchers forage with a distinctive bill-probing action. Their rapid perpendicular thrusts resemble the up-and-down stitching of a sewing-machine needle.

**APPEARANCE:** Long, straight, heavy black bill. Breeding adults have blackish brown upperparts with feathers edged with reddish buff. Whitish eyebrow and dark eye-line. Tail barred with light and dark brown. White wedge on rump and lower back. Underparts reddish with blackish spotting on breast and some white on belly. Flanks barred with dark brown. Legs yellowish green. **Winter adults** greyish brown above and white below with greyish breast. **Immatures** resemble breeding adults but paler overall with greyish face. Mantle feathers more heavily edged with rust.

▶ Long-billed Dowitcher very similar; in breeding plumage, bars on flanks may extend to breast; throat may be more heavily spotted; broad white tips on scapular feathers in spring; rarely white on belly; grey breast more extensive in winter. Red Knot has shorter bill; reddish breast unmarked in breeding plumage; lacks white rump wedge in flight. Common Snipe has heavy streaking on neck and breast, shorter legs, light stripe on crown, and two-toned bill.

**VOICE:** Often silent. Utters mellow, repeated *toodulu toodulu* in flight.

**HABITAT AND BEHAVIOUR:** Breeds on coastal tundra and muskeg. Lakeshores and marshes during migration. Flight strong and swift with relatively rapid wingbeats. Forages by probing methodically in mud, sand, or shallow water. Feeds in compact groups.

**STATUS:** Rare breeder. Common spring and fall migrant.

# LONG-BILLED DOWITCHER F
*Limnodromus scolopaceus*

L 28–32 cm / 11.0–12.6" Wt 110–140 g / 4–5 oz

The less common Long-billed Dowitcher is difficult to distinguish from the Short-billed Dowitcher in the field with confidence. Where they occur together in migration, vocalizations may be useful in telling them apart.

**APPEARANCE:**
Long, straight, heavy black bill. Pale eyebrow and dark eye-line. White, wedge-shaped patch on rump and uppertail coverts. Legs yellowish green. Breeding adults have brownish black upperparts with feathers narrowly edged

WINTER

with rust and sometimes tipped with white. Underparts reddish with heavily spotted throat and black barring on flanks and sides. Tail striped with light and dark brown. **Winter adults** dingy greyish brown, somewhat lighter below, particularly on belly and undertail coverts. Pale eyebrow. Flanks barred with grey. **Immatures** resemble breeding adults but with greyer face and throat.

▶ Short-billed Dowitcher very similar but has more white on flanks and belly; dark bars on flanks less extensive; upperparts have somewhat brighter feather edges; grey breast less extensive in winter plumage. Red Knot has much shorter bill; reddish breast unmarked in breeding plumage; lacks white rump wedge in flight. Common Snipe has heavy streaking on neck and breast, shorter legs, light median stripe on crown, and bicoloured bill.

**VOICE:** Utters series of loud, high-pitched *keek*s when alarmed.

**HABITAT AND BEHAVIOUR:** Lakeshores, marshes, and mud flats. Flight strong and rapid, and relatively high above ground when moving between feeding locations. Probes with rapid jabbing motion while foraging.

**STATUS:** Very rare spring and fall migrant.

# OMMON SNIPE *Gallinago gallinago*

27–29 cm / 10.5–11.5" Wt 90–120 g / 3.2–4.3 oz

ipe populations were drastically reduced by overhunting in the
neteenth century. Although the species appears to have recovered,
e may question if annual takes of 500,000 to 1,000,000 individuals in
cent decades, in concert with loss of wetland habitat, are sustainable.

## PPEARANCE:

ry long, straight
ll. Crown striped
th brownish black
d buff. Buff
ebrow and dark
own eye-line.
perparts spotted
d barred with
own, black,
fous, and buff.
ght spots form
ur lines down
ck. Sides of head
ff streaked with
rk brown. Wings
rk brown mottled with buff and tipped with white. Central tail
athers black and cinnamon; outer tail feathers whitish spotted with
own. White tips visible in flight. Neck, breast, and flanks buffy white
reaked with dark brown. Belly white. **Immatures** similar with
mewhat buffier upperparts and cinnamon rump.

▶ American Woodcock chunkier with unmarked, buffy
nderparts and transverse bars on head, not longitudinal stripes; occurs
more-wooded habitat. Dowitchers larger with longer legs, narrowly
rred tail, and white rump patch visible in flight; lack striped crown.

**OICE:** Repeated *chip-per chip-per.* Vibrating tail feathers produce
pid, hollow *huhuhuhuhuhuhu* during aerial display. Hoarse, rasping
*scaap* given outside breeding season.

**HABITAT AND BEHAVIOUR:** Freshwater
marshlands, bogs, moist meadows, and swamps.
Flies zigzag when flushed; otherwise, flight
strong and straight. Usually walks but can
run. Swims and dives occasionally.

**STATUS:** Common breeder and migrant.
Rare winter visitor.

# ✓AMERICAN WOODCOCK *Scolopax minor*

L 25–31 cm / 10–12" Wt 155–250 g / 5.5–9.0 oz

During his courtship flight display, the male "timberdoodle" spirals as high as 100 m (330') with twittering wings accompanying his melodious chirping. He circles back to the ground with a zigzagging, diving, and banking descent.

**APPEARANCE:**
Very plump upland shorebird with no apparent neck. Upperparts mottled with brown, buff, and gray. Transverse colour bars on crown. Blackish line through large, dark eyes set high on head. Very long, brownish red bill with dark tip. Rounded wings

mottled brown. Tail black with brownish spots and tipped with light gray. Underparts unmarked, bright cinnamon. **Female** considerably larger than male. **Juveniles** similar but somewhat grayer with less-intense markings.

▶ Common Snipe has striped head and back, and pointed wings; usually calls when flushed.

**VOICE:** Most vocal at dawn and dusk. Ground call a buzzy, nasal *peer*, repeated many times, given only by male. Flight call is fast, repetitive series of four to six melodious notes: *chirp-chirp-chirpchirpchirp*. Also utters rapid, harsh cackle: *ca-ca-ca-ca-ca*. Wings make twittering sound in flight and when flushed.

**HABITAT AND BEHAVIOUR:** Moist forests, wet thickets, brushy swamps, and open fields. Very secretive during day. Flushes vertically until through branches, then moves forward. Walks on ground with bill pointing down. Uses bill to probe for earthworms.

**STATUS:** Common breeder. Common spring and fall migrant.

158

# ILSON'S PHALAROPE *Phalaropus tricolor*
1.5–24.0 cm / 8.5–9.5" Wt 50–70 g / 1.8–2.5 oz

laropes are well known for their reversed sex-role mating system.
males are the aggressors in courtship and play no part in raising
ng after the eggs have been laid. Consequently, they sport the more
ghtly coloured plumage.

**PEARANCE:**
eding female
pale grey crown
nape. White
eks and hind
k. Needle-like
ck bill longer
n head. Broad,
ck stripe through
and down neck;
dered by
stnut on lower
k. Foreneck
hed with
namon. Back

♀

k grey with chestnut stripes. Wings greyish brown. Tail pale grey.
ast, belly, and undertail coverts white. Legs greyish black.
**eding male** smaller with brown crown, and white eyebrow and
ek. Brown and chestnut line extends from eye down neck. Back
ttled brown and chestnut with pale feather edges. Underparts
tish. Foreneck tinged with pale cinnamon. **Winter adults** plain pale
y above and white below. Face white with pale stripe through eye.
**matures** brown above with buff feather edges. Greyish eye-stripe
white eyebrow. Underparts white with buffy tinge on sides of
ast. Legs yellow.
► Only phalarope with white rump and without wing stripe.
eding Red-necked Phalarope has dark crown and prominent
stnut patch on foreneck; upper wings boldly marked with grey and
white in winter. Breeding Red Phalarope has deep reddish
neck and underparts; distinguished in winter by
grey tail, white wing stripe, and dark stripe
through rump.

**VOICE:** Utters low, nasal *wurk* on breeding
grounds. Generally silent in winter.

**HABITAT AND BEHAVIOUR:** Shallow lakes,
marshes, ponds, and mud flats. Fast flight.
Walks well on land. Often stands
on one foot to sleep.

**STATUS:** Rare breeder. Rare to
uncommon spring and fall migrant.

159

# RED-NECKED PHALAROPE *Phalaropus lobatus*

L 18–20 cm / 7–8" Wt 24–28 g / 0.9–1.0 oz

When feeding on the water's surface, phalaropes often spin like tops, then stab repeatedly at aquatic insects that are disturbed by their rapid dabbling feet.

**APPEARANCE:**
Breeding female has blackish hood. White eye crescents and throat. Thin, black bill. Large chestnut patch on neck bordered below with grey band. Dark grey back conspicuously streaked with buffy rust. Rump grey. Wings and tail grey. White wing stripe. Underparts white

♂ SUMMER

with greyish wash on sides and flanks. **Breeding male** has similar plumage pattern but duller and browner overall with buffy eye-line. **Winter adults** grey above with conspicuously streaked back. Dark crown and eye-line. Underparts white. **Immatures** resemble winter adults but somewhat browner with buffy streaks on back. Dark brown crown, hindneck, and eye-line.

▶ Wilson's Phalarope lacks chestnut patch on neck. Lacks white wing stripe in all plumages. Red Phalarope larger with stouter bill, reddish underparts, and less conspicuous wing stripes and back streaks in breeding plumage; paler grey mantle in winter. Winter Sanderling has pale head and unmarked back.

**VOICE:** Soft *prip* given in flight resembles call of Sanderling.

**HABITAT AND BEHAVIOUR:** Bays, lakes, and ponds. Tundra in summer. Flight erratic and darting. Spins on water's surface while feeding. Does not dive. Young swim immediately following hatching.

**STATUS:** Rare to uncommon breeder. Rare spring and uncommon fall migrant.

# RED PHALAROPE *Phalaropus fulicaria*

19–23 cm / 7.5–9.0" Wt 50–65 g / 1.7–2.3 oz

he rich red colour of the breeding Red Phalarope is rarely seen in Ontario. The phalaropes are best distinguished from other greyish horebirds in fall and winter by their characteristic mode of foraging n water.

**APPEARANCE:**
Breeding female has lack crown and orehead and white ace. Bill yellow ith black tip. hroat, neck, and nderparts rufous ed. Feathers of antle brownish lack tipped with right buff.
Breeding male like emale but paler, articularly on head nd underparts.

♀

Winter adults have white head, neck, and underparts. Black line xtends from eye to ear. Bill and nape blackish. Mantle bluish grey. Moulting adults appear blotchy. **Immatures** resemble winter adults ut with buffy neck and mantle, and dark streaking n upperparts.

► Only phalarope predominantly rufous red in breeding plumage. winter, Red-necked Phalarope distinguished by thinner bill, and rongly striped upperparts. Winter Wilson's Phalarope has paler head cking dark mask; wings paler in flight with no wing stripe.

**VOICE:** Sharp *whit* similar to but higher-pitched than call of ed-necked Phalarope. Also gives low *clink clink.*

**HABITAT AND BEHAVIOUR:** Lakes and large wetlands. Swift, light, sandpiper-like flight. Flies faster than other phalaropes. Swims well with lobed toes in still or rough water. Spins like top when feeding on surface. Upends to feed in shallow water.

**STATUS:** Very rare spring and rare fall migrant.

# POMARINE JAEGER *Stercorarius pomarinus*

L 51–58 cm / 20.0–22.8" Wt 700–1060 g / 1.6–2.4 lb

Jaegers have been described as "falcons of the seas" because they pursue gulls and terns in flight to steal their fresh fish catch. They also consume small birds and mammals, eggs, and carrion.

**APPEARANCE:** Long, pointed, angled wings. Long, blunt, twisted streamers on black tail. Slightly hooked bill. **Light-morph adults** have black cap, mantle, wings, and tail. Yellowish cheeks. Throat to upper belly white with dark, mottled breast band, sides, and flanks. Lower belly and undertail coverts black. Base of primaries white. **Dark morph** entirely blackish except for white underwing. **Immatures** have variable barring on backs, underparts, and underwings. Dark wings and tail. Blunt central tail feathers extend just beyond remainder of tail.

▶ Adults best distinguished from other jaegers by blunt, twisted tail streamers. Adult Parasitic Jaeger lacks mottling on sides and flanks; less white on primaries. Adult Long-tailed Jaeger has thin, pointed tail streamers, less white on primaries; lacks dark breast band; immatures can be distinguished only by tail shape.

**VOICE:** Generally silent. Occasionally utters sharp *which-yew* in flight.

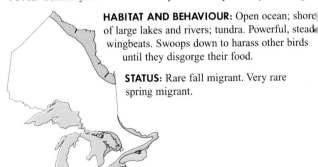

**HABITAT AND BEHAVIOUR:** Open ocean; shore of large lakes and rivers; tundra. Powerful, steady wingbeats. Swoops down to harass other birds until they disgorge their food.

**STATUS:** Rare fall migrant. Very rare spring migrant.

# PARASITIC JAEGER *Stercorarius parasiticus*

46–56 cm / 18–22" Wt 400–500 g / 14.3–17.8 oz

The Parasitic Jaeger is so named because it forces other birds, such as gulls and terns, to disgorge their food in flight. Once the prey is released, it expertly swoops down to snatch the item as it falls.

**APPEARANCE:**
Breeding adults
occur in light and
dark morphs with
some intermediates.
**Light morph**
brown above with
blackish cap and
white collar. Neck
yellowish. Wings
dark brown with
conspicuous white
patch at base of
primaries. Pointed
central tail feathers

project 6.5–9 cm (0.5–3.5") beyond rest of blackish tail. Partial or complete brownish breast band. Underparts whitish except for greyish brown undertail coverts. **Dark morph** similar but with brown underparts. **Immatures** have brown barring on underwing coverts and underparts. Pointed tail feathers project slightly beyond the rest. Backs barred with white. Some individuals tinged with cinnamon on head and back.

▶ Adult Pomarine Jaeger has spoon-shaped central tail feathers; dark breast band more distinct. Central tail feathers of Long-tailed Jaeger much longer; lacks breast band; immatures are highly variable and difficult to distinguish, but best identified by tail shape.

**VOICE:** Long call comprises one to twelve rising bi-syllabic notes. Also gives yelping call that resembles small dog. Various other mewing, purring, or squeaking notes.

**HABITAT AND BEHAVIOUR:** Open ocean, coastal bays, and large lakes (rarely). Tundra in summer. Flight fast and buoyant on narrow, angled wings. More agile than Pomarine Jaeger. Usually flies near water's surface. Swims readily but does not dive.

**STATUS:** Rare breeder. Very rare spring and rare fall migrant.

# LONG-TAILED JAEGER *Stercorarius longicaudus*

L 50.0–58.5 cm / 19.5–23" Wt 260–350 g / 9.3–12.5 oz

The Long-tailed Jaeger makes long trans-equatorial migrations from breeding grounds in arctic Canada, Greenland, and Alaska south to Chile. Due to its predominantly pelagic migration route, it is only occasionally observed inland.

**APPEARANCE:**
Breeding adults have black cap. Otherwise, head and underparts white. Neck yellowish on sides. Back and rump dark grey. Pointed black wings may have white on primaries. Underwings plain dark brown. Black tail has diagnostic elongated, pointed

central feathers (length 2–6 cm; 0.8–2.4"). **Immatures** have variable barring on underwings and undersides.

▶ Adult Parasitic and Pomarine jaegers have dark breast band, shorter central tail feathers, and more obvious white wing patches; immatures more difficult to distinguish. Long-tailed Jaeger slimmer with narrower underwings; central tail feathers noticeably project beyond tail and are rounded at ends.

**VOICE:** Long, shrill *kri kri-kri-kri* followed by rattling *kr-r-r-r kr-r-r-r.* Also utters *kreck.* Female gives *kuep* note.

**HABITAT AND BEHAVIOUR:** Open ocean; rarely large lakes. Tundra in summer. Graceful tern-like flight most agile of all jaegers. Slower in direct flight than Parasitic Jaeger. Frequently hovers like kestrel. Swims well.

**STATUS:** Extremely rare to uncommon spring and fall migrant.

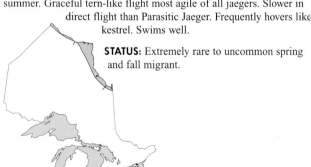

# LAUGHING GULL *Larus atricilla*

40.5–43.0 cm / 16–17" Wt 290–320 g / 10.4–11.4 oz

Typical of many gulls, the Laughing Gull pesters boaters, campers, and beach visitors for food handouts. Unlike its greedy congeners, however, this species will rarely accept bread unless it is buttered.

**APPEARANCE:**
Breeding adults
have black head
with white eye
crescents. Long,
drooped red bill.
Body white with
dark grey mantle.
Wings have black
tips and white
trailing edge.
Tail white. Legs
orangish black.
**Winter adults**
and **immatures**
have grey mottling

on head, particularly at nape. Bill and legs black. **First-year** birds have greyish breast and flanks. Wings brownish with black tips. Rump white. Tail white with broad black band. **Second-year** birds more like adults with partial hood present in summer.

▶ Franklin's Gull smaller with red legs; adults have black mask in winter; immatures have greyish crown. Black-headed and Bonaparte's gulls paler with slimmer bill, white wedge on extended wing, and reddish legs; adults have white heads with black spot behind ear in winter. Little Gull paler with reddish legs and small, black bill; lacks black wing tips and eye crescents.

**VOICE:** Strident, high-pitched laughing *ha-ha-ha-ha-ha-haah-haah-haaah.* Also utters loud, staccato *kuk-kuk-kuk-kuk* and softer *woooof-woof-wooof.*

**HABITAT AND BEHAVIOUR:** Shorelines, piers, and landfills. Flight buoyant, agile, and powerful. Soars on thermals and hovers to feed on insects. May skim surface of water to drink. Walks with slight waddle. Strong swimmer.

**STATUS:** Rare visitor from March to October, but has occurred in all months.

165

# FRANKLIN'S GULL *Larus pipixcan*

L 33–38 cm / 13–15" Wt 250–265 g / 8.8–9.5 oz

The dovelike profile of Franklin's Gull has earned it the vernacular name "Prairie Dove." This gull is frequently observed following tractors across newly ploughed fields in search of insects.

**APPEARANCE:** Breeding adults have black head with goggle-like white eye crescents. Body and nape white. Mantle grey. Wings have white bar that separates grey of mantle from black, crescent-shaped patch near tips. White tips of primaries visible at rest. Centre of tail pale grey. Breast sometimes tinged with pink. Bill and legs orangish red. **Winter adults** have blackish half-

WINTER

hood. **Juveniles** and **first-winter** birds like winter adults but have broad blackish band on tail.

▶ Bonaparte's Gull has black bill and white, wedge-shaped patch on forewing. Laughing Gull larger and chunkier with thinner eye crescents; lacks white bar and tips on wings and grey central tail feathers; blackish half-hood less extensive in winter. Little Gull paler and lacks white eye crescents. Black-headed Gull paler with smaller dark brown hood in breeding plumage; conspicuous white wedge in forewing; lacks black mask in winter. Sabine's Gull has yellow-tipped black bill, and prominent black, white, and grey triangles on wings.

**VOICE:** Gives shrill *weeeh-ah weeeh-ah* while feeding. Utters *po-lee po-lee* only on breeding grounds.

**HABITAT AND BEHAVIOUR:** Agricultural fields, marshes, shorelines, and landfills. Steady, buoyant flight. Usually migrates in huge mixed flocks of Bonaparte's and other gulls.

**STATUS:** Rare to uncommon spring and fall migrant.

# LITTLE GULL *Larus minutus*

29.0–30.5 cm / 11.5–12.0" Wt 100–150 g / 3.5–5.4 oz

The first recorded nesting attempt of this small Eurasian gull in the New World occurred at Oshawa's Second Marsh in 1962. Nine years later, offspring fledged from Cranberry Marsh, 13 km (8 miles) to the west. Since that time, nesting reports have increased slowly.

**APPEARANCE:**
Breeding adults have black hood. Lacks white eye crescents. Bill reddish brown. Wings pale grey above and black below; tips and trailing edge have broad white border. Underparts and nape white, tinged with pink. Legs red. **Winter adults** have blackish grey on hind crown, nape, and ear coverts, and around eye. Pink on underparts and

nape often lacking. Bill black. **Juveniles** have blackish brown crown, ear coverts, and eye crescent. White tips on blackish brown mantle confer scaly appearance. Extended wing shows dark brown M-pattern on upper surface; underwing whitish with black-tipped primaries. Rump grey barred with black; underparts white. Tail white with brownish tip. **First-year** birds lack dark upper nape and scaly feathers, and have more grey on mantle.

▶ Bonaparte's and Black-headed gulls larger with prominent white wedge on upper wing, pale underwings, and white eye crescents. Laughing and Franklin's gulls also larger with dark grey mantles and paler underwings. Sabine's Gull has greyish head and triangular white wing-patches.

**VOICE:** Harsh *kay-kay-kay*. Also gives *tick-ka-tick-ka-tick-ka*. Alarm call: *kvee-oo*. Silent during migration and in winter.

**HABITAT AND BEHAVIOUR:** Lakes and bays. Flight buoyant and agile with deep wingbeats. Hesitates and looks downward or hovers while foraging. Also forages while swimming. Patters on surface of water with wings outstretched.

**STATUS:** Rare breeder. Uncommon spring and fall migrant. Rare winter resident.

# BLACK-HEADED GULL *Larus ridibundus*

L 35.5–40.5 cm / 14.2–16.0"  Wt 210–295 g / 7.5–10.5 oz

It is ironic that among all dark-headed gulls in North America, the one called "Black-headed" actually has a brown head. This vagrant from the Old World is often observed in flocks of Bonaparte's and Ring-billed gulls.

**APPEARANCE:** Breeding adults have chocolate-brown on head that does not extend down nape. White eye crescents. White body. Grey mantle. Wings have white outer primaries (forming wedge) tipped with black. Inner underwing primaries greyish from below. Bill and legs dark red. **Winter birds** have white head with blackish eye crescent and ear spot. Bill often tipped with black. **Immatures** have pale legs and dark tail band. Wings have dark brownish bar on inner wing from scapulars to wrist, and black bar along trailing edge. Flight feathers dusky below. Pinkish orange bill has black tip. **First-year** birds may have incomplete dark hood.

SUMMER IMMATURE

WINTER

▶ Bonaparte's Gull very similar but can be separated by smaller size, thin black bill, darker and more extensive hood, and paler underwing primaries. Franklin's and Laughing gulls have black hood extending over nape and lack white wedge on leading edge of wing. Little Gull lacks black-tipped primaries and eye crescents; dark cap an bill in winter. Sabine's Gull has black wedge on forewing and yellow-tipped, black bill.

**VOICE:** Usually silent away from breeding grounds. Occasionally utters high-pitched *craah.*

**HABITAT AND BEHAVIOUR:** Marshes, and shorelines of lakes and rivers. Forages at water's surface or gleans invertebrates from the ground. Sometimes catches insects in flight. May steal food from other birds.

**STATUS:** Rare fall visitor. Very rare winter and spring visitor.

# BONAPARTE'S GULL *Larus philadelphia*
30–36 cm / 11.8–14.2" Wt 200–250 g / 7.1–8.9 oz

Unlike its raucous, unseemly congeners, this delicate little gull does not fight with its neighbours, loiter in parks, or dine in landfills. On the contrary, it dabbles and gleans for food along shorelines and nests high above the ground in coniferous trees.

**APPEARANCE:** Breeding adults have black head with white eye crescents. Black bill. Grey mantle and white body. Underparts flushed with pink. Wings have white forewing wedge and black-tipped primaries. Wing tips pale below. Legs orangish red. **Winter adults** have white head with greyish nape, dark ear-patch, and blackish eye crescent. **Immatures** similar to winter adults but with narrow black tail band, dark brown bar on leading edge of wing, black band on secondaries, and black outer primaries. **First-year bird** may have partial dark hood.

SUMMER

WINTER

► Franklin's Gull has orange bill and lacks white forewing wedge; black face mask in winter. Black-headed Gull has brownish head, reddish bill, and dark underwing primaries. Little Gull lacks white eye crescents; black hood extends over nape. Sabine's Gull has large white, black, and grey triangles on wings; black bill has yellow tip.

**VOICE:** Sparrow-like chattering. Utters soft *ear ear* while feeding.

**HABITAT AND BEHAVIOUR:** Breeds in boreal forest. Lakes, rivers, and marshes during migration. Graceful, tern-like flyer with fast wingbeats.

**STATUS:** Uncommon breeder. Very common spring and fall migrant. Locally common winter visitor.

169

GB common

# MEW GULL *Larus canus*

L 38.0–40.5 cm / 15–16" Wt 350–545 g / 12.5–19.5 oz

This native of the Pacific Northwest and northern Eurasia best resembles a diminutive Herring Gull. It is most frequently observed in Ontario along the lower Great Lakes in fall.

**APPEARANCE:**
White body and grey mantle. Small, unmarked, yellow, plover-like bill. Eyes brown. Black wing tips have extensive white mirrors. Legs and feet greenish yellow. Head washed with brown in winter. Bill dusky green. **Juveniles** mottled pale greyish brown

WINTER

above and below. Pinkish grey legs. Bill pinkish grey with dark tip. **First-** and **second-winter** birds increasingly like adults but retain two-toned bill, dusky primaries, and dark greyish brown terminal band on tail.

▶ Thin bill and small size distinctive in all plumages. Adult Ring-billed Gull large with pale eyes, lighter mantle, and dark band near end of bill; first-winter bird has whiter underparts with heavier spotting. Herring Gull much larger; heavy bill has red spot on lower mandible. Immature Thayer's Gull larger with paler wing tips and black bill.

**VOICE:** Utters low, mewing *mee-u.* Also gives typical gull call, *hiyah-hiyah-hiyah,* that is higher pitched than other gull species.

**HABITAT AND BEHAVIOUR:** Lakes in summer. Coastal areas and rivers in winter. Flight light and buoyant. Rarely far from land. Forages near water's surface, rarely plunges beneath. Flocks sometimes feed in ploughed fields.

**STATUS:** Rare fall visitor.

# [R]ING-BILLED GULL *Larus delawarensis*

45.5–51.0 cm / 18–20" Wt 405–540 g / 14.5–19.3 oz

[W]idespread on lakes and rivers throughout the province, the Ring-[bi]lled Gull frequents garbage dumps, city parks, and fast-food [re]staurants. Populations have increased dramatically because of its [to]lerance for human habitation.

**[A]PPEARANCE:**
[B]reeding adults
[w]hite with grey
[m]antle. Yellow bill
[ha]s black ring near
[ti]p. Eyes and legs
[ye]llow. Wing tips
[bl]ack with
[pr]ominent white
[sp]ots. Head streaked
[w]ith brown in
[w]inter. **Juveniles**
[m]ottled brown
[ab]ove. Head and
[br]east streaked
[w]ith greyish brown.

[R]ump, inner wings, and tail spotted with brown. Primaries and broad
[tai]l band blackish brown. Bill pinkish with black tip. Legs pink. **First-
[an]d second-year** birds increasingly like winter adults.

▶ California Gull larger with dark eyes, and red and black spots
[in] bill. Herring, Thayer's, Iceland, and Glaucous gulls larger with
[pi]nkish legs; yellow bill has red spot on lower mandible. Mew Gull has
[da]rk eyes and less black on wing tips; lacks bill ring. Lesser Black-
[ba]cked Gull darker and lacks bill ring.

**[V]OICE:** High-pitched *kakakaka-akakaka. Kree kree kree* given during
[fo]od squabbles. Also utters low, laughing *yook-yook-yook.*

**[H]ABITAT AND BEHAVIOUR:** Lakes, rivers, landfills, beaches,
parks, and fields. Flight buoyant with rapid wingbeats.
More manoeuvrable than larger, similarly
plumaged gulls. Alights on water with feet
dangling and wings held above head.

**STATUS:** Uncommon to locally abundant
breeder. Locally common migrant and
winter visitor.

# CALIFORNIA GULL *Larus californicus*

L 50–58 cm / 20–23" Wt 700–850 g / 1.6–1.9 lb

An unmated bird of this western species twice attempted nesting among the large Ring-billed Gull colony of Toronto's outer harbour. Their similarity to Herring and Ring-billed gulls may cause California Gulls to go unnoticed in the province.

**APPEARANCE:**
Adults white with grey mantle. Wings have black tips with white mirrors. Head and neck has dusky mottling in winter. Bill yellow with black and red spots. Black spot may be absent during breeding. Legs yellowish green.

WINTER

**Juveniles** very dark overall with whitish edging on mantle. Bill black. Pinkish legs. **First-winter** birds mottled greyish brown, somewhat lighter below. Pinkish bill has dark tip. Primaries and band across secondaries dark dusky brown. Rump barred brown and white. Unbanded dusky brown tail. **Second-** and **third-winter** birds have progressively more grey on mantle and white on underparts. Bill has blackish ring. Legs greyish green.
▶ Ring-billed Gull smaller with shorter bill, paler mantle, yellow eyes, and black ring on bill; less white on wing tips in flight; first-winter birds paler; bill resembles that of third-winter California Gull but latter darker with dark eyes. Herring Gull larger and paler with stout bill, light eyes, and pink legs. Mew Gull much smaller with shorter, thinner bill. Adult Thayer's Gull has pink legs and greyish wing tips.

**VOICE:** Variable call notes including loud, ringing *yeow,* soft *waaaaaaah,* and long *kyow*. Head often in vertical position when calling, and lowered with each note. Voice ranges in pitch between higher, harsh Ring-billed Gull and lower, richer Herring Gull.

**HABITAT AND BEHAVIOUR:** Islands and shores of lakes. May jump directly into flight but generally takes a few steps. Wing strokes deeper and quicker than larger gulls. Glides in high winds or updrafts.

**STATUS:** Vagrant breeder. Rare fall and winter visitor.

# HERRING GULL *Larus argentatus* ✓ ┬ ┬

58–65 cm / 22.8–25.6" Wt 900–1200 g / 2.0–2.7 lb

During the nineteenth century, excessive feather and egg hunting caused the extirpation of the Herring Gull from some southern Ontario counties. Its recovery in recent decades has been due largely to its exploitation of human refuse as a food source.

**APPEARANCE:** Large gull with white body and grey mantle. Yellow eyes. Heavy yellow bill has red spot near tip. Black wing tips have white mirrors. Legs pink. **Winter adults** streaked with dusky brown on crown, hindneck, and sides of upper breast.

**Immatures** and **first-winter** birds dark greyish brown, streaked and mottled with dusky brown. Blackish primaries. Wide subterminal black band on tail. Bill pinkish with black tip. Eyes dark brown. Pinkish grey legs. **Second- and third-winter** birds paler with whitish head and underparts. Whitish rump contrasts with dark-brown-tipped tail. Bill buff with broad black bar near tip. Eyes and bill become yellowish in third year.

▶ Adult Thayer's Gull similar but can be distinguished by brown eyes, and little or no black on underside wing tips. Smaller Ring-billed Gull has black ring on bill and yellow legs. California Gull distinguished by black and red bill spots and yellow legs; immatures more difficult to separate. Herring Gull darker than most other species. Immature Greater Black-backed Gull less mottled with less distinct black band on tail.

**VOICE:** Trumpeting *keeyou* or *kyow-kyow-kyow* given as bird lowers and elevates head. *Eeeyou* given when flushed. Alarm call: *kek-kek*.

**HABITAT AND BEHAVIOUR:** Beaches, lakes, farmland, and garbage dumps. Glides, circles, and dives on outstretched wings. Walks or runs on land. Jumps to perches with single flap of wings. Runs to take off. Swims well. Dives from surface or low altitudes to depths under 2 m (6').

**STATUS:** Common breeder. Abundant migrant and winter visitor.

## THAYER'S GULL *Larus thayeri*

L 56–64 cm / 22.0–25.2" Wt 810–950 g / 1.8–2.1 lb

Thayer's Gull was formerly considered a subspecies of the Herring Gull. Its similarities to this species, particularly in immature plumage, often make it difficult to identify in the field.

**APPEARANCE:** Breeding adults white with grey mantle. Brown eyes. Yellow bill has red spot on lower mandible. Wings have black tips and white mirrors. Little or no black on underside of wing tips. Feet pinkish. **Winter adults** heavily mottled with greyish brown on head and neck, conferring almost hooded appearance. **Immatures** mottled above and below with greyish brown. Bill black. Outer primaries pale, particularly on underside. Tail has dark tip. **Second-** and **third-year** birds increasingly resemble winter adults but retain dark-tipped tail and brownish wing tips.

SUMMER

WINTER

▶ Herring Gull has darker mantle, light eyes, and more black on wing tips. Iceland and Glaucous gulls have light eyes and more white on wing tips. Ring-billed Gull has yellow eyes and legs, and dark ring around bill.

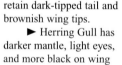

**VOICE:** Laughing, raucous calls resemble those of Herring Gull. Guttural, dry *kak-kak-kak* most frequently heard.

**HABITAT AND BEHAVIOUR:** Large lakes and rivers, and landfills. Flight strong but not particularly swift. Frequently rises vertically in flight and soars at height. Usually observed in mixed flocks with Herring and Ring-billed Gulls.

**STATUS:** Rare visitor from October to May.

# ICELAND GULL *Larus glaucoides*

57–66 cm / 22–26" Wt 810–1000 g / 1.8–2.2 lb

Identifying the Iceland Gull in the field is often a difficult task. Typically, adults differ from the Glaucous Gull only in size. In addition, first-year Iceland Gulls are almost identical to pale Thayer's Gulls.

**APPEARANCE:**
Breeding adults have white body and pale grey mantle. Yellow bill has red spot on lower mandible. Eyes yellow with dark eye-ring. Flight feathers greyish with white or pale grey wing tips. Legs pink. **Winter adults** have head and breast streaked with

greyish brown. **Immatures** mottled with pale greyish brown except on pale grey flight feathers. Bill black. **First-** and **second-year** birds whitish overall with increasingly less brown mottling. Bill pale at base with black tip in second year.

▶ Glaucous Gull stouter with longer, heavier bill and pure white wing tips; first-year bird has pink bill with dark tip. Herring Gull darker above with black wing tips. Thayer's Gull has dark eyes and more grey on wing tips. Ring-billed Gull smaller and darker with black ring around bill near tip.

**VOICE:** Utters shrill, laughing, high-pitched *kee-orrh korrh-korrh-korrh-korrh*. Also gives *ack-ack-ack-ack-ack* when alarmed.

**HABITAT AND BEHAVIOUR:** Large lakes and rivers, and landfills. Agile and buoyant on wing despite large size.

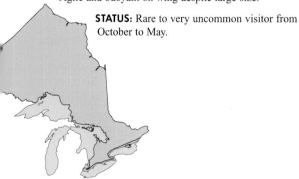

**STATUS:** Rare to very uncommon visitor from October to May.

# LESSER BLACK-BACKED GULL *Larus fuscus*

L 53.5–56.0 cm / 21–22"  Wt 770–1000 g / 1.7–2.2 lb

In North America, the Lesser Black-backed Gull is most commonly observed with the brown-streaked foreparts of winter plumage. Recently, however, summer reports of this European native in Ontario have increased dramatically, suggesting that nesting attempts may soon be recorded.

**APPEARANCE:**
Adults have white body and dark grey mantle. Bill yellow with red spot on lower mandible. Eyes and legs yellow. Wing tips extensively black with one or two white spots.
**Winter adults** have head and neck heavily streaked with brown. Dark brownish smudge

WINTER

surrounds eyes. **Immatures** mottled greyish brown with heavily streaked head, neck, and underparts. Dark tail band. Legs pink. Bill and eyes dark. **First-** and **second-year** birds have dark brownish grey wings but increasingly whiter bodies and grey backs. Eyes yellowish and bill pale with dark tip in second and third year.

&#9654; Adults distinguished from other large gulls by mantle colour midway between light grey of Herring Gull and dull black of Great Black-backed Gull. Slaty-backed Gull has pink legs and more white on trailing edge of wings. Greater Black-backed Gull much larger with pink legs; first- and second-year birds resemble young Herring Gull but have much darker backs and underwings.

**VOICE:** Screeching call, *keeyu keeyu keeyu,* lower-pitched than Herring Gull's.

**HABITAT AND BEHAVIOUR:** Landfills, and large lakes and rivers. Slender wings confer more buoyant flight than Great Black-backed Gull.

**STATUS:** Rare to uncommon visitor from September to May. Rare summer resident.

# GLAUCOUS GULL *Larus hyperboreus*
66–76 cm / 26.0–29.5" Wt 1.2–1.8 kg / 2.6–4.0 lb

Immature Glaucous Gulls are more frequently observed in Ontario than are adults. Fortunately, their pale plumage and large size allows them to be quickly identified among a mixed-species flock.

**APPEARANCE:** Very large, bulky, pale gull. Breeding adults have white body with pale grey mantle. Eyes yellow. Long, heavy yellow bill has red spot on lower mandible. White wing tips. Pink legs. Some brownish streaking on head and breast in winter. **Immatures** mottled and barred with pale greyish buff. Primaries pale grey with white tips. Bill pinkish with black tip. Legs pink. **Second-** and **third-year** birds increasingly pale with less mottling, particularly on mantle, and less black in bill tip.

▶ Large size and pale colour distinctive. Iceland and Thayer's gulls smaller with darker mantle. Other large gulls have much darker mantles and black wing tips.

**VOICE:** Screeching call resembles that of Herring Gull: *kak-kak-kak.* Also utters harsh, nasal croaks like a Northern Raven.

**HABITAT AND BEHAVIOUR:** Landfills, and large lakes and rivers. Flight strong and sometimes swift. Seizes birds on the wing and consumes them whole. Holds prey under one foot while using powerful bill to shred it. Steals food from ducks and other gulls.

**STATUS:** Rare to uncommon visitor from November to May. Exceptionally rare summer visitor.

# GREAT BLACK-BACKED GULL *Larus marinus*

L 71–79 cm / 28.0–31.1" Wt 1.3–2.0 kg / 2.9–4.4 lb

The Great Black-backed Gull's large size and aggressive disposition allow it to dominate in mixed flocks both on land and in flight. This species frequently steals food from other species and preys directly on their chicks.

**APPEARANCE:**
Adults white with black back and wings. Wings have white trailing edges and white spots near tips. Bill yellow with red spot on lower mandible. Eyes pale yellow with red eye-ring. Wing linings greyish. Legs pink. **Winter adults** have diffuse brownish streaking

on back of head. **Immatures** checkered with greyish brown, darkest on wings and back. Whitish head and upper breast. Bill black. Whitish rump visible in flight. Tail has broad, black subterminal band. Plumage becomes more like adults' through **second and third year** with increasing black feathering on back and wings, and bill turning yellow from base to tip.

▶ Distinguished from other gulls by large size and dark mantle. Adult Lesser Black-backed Gull much smaller with yellow legs and feet; face and neck streaked with black in winter. Immature Great Black-backed Gulls resemble immature Herring and Lesser Black-backed gulls in coloration but much larger.

**VOICE:** Gives hollow, harsh *cowwp cowwp*. Also utters deep *err-ul*.

**HABITAT AND BEHAVIOUR:** Breeds on islands. Large lakes and rivers, and landfills in winter. Strong flyer; frequently soars. Attacks with steep dive. Walks or runs with lumbering gait. Jumps to high perch assisted with single beat of wings.

**STATUS:** Very rare breeder. Uncommon to common migrant and winter visitor.

# SABINE'S GULL *Xema sabini* Scotland

32–34 cm / 12.6–13.4" Wt 150–175 g / 5.5–6.3 oz

Most Sabine's Gulls migrate from their high arctic breeding sites to wintering grounds in South America over the open waters of the Pacific Ocean. Rare individuals are observed on the southern Great Lakes.

**APPEARANCE:**
Breeding adults have slate-grey hood outlined with black. Black bill has yellow tip. Body white with grey mantle. Wings have black outer primaries tipped with large, triangular, white patch mid-wing, and grey inner wing. Forked tail. Legs black.

**Winter adults** have white head with dark grey nape and hind crown.
**Immatures** browner on upperparts with pale feather edging. Sides of breast greyish brown. Bill black. Wing pattern like adults but somewhat muted in coloration. Shallowly forked tail has dark tip.

▶ Tricolour wings and forked tail diagnostic in all plumages. Bonaparte's and Black-headed gulls have white primaries with narrow black tips. Immature Black-legged Kittiwake lacks greyish brown on head and breast, and large white triangular patch on wing.

**VOICE:** Tern-like *kee-kee* usually given only on breeding grounds. Generally silent during migration.

**HABITAT AND BEHAVIOUR:** Tundra in summer. Large lakes and rivers during migration. Flight graceful, buoyant, and swift with deep wingbeats. May be slower when flying close to water. Does not dive but picks food from surface of water while in flight.

**STATUS:** Very rare spring and fall migrant.

England

# BLACK-LEGGED KITTIWAKE *Rissa tridactyla*

L 40–46 cm / 15.5–18.0" Wt 365–410 g / 13.0–14.5 oz

Unlike many other gull species, the Black-legged Kittiwake does not feed in garbage dumps. Consequently, its reproductive success is strongly influenced by availability of small fish and marine invertebrates and not by human habitation.

**APPEARANCE:** Breeding adults have grey mantle and white body. Small, unmarked yellow bill. Dark brown eyes. Black wing tips cut straight across upper and lower wing as if "dipped in ink." Otherwise, underwing white. White tail square or slightly notched. Black legs. **Winter adults** tinged with grey across back of head and nape. **Immatures** and **first-year** birds more strongly marked with dark spot behind eye and dark bar on nape. Black "M" on open wings formed by dark outer primaries and bar across inner wing. Slightly notched tail has black terminal band. Bill black. **Second-year** birds have yellow bill and less distinct upper wing pattern.

▶ Other black-headed gulls lack combination of black legs, yellow bill, grey nape, and unpatterned, black wing tips. Immature Sabine's Gull has triangular dark patch on upper wing, duskier nape, and forked tail.

**VOICE:** Utters raucous, nasal *kitti-waak* at nesting colony. Also gives barking *vapf vapf vapf* and various other squeaking, coughing, and cooing calls.

**HABITAT AND BEHAVIOUR:** Breeds on coastal cliffs. Occurs rarely inland on beaches and shorelines. Flight highly manoeuvrable. Wingbeats stiff, almost tern-like. Dives only to depth of 0.5–1.5 m (1.6–4.9') to feed on surface-swarming fish.

**STATUS:** Rare migrant and visitor in fall. Extremely rare visitor remainder of year.

# IVORY GULL *Pagophila eburnea*

38–43 cm / 15–17" Wt 450–650 g / 16.1–23.2 oz

This somewhat pigeon-like gull is observed occasionally on the Great Lakes and Lake Simcoe. If its all-white plumage is not readily visible, it can be identified by its distinctive, tern-like call.

IMMATURE

**APPEARANCE:** Entirely white gull has blackish legs and slate-grey bill with yellow tip. Dark brown eyes. **Immatures** predominantly white with blackish face and bill. Wing coverts, wing flight feathers, and tail topped with black, conferring spotted appearance when at rest. In flight, wings have black spots on trailing edges and tail has distinctive black border.

► Only all-white gull with dark legs. Iceland and Glaucous gulls white with pale grey mantle and pinkish legs; yellowish eyes and bill.

**VOICE:** Diagnostic harsh, shrill, bi-syllabic, tern-like *keearr.* Also gives descending scream, *keeeeeeeeer,* repeated two or three times. Alarm or threat call a low *pseeoo* or growling *roor-oh-roor-oh-roor.*

**HABITAT AND BEHAVIOUR:** Pack ice, rocky islands, and cliffs. Flight graceful and powerful. Walking gait resembles that of plover. Swims less frequently than most other gulls. Does not dive under surface completely.

**STATUS:** Rare winter visitor.

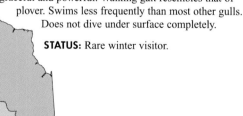

# CASPIAN TERN *Sterna caspia* +F

L 47–54 cm / 18.5–21.3" Wt 560–700 g / 20–25 oz

North America's largest tern is rare in Ontario and vulnerable to extinction in Canada. Populations have been reduced by fluctuating water levels, habitat encroachment by Ring-billed Gulls, predation, and human disturbance.

**APPEARANCE:** Large head, thick neck, and heavy red bill in all plumages. Breeding adults have black cap with small crest. Mantle pale grey. Wings white above. Black underside of primaries visible in flight. At rest,

wing tips extend beyond short, notched, white tail. Legs and feet black. Underparts white. **Winter adults** and **immatures** have black caps streaked with white. Immatures also have orangish bills and, sometimes, reddish legs.

▶ Other terns smaller with thinner bills and deeply forked tails. Accidental Royal Tern has yellowish orange bill, prominent black crest and paler wing tips. Common Tern has red legs and feet, and grey on outer tail feathers. Arctic Tern much greyer above; also has red legs and feet. Forster's and accidental Least terns have yellowish orange to yellow bills, legs, and feet. Sandwich Tern has black bill.

**VOICE:** Hoarse, raucous *kraa* or *ka-ka-kraaaa*. Utters hard, whirring *rro-rro-rra-rrererre* during aggressive encounters.

**HABITAT AND BEHAVIOUR:** Open areas near lakes, rivers, and beaches. Flight heavy and gull-like with deep, powerful wingbeats. Flies with bill down when foraging, dives, and submerges completely. Often feeds from surface. Waddling walk.

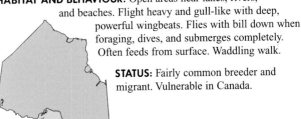

**STATUS:** Fairly common breeder and migrant. Vulnerable in Canada.

# COMMON TERN *Sterna hirundo* ✓

33–41 cm / 13.0–16.1" Wt 110–140 g / 3.9–5.0 oz

Common Terns usually nest colonially on sparsely vegetated islands or beaches. Individuals not tending young will drive off intruders by vigorously diving at them or defecating on them.

**APPEARANCE:** Breeding adults have black cap and nape. Thin, red bill has black tip. White body with grey mantle. Underparts tinged with grey. White rump. Upper wing has dark wedge on primaries. Dark, trailing edge visible from below. Forked tail white with grey outer feathers. Does not extend beyond folded wing. Legs and feet red. **Winter adults** have black on head restricted to nape and more black on bill. **Immatures** resemble winter adults but somewhat brownish above with dark shoulder bar visible in flight or at rest. Bill mostly black.

▶ Arctic Tern has all-red bill and more deeply forked tail; upper wing lacks dark grey primaries; underparts greyer. Forster's Tern has grey tail with white outer edges; upper primaries silvery; adults in winter and immatures have blackish eye-patch. Caspian Tern larger overall with heavier red bill.

**VOICE:** High-pitched, drawn-out *kee-ar.* Also utters staccato *kip.* Low, nasal *aanh* given singly or as bi-syllabic *aa-unh aa-unh aa-unh.*

**HABITAT AND BEHAVIOUR:** Islands, breakwaters, and beaches. Flight strong, buoyant, and graceful. Often hovers while foraging, then drops below surface to seize small fish.

**STATUS:** Common breeder. Common spring and fall migrant.

*Confront*

# ARCTIC TERN *Sterna paradisaea*

L 36–43 cm / 14.2–16.9" Wt 100–118 g / 3.5–4.2 oz

The Arctic Tern is renowned for its annual round-trip migration from the Arctic to Antarctica, which may measure 32,000 km (19,200 miles) or more. It generally follows a pelagic route and is rarely seen near shore south of its breeding grounds.

**APPEARANCE:**
Rounded head and short neck. Breeding adults have black cap and nape. Bill deep red. Mantle grey. Upper wings unmarked grey. Long, forked tail and undertail coverts white. Underparts pale grey. Underwing appears translucent except for narrow,

black, trailing edge. Legs and feet orangish red. **Winter adults** and **immatures** have white forehead, black bill and nape, and white underparts.

▶ Common Tern has black-tipped bill and whiter underparts; upper primaries show dark grey wedge in flight; immatures browner above with some orange on bill. Forster's Tern has grey tail with white outer feathers, black-tipped bill, and silvery appearance to upper primaries; flight feathers lack black, trailing edge on underside.

**VOICE:** Utters harsh, high-pitched *kee-ya* with descending inflection. Also gives repeated *kee-kee-kee-kee.*

**HABITAT AND BEHAVIOUR:** Tundra, islands, beaches, and rocky shorelines. Flight strong, effortless, graceful, and buoyant. Frequently forages by plunging from a hovering position. Aggressively defends nest from intruders.

**STATUS:** Uncommon breeder. Rare spring and fall migrant.

# FORSTER'S TERN *Sterna forsteri*
36–41 cm / 14.2–16.1" Wt 125–150 g / 4.5–5.5 oz

Unlike other terns, Forster's Terns may be extending their range in Ontario. This expansion may be correlated with above-average water levels in many southwestern marsh areas, which have an adverse impact on competing nesting Common Terns.

**APPEARANCE:**
Breeding adults
have black cap,
black-tipped orange
bill, and long
orange legs. Neck
and underparts
white. Inner wing
and back light grey.
Upper surface of
primaries silvery.
Rump white. Tail
grey with white
outer feathers.
Underwing has

poorly defined darkish wedge. **Winter adults** have white head with thick black band through eye to greyish nape. Bill black with rusty base. **Juveniles** resemble winter adults but with brownish grey upperparts. Bill brownish black. Legs yellowish.

▶ Common Tern has dark wedge near tips of primaries, darker bill and legs, grey tinge to underparts, and predominantly white tail; lacks band through eye in winter. Arctic Tern greyish below; white tail has grey outer feathers; lacks black tip on bill; no mask in winter. Caspian Tern larger with heavier reddish orange bill.

**VOICE:** Nasal, high *keer* given in flight. Also gives grating, low-pitched, nasal *tzaap*.

**HABITAT AND BEHAVIOUR:** Breeds in marshes. Lakes and marshes in migration. Flight graceful and swallow-like with shallow, rapid wingbeats. Snatches insects in flight.

**STATUS:** Rare to uncommon breeder. Rare to locally common spring and fall migrant.

185

# BLACK TERN *Chlidonias niger*

L 23–26 cm / 9–10"  Wt 50–60 g / 1.8–2.1 oz

Throughout the breeding season, this tern favours freshwater habitats. However, during its protracted southbound migration, it occurs primarily near salt water and is frequently observed far out at sea.

**APPEARANCE:** Head and body black grading to grey rump, in breeding plumage. Wings and tail uniformly grey except for white leading edge on wings. Breast and belly black with contrasting white undertail coverts. Pale grey wing linings. Bill black. Legs dark red.

**Winter plumage** has white head with blackish cap, grey back, and wholly white underparts except for diagnostic small dark patch on each side of breast. Individuals undergoing moult mottled black and white on head and underparts. **Juveniles** similar to winter adults but with browner back and wing coverts.

▶ Distinctive in breeding plumage. Distinguishable from other terns in winter plumage by small size, grey rump and tail, and dark spots at sides of breast.

**VOICE:** Short, metallic *krik* heard among flocks and foraging birds. Alarm call a high-pitched *keek*. Female utters soft, rapid *eew*.

**HABITAT AND BEHAVIOUR:** Marshes, wet meadows, and ponds. Agile in flight. Flies swallow-like over surface of water or land foraging for insects and small fish. Migrating flocks form horizontal arc.

**STATUS:** Uncommon breeder. Uncommon to common spring and fall migrant. Vulnerable in Ontario because of destruction of marsh habitat.

# LACK GUILLEMOT *Cepphus grylle*

30-36 cm / 11.8-14.2" Wt 420-500 g / 15-18 oz

ntario boasts only a single nesting record for the "Sea Pigeon."
atched eggshells were discovered in 1957 on a small island in
udson Bay that falls within provincial boundaries only because it is
ined to the mainland at low tide.

**PPEARANCE:**
reeding adults
lvety black with
hite wing-patch.
ing linings white.
lack bill. Feet and
outh lining bright
ange. **Winter adults**
ve white head and
nderparts. Back
ottled black and
hite. Wing-patch less
stinct. **Immatures**
oty brown above,
rticularly on head,
des, and wings.
hite wing-patch smaller.

▶ Breeding plumage distinctive. Accidental murres, Razorbills,
urrelets, and Atlantic Puffins have white underparts in all plumages.
o other species so extensively white on head in winter. Also, all lack
ng-necked, duck-like profile of guillemots. White-winged Scoter
rger and stouter with small white wing-patch visible while swimming.

**OICE:** Utters high-pitched, wheezing *squeee*. Also gives whistling calls.

**ABITAT AND BEHAVIOUR:** Rocky shores, open sea. Flight swift on
pidly beating wings. Prefers shallow water. Upright stance.
equently dips head while swimming. Courtship display involves
ad-bobbing and wing-raising. Usually nests in small colonies.

**STATUS:** Extremely rare breeder. Rare winter visitor.

# COLUMBIFORMES
## Pigeons and Doves

Pigeons and doves are plump, small-headed birds with distinctive cooing calls. Their predominantly greyish or brownish plumage may show colourful iridescent patches under closer examination. Pigeons and doves eat primarily seeds, waste grain, and fruit, and are generally observed feeding on the ground. However, they are capable of very fast flight on pointed wings. The introduced Rock Dove, a common inhabitant of city streets, is noted for its racing prowess. Eight columbiform species have been recorded in Ontario, including five accidental species (Band-tailed Pigeon, Eurasian Collared-Dove, White-winged Dove, Inca Dove, and Common Ground-Dove, see pp. 389–90). One species is extinct (Passenger Pigeon, see p. 399).

# ROCK DOVE *Columba livia*

30.5–33 cm / 12–13" Wt 340–360 g / 12–13 oz

Colonists brought the Rock Dove, also known as the Domestic Pigeon, to North America during the seventeenth century. Many escaped captivity to establish feral populations that continue to flourish in human-modified environments. Such birds frequently exhibit huge variations in plumage coloration.

**APPEARANCE:** Large, plump pigeon. Wild type has dark grey head and tail. Wings lighter grey with two broad black bars. Iridescent neck. White rump visible in flight. Underparts medium to dark grey. Also reddish, whitish, and blackish colour variants that sometimes retain some markings of wild type. **Immatures** resemble adults but browner overall and lack iridescent feathering on neck.

▶ Mourning Dove, Eurasian Collared-Dove, and Common Ground-Dove smaller and browner with pointed tails. Other accidental pigeons somewhat darker above and lack white rump.

**VOICE:** Primary call a soft, gurgling, complex series of coos: *coo roo-c oo-coo.* Often accompanied with strutting, bowing, and tail-fanning. Also: *oh-oo-oor* given when nesting, and grunting alarm call *oorhh.* Makes snapping noise with bill.

**HABITAT AND BEHAVIOUR:** Cities, farms, and towns. Almost exclusively among human habitation. Flight fast, strong, and direct. A homing pigeon can average 69 km/h (41 mph) for many hours. Makes wing-clapping display flight. Walks or runs with head moving back and forth. Forages on open ground.

**STATUS:** Very common year-round resident. Native to Old World.

# MOURNING DOVE *Zenaida macroura*

L 28–33 cm / 11–13" Wt 112–140 g / 4–5 oz

The mournful call of this dove is well known in residential communities throughout its range. Calling frequently begins before dawn and may continue for hours at a time.

**APPEARANCE:** Elongate dove with small head, slim neck, and long, pointed tail. Generally greyish brown above. Male has distinctive bluish grey cap and pinkish hue over foreparts; neck tinged with pink iridescence. Black spot on side of head. Bill small and black. Wings darker greyish brown, marked with numerous black spots. Underparts buff. Tail graduated, with long, greyish brown central feathers. Shorter outer grey feathers have black bars and white tips. **Female** similar but with foreparts mostly olive. **Immatures** have brownish plumage. Whitish edging on feathers gives upperparts scaly appearance.

▶ Rock Dove stockier with shorter tail, white rump, and iridescent neck. Accidental White-winged Dove has prominent white wing-patch. Common Ground-Dove has scaly foreparts. Accidental Eurasian Collared-Dove paler with black collar on hindneck.

**VOICE:** Most commonly heard call a mournful *who-ah whoo-whoo-who* with sharply rising, inflected second syllable. Given by male, often from conspicuous perch. Female utters faint coos. Both may give soft *ork* and *roo-oo*.

**HABITAT AND BEHAVIOUR:** Agricultural fields, open woodlots, and residential areas. Capable of swift, direct flights with rapid changes in pace and altitude. Wingbeats make obvious whistling noise, particularly at takeoff. Walks or runs on ground.

**STATUS:** Very common year-round resident

# UCULIFORMES
## uckoos

like their Old World kin, North American cuckoos are
t obligate brood parasites. However, Yellow-billed and
ack-billed cuckoos occasionally lay their eggs in other
ds' nests when certain environmental conditions prevail.
ese long-distance migrants return rather late to breeding
ounds in Ontario and, because of their elusive nature,
sting may be well underway before it is detected.
though these birds are generally silent and secretive, their
m, long-tailed, and somewhat hunch-backed posture will
nfirm their presence, if observed. Two cuckoo species
eed in Ontario. One accidental species has been reported
roove-billed Ani, see p. 390).

# BLACK-BILLED CUCKOO *Coccyzus erythropthalmu*

L 28–30 cm / 11–12" Wt 45–55 g / 1.6–2.0 oz

The Black-billed Cuckoo is a voracious consumer of destructive, noxious caterpillars. Its local distribution and abundance is often correlated with outbreaks of such insects.

**APPEARANCE:** Slender and long-tailed. Upper-parts plain greyish brown. Underparts dull white, shaded with pale greyish buff. Underside of graduated tail dark brown tipped with white, giving appearance of eight crescent-shaped spots. Moderately long, curved bill entirely black. Orbital ring bright red in adults. Two inner toes point
forward, two outer toes reversed. **Immatures** have rich cinnamon ting on wings and less distinct undertail pattern. Orbital ring greenish grey

▶ Distinguished from Yellow-billed Cuckoo by red eye-ring, black bill, and small tail spots. Adult Black-billed Cuckoo lacks rufou wing-patch in flight.

**VOICE:** Fast, rhythmic series of two to five notes with brief pause between sets: *cucucu cucucu cucucu.* Often repeated many times. Ma be preceded by five short gurgling notes: *krak-ki-ka-kruk-kruk.* Calls night, particularly in summer. Calls quieter and more dove-like than Yellow-billed Cuckoo.

**HABITAT AND BEHAVIOUR:** Groves, abandoned farmland, forest edges, and riparian thickets. Occurs in coniferous forest and suburban areas more frequently than Yellow-billed Cuckoo. Flight graceful and hurtling with deep wingbeats; glides and jumps into cover. Furtive an retiring; often difficult to detect unless calling. While foraging, remains motionless and scans surrounding vegetation, then makes hopping dashes to capture prey.

**STATUS:** Rare to fairly common breeder.

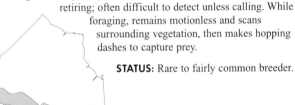

# YELLOW-BILLED CUCKOO *Coccyzus americanus*

28–33 cm / 11–13" Wt 55–65 g / 2.0–2.3 oz

Skulky and secretive by nature, the Yellow-billed Cuckoo may first reveal its presence by its hollow, wooden call. Often dubbed "Raincrow" because of its tendency to call before inclement weather.

**APPEARANCE:**

Slender and long-tailed. Head and upperparts plain greyish brown. Bill moderately long and curved; upper mandible black, lower bright yellow in adults. Orbital ring yellow or grey. Underparts dull white, faintly shaded white or pale buff. Underside of graduated tail feathers broadly tipped with white, giving appearance of six large spots. Large rufous wing-patch diagnostic in flight. Two inner toes point forward, two outer toes reversed. **Immatures** similar with somewhat less distinct markings.

▶ Easily confused with Black-billed Cuckoo; however, latter species lacks rufous wing-patch, yellow lower mandible, and large, roundish tail spots. Immature Black-billed Cuckoos may have buff wash on throat and undertail coverts.

**VOICE:** Most frequently heard call: *ka-ka-ka-ka-ka-kow-kow-kowlp-kowlp-kowlp.* Also harsh, rattling *kow-kow-kow-kow-kow* that resembles sound of metal door knocker hitting strike plate. Calls louder and more guttural than Black-billed Cuckoo.

**HABITAT AND BEHAVIOUR:** Open woodland, abandoned farmland, overgrown orchards, and dense thickets along streams and marshes. Flight fairly swift and direct, but appears laboured. Somewhat slower in flight than Black-billed Cuckoo. Usually perches with back hunched and body held low to avoid detection. Slinks away into vegetation when disturbed.

**STATUS:** Rare to fairly common breeder.

# STRIGIFORMES
## Owls

Owls have been called the "nocturnal birds of prey," although a few species are active during daylight hours. Members of this order are characterized by large heads with prominent forward-directed eyes set into feathered facial discs. Hooked bills and talons are well suited to the birds' predatory lifestyle. Some species have distinctive ear tufts. Owls are noted for their silent flight, which is conferred by the softly feathered leading edge of their wings. Twelve owl species occur in Ontario, including one accidental species (Burrowing Owl, see p. 390).

# ARN OWL *Tyto alba*

37–44 cm / 14.5–17" Wt 475–560 g / 1.1–1.3 lb

s suggested by its common name, the Barn Owl usually nests in man-made structures, such as barns, silos, church steeples, and other occupied buildings. It is the only Ontario owl with a heart-shaped face.

**PPEARANCE:**
onspicuous heart-shaped
cial disc. Eyes dark brown.
o ear tufts. Upperparts
ff, heavily marked with
ack and white. Underparts
riable, ranging from pale
imarked buff to dark buff
avily spotted in black.
ings long and rounded in
ght; tail short. Legs long
th sparse feathering to
es. Underparts of **female**
pically darker and more
otted than those of male.
**amatures** resemble adults
t somewhat buffier with
ss extensive spotting
upperparts.
▶ Heart-shaped
cial disc diagnostic in
plumages.

**OICE:** Long, drawn-out, raspy screech, *kar-r-r-r-ick,* heard during eeding season. Also utters highly variable snores, *scheuh,* and hisses, *iish,* particularly during flight and in non-breeding season. ccasionally makes bill-snapping sounds.

**ABITAT AND BEHAVIOUR:** Open woodlands, farmland, and grassy eadows. Also residential and urban areas. Buoyant, deep wingbeats. Rather slow when hunting, but capable of rapid flight. Strictly nocturnal; most active just after sunset and shortly before sunrise. Perches silently between foraging excursions. Hunts over open fields and orchards and around farms.

**STATUS:** Extremely rare. Threatened (possibly extirpated) in Ontario due to urbanization and intensive agricultural practices.

# EASTERN SCREECH-OWL *Otus asio*

L 16.5–25.0 cm / 6.5–10.0" Wt 160–190 g / 5.7–6.8 oz

The Eastern Screech-Owl occurs in two distinct colour phases, one prominently grey and the other rufous. Both colour morphs may be found within populations throughout the species' range.

**APPEARANCE: Grey morph** has variegated greyish-brown upperparts streaked with dark brown. Eyes yellow. Eyebrows and lores white. Broad black stripe outlines whitish facial disc. Conspicuous ear tufts. Scapulars and wing coverts broadly tipped with white, forming two conspicuous lines of spots on wings. Primaries barred with grey and white. Dark and light grey bars on tail. Underparts whitish with dark vertical streaks, heaviest on throat and upper breast. **Rufous morph** is deep cinnamon above with narrow black streaks. Wings reddish brown with two rows of white spots. Tail rufous with fine brown barring. Facial discs rufous. **Immatures** of both morphs barred with white and brown. Rufous-phase immatures have rufous edging on bars.

▶ Rufous individuals distinctive. Grey morph individuals only small owl species in Ontario with conspicuous ear tufts.

**VOICE:** Mournful, tremulous wail, descending in pitch; resembles whinny of horse. Also utters slow, single-pitched trill that gradually increases in volume. Call notes include variable, low-pitched hoot and loud, piercing screech.

**HABITAT AND BEHAVIOUR:** Open deciduous woodland, and shade trees within cities or along streams. Rapid, uniform wingbeats. Flights usually short and direct through tr canopy. May hover briefly when hunting.

**STATUS:** Uncommon year-round resident.

# GREAT HORNED OWL *Bubo virginianus*

46–63 cm / 18.1–24.8" Wt 1.0–2.5 kg / 2.2–5.5 lb

This powerful and aggressive owl hunts at night for prey as large as rabbits, geese, and herons. Its strong talons may exert a force in excess of 13 kg (29 lb).

**APPEARANCE:** Upperparts dark brown mottled with greyish white and dusky brown. Tawny facial discs bordered black except at throat. Large yellow eyes. Conspicuous whitish eyebrow and bib. Widely spaced, brownish black ear tufts. Wings brown barred with black and spotted with greyish brown and buff. Tail tawny barred with dusky brown. Breast and belly whitish; somewhat tawny at sides. Underparts, except centre of breast, heavily barred with brownish black. Bars widely spaced on undertail coverts. Feathered buffy legs and toes. Paler subarctic birds have greyish buff plumage mottled with whitish grey. **Immatures** buffy with brown barring and dark facial discs. Ear tufts indistinct.

► Long-eared Owl much smaller with closely spaced ear tufts and lengthwise streaking on underparts; lacks white bib. Great Gray and Snowy owls large but lack ear tufts and tawny facial discs bordered black.

**VOICE:** Deep-toned, tremulous hoot of three to six notes, *who-hoo-ho-oo,* given by male and female. Calls include hawk-like, whistling *oo-who-o-o-o-ooh* and hissing, cat-like *meee-owwwwww.*

**HABITAT AND BEHAVIOUR:** Open woodlands, swamps, and agricultural areas. Flight powerful, direct, and manoeuvrable. Occasionally walks on ground with pronounced side-to-side gait.

**STATUS:** Common year-round resident.

197

# SNOWY OWL *Nyctea scandiaca*

L 55–70 cm / 22–28" Wt 1.8–2.5 kg / 4.0–5.6 lb

The Snowy Owl is the only predominantly white owl. However, many other owl species, flying overhead at night, may appear white when li from below with a flashlight or car headlight beams.

**APPEARANCE:** White; variably spotted or barred with dusky brown. Some appear pure white. Lacks ear tufts. Feathers surrounding eyes nearly conceal black bill. Eyes yellow. **Female** has more extensive brown markings, particularly on breast and wings, and are much larger. **Immatures** resemble adult female but more heavily barred.

▶ White-phase Gyrfalcon slimmer with longer tail and pointed wings. Barn Owl white below, but has mottled brown upperparts.

**VOICE:** Usually silent. Sometimes gives booming, low hoot of usually two, but sometimes six or more, notes: *hoo hoo.* Male commonly hoots, but female does so only rarely. Hoots carry over long distance and may be answered by other Snowy Owls. Other calls include rattling *rick rick rick,* barking *quawk quawk quawk,* and low, rapid, cackling *ka-ka-ka-ka-ka-ka.*

**HABITAT AND BEHAVIOUR:** Open country; fields, marshes, beaches, dunes, and tundra. Differs from most owls in being somewhat diurnal Flight strong and steady, but not rapid. Downward stroke a long, deliberate sweep; upward stroke quick and jerky. May glide on horizontal wings for some distance. Frequently observed perching quietly on posts, haystacks, and dunes.

**STATUS:** Very rare summer visitor. Uncommon winter visitor.

# NORTHERN HAWK OWL *Surnia ulula*
36–44 cm / 14.5–17.5" Wt 295–350 g / 10.5–12.5 oz

This predominantly diurnal owl hunts from exposed perches, suggesting that it relies on eyesight as well as hearing to locate its prey. Once prey is observed, the owl dives from its perch with a rapid, low swoop.

**APPEARANCE:** Flat head. Small facial disc whitish with distinctive, heavy black border conferring fierce expression. Small yellow eyes. Forehead conspicuously spotted with white. Hindneck has dark V-shaped pattern. Upperparts brownish black with heavy white spotting and streaking. Wings greyish brown with faint brown bars and large white spots.

Long, greyish brown tail somewhat wedge-shaped and crossed with seven to eight white bars. Underparts white with heavy brown barring. Legs fully feathered. **Immatures** similar to adults but somewhat greyer overall and less extensively marked with white.

▶ Overall appearance distinctive. Smaller Boreal Owl has black-bordered facial discs but lacks horizontal barring on underparts; forehead narrower and eyes larger.

**VOICE:** Usually silent. Male utters trilling whistle: *tu-wita-wit tiwita-wita wita wita.* Female gives hoarse *chat.* Alarm call a rapid hawk-like series, *kee-kee-kee-kee,* given in flight.

**HABITAT AND BEHAVIOUR:** Open coniferous and mixed woodlands, and muskeg. Flight rapid, strong, and agile through dense vegetation. Able to soar and hover. Rarely walks on ground. Perches with body inclined forward. Flicks tail.

**STATUS:** Rare to locally uncommon year-round resident. Rare visitor to southern Ontario in winter.

# BARRED OWL *Strix varia*

L 43–60 cm / 17–24" Wt 615–755 g / 1.4–1.7 lb

Despite its predominantly nocturnal habits, this vocal owl frequently gives its distinctive, emphatic call during daylight hours. When appropriate nesting cavities are unavailable, Barred Owls will use old Red-shouldered and Cooper's hawks' nests.

**APPEARANCE:** Large, big-headed owl lacking ear tufts. Upperparts greyish brown; feathers barred and edged with buffy white. Brown eyes. Yellowish bill. Roundish facial discs greyish brown with indistinct concentric whitish and brownish rings. Short, broad wings and tail barred broadly with dull white and dark brown. Neck and upper breast transversely barred with brown and dull white. Belly streaked vertically. **Immatures** resemble adults but are somewhat more reddish brown.

▶ Other owls, except distinctive heart-faced Barn Owl, have yellow eyes. Great Gray Owl larger with longer tail and white bow tie; lacks transverse barring on neck. Other "earless" owls much smaller with more boldly marked foreheads and facial discs.

**VOICE:** Hooting call of nine notes: *who-cooks-for you who-cooks-for-you-all.* Somewhat higher pitched than Great Horned Owl. Also utters screaming, chuckling, and barking notes. Calls end frequently with descending *ooo-aaarrrr.*

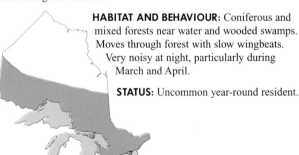

**HABITAT AND BEHAVIOUR:** Coniferous and mixed forests near water and wooded swamps. Moves through forest with slow wingbeats. Very noisy at night, particularly during March and April.

**STATUS:** Uncommon year-round resident.

# GREAT GRAY OWL *Strix nebulosa*
1-84 cm / 24-33" Wt 700-1700 g / 1.6-3.8 lb

like many owls, the principally nocturnal Great Gray Owl will hunt ring daylight hours on overcast days. It is easiest to observe during nter when its cryptic plumage is not concealed by foliage.

**PEARANCE:** Very large. rcular facial discs finely rred with brown and greys form six or more nearly ncentric rings on white ckground. White patches foreneck resemble bow . Bill yellow with black tch below. Lacks ear tufts. herwise, body streaked th browns and greys. ng, wedge-shaped tail ttled with grey and own. Yellow eyes appear all. Legs fully feathered. **imatures** resemble adults. ► Easily distinguished m other owls by large e. Barred Owl has similar mage but is much smaller, s dark eyes, and lacks ite bow tie.

**OICE:** Low, booming, evenly spaced *hoos* given in repetition. Notes ly audible at short range. Male calls at lower pitch than female. Also, i single *whoop* or *who-oop.*

**HABITAT AND BEHAVIOUR:** Dense coniferous forest. Hunts in open is, bogs, meadows, and muskeg. Flight agile and sometimes rapid; ngbeats slow and deep. May hover above suspected prey location, then pounce once prey is observed. Usually roosts in trees near trunk to avoid detection. Rarely walks on ground.

**STATUS:** Rare to very uncommon year-round resident. Rare visitor to southern Ontario in winter.

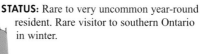

# LONG-EARED OWL *Asio otus*

L 34–39 cm / 13.5–15.5" Wt 250–405 g / 9.0–14.5 oz

Long-eared Owls hunt only at night, remaining quiet and concealed during daylight hours. Although they defend their nest against conspecifics when breeding, these owls roost communally in winter.

**APPEARANCE:** Chestnut facial discs. Long, closely spaced dark brown ear tufts. Eyebrows and moustache whitish. Eyes orangish yellow. Lores and bill black. Upperparts mottled with black, brown, grey, buff, and white. Long, rounded wings extend beyond tail when perched. Upper wing dark grey with orangish base. Tail buffy with seven to ten brown bars. Breast brownish grey with white spots. Belly whitish, cross-hatched and streaked with dark brown. Flanks and wing linings tawny. Legs and toes densely feathered. **Female** darker brown than male.

**Immatures** resemble adults but somewhat more rufous.

▶ Great Horned Owl larger with white throat-patch and more widely spaced ear tufts. Short-eared Owl paler with streaking restricted to breast; also facial discs tawny and ear tufts less prominent.

**VOICE:** Male utters series of two to two hundred low, moaning, evenly spaced hoots. Female gives soft, nasal *shh-oogh* at nest. Barking alarm call, *ooack ooack ooack,* higher pitched in female.

**HABITAT AND BEHAVIOUR:** Moist coniferous or mixed forest. Extremely agile flier. When hunting, flies with long glides interrupted by deep wingbeats. Often hovers over prey. Spreads wings in imposing threat display when disturbed at nest.

**STATUS:** Uncommon spring and fall migrant and winter visitor

# SHORT-EARED OWL *Asio flammeus*

33–43 cm / 13–17" Wt 280–500 g / 10–18 oz

When hunting, the Short-eared Owl can be recognized by its low, easy flight, which resembles that of a giant butterfly. Consequently, this species has garnered the vernacular name "Loper."

**APPEARANCE:** Upperparts dark brown, heavily mottled with buff. Round, grey and white facial discs. Orbital area black; eyes yellow. Small, closely set ear tufts. Wings long and broad with pale buff patches at base of primaries. Wings extend beyond tail when perched. Tail buff with dark horizontal barring. Underparts whitish to pale rust. Neck and upper breast streaked with dark brown. Belly and flanks have distinct dark stripes. Underside of wings has dark wrist-patches and wing tips. **Female** browner dorsally, with rustier underparts and heavier streaking. **Immatures** similar to adults but darker above and buffier below.

► Long-eared and Great Horned owls have long ear tufts. Barred Owl has dark eyes and horizontal barring on breast.

**VOICE:** Generally silent except in breeding season. Male gives *hoo-hoo-hoo-hoo-hoo* during aerial courtship display, accompanied with wing clap. Both sexes give emphatic, barking *keee-ow*.

**HABITAT AND BEHAVIOUR:** Open areas, particularly meadows, marshes, bogs, and tundra. Flight buoyant with slow, irregular wingbeats. Shifts back and forth on long wings. Hovers with or without wind; also soars. Hunts low to ground. Most active around dusk.

**STATUS:** Rare breeder. Uncommon migrant and winter visitor. Vulnerable in Canada due to destruction of wetlands.

203

## BOREAL OWL *Aegolius funereus*
L 21.5–30.5 cm / 8.5–12.0" Wt 100–140 g / 3.5–5.0 oz

The Boreal Owl is rarely seen because it avoids open country and conspicuous activity during daylight hours. This obligate cavity nester will accept artificial nest boxes, if made available.

**APPEARANCE:** Prominent black frames surrounding greyish white facial disc confer square-headed profile. Forehead and crown dark brown with numerous small white spots. No ear tufts. Back dark brown with large white spots. Wings and tail have rows of white spots that are visible even when perched. Underparts white broadly streaked with brown and russet. Bill buffy white. Legs and toes feathered to claws. **Immatures** chocolate-brown, with whitish eyebrows and cheek-patches.

► Northern Saw-whet Owl lacks black frames on facial discs, and has dark bill and white streaks, not spots, on brown crown.

**VOICE:** Loud call, uttered only by male, a series of trills comprising eleven to twenty-three notes that increase in volume. Call may be repeated for twenty minutes or more. Male and female also give loud, hoarse, screeching *kuwaak.*

**HABITAT AND BEHAVIOUR:** Boreal forest. Moves among trees with flapping flight, but attacks prey using direct glide. Can hover for brief periods. May also hop along ground in pursuit of prey. Adults and young climb well using bill, feet, and wings.

**STATUS:** Rare to locally common year-round resident. Uncommon visitor to southern Ontario in winter.

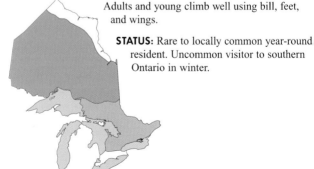

# NORTHERN SAW-WHET OWL *Aegolius acadicus*

18–21 cm / 7.0–8.5" Wt 75–100 g / 2.7–3.6 oz

The Northern Saw-whet Owl is Ontario's smallest owl. It is quite tame and inquisitive, and can frequently be attracted into view by imitating its whistled call.

**APPEARANCE:** Small owl. Large, round head brown, streaked with white on crown and nape. Facial discs white above and between eyes; otherwise, pale brown streaked with dark brown and white. Black bristle-like feathers between large yellow eyes. Black bill. Lacks ear tufts. Back, wings, and tail brown spotted with white. Underparts white, broadly striped with brown. Legs heavily feathered. **Immatures** darker brown with conspicuous white, V-shaped patch between and above eyes.

► Larger Boreal Owl similar but has prominent black feathers surrounding facial disc and a yellowish bill.

**VOICE:** Monotonous, rapid series of whistled notes at constant pitch: *too-too-too-too*. Resembles sound of small bell or dripping water. Also rarely gives loud, sharp, squeaking "saw-whetting" call, always in sets of three: *skreigh-aw, skreigh-aw, skreigh-aw.*

**HABITAT AND BEHAVIOUR:** Forest and woodlands of all types, but most abundant in coniferous and riparian forest. Hunts along forest edges or openings. Flies low to ground with rapid wingbeats, swooping up to perches. Flight similar to that of woodpecker.

**STATUS:** Fairly common breeder. Uncommon spring and fall migrant. Rare winter visitor.

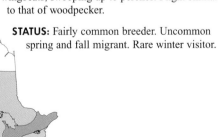

# CAPRIMULGIFORMES
## Nightjars

Nightjars are nocturnal or crepuscular birds with large eyes and long wings and tails. Despite its small apparent size, the typical nightjar bill has an exceedingly large gape, which is used to hawk flying insects. During the day, nightjars rest horizontally on tree limbs or on the ground where they are well camouflaged by their cryptic grey and brown plumage. Many species are best revealed by their calls. Five nightjar species have been reported in Ontario, including two accidentals (Lesser Nighthawk, Common Poorwill, see pp. 390–91).

# COMMON NIGHTHAWK *Chordeiles minor*
L 21.5–25.5 cm / 8.5–10.0" Wt 70–98 g / 2.5–3.5 oz

The Common Nighthawk feeds on flying insects, primarily at dusk and dawn. It may forage more than 175 m (568 feet) above the ground, descending in large circles until additional prey is encountered.

**APPEARANCE:** Upperparts blackish, mottled with grey, brown, buff, and white. Large flattened head with large eyes and small bill. Long, pointed wings with white patch across primaries best observed in flight. Long, rectangular tail notched at tip with white band in male. Underparts whitish, heavily barred with dark grey, particularly on breast. Conspicuous white throat-patch. **Female** somewhat browner, with buff throat and no white on tail. **Immatures** similar with less-conspicuous throat-patch.

▶ Similar Lesser Nighthawk has more rounded wings, buffy bands on primaries, and buff undertail coverts; white wing-patch closer to wing tip; tends to forage closer to ground. Other nightjars have rounded wings and tails, and lack white wing-patches and dark barring on undersides; also flight more moth-like.

**VOICE:** Nasal *peent* given in flight. Female also gives throaty *cluck*. Male utters croaking *auk auk auk* during courtship. Lesser Nighthawk gives rapid trilling in flight.

**HABITAT AND BEHAVIOUR:** Open country, cities, and towns. Flight graceful; continuous flapping with occasional periods of gliding. Walks little. Perches motionless with eyes shut on posts, tree limbs, and rocks during the day.

**STATUS:** Uncommon breeder. Uncommon to locally common spring and fall migrant.

# CHUCK-WILL'S-WIDOW *Caprimulgus carolinensis*

L 28.0–30.5 cm / 11–12" Wt 80–120 g / 2.8–4.2 oz

The Chuck-will's-widow is a recent addition to Ontario's avifauna; its breeding was not confirmed until 1977. This nightjar is best observed at dusk when it leaves its cryptic daytime perch in search of flying insects.

**APPEARANCE:** Upperparts cinnamon brown mottled with buff and black. Throat pale rufous with white half-collar in male and pale buff in **female** and **immatures.** Tail long and rounded. Male has white on inner webs of outer three tail feathers. Breast mottled black and brownish olive. Otherwise, underparts buffy cinnamon barred with dark brown.

▶ Whip-poor-will and Common Poorwill smaller and somewhat greyer, and male has broad white tail-patches. Whip-poor-will also has blackish chin. Nighthawks have narrow pointed wings with prominent white wrist bands; underparts and tail barred with blackish grey and white.

**VOICE:** Common name describes most frequently heard call: *chuck-will's-widow.* First note barely audible. Second and third notes have increasing emphasis. May call continuously for extended periods. Also gives guttural growling and clucking notes.

**HABITAT AND BEHAVIOUR:** Riparian woodlands, and forest and swamp edges. Flies silently with numerous flaps followed with glide. Highly manoeuvrable when in pursuit of prey. Roosts among scattered leaves on forest floor or on horizontal tree branches during the day.

**STATUS:** Rare breeder. Spring and summer visitor.

# WHIP-POOR-WILL *Caprimulgus vociferus*
23–25 cm / 9.1–9.8" Wt 55–70 g / 2.0–2.5 oz

Whip-poor-wills and their kin are collectively known as "goatsuckers." This name stemmed from an age-old superstition that suggested these birds sucked milk from the udders of goats, a crime purportedly causing blindness in their victims.

**APPEARANCE:** Mottled greyish brown overall with black spots and streaks. Large dark eyes. Rounded wings have reddish tinge. Black chin. Male has white throat-patch and large white patches on long, rounded tail. **Female** has buff throat-patch and buffy tips on outer tail feathers. **Immatures** resemble female but more uniformly brown above.

Immature male has buff tail-patches.

▶ Chuck-will's-widow larger and more reddish overall with brownish throat and whitish necklace; breast darker; much less white in tail of male. Common Nighthawk has forked tail and white patches on wings; throat white in male and buff in female; behaviour much more conspicuous.

**VOICE:** Loud, rolling, repeated *whip-poor-will,* with accent on first and third syllables. Faster tempo than call of Chuck-will's-widow. Also utters single, sharp *whip.*

**HABITAT AND BEHAVIOUR:** Open woodlands, often along forest edges; pine plantations. Flight silent and smooth, unlike jerky flight of nighthawks. Calls repeatedly in the evening. Nocturnal. Feeds on flying insects. Roosts during the day on ground or horizontal branch.

**STATUS:** Rare to fairly common breeder.

# APODIFORMES
## Swifts and Hummingbirds

Swifts (Apodidae) and hummingbirds (Trochilidae) are noted for their extraordinary powers of flight. Both families have narrow, pointed wings with wrist joints positioned relatively close to the body. Swifts frequently remain airborne throughout the day, alternating rapid "twinkling" flight with gliding. They never perch, but rest by clinging to vertical surfaces. Hummingbirds beat their stiff wings with such rapidity that they can hover or fly backwards. Many species undergo torpor during cold weather to conserve energy. Two apodiform species breed in Ontario. Four additional species occur as accidentals (Green Violet-ear, Broad-billed Hummingbird, Black-chinned Hummingbird, and Rufous Hummingbird, see p. 391).

# CHIMNEY SWIFT *Chaetura pelagica*

12–14 cm / 4.7–5.5" Wt 25– 28 g / 0.9–1.0 oz

The Chimney Swift acquired its common name from its proclivity to nest in the interior of brick chimneys. Small flocks of swifts can be observed foraging on wing at dusk in most towns and cities of southern and central Ontario.

**APPEARANCE:** Cigar-shaped body entirely brown with somewhat lighter throat and upper breast. Narrow, pointed, swept-back brown wings. Short, stiff brown tail has spines at feather tips. **Immatures** resemble adults but have somewhat darker throat and upper breast.

► Swifts distinguished from swallows by their longer, narrower, and more tapered wings, and their distinctive erratic manner of flight. Also, swallows generally paler below with forked or notched tails.

**VOICE:** Loud, rapid chattering or ticking call given in flight. Utters quick series of *chip* notes.

**HABITAT AND BEHAVIOUR:** Forages above towns and cities. Nests and roosts in chimneys, abandoned attics, and barns, and occasionally tree cavities. Flight rapid and bat-like. Glides between bursts of "twinkling" flight. Wings held bowed like a boomerang. Forages, drinks, bathes, and mates on the wing. Does not perch but uses feet to cling to vertical surfaces.

**STATUS:** Fairly common breeder. Common spring and fall migrant.

# RUBY-THROATED HUMMINGBIRD

*Archilochus colubris*

L 7.5–9.0 cm / 3.0–3.5" Wt 2.8–4.5 g / 0.1–0.2 oz

The Ruby-throated Hummingbird is the only hummer found regularly in Ontario. This feisty little dynamo is a welcomed visitor to nectar feeders in backyard gardens.

**APPEARANCE:** Upperparts iridescent green. Adult male has brilliant red throat that may appear black in poor light. Sides and flanks washed with olive. Otherwise, underparts whitish. Forked tail green with blackish outer feathers. **Female** lacks red throat-patch. Tail rounded with green centre and black outer feathers broadly tipped with white. **Immatures** similar; immature male may have dusky and reddish streaks on throat.

▶ Accidental Male Black-chinned Hummingbird has black and purple throat, and whitish collar between throat and olive sides; female not easily distinguished. Accidental Rufous Hummingbird extensively rufous or buff. Occasionally large sphinx moths are mistaken for hummingbirds; however, moths rarely feed before dusk.

**VOICE:** Rapid, squeaky, chirping *chick* given with threat display. Both sexes give repetitive *chee-dit* during migration. Female utters *mew.* Distinctive humming sound produced by beating wings.

**HABITAT AND BEHAVIOUR:** Mixed woodlands, wetlands, parks, and suburban gardens. Locomotion restricted to flying. Frequently hovers and flies backwards. Feeds during daylight.

**STATUS:** Fairly common breeder. Common migrant.

# CORACIIFORMES
## Kingfishers and Allies

Worldwide, the order Coraciiformes comprises ten diverse families, including hornbills, rollers, motmots, and bee-eaters. However, Ontario is home to only a single coraciiform species—the Belted Kingfisher. Despite its singularity, this species exhibits the long, strong bill and fused second and third toes that characterize most of its confamilials. Kingfishers are usually associated with water. They nest in burrows that they dig in stream banks.

# BELTED KINGFISHER *Ceryle alcyon* ✝F

L 28–36 cm / 11–14" Wt 140–170 g / 5.0–6.1 oz

The Belted Kingfisher feeds primarily on small fish. To catch its prey, it may dive obliquely into the water from an overhanging perch or while hovering 6–12 m (20–40 feet) above the surface.

**APPEARANCE:** Upperparts bluish grey. Head has shaggy, double-peaked crest and broad white collar. Small white spot near dark eyes. Large black bill. Wings dark bluish grey to black with irregular white markings on coverts and flight feathers visible in flight. Bluish grey to black tail feathers have white tips. Underparts generally white except for prominent bluish grey band on upper breast. **Female** also has rufous band on lower breast. Rufous flanks more extensive in female. **Immatures** resemble male; however, plumage somewhat darker, with more prominent white spots and brown breast band.

♀

▶ Distinctive in all plumages.

**VOICE:** Most frequently heard call a sharp, metallic rattle, *tick-tick-tick-tick-tick-tick,* given while perched or in flight. Also utters harsh screaming and squeaking calls.

**HABITAT AND BEHAVIOUR:** Streams, rivers, ponds, and lakes. Flight strong and direct; glides following two or three flapping strokes. Often flies close to water surface. Can hover while searching for prey. Shuffles poorly on short legs, primarily into and out of nesting burrows.

**STATUS:** Common breeder. Rare winter resident.

# PICIFORMES
## Woodpeckers

Most Ontario woodpeckers are boldly patterned, black-and-white birds with variably sized, chisel-shaped bills. They are commonly seen inching their way up the trunks of trees, using their stiff tails as props, as they search for hidden insects. One exception is the brownish Northern Flicker, which prefers to forage on the ground for ants. Most woodpeckers demonstrate a distinctive undulating flight pattern. Males can usually be distinguished from females by the extent of red or yellow feathering on their heads. Nine woodpecker species breed in Ontario. One species occurs as an accidental (Lewis's Woodpecker, see p. 391).

# RED-HEADED WOODPECKER
## *Melanerpes erythrocephalus*
L 22–25 cm / 8.5–10" Wt 55–85 g / 2–3 oz

Red-headed Woodpecker densities are subject to local fluctuations. Furthermore, continental populations, once spurred on by the forest-clearing of early settlers, have recently declined as dead and dying tree removal has become standard forest-management practice.

**APPEARANCE:** Adults have bright red head. Upperparts black with large white wing-patch and white rump. Tail blackish brown. Breast and belly white. **Immatures** have dull brown head and upper breast. Some individuals have red tinge on head. Upperparts blackish barred with brown. Wings and tail brown. Two dark bars on white secondaries. Underparts dull white and variably streaked with brown.

▶ Adults unmistakable. Immatures somewhat like young Yellow-bellied Sapsuckers but can be separated by white patch on wing and brown upper breast contrasting with whitish lower breast.

**VOICE:** Loud *kwee-arr* uttered singly or in short series. Also gives chattering and rattling notes. Drums weakly in short bursts.

**HABITAT AND BEHAVIOUR:** Open deciduous woodland, city parks, and groves. Usually flies with typically undulating woodpecker style; however, also able to fly directly. Frequently seen flying across open areas. Fly-catches from high perches. Aggressively pursues other woodpeckers. Stashes food in cavities in trees, utility poles, and buildings.

**STATUS:** Uncommon breeder. Fairly common spring and fall migrant. Rare winter visitor. Vulnerable in Ontario and Canada likely owing to loss of habitat.

# RED-BELLIED WOODPECKER
## *Melanerpes carolinus*
21.5–24.0 cm / 8.5–9.5" Wt 60–90 g / 2.1–3.2 oz

The Red-bellied Woodpecker is not generally considered a migrant, but Great Lakes populations of this species may be driven south during unusually cold winters. In Ontario, this species occurs primarily in remnant stands of Carolinian forest.

**APPEARANCE:** Adult male has red crown. Otherwise, upperparts and central tail feathers barred black and white. Outer tail feathers mostly black. Uppertail coverts white. Face and underparts greyish white except for reddish or pinkish patch on belly. Belly-patch often difficult to observe in field. **Female** similar except with red restricted to nape, hind crown, and base of bill. **Immatures** similar but lack red on head and have dusky, not black, bills.

▶ Distinguished from other woodpeckers by black and white barring on back and red patch on head. Northern Flicker has brownish back with black bars and grey crown. Red-headed Woodpecker has completely red head and unbarred lack back.

**VOICE:** Very vocal. Gives rolling *churr* call and long, rattling *cha-aa-aa*. Female gives soft *grr* when approaching nest. Also gives *chip, chup,* and *yuk* notes. Drums on dead trees or utility poles in one-second bursts.

**HABITAT AND BEHAVIOUR:** Mature deciduous forest; occasionally towns. Flight undulating. Lands with short, downward glide followed by rapid, upward glide to perch. Climbs up tree trunks with alternating hops and pauses.

**STATUS:** Uncommon year-round resident.

# YELLOW-BELLIED SAPSUCKER *Sphyrapicus varius*

L 19.5–22 cm / 7.6–8.6" Wt 45–50 g / 1.6–1.8 oz

Sapsuckers drill parallel lines of pit-like holes in the bark of trees during winter and spring. Insects are attracted to the "wells" as they fill with sap. The sapsucker makes regular rounds of the trees in its territory to lap up both the pooled sap and the insects trapped in it.

**APPEARANCE:** Adult male has red forehead and crown. Face black-and-white striped. Red throat-patch outlined with black. Upperparts barred with black, white, and brown. Black wings have large white patches. White rump. Tail black with white bars on central feathers. Underparts whitish with yellow wash. **Female** resembles male but has red restricted to forehead and crown. Throat white. **Immatures** browner overall with whitish eyebrow and moustache streak. Wings, rump, and tail like adults.

▶ Downy and Hairy woodpeckers lack white wing-patch and red forehead and crown. Three-toed Woodpecker has yellow crown and lacks white wing-patch. Pileated Woodpecker much larger with robust bill.

**VOICE:** Utters series of *chur* notes. Also gives *weep-weep* calls. Bill-hammering in irregular series of single, double, and triple beats resembles Morse code.

**HABITAT AND BEHAVIOUR:** Deciduous and mixed forest. Strong, swift, undulating flight. Seldom goes to ground. Noisy and conspicuous on breeding grounds but generally less active than most woodpeckers.

**STATUS:** Uncommon to common breeder. Uncommon to common spring and fall migrant.

# DOWNY WOODPECKER *Picoides pubescens*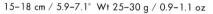

15–18 cm / 5.9–7.1" Wt 25–30 g / 0.9–1.1 oz

The common and widespread Downy Woodpecker is the most familiar woodpecker species to people who feed birds in their backyard. Its foraging behaviour can often be observed as it is quite tolerant of human activity.

**APPEARANCE:** Short, black bill with white feather tufts at base. Head black-and-white striped. Male has small red patch on back of head. Back white. Wings black barred with white. Rump black. Tail mostly black. White outer tail feathers barred with black. Underparts white. **Female** has no red patch on head. **Immatures** resemble adults but have red on crown and black streaks on sides and flanks.

▶ White back in flight distinguishes Downy Woodpecker from all other small woodpeckers except Hairy Woodpecker. Hairy Woodpecker can be distinguished by much longer bill (as long as head), lack of black barring on outer tail feathers, and more timid behaviour. Yellow-bellied Sapsucker has red forecrown, large white wing-patch, and black bib. Three-toed Woodpecker has yellow forecrown and black-and-white barring on back and sides.

**VOICE:** Most frequently heard call a flat *pik*. Also utters a long, rattling *ki-ki-ki-ki-ki* that drops in pitch and accelerates toward end. Hammers in bursts of one to one and a half seconds.

**HABITAT AND BEHAVIOUR:** Deciduous and mixed woodlands. Usually seen during short, undulating flights from tree to tree. Feeds with loose aggregation of other woodland bird species in winter. Sometimes hangs in foliage like a chickadee.

**STATUS:** Common year-round resident.

# HAIRY WOODPECKER *Picoides villosus*

L 19–24 cm / 7.5–9.5" Wt 70–85 g / 2.5–3.0 oz

Like other members of its family, the Hairy Woodpecker is well equipped for a life of tree-hammering. Feathered nostrils serve to filter sawdust, strong neck muscles support the head and bill, and a reinforced skull protects the tightly packed brain from concussion.

**APPEARANCE:** Head black-and-white striped. Male has small red patch on back of head. Black bill as long as head. Back white. Wings black barred with white. Rump black. Tail black with white outer tail feathers. Underparts white. **Female** has no red patch on head. **Immatures** resemble adults but have red on crown and black streaks on sides and flanks.

▶ White back in flight distinguishes Hairy Woodpecker from all other small woodpeckers except Downy Woodpecker. Downy Woodpecker identified by much shorter bill, black barring on white outer tail feathers, and more conspicuous behaviour. Yellow-bellied Sapsucker has red forecrown, large white wing-patch, and black bib. Three-toed Woodpecker has yellow forecrown and black-and-white barring on back and sides.

**VOICE:** Utters loud, sharp *peek.* Also gives rattling call, *keek-ki-ki-ki,* that is faster than that of Downy Woodpecker. Other calls include *wick a* and *tewk.* Drums variably, but always louder than Downy Woodpecker drumming.

**HABITAT AND BEHAVIOUR:** Deciduous and mixed forests. Swift, undulating flight. Shyer than Downy Woodpecker; usually flies ahead when approached.

**STATUS:** Uncommon to fairly common year-round resident.

# THREE-TOED WOODPECKER *Picoides tridactylus*

21–24 cm / 8.3–9.5" Wt 50–60 g / 1.8–2.1 oz

Generally considered a boreal species, the Three-toed Woodpecker was widespread throughout the south during the 1950s and 1960s when the Dutch elm disease epidemic provided an abundance of dead trees and bark beetles.

**APPEARANCE:** Head black with white eyebrow and moustache. Male has yellow crown; black in female. Black bill. Back barred black and white. Wings black with narrow white bars on flight feathers. Rump black. Black tail has black-and-white barred outer feathers. Underparts white with black bars on sides and flanks. Three toes. **Immatures** resemble adults but duller and browner with yellowish crown.

► Black-backed Woodpecker similar but can be separated by solid black back, and unbarred, white outer tail feathers. Hairy and Downy woodpeckers have white back and lack black barring on sides. Yellow-bellied Sapsucker has red forecrown, large white wing-patch, and black bib.

**VOICE:** Often silent. Call note, *pik,* resembles call of Downy Woodpecker but lower-pitched. Also gives rattling *pik-ik-ik-ik.* Drums regularly in short bursts.

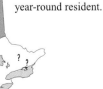

**HABITAT AND BEHAVIOUR:** Coniferous forest, bogs, and burned-over areas. Flight swift and undulating. Generally inconspicuous but quite tame when approached. Forages by chiseling off flakes of bark from dead or dying trees.

**STATUS:** Rare to uncommon year-round resident.

221

# BLACK-BACKED WOODPECKER *Picoides arcticus*

L 23–25 cm / 9.0–9.8" Wt 70–85 g / 2.5–3.0 oz

In Ontario, the Black-backed Woodpecker is the more common of the two three-toed woodpecker species. However, it is rarely observed because its sombre plumage provides excellent camouflage against the blackened trunks of burned trees that are its preferred foraging sites.

**APPEARANCE:** Head and back glossy black. White moustache. Male has yellow crown. Black bill. Wings black with narrow white bars on flight feathers. Rump black. Black tail has white outer feathers. Underparts white with black bars on sides and flanks. Three toes. **Female** has black crown. **Immatures** resemble adults but duller and browner with yellowish crown.

▶ Three-toed Woodpecker similar but can be distinguished by white eyebrow and black-and-white barred back and outer tail feathers. Hairy and Downy woodpeckers have white back and lack black barring on sides. Yellow-bellied Sapsucker has red forecrown, large white wing-patch, black-and-white back, and black bib.

**VOICE:** Call a fast, sharp *kyik*. Also gives distinctive screaming rattle, *wet-et-ddd-eee-yaaa,* during agonistic encounters. Drums in prolonged series of short bursts.

**HABITAT AND BEHAVIOUR:** Coniferous forest, particularly burned-over areas. Highly manoeuvrable, undulating flight; generally flies from tree to tree. Very vocal and aggressive at times. Quite tame when approached.

**STATUS:** Uncommon to locally common year-round resident.

# NORTHERN FLICKER *Colaptes auratus*

28–32 cm / 11.0–12.5" Wt 130–145 g / 4.6–5.2 oz

This large woodpecker is most commonly seen on the ground, where it forages primarily for ants. It plays an important role in woodland communities because it excavates many tree cavities which are subsequently used by other species.

**APPEARANCE:** Grey crown and nape. Sides of head and throat sandy brown. Male has black moustache and red nape-patch. Both sexes have broad, black necklace. Back and wings brown barred with black. Shafts of flight feathers yellow. Conspicuous white rump visible in flight. Black tail feathers stiff and pointed. Underparts buff with black spotting. Wing linings and undertail coverts yellow. **Immatures** resemble adults but somewhat duller, with broader black barring and paler breast and belly.

► Plumage distinctive. Also only woodpecker to feed on open ground.

**VOICE:** Most commonly heard call in spring a loud, rapid *wik-wik-wik-wik-wik*. Faster and higher pitched than Pileated Woodpecker. Other calls include sharp *peah,* and variable, rhythmic *ta-week ta-week ta-week*. Drumming sounds like miniature pneumatic drill.

**HABITAT AND BEHAVIOUR:** Open deciduous and mixed forest, forest edges, farmland, wetlands, and suburban areas. Flight somewhat undulating, with bursts of wing-flapping alternating with gliding with wings folded against body. Hops slowly while foraging.

**STATUS:** Very common breeder and spring and fall migrant. Rare winter visitor.

# PILEATED WOODPECKER *Dryocopus pileatus*

L 42–49 cm / 16.5–19.0" Wt 250–350 g / 8.9–12.5 oz

The crow-sized Pileated Woodpecker is Ontario's largest woodpecker. Its loud, distinctive call may be most familiar as a stock background noise in old jungle movies.

**APPEARANCE:** Body largely black. Broad white stripe on head of adult male extends from nostrils across cheek, sides of neck, and under wing. Black eye-line; white line above eye. Bright red moustache continues as black line across lower cheek and down foreneck. Red forehead extends to prominent, pointed, red crest. Bill blackish above; yellowish at base of lower mandible. Broad white wing linings are conspicuous in flight. **Female** similar except for black moustache and black or buff on forehead and forecrown. **Immatures** greyer than adults with orange, rather than red, on head.

♀

▶ Red-headed Woodpecker much smaller with prominent red hood.

**VOICE:** Loud, repeated, and irregular *kik-kikkik-kik-kik-kikkik* series. More hollow and slower than call of Northern Flicker. In flight, gives intermittent *wuk* notes that rise and fall in pitch. Other call notes include loud, shrill *g-waick g-waick* and whining *hn-hn*. Loud, slow, resonant drumming.

**HABITAT AND BEHAVIOUR:** Mature forest; occasionally agricultural areas and parks with large trees. Flight strong and direct but rather slow. Feet adapted primarily for climbing vertical surfaces.

**STATUS:** Rare to uncommon year-round resident.

# PASSERIFORMES
## Perching Birds

More than one half of all bird species belong to the Passeriformes. Although anatomically distinct in many ways, all passerines share a "perching foot," with three toes pointing forward and one extending backward. Many also share specific adaptations of the vocal apparatus, which allow these birds to produce the elaborate and beautiful songs for which they are renowned.

Twenty-five passerine families, comprising 213 species, occur in Ontario. Fifty-seven species have been recorded as accidentals (Western Wood-Pewee, Gray Flycatcher, Dusky Flycatcher, Say's Phoebe, Vermilion Flycatcher, Ash-throated Flycatcher, Sulphur-bellied Flycatcher, Variegated Flycatcher, Tropical/Couch's Kingbird, Cassin's Kingbird, Gray Kingbird, Fork-tailed Flycatcher, Bell's Vireo, Black-capped Vireo, Plumbeous Vireo, Clark's Nutcracker, Eurasian Jackdaw, Fish Crow, Violet-green Swallow, Cave Swallow, Carolina Chickadee, Rock Wren, Siberian Rubythroat, Bicknell's Thrush, Eurasian Blackbird, Fieldfare, Sage Thrasher, Sprague's Pipit, Phainopepla, Virginia's Warbler, Black-throated Gray Warbler, Townsend's Warbler, Hermit Warbler, Swainson's Warbler, MacGillivray's Warbler, Painted Redstart, Green-tailed Towhee, Spotted Towhee, Cassin's Sparrow, Bachman's Sparrow, Black-throated Sparrow, Baird's Sparrow, Golden-crowned Sparrow, Chestnut-collared Longspur, Black-headed Grosbeak, Lazuli Bunting, Varied Bunting, Painted Bunting, Great-tailed Grackle, Hooded Oriole, Bullock's Oriole, Scott's Oriole, Brambling, Gray-crowned Rosy-Finch, Cassin's Finch, Lesser Goldfinch, Eurasian Tree Sparrow, see pp. 391–99).

## OLIVE-SIDED FLYCATCHER *Contopus cooperi*

L 18–20 cm / 7.1–7.8" Wt 32–37 g / 1.1–1.3 oz

A mated pair of Olive-sided Flycatchers will aggressively defend a nesting territory 40 hectares (100 acres) or more in size. The male's loud, distinctive song—a familiar summer sound throughout northern Ontario—may serve to establish territory boundaries.

**APPEARANCE:** Olive-brown above with somewhat darker wings and tail. Wing bars and eye-ring indiscernible. Bill black with dull orange at base of lower mandible. Distinctive white tufts on lower back may be hidden by wings. Throat white. Streaked olive-brown sides and flanks separated by stripe of white down the centre of underparts, suggests "unbuttoned vest." Undertail coverts white. **Immatures** similar but more brownish with buffy wash on wings.
► Best distinguished from other flycatchers by large size and "vested" appearance. Wood-pewees much smaller with white wing bars.

**VOICE:** During courtship male gives incessant *quick-three-beers! quick-three-beers!* Call a series of three evenly spaced, high *pip pip pip* given by both sexes.

**HABITAT AND BEHAVIOUR:** Open coniferous and mixed forest; often in burned areas and wetlands. Flight fast, agile, and direct with deep wingbeats when pursuing prey; more fluttery when returning to perch. Often perches conspicuously on treetops while vocalizing. Forages by flying out from high perches to snatch insects in flight, then returns to the same or another prominent perch.

**STATUS:** Locally common breeder. Fairly common spring and fall migrant.

# EASTERN WOOD-PEWEE *Contopus virens* ✓ heard
15–16 cm / 6.0–6.5" Wt 11–17 g / 0.4–0.6 oz

*(handwritten: ✗ F / heard by another birdwatcher)*

This small flycatcher is best known for its distinctive call heard most frequently at dawn and dusk in summer. It prefers to perch on an exposed branch from which it makes short sallies to capture flying insects.

**APPEARANCE:** Upperparts dark greyish olive. Light greyish olive below with somewhat darker olive on breast and sides. Two whitish wing bars. Tail blackish. Upper mandible blackish; lower mandible yellowish. **Immatures** similar but darker with yellowish belly and buff-edged feathers on upperparts. Wing bars buff.

► Almost identical to accidental Western Wood-pewee; distinguished only by song. Eastern Phoebe lacks white wing bars; also, bobs tail. Olive-sided Flycatcher larger with dark olive sides. Lacks wing bars. *Empidonax* flycatchers smaller and have white eye-rings. Accidental Say's Phoebe has pale, rusty belly.

**VOICE:** Sweet, slurred *pee-ah-wee,* diagnostic. Other calls include terse *tip* and rapid, shrill *pe-e-e-e-e.* Primary song of Western Wood-pewee harsh, buzzy *pheer-reet.*

**HABITAT AND BEHAVIOUR:** Deciduous and mixed forest, and shade trees of farms, parks, and yards. Flight generally fluttering and slow. Makes looping sallies from exposed perches to hawk flying insects. Sits upright on perch. Does not flick or wag tail.

**STATUS:** Common breeder. Common spring and fall migrant.

227

# YELLOW-BELLIED FLYCATCHER
*Empidonax flaviventris*

L 12.5–14.5 cm / 4.9–5.7" Wt 11–13 g / 0.4–0.5 oz

Species of *Empidonax* flycatchers ("empids") are notoriously difficult to tell apart because of their similar plumages. Fortunately, the decidedly yellowish underparts of the Yellow-bellied Flycatcher ensure that at least one "empid" can be identified by sight alone.

**APPEARANCE:** Upperparts olive-green. Yellowish eye-ring. Upper mandible blackish; lower entirely orange. Wings and tail blackish, edged with olive-green. Two whitish wing bars. Underparts yellow, somewhat brighter on belly. Breast tinged with olive. **Immatures** resemble adults but browner overall with buffy wing bars.

▶ Acadian, Willow, Alder, and Least flycatchers have white eye-rings and lack bright yellow underparts. All but Acadian have browner upperparts. Immature Acadian Flycatchers somewhat yellowish below but have white throat. All other flycatchers with yellow underparts much larger. Song also useful to identify species.

**VOICE:** Most common song by male on breeding grounds an abrupt, unmusical, metallic *chelink*. Resembles call of Least Flycatcher but delivered less frequently and with less force. Calls include whistled *che-wee* that rises in pitch.

**HABITAT AND BEHAVIOUR:** Coniferous woods, muskeg, and bogs. Flight weak except for quick fly-catching forays. Shy and retiring; usually does not perch in the open. Habitually flicks tail (but not wings).

**STATUS:** Uncommon to fairly common breeder. Fairly common spring and fall migrant.

# ACADIAN FLYCATCHER *Empidonax virescens*

14.0–16.5 cm / 5.5–6.5" Wt 12–14 g / 0.4–0.5 oz

Extreme southern Ontario is the northern limit of the breeding range for this little flycatcher. Breeding densities have been reduced significantly in recent decades as favoured habitat has been cleared for farmland and forest products.

**APPEARANCE:** Olive-green above. White eye-ring. Large bill black above and pinkish below. Wings and tail brownish-blackish edged in olive. Two yellowish wing bars (buff in fall). Very long primaries. White throat. Underparts whitish with pale yellow tinge on flanks, lower belly, and undertail coverts. **Immatures** and **fall adults** somewhat more yellow below. Immature has buff feather edges on back and head that confer scaly appearance.

► Yellow-bellied Flycatcher more extensively yellow below in adult and immature plumages. Alder and Willow flycatchers browner overall with faint, whitish eye-ring. Least Flycatcher has prominent eye-ring, rounded head, and shorter wings. "Empids" best identified by song.

**VOICE:** Male sings explosive, whistling *peet-sa* or *pizza* with second syllable accented and higher in pitch. During breeding season, utters loud Northern Flicker-like *ti-ti-ti-ti-ti.* Call note a soft *peet.*

**HABITAT AND BEHAVIOUR:** Mature deciduous forest, riparian woodlands, and wooded swamps. Flight weak and fluttery unless fly-catching. Perches inconspicuously among vegetation. Sometimes flicks tail when calling.

**STATUS:** Rare breeder.

# ALDER FLYCATCHER *Empidonax alnorum*

L 13–17 cm / 5.1–6.7" Wt 12–14 g / 0.4–0.5 oz

Alder and Willow flycatchers were formerly lumped into a single species. However, detailed examinations of their two distinct song forms during the 1960s and 1970s have resulted in this taxonomic partitioning.

**APPEARANCE:** Upperparts dull greyish olive; crown somewhat darker. Whitish eye-ring may be absent or indistinct. Bill blackish above; yellowish below. Wings dark greyish olive with two whitish wing bars. Tail dark olive-grey washed with brown and edged with olive. Throat white. Breast, sides, and flanks greyish olive tinged with dull yellow. Belly and undertail coverts whitish. **Immatures** somewhat browner with buffy wing bars.

▶ Willow Flycatcher distinguished only by song (song is sneezy *fitz-bew;* call is liquid *whit*) and preference for drier brushy fields and thickets. Least Flycatcher smaller with greyer upperparts, whiter underparts, and more distinct eye-ring. Yellow-bellied Flycatcher more yellowish below, including throat. Acadian Flycatcher bright green above with yellowish eye-ring and wing bars. Phoebes and wood-pewees larger. Similarly plumaged flycatchers distinguished by song.

**VOICE:** Male sings burry *fee-bee-o* with accented second and descending third syllables. Given most frequently in morning and evening. Calls include low, flat *kep* and loud, extended *wee-oo*.

**HABITAT AND BEHAVIOUR:** Wet alder swamps and thickets, often bordering on lakes and streams. Spreads and flicks tail up and down during agonistic encounters. Displaces adversaries from perch.

**STATUS:** Common breeder. Common spring and fall migrant.

# WILLOW FLYCATCHER *Empidonax traillii*
13.0–16.5 cm / 5.1–6.5" Wt 12–14 g / 0.4–0.5 oz

The breeding ranges of the Willow Flycatcher and its sister species, the Alder Flycatcher, overlap in the transition zone between prairie and boreal forest. Of the two species, the Willow Flycatcher has the more southern distribution.

**APPEARANCE:** Upperparts dull greyish olive tinged with brown; crown somewhat darker. Narrow, indistinct, whitish eye-ring may be absent. Lores may be whitish. Bill blackish above, yellowish or orangish below. Wings dark greyish olive with two whitish wing bars. Tail dark brownish olive-grey edged with olive. Throat white. Breast, sides, and flanks greyish olive tinged with dull yellow. Belly and undertail coverts yellowish white. **Immatures** somewhat browner with yellowish belly.

► Identical Alder Flycatcher distinguished only by song (accented *fee-bee-o;* call a low *kep*) and preference for somewhat wetter willow, alder, and swampy habitat. Least Flycatcher smaller; greyer above and whiter below with more distinct eye-ring. Yellow-bellied Flycatcher has more yellowish underparts. Acadian Flycatcher bright green above with yellowish eye-ring and wing bars. Phoebes and wood-pewees larger and can be distinguished by song.

**VOICE:** Male sings sneezy *fitz-bew.* Both syllables accented. Call notes dry *fitz* and whistled *whit.* Less sharp than calls of Alder Flycatcher.

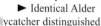

**HABITAT AND BEHAVIOUR:** Open shrubby vegetation, brushy fields, and abandoned farmland. Forages by short sallies to glean insects from leaves.

**STATUS:** Uncommon to locally common breeder.

# LEAST FLYCATCHER *Empidonax minimus*
L 12.5–14.0 cm / 5.0–5.5" Wt 8–13 g / 0.3–0.5 oz

The Least Flycatcher is the smallest and most common member of the *Empidonax* flycatcher group. In addition, it occupies a broader range of habitats than its congeners, and is often found nesting close to human habitation.

**APPEARANCE:** Upperparts greyish green. White eye-ring and throat. Bill dark with yellowish orange base on lower mandible. Wings have two white-to-pale yellow wing bars. Underparts whitish washed with pale grey on breast. Flanks and lower belly may have yellow tinge. **Immatures** similar but somewhat browner with buff wing bars.

► Smaller than other *Empidonax* species, with stubbier bill and slightly forked tail; also greyer than most other *Empidonax* flycatchers. Alder and Willow flycatchers lack eye-ring. Other greyish flycatchers, pewees, and phoebes much larger.

**VOICE:** Song diagnostic. Sharp, emphatic *che-bek* with accent on second syllable. Also gives rapid chatter, *weep-weep-weep-weep,* and short, soft call note, *wit.*

**HABITAT AND BEHAVIOUR:** Open deciduous woodlands and forest edges. Flight rapid and direct. Makes short, frequent sallies from perch to perch while foraging, frequently with abrupt mid-air turns. Flicks tail upward only, not downward or laterally.

**STATUS:** Common breeder. Common migrant.

# ASTERN PHOEBE *Sayornis phoebe*

14.5–16.5 cm / 5.7–6.5" Wt 16–20 g / 0.6–0.7 oz

he Eastern Phoebe is among the first migrants to return to Ontario
ach spring. It demonstrates strong nest-site attachment and frequently
uses or renovates nests from previous years.

**PPEARANCE:** Upperparts
rk grey. Head, wings, and
il slightly darker than back.
ill black. Lacks eye-ring
d distinct wing bars in
dult plumage. Underparts
hitish with pale yellowish
ash. **Immatures** similar
it have two buff wing bars
d somewhat more obvious
ellow colour on underparts.
▶ Distinguished from
any other flycatchers by
ck of eye-ring. Also
astern Wood Pewee and
all *Empidonax* flycatchers
ave wing bars, light-
loured lower mandibles,
d shorter tails.

OICE: Easily identified by
e-bee song given by male
aring breeding season. Phrase repeated many times with alternately
sing and falling notes. Male rarely gives rapid, harsh, nasal *tree-tree-
ee-tree-tree.* Both sexes give distinctive clear, sweet, weak *chip*
roughout the year. Other call notes include *twee-t* and *t-yooh.* Also
aps bill.

**ABITAT AND BEHAVIOUR:** Deciduous and mixed woodland edges,
rmland, gardens, marshes, and shorelines. Flight direct with steady
wingbeats, not undulating. Hovers occasionally. Rarely
hops; generally moves from one perch to another
by flying. Habitually wags long tail, with up-and-
down and lateral movement.

**STATUS:** Common breeder. Common spring
and fall migrant.

?

233

# GREAT CRESTED FLYCATCHER *Myiarchus crinitus*

L 20–23 cm / 7.8–9.0" Wt 30–36 g / 1.1–1.3 oz

This large, raucous species is the only cavity-nesting flycatcher in eastern North America. It frequently uses old woodpecker holes but will also nest in appropriately sized stovepipes, tin cans, and hollow posts.

**APPEARANCE:** Upperparts olive-brown; somewhat darker on crown. Chin, cheeks, throat, and breast medium grey. Bill dark brown above, paler below. Wings greyish brown. Outer edges of primaries rufous; other wing feathers edged with buff or pale yellow. Central tail feathers olive-brown; outer feathers distinctly rufous. Belly and undertail coverts yellow. **Immatures** similar to adults but somewhat duller overall.

▶ Accidental Ash-throated Flycatcher less olive above with much paler underparts, particularly yellow belly. Rare Sulphur-bellied Flycatcher has bold facial pattern and streaked breast. Western, and accidental Cassin's and Tropical kingbirds somewhat paler with blackish wings and tail. Other large flycatchers lack yellow underparts. *Empidonax* and related flycatchers much smaller.

**VOICE:** Song two alternating phrases, *wheerrup* and *whee-uh,* repeated frequently at dawn in spring. Loud, whistled, ascending *whee-eep* diagnostic. Other calls include throaty, rolling *purr-it,* sharp *wit-whit,* and noisy, grating *rree-rree-rree-rree.*

**HABITAT AND BEHAVIOUR:** Woodland edges and clearings. Flight swift and agile. Glides effortlessly from perch to perch. Rarely walks on ground. Raises crown feathers when excited.

**STATUS:** Common breeder. Common spring and fall migrant.

# WESTERN KINGBIRD *Tyrannus verticalis*

20.5–24.0 cm / 8.0–9.5" Wt 37–41 g / 1.3–1.5 oz

This western species expanded its range eastward throughout the twentieth century, but breeding in Ontario was not verified until 1983. The Rainy River district remains the most likely region for regular breeding of this "tyrant" flycatcher.

**APPEARANCE:** Head, nape, and breast pale grey. Indistinct mask formed by dark grey lores and ear coverts. Narrow red or orange patch on crown (smaller in female) usually concealed. Throat white. Back grey with greenish wash. Wings dark brownish grey. Long black tail has white on outer feathers. Belly and undertail coverts bright yellow. **Immatures** similar but generally paler and tinged with brown.
► Accidental Cassin's Kingbird distinguished by darker breast; tail lacks white outer feathers but has white tip. Great Crested Flycatcher much darker with cinnamon wings and tail.

Accidental Gray Kingbird and Ash-throated Flycatcher lack bright yellow underparts. Eastern Kingbird has black-and-white plumage; distinguished from most other flycatchers by larger size, elongate body, stout bill, and long, square tail.

**VOICE:** Flight song *pkit-pkit-deedle-ot* has emphasis on high-pitched third syllable. Utters loud *pkit* alone or in combination with other rapid, chattering notes.

**HABITAT AND BEHAVIOUR:** Open scrub land with scattered brushy areas. Very agile flyer. Forages on wing. Pursues predators, such as hawks and falcons, during nesting season. Perches conspicuously on fence posts and treetops.

**STATUS:** Very rare breeder. Rare spring and fall migrant.

# EASTERN KINGBIRD *Tyrannus tyrannus*

L 21.5–23.0 cm / 8.5–9" Wt 39–46 g / 1.4–1.6 oz

Conspicuously perching on fences and overhead wires, the Eastern Kingbird is Ontario's best-known tyrant flycatcher. A "sit-and-wait" predator, this species makes frequent, rapid sallies to capture large flying insects.

**APPEARANCE:** Upperparts black. Head slightly crested, particularly in male. Narrow red or orange crown-patch rarely visible. Two indistinct whitish wing bars. Tail has diagnostic broad, white terminal band. White below with a pale greyish wash on upper breast and sides. **Immatures** have buffy edging on upper part feathers, and lack crown-patch.

▶ No other North American Flycatcher entirely black above and white below. Western Kingbird, accidental Cassin's Kingbird, and Great Crested Flycatcher greyish above and yellow below. Accidental Grey Kingbird and Ash-throated Flycatcher grey and white, and lack white-tipped tail.

**VOICE:** Male utters long, repeated song with two alternating phrases, *t-t-tzeer* and *t-tzeetzeetzee,* primarily at dawn. Male also gives harsh *chatter-zeer.* Both sexes utter high-pitched, crisp *zeer* and *t-zeer.*

**HABITAT AND BEHAVIOUR:** Agricultural lands, forest clearings, and along roadsides. Flies only; rarely goes to ground. Flaps wings continuously and rapidly in flight, especially when hawking insects. Also hovers.

**STATUS:** Very common breeder. Common spring and fall migrant.

# CISSOR-TAILED FLYCATCHER
*yrannus forficatus*

28–38 cm / 11–15" Wt 38–43 g / 1.4–1.5 oz

nfortunately, the Scissor-tailed Flycatcher is only a casual visitor in ntario. Its beautiful plumage and calm, graceful demeanour are a eat pleasure to observe.

**PPEARANCE:** Pale grey head and grey mantle. Scarlet crown-patch sually obscured. Wings black with narrow white edges. Extremely ng, forked tail (male: 22 cm; 8.7") has black central feathers; white ter feathers broadly tipped with black. Underparts greyish white with le salmon-pink on belly, flanks, and undertail coverts. Sides and nderwing bright salmon-pink. **Female** less brightly coloured than ale with slightly shorter tail (15 cm; 5.9"). **Immatures** somewhat ller than female. Dull dark above and buffy white below with pinkish des. Short tail blackish brown with white outer feathers.

▶ Adults distinguished from other North American flycatchers by ng, forked tail. Accidental Fork-tailed Flycatcher has prominent black ad and lacks salmon-pink on underparts and wing linings. Immatures stinguished from Western Kingbird by paler breast and pinkish sides.

**VOICE:** Male sings variable number of *pup* notes followed by *perleep* or *perroo.* Both sexes give loud chattering and sputtering notes that resemble calls of Western Kingbird. Call note a harsh *keck* or *kew.*

**HABITAT AND BEHAVIOUR:** Open grassland with occasional trees and shrubs; farms and roadsides. Flight direct on rapid wingbeats with folded tail. Tail spread while hovering. Perches conspicuously on wires and fences. Rarely walks.

**STATUS:** Rare spring and fall visitor.

# LOGGERHEAD SHRIKE *Lanius ludovicianus* ⌐

L 20.5–25.5 cm / 8–10" Wt 40–54 g / 1.4–1.9 oz

Like its congener the Northern Shrike, the Loggerhead Shrike is a predatory species that dives at its prey from a high perch. It is endangered in Ontario owing to changes in land use, pesticides, and competition with more human-tolerant species.

**APPEARANCE:** Large head. Grey crown, nape, back, and rump. Black facial mask bordered below by white chin, throat, and malar region. Hooked bill black. Wings black with large, white wing-patch best observed in flight. Rounded tail black with white outer feathers. Underparts pale grey. **Female** smaller than male with somewhat browner wings.

**Immatures** have paler grey plumage with faintly barred underparts.
▶ Larger Northern Shrike distinguished by narrower black mask, paler grey upperparts, and more powerful bill; immatures brownish with finely barred underparts. Northern Mockingbird similar but lacks contrasting black mask and wings, and hooked bill.

**VOICE:** Usually silent. Male sings series of varied trills, and clear notes in spring. Often repeated several times spaced with long pauses. Frequently heard phrase is mechanical *zee-ert*. Call notes include *jaa* and *bzeek*.

**HABITAT AND BEHAVIOUR:** Pastures, marginal farmland, and wetlands, with associated high perches. Moves from perch to perch by swooping down, flying low to ground, then climbing abruptly to new location. Dives at prey from perch. Hops on ground.

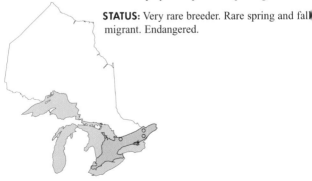

**STATUS:** Very rare breeder. Rare spring and fall migrant. Endangered.

# NORTHERN SHRIKE *Lanius excubitor*

L 23–28 cm / 9–11" Wt 55–73 g / 2.0–2.6 oz

The Northern Shrike is a predatory songbird that hunts from exposed perches, using its sharp bill to sever the spinal cord of its prey. Lacking the grasping talons of raptors, the shrike impales its prey on thorns and barbed wire fences to facilitate its consumption.

**APPEARANCE:** Pale grey above; palest on crown and rump. Relatively narrow black mask bordered above with thin white line. Powerful, hooked, black bill. Pale region at base of lower mandible darkens in late winter. Throat, chin, and malar area white. Wings black with white wing-patches visible in flight. Rounded black tail tipped with white. Underparts  very pale indistinctly barred with darker grey. **Immatures** have brownish upperparts with subtle brown barring on underparts. Facial pattern less distinct.

▶ Loggerhead Shrike smaller with wider black mask, darker upperparts, and smaller bill; often difficult to distinguish these species using only one or two characters. Northern Mockingbird similar but lacks contrasting black mask and wings, and hooked bill.

**VOICE:** Usually silent. Occasionally utters long, varied, thrasher-like series of both harsh and musical notes. Call notes include *shek shek* and grating *jaaeg.*

**HABITAT AND BEHAVIOUR:** Sparse coniferous forest, open country with high perches. Flies off rapidly in a straight line when approached. Uses higher and more conspicuous perches than Loggerhead Shrike.

**STATUS:** Rare breeder. Uncommon spring and fall migrant and winter visitor.

# WHITE-EYED VIREO *Vireo griseus*

L 10–13 cm / 4–5" Wt 10.5–13.0 g / 0.4–0.5 oz

This little songster produces a dozen or more distinct songs, each comprising up to ten variable elements. It is frequently the subject of studies in avian vocal communication.

**APPEARANCE:** Upperparts greyish green tinged with yellow. Wide yellow stripe extends from base of upper mandible to and around eye. Indistinct brown line between bill and eye. Iris white in adults. Neck grey. Wings and tail greyish brown edged with yellow and olive. Wings have two white to yellowish white wing bars. Underparts whitish with yellow sides and flanks. **Immatures** similar but slightly darker brownish olive. Two yellow wing bars. Underparts dull greyish white with sides and undertail coverts yellow or buff. Eyes brownish.

▶ All other vireos have dark eyes. Underparts of Yellow-throated Vireo more extensively yellow. Blue-headed Vireo has greyish head with white eye-ring and lores, and snowy white throat. *Empidonax* flycatchers have broad, flat bills.

**VOICE:** Song a loud, enthusiastic *chick-a-per-weeoo-chick.* Male also utters rambling, warbling song of harsh, squeaky notes. Call notes include raspy, chattering *chee* or *ehh,* and soft *pik.*

**HABITAT AND BEHAVIOUR:** Deciduous thickets, second-growth forest, swampy woodlands, and brambles. Flights short with rapid wingbeats. Manoeuvres with tail. Uses fluttery flight during courtship. Hops among foliage.

**STATUS:** Rare breeder. Rare spring and fall migrant.

# YELLOW-THROATED VIREO *Vireo flavifrons* F

12.5–15.0 cm / 5–6" Wt 15–21 g / 0.5–0.75 oz

This vireo is easily overlooked because it usually nests and forages high in the forest canopy. Males sing much less once mated.

**APPEARANCE:** Crown, nape, and back olive-green. Bright yellow eye spectacles. Wings dark greyish with two broad, white wing bars. Rump grey. Tail blackish edged with white. Bright yellow throat and breast. Belly and undertail coverts white. **Immatures** more brownish olive above with paler buffy yellow on underparts.

▶ Only vireo with bright yellow throat and breast, yellow around eye, and bright wing bars. Philadelphia Vireo yellowish below but has dark eye-line and lacks wing bars. White-eyed, Blue-headed, and accidental Bell's vireos have yellowish sides with whitish throat and breast. Pine Warbler similar but browner with smaller bill and faintly streaked underparts. Larger Yellow-breasted Chat has black lores with white spectacles, and lacks wing bars.

**VOICE:** Primary song by male a variable series of low-pitched, buzzy phrases separated by pauses: *ahweeo, eeyay, ayo, away, oweeah, eeoway.* Calls include harsh scolding, *cha-cha-cha;* quick, sharp *heeeat;* and low *merr-mr-mr-mr.*

**HABITAT AND BEHAVIOUR:** Relatively mature deciduous woodlands with spreading canopy. Flights short and deliberate from branch to branch. Hops along branches, rarely goes to ground.

**STATUS:** Uncommon breeder. Uncommon spring and fall migrant.

241

# BLUE-HEADED VIREO *Vireo solitarius*

L 13–15 cm / 5.1–5.9" Wt 13–19 g / 0.5–0.7 oz

The Blue-headed Vireo comprises the eastern portion of the Solitary Vireo complex. This three-species group, which also includes the accidental Plumbeous Vireo and the western Cassin's Vireo, was recently divided based on the results of molecular genetic analyses.

**APPEARANCE:** Crown, nape, and face deep bluish grey. Bold, white spectacles and lores. Otherwise, upperparts olive-green. Wings and tail black, narrowly edged with olive. Two yellowish white wing bars. Throat, breast, and belly white. Sides and flanks yellowish, indistinctly streaked with olive. **Immatures** resemble adults.

▶ Plumbeous Vireo has grey upperparts with olive restricted to rump. Yellow on sides faint or lacking. Accidental Black-capped Vireo female has greyish head with conspicuous red eyes. Red-eyed Vireo has greyish crown but face markedly different; also lacks wing bars. Other vireos have olive or greyish olive upperparts with little or no colour contrast between head and back.

**VOICE:** Clear, sweet phrases separated by pauses: *teeaytoay.* Occasionally phrases run together into warble. Song higher pitched and slower than that of Red-eyed Vireo. Also utters harsh, scolding, wren-like *cha-cha-cha-cha* and nasal *neah-neah-neah.*

**HABITAT AND BEHAVIOUR:** Coniferous or mixed woodlands often near water. Flight slow and deliberate between perches. Hops short distances along branches. Seldom goes to ground.

**STATUS:** Common breeder. Fairly common spring and fall migrant.

# WARBLING VIREO *Vireo gilvus*

2.5–15.0 cm / 4.9–5.9" Wt 10–13 g / 0.4–0.5 oz

...e Warbling Vireo may be difficult to detect solely on the basis of its ...ndescript plumage. Fortunately, its presence is revealed by its ...guid, melodious song, which is delivered almost unceasingly from ...e tops of deciduous trees.

...PEARANCE: Upper-...rts light grey tinged ...th olive. No wing bars. ...ey crown. Whitish ...res and eyebrow. Eyes ...own. Underparts whitish ...shed with yellowish ...een on sides and flanks. ...matures often more ...llowish below and may ...ve single, faint buffy ...ng bar.
► Philadelphia ...reo somewhat more ...ve above with yellow ...derparts and prominent black eye-line. Red-eyed Vireo more olive ...ove and has black borders on crown. Other Ontario vireos have ...ominent white or yellowish wing bars and "spectacled" appearance. ...nnessee Warbler much smaller with slimmer bill and greenish back. ...range-crowned Warbler more yellow overall with slimmer bill.

...DICE: Male gives long, warbling song that vaguely resembles those ...'Purple and House finches, but softer. May end abruptly on ...cending note. Sings throughout day. Scolding, wheezy call, *tshay ...hay,* may be delivered between songs.

...ABITAT AND BEHAVIOUR: Deciduous and mixed woodland edges, ...rks, and gardens. Usually stays well hidden in tree canopy. Gleans ...sects from foliage while perched or hovering.

STATUS: Common breeder. Uncommon spring and fall migrant.

## PHILADELPHIA VIREO *Vireo philadelphicus*

L 10–13 cm / 4–5" Wt 11–13 g / 0.4–0.5 oz

The poorly known Philadelphia Vireo is often overlooked in density estimates, partly because of overwhelming local abundance of the Red-eyed Vireo, which has similar plumage and vocalizations.

**APPEARANCE:** Upperparts greyish olive. Greyish cap. Dusky lores and eye-line. White eyebrow. Eyes dark brown. Short, dusky bill. Underparts pale yellow, darkest on breast and palest on throat. **Immatures** similar but somewhat more richly coloured in fall.

► Distinguished from other vireos by combination of unmarked wings and yellow underparts. Warbling Vireo sometimes has yellow wash on flanks but not breast; also has less distinct facial pattern. Red-eyed Vireo has red eyes, black borders on white eyebrow, and whitish underparts. Fall Tennessee Warbler smaller with greenish yellow upperparts and narrower, less defined eyebrow stripe. Female Black-throated Blue Warbler has white wing spot and dark cheek.

**VOICE:** Only male sings. Short, variable, often repeated phrases. Some notes bubbling, others raspy. Similar to song of Red-eyed Vireo but higher pitched, sweeter, and delivered more slowly. Scolding call note, *ehhh,* resembles that of Warbling Vireo.

**HABITAT AND BEHAVIOUR:** Deciduous woodlands, particularly where trembling aspen dominant. Flight strong but not rapid. Uses short flights and hops to move through foliage. Captures prey on the wing or when perched. Rarely goes to ground.

**STATUS:** Uncommon breeder. Uncommon spring and fall migrant.

# RED-EYED VIREO *Vireo olivaceus*

L 14.0–16.5 cm / 5.5–6.5" Wt 16–18 g / 0.5–0.6 oz

The Red-eyed Vireo is Ontario's most common vireo species. This persistent songster has been known to deliver more than 20,000 songs in a single day.

**APPEARANCE:** Crown bluish grey. Prominent white eyebrow bordered above and below with black line. Bright red eyes visible at close range. Otherwise, upperparts olive; somewhat darker on wings and tail. No wing bars. Underparts white. **Immatures** resemble adults but with brown eyes and pale yellow wash on flanks and undertail coverts.

► Smaller Philadelphia Vireo strongly yellow below with dark eyes; grey cap lacks black border on lower edge. Warbling Vireo paler with olive crown and dark eyes; lacks black stripe bordering white eyebrow. Other Ontario vireos have prominent white or yellowish wing bars and "spectacled" appearance. Tennessee Warbler much smaller with slimmer bill and greenish back.

**VOICE:** Male sings continuous, monotonous series of robin-like phrases, repeated forty times per minute, separated by deliberate pauses. Given almost continuously throughout the day in spring and early summer. Call a nasal, scolding *chway.*

**HABITAT AND BEHAVIOUR:** Deciduous woodlands and shade trees. Hops along branches with body diagonal to direction of travel. Perches with hunched posture. Generally more sluggish in behaviour than warblers.

**STATUS:** Very common breeder. Very common spring and fall migrant.

## GRAY JAY *Perisoreus canadensis*

L 27–31 cm / 10.5–12.0" Wt 62–82 g / 2.2–2.9 oz

These tame jays of the boreal forest are well known to campers as they boldly attempt to steal food from campsites and picnic tables. Items that are not consumed immediately are broken into bits and cached for future use behind flakes of bark, under tufts of lichen, among coniferous needles, and in tree forks.

**APPEARANCE:** Small, long-tailed jay without crest. Head white with diagnostic large black patch at nape that continues forward to crown and eyes. White throat extends to collar around neck. White feathers cover base of black bill. Back, wings, and tail medium grey. Flight feathers variably tipped with white. Underparts white to buffy grey. **Immatures** uniformly dark grey with distinct white whisker mark. Bill initially white, then turning black.

▶ Northern Mockingbird has darker wings and tail, white wing-patch, and longer bill. Shrikes have black mask, black-and-white wings and tail, and hooked bill.

**VOICE:** Usually silent. Occasionally utters a variety of soft, short whistling and chattering notes, including *whee-ah, whu-whu-whu,* and *whuit-whuit-whuit-whuit.* Harsh, grating, and rapid *cha-cha-cha-cha* associated with mobbing of predators.

**HABITAT AND BEHAVIOUR:** Coniferous and mixed coniferous-deciduous forest. Slow flight straight and direct with rapid wingbeats alternating with sustained glides. Rarely observed alone, more frequently in pairs or small groups. Occasionally carries large food items with feet.

**STATUS:** Common year-round resident.

# BLUE JAY *Cyanocitta cristata* ✓ + F

28-32 cm / 11.0-12.5" Wt 82-94 g / 2.9-3.4 oz

The loud, showy Blue Jay is among Ontario's best-known birds. Blue Jays are most active and vocal in spring, but become much less conspicuous during nest-building and incubation. They may feed in flocks in the fall.

**APPEARANCE:** Blue crest. Heavy black bill. Black lores. White face outlined with black. Upperparts blue. Wings finely barred with black, and have large white bars and spots. Underparts white or dull grey with black necklace. Rounded blue tail, barred with black, has white corners. Individuals recognizable by characteristic head patterns. **Immatures** resemble adults but somewhat duller white-and-black markings.
► Unmistakable in all plumages.

**VOICE:** Extremely varied. Calls include harsh, screaming *jay-jay,* whistled, yodelling *too-wheedle too-wheedle,* and guttural, rattling *trrrrrr.* Also imitates calls of Red-shouldered and Red-tailed hawks.

**HABITAT AND BEHAVIOUR:** Oak and pine forests, agricultural areas, suburban gardens, and groves. Flight steady, direct, and deliberate with slow, shallow wingbeats alternating with swooping glides. Common visitor to bird feeders, particularly if they are filled with peanuts. Also forages on ground and among foliage. Often migrates in large flocks.

**STATUS:** Very common breeder. Very common spring and fall migrant. Fairly common winter visitor.

# BLACK-BILLED MAGPIE *Pica hudsonia*

L 46–56 cm / 18.1–22.0"  Wt 135–200 g / 4.8–7.1 oz

The Black-billed Magpie is probably a recent addition to Ontario's avifauna. More widespread in western Canada, nesting magpies were first recorded in Ontario near the Manitoba border in 1980.

**APPEARANCE:** Head, breast, and back black. Bill black. Rounded black-and-white wings. White scapulars. Long, black, graduated tail. Wings and tail glossed with blue and green. White belly. Undertail coverts black. Legs black. **Immatures** resemble adults but more brownish with dull white markings.

▶ Distinctive in all plumages. Crows and ravens entirely black. Jays more extensively blue or grey.

**VOICE:** Loud, repeated, high-pitched *chek-chek-chek-chek.* Also utters whiny, inquisitive *mmag?* May imitate other sounds.

**HABITAT AND BEHAVIOUR:** Groves of aspen, willow, or alder on open farmland. Flight from tree to tree slow and wavering; often hampered by long tail. Gregarious and aggressive. Noisily mobs potential predators, such as roosting owls. Walks jerkily with twitching, slightly uplifted tail.

**STATUS:** Very rare and extremely local year-round resident.

# AMERICAN CROW *Corvus brachyrhynchos* ✓+F

43–53 cm / 16.9–20.9" Wt 430–530 g / 15.4–18.9 oz

This adaptable species was already common when Europeans settled Ontario, and as forest was cleared for agricultural purposes, crow populations increased dramatically. Despite measures taken in the last two centuries to eliminate them, crows continue to thrive in most parts of the province.

**APPEARANCE:** Entirely black with slight purplish gloss. Black bill and legs. Smooth throat. Square-shaped tail. **Immatures** resemble adults but somewhat duller black with no metallic sheen.

▶ Common Raven much larger with wedge-shaped tail, heavier bill, and shaggy throat. Accidental Fish Crow nearly identical but can be distinguished by smaller size, longer tail, stiff wingbeats, and different call.

**VOICE:** Distinctive, loud *caw-caw-caw* given repeatedly. Young birds sound more nasal. Various other notes and calls used in flock communication.

**HABITAT AND BEHAVIOUR:** Cities and towns, farmland, open areas with scattered trees, and marshes. Flight direct and steady, but not swift. Typically only flies from tree to tree. Gregarious; more than 90,000 individuals reported to roost together at one site in winter. Walks deliberately on ground. Uses wings to accelerate to running speed.

**STATUS:** Common to abundant breeder and spring and fall migrant. Common winter visitor.

# COMMON RAVEN *Corvus corax*

L 55–68 cm / 22–27" Wt 700–1500 g / 1.5–3.3 lb

The intelligence of the raven is renowned, and many indigenous cultures traditionally consider this species a trickster or cheat. More recently, a few experimental studies have demonstrated the raven's ability to count, solve problems, and use rudimentary tools.

**APPEARANCE:** Entirely glossy black. Large chisel-like black bill. Throat has elongated feathers. Long, rounded wings. Wedged-shaped tail. **Immatures** and **first-year adults** have dull brownish black body plumage with glossy black flight feathers.

▶ Distinguished from other crows primarily by size. American Crow and Fish Crow are smaller with thinner bills and squarish tails visible in flight. Blackbirds much smaller and thinner with pointed bills and long tails.

**VOICE:** Hoarse, low-pitched, croaking *crock*. Alarm call given at nest: *keck-keck-keck*.

**HABITAT AND BEHAVIOUR:** Boreal and mixed forest. Long-distance flight on even wingbeats. Dives and rolls in flight by tucking in one wing. Able to fly upside down briefly. Walks on ground. Nests in artificial structures, such as utility towers, if natural sites lacking.

**STATUS:** Common year-round resident.

# HORNED LARK *Eremophila alpestris*
18.0–20.5 cm / 7–8" Wt 28–40 g / 1.0–1.4 oz

The Horned Lark was probably rare in southern Ontario until forests were cleared for cultivation. Recent abandonment of agriculture in south-central counties has caused some local population declines.

**APPEARANCE:** Small ground-dwelling songbird with "horns." Upperparts warm brown streaked with dusky brown and black. Yellow face has striking black lores, cheek-patches, and crescent on crown. Small, horn-like, black tufts on crown can be raised and lowered. Usually erect in male. Yellow throat bordered below with wide black bar. Breast and belly pale  cinnamon to white. Blackish tail has white outer feathers. Wing linings grey. Male slightly darker than female. **Juveniles** dark brown with spotting and scaling on upperparts. Face dusky brown with buff eyebrow, throat, and chin. Underparts buff to dusky brown. Tail brownish grey with white outer feathers.

▶ In winter, may occur in mixed flocks of pipits and Snow Buntings. Easily distinguished by horns and distinctive facial markings.

**VOICE:** Sweet, delicate, tinkling song often given in flight. Resembles sound of squeaky fence. Also gives clear, distinctive *tsee-titi* and loud *su-weet.*

**HABITAT AND BEHAVIOUR:** Pastures, sparsely vegetated fields, and tundra. Flight somewhat undulating with wing-beating alternating with gliding with closed wings. Adults walk, fledglings hop.

**STATUS:** Common breeder. Common spring and fall migrant. Uncommon winter visitor.

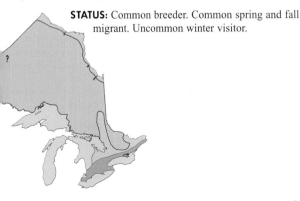

# ✓ PURPLE MARTIN *Progne subis*

L 18.0–21.5 cm / 7.0–8.5" Wt 45–58 g / 1.6–2.1 oz

In eastern North America, this large swallow relies almost entirely on artificial colonial nesting boxes. A backyard boon, each martin consumes thousands of flying insects daily.

**APPEARANCE:** Small bill, pointed wings, and long, notched tail. Male uniformly glossy bluish black above and below; somewhat darker on wings and tail. **Female** has dull bluish black upperparts with blackish wings and tail. Often has faint greyish collar across nape; sometimes forehead greyish. Underparts generally grey with dull white feather edging. Belly white. **Immatures** similar to female but duller and somewhat browner. **First-year male** frequently has some blue feathering on underparts.

► Much larger than other swallows. Dark underparts of male diagnostic. Female martin somewhat similar to Tree Swallow, but latter much smaller with immaculate white, not grey, underparts. European Starling in flight superficially resembles male Purple Martin. However, starling has more triangular wings and much longer bill.

**VOICE:** Complex, gurgling song that begins with several clear notes and ends with extended twitter. Calls include descending *swee-swuh-swuh* and rich *tyu* given in flight.

**HABITAT AND BEHAVIOUR:** Towns, farms, and open country. Often near water. In flight, sails in large circles with regular alternation between quick flapping and gliding. Holds wings horizontally during glides. Goes to ground only to collect nesting material.

**STATUS:** Locally common breeder. Common spring and fall migrant.

# REE SWALLOW *Tachycineta bicolor*

2.5–15.0 cm / 5–6" Wt 18–24 g / 0.6–0.9 oz

e handsome Tree Swallow returns to its breeding grounds in early ring. Although it usually feeds on flying insects, this swallow relies seeds and berries until its preferred food becomes plentiful.

**PPEARANCE:** Adult ale dark greenish blue ove and white below. ead shows clear, sharp e from white throat to rk cap. Adult **female** mewhat duller than ale; sometimes brown ith greenish sheen. ide-based, triangular ngs. Slightly notched l. Bill very small and ack. **Immatures** have sky brown back and fuse breast band.

▶ Purple Martin larger with darker underparts. Barn Swallow ff to rufous below and has deeply notched tail. Northern Rough- inged Swallow and Bank Swallow have brown upperparts; immatures ve more prominent breast bands than immature Tree Swallows.

**DICE:** Several variable, bubbly, high-pitched notes or phrases: *chi- it, blup-plup-plup, klweet-klweet.* Call note a loud, harsh, single or uble *cheet* or *chi-veet.*

**ABITAT AND BEHAVIOUR:** Open woodlands, marshes, roadsides, stures and fields, and gardens. Spends much of time in flight. Very ept flyer; glides in circles, each glide ending with a few quick flaps. arely walks, but flies from perch to perch. Perches on reeds and res. Usually forages above ponds, small lakes, and marshes.

**STATUS:** Common breeder. Common spring and fall migrant.

# √NORTHERN ROUGH-WINGED SWALLOW +F
## *Stelgidopteryx serripennis*
L 12.5–14.5 cm / 5.0–5.7" Wt 11–18 g / 0.4–0.6 oz

The Northern Rough-winged Swallow is so named because of the stiffened barbs on the leading edge of its outer primary wing feathers

**APPEARANCE:** Greyish brown above. Dull to creamy white below with pale greyish brown throat, breast, sides, and flanks. Tail slightly notched. **Immatures** have warm brown upperparts. Underparts dull white with buffy-brown on throat and breast. Wings dark greyish brown edged in pale rufous and buff. **Second-year** birds often have buffy feathers retained on throat and chin.

► Distinguished from other brown-and-white swallows by diffus greyish brown wash on throat, breast, and sides. Bank Swallow has white throat and sharply defined brownish breast band. Cliff Swallow has rufous throat. Immature Tree Swallows have dull greyish breasts but can be distinguished by white throat and dark grey backs. Other swallows have distinctly different coloration.

**VOICE:** Most frequent call a series of short, rapid *brrrt* notes or buzz *jee-jee-jee.* Alarm note harsh, grating *brzzzzzzt.*

**HABITAT AND BEHAVIOUR:** Nests in bridges, sandy roadbanks, and gravel pits. Flies with slow, deliberate wingbeats. When gliding, holds wings straight out from body, not with sharp bend at wrist. Lacks fluttery wingbeat of Bank Swallow. Descends to ground only to gather nesting material. Frequently feeds over water.

**STATUS:** Rare to common breeder. Common spring and fall migrant.

# BANK SWALLOW *Riparia riparia*
11–14 cm / 4.5–5.5" Wt 12–18 g / 0.4–0.6 oz

The highly gregarious Bank Swallow nests in large colonies in excavated burrows in riverbanks, road cuttings, gravel quarries, and railroad embankments. Its Latin name alludes to its traditional preference for riparian sites.

**APPEARANCE:** Greyish brown upperparts. Long, pointed wings and notched tail dark brown. White throat contrasts with prominent brown breast band, which is widest in centre and may extend to belly as sharp spike. Belly and undertail coverts white. **Immatures** distinguished from adults by buffy-edged upperparts and buffy wash on throat.

► Northern Rough-winged Swallow somewhat larger with diffuse brown wash over throat and breast; no distinct line between dark crown and paler lower cheek. Immature Tree Swallows larger with indistinct brownish breast band that is palest in centre; white underparts extend to sides of rump. During flight, Bank Swallows hold wings more sharply angled at wrist, and have more flicking wingbeats than Tree or Northern Rough-winged swallows.

**VOICE:** Harsh, bubbling, rapid *chik-ik chik-ik cheik cherk cherk cherk* continuous chattering *chi-chi-chi-chi-chi-chi-i-i-i-i.* Alarm call a clear *tsee-ip.*

**HABITAT AND BEHAVIOUR:** Vertical banks near water. Forages over fields, marshes, and lakes. Flight fluttery with shallow, rapid wingbeats. Rarely glides. Descends to ground to collect nesting material. Climbs vertical banks using feet and aided by flapping wings.

**STATUS:** Common breeder. Common spring and fall migrant.

# CLIFF SWALLOW *Petrochelidon pyrrhonota*

L 12.5–15.0 cm / 5–6" Wt 22–25 g / 0.8–0.9 oz

This chunky swallow is most readily identified from below by its square-tipped tail as it forages over water and grassy pastures. It buil a jug-like mud nest against an overhanging or vertical surface.

**APPEARANCE:** Strongly patterned. Upperparts generally blue-black with fine, whitish streaking on back. Triangular beige patch on forehead. Narrow collar of light brown on neck. Rump buff to tawny orange. Wings and square-tipped tail dark with slight metallic sheen. Chin, throat, and sides of neck chestnut. Base of throat metallic green or blue. Otherwise, underparts greyish buff. **Immatures** have darker or dulle forehead, and some white feathers on throat.

▶ Most other Ontario swallows distinctly brownish. Barn Swallow similar to Cliff Swallow but lacks buffy rump, buff collar a forehead, and has deeply forked tail. Accidental Cave Swallow distinguished by sharply defined black cap above chestnut forehead, pale throat, and darker rufous rump. Tree Swallow greenish and lack chestnut throat.

**VOICE:** Song given in flight is twittering, squeaking, harsh series of notes. Calls include low *chrrr* and nasal *nyew.*

**HABITAT AND BEHAVIOUR:** Grasslands, towns, open woodland, an riparian-edge habitat. Flapping flight frequently interspersed with lor glides. Only swallow to slant wings downward when gliding. Walks c ground to collect mud for nests. Shuffles sideways to move along perch.

**STATUS:** Uncommon breeder. Uncommon spring and fall migrant.

# BARN SWALLOW *Hirundo rustica*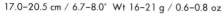

17.0–20.5 cm / 6.7–8.0" Wt 16–21 g / 0.6–0.8 oz

Barn Swallows build their cup-shaped, mud-and-grass nests on any structure that offers overhead protection. Many cultures believe that a swallow's nest on one's house confers good luck to its occupants.

**APPEARANCE:** Upper-parts metallic bluish black; wings and tail somewhat darker. Forehead chestnut. Lores and cheeks dark brown. Very long, deeply forked tail has white or buffy spots on inner webs. Chestnut chin and throat separated from buffy underparts by incomplete blackish blue breast band. **Immatures** have slightly forked tail. Upperparts somewhat duller black with reddish brown edging on wing coverts. Forehead and underparts buffy cinnamon.

▶ Cliff Swallow has similar plumage pattern but has buffy rump and forehead, and square tail. Larger Purple Martin bluish or greyish below and has shallowly notched tail. Other swallows much paler below with brownish upperparts; lack deeply notched tail.

**VOICE:** Emphatic, clear *sip sip sip sip* notes interspersed with harsh, twittering rattle. Call notes include excited *tsi* and softer *wit wit* usually given in flight.

**HABITAT AND BEHAVIOUR:** Farmlands, marshes, and lakes. Usually near human habitation. Swoops back and forth in flight with little gliding. Wing tips pulled back on each downstroke. Goes to ground to collect nesting material or to sunbathe.

**STATUS:** Common breeder. Common spring and fall migrant.

257

# BLACK-CAPPED CHICKADEE *Poecile atricapilla*

L 12.3–14.6 cm / 4.8–5.7" Wt 10–14 g / 0.35–0.5 oz

This tame and inquisitive little acrobat is known to those who fill their bird feeders with black sunflower seeds. Chickadees occur in Ontario year-round, and on cold winter nights, they lower their body temperature to conserve energy.

**APPEARANCE:** Small size. Black cap that obscures dark eyes. Black bib. Large white cheeks. Back, wings, and long tail grey. Wing coverts and flight feathers edged in white. Underparts whitish with buffy sides and flanks. Small black bill. **Immatures** resemble adults but somewhat more brownish.

► Accidental

Carolina Chickadee similar but smaller and lacks white feather edges on wings. Boreal Chickadee distinguished by brown cap and flanks. Tufted Titmouse lacks black cap and bib.

**VOICE:** Most distinctive song a clear *chick-a-dee-dee-dee;* sometimes only gives *dee-dee-dee.* Also utters loud, whistled *fee-bee-ee* or *fee-bee,* with first note higher in pitch.

**HABITAT AND BEHAVIOUR:** Deciduous and mixed deciduous-coniferous woodland, pastures, hedgerows and thickets, orchards, gardens, and marshes. Flight slightly undulating with rapid wingbeats. Seldom flies long distances. Hops along branches while foraging, sometimes upside down. Also creeps along vertical trunks. Caches seeds and insects in tree bark, dead leaves, clusters of conifer needles, and knotholes in autumn.

**STATUS:** Very common year-round resident.

# BOREAL CHICKADEE *Poecile hudsonica*

. 12.5–14.0 cm / 5.0–5.5" Wt 9–11 g / 0.3–0.4 oz

The Boreal Chickadee shares many endearing qualities with the more familiar Black-capped Chickadee. This active little bird is one of the few songbird species that are permanent residents of the northern boreal forest.

**APPEARANCE:** Crown and nape brown. Cheeks white. Black bib. Small black bill. Sides of head greyish. Back and rump brown. Wings and tail grey with pale grey edging. Breast and belly greyish white. Sides, flanks, and undertail coverts rufous. **Immatures** somewhat duller and paler.

► Black-capped and accidental Carolina chickadees have black caps, grey backs, and white to buffy sides and flanks.

**VOICE:** Primary song wheezy, drawn-out *chick-che-day-day.* Less lively than Black-capped Chickadee's song. Also gives *see see see* and *dit dit dit.*

**HABITAT AND BEHAVIOUR:** Coniferous forests, but also mixed forest with limited deciduous component. Flight usually straight, not undulating. Nervous flicking of wings when flitting from perch to perch. Hops on ground and within foliage. Seldom hangs upside down.

**STATUS:** Fairly common year-round resident.

# TUFTED TITMOUSE *Baeolophus bicolor*

L 15.5–16.5 cm / 6.0–6.5" Wt 18–22 g / 0.6–0.8 oz

The acrobatic foraging behaviour of the Tufted Titmouse is reminiscent of its more widely known relative, the Black-capped Chickadee. During the winter, titmice join small, mixed-species flocks.

**APPEARANCE:** Small, crested bird. Upperparts dark grey, including shaggy, erect crest. Forehead and bill black. Dark eyes appear large and round. Wings and tail unmarked grey. Underparts pale grey, with rusty flanks. **Immatures** similar with somewhat browner, darker plumage.

► Distinguished from Black-capped and accidental Carolina chickadees by erect crest and lack of black crown and bib. Boreal Chickadee brownish above and lacks crest.

**VOICE:** Very vocal in all seasons. Chickadee-like call a terse, scratchy *tsee-day-day-day,* with high-pitched first note. Variable scolding calls include sharp *vet-vet-vet* and *see-jert-jert.* Male sings series of loud, clear, whistled notes, typically of two-note phrases, *peter-peter-peter,* usually repeated two to ten times.

**HABITAT AND BEHAVIOUR:** Deciduous and mixed forests of southern counties. Also wooded sand dunes and residential gardens. Sustained flight direct and not undulating; most commonly observed flying actively from branch to branch. Jumps along branches or hops on ground while foraging for small insects and seeds. Often hangs upside down from twigs.

**STATUS:** Rare year-round resident.

# ED-BREASTED NUTHATCH *Sitta canadensis* ✓

1.5–12.0 cm / 4.5–4.7" Wt 10.5–13.0 g / 0.4–0.5 oz

thatches are renowned for their ability to walk either with head up head down on vertical tree trunks. This behaviour is facilitated by a atively large hind toe, or hallux, and laterally compressed claws.

**PEARANCE:** Adult male has
ck crown and nape; dark
ish grey in **female.**
ominent white eyebrow. Black
e-line somewhat broader on
le. Bill dark bluish black.
maining upperparts bluish
y. Chin, cheeks, ear coverts,
d sides of neck whitish to
e buff. Breast, flanks, sides,
lly, and undertail coverts
namon in male, buffy in
nale. **Immatures** similar to
ults but with duller and less
arply defined crown.
derparts somewhat paler.
perparts faintly fringed with
ck on male.

► White-breasted Nuthatch has white face without prominent
ck eye-line; also distinguished by black stripe on hindneck and
ite underparts.

**OICE:** Most common vocalization a nasal *yank yank* that resembles
all toy horn. Quicker and lower pitched than call of White-breasted
thatch. Also utters plaintive, repeated *waa-aa-ns.* Male gives aggressive
sh, buzzy *hn-hn-hn-hn-hn.* Female utters series of *we-we-we* notes
ring courtship and incubation.

**ABITAT AND BEHAVIOUR:** Coniferous and mixed forest, particularly
ere fir and spruce are dominant. May visit feeders in winter. Flight
irregular and bounding. Long-distance flights have
pronounced undulations. Some individuals
overwinter in Ontario, whereas others make
short migrations.

**STATUS:** Fairly common year-round resident.

# WHITE-BREASTED NUTHATCH
## *Sitta carolinensis*

L 14–15 cm / 5.5–6"  Wt 18–26 g / 0.65–1.0 oz

This small songbird is a common visitor to backyard bird feeders. Nuthatches, as their name suggests, frequently wedge food items into tree bark crevices, then use their bills to hammer them open.

**APPEARANCE:** Small and short-tailed. Crown, nape, and foreback black in adult male. Back, rump, and tail coverts bluish grey. Wing coverts and flight feathers grey, tipped with white. Sides of head, breast, and belly white. Undertail coverts rust. Adult **female** similar to male but has grey crown. **Immatures** resemble adults but are darker and tinged with brown.

▶ Less stocky than Black-capped Chickadee, and lacks black b Red-breasted Nuthatch distinguished by thick black line through eye, and rusty underparts.

**VOICE:** Only male sings simple, rapid series of six to eight notes, heard most commonly in late winter and spring: *to-what what what what what what.* Both male and female frequently utter nasal *yank ya yank* that resembles small toy horn. Call more prolonged and higher pitched than that of Red-breasted Nuthatch.

**HABITAT AND BEHAVIOUR:** Mature deciduous woodlands and shade trees in residential areas. Bounding flight resembles that of a small woodpecker. Forages for insects and plant matter predominantly on trunks and main branches of trees; moves downward as well as upward while feeding. Caches food und loose tree bark.

**STATUS:** Common year-round resident.

# BROWN CREEPER *Certhia americana* ✓

12.5–14.5 cm / 4.9–5.7" Wt 7–8 g / 0.25–0.3 oz

The small and solitary Brown Creeper is inconspicuous in appearance, manner, and voice. Rather than launch an aggressive or otherwise conspicuous display when threatened, this little bird remains motionless against the tree trunk, allowing its cryptic plumage to conceal its presence.

**APPEARANCE:** Bill thin and decurved. Crown and upperparts brown streaked with greyish white. Whitish eyebrow. Long, pointed, brown tail feathers. Underparts whitish. Flanks and undertail coverts tinged with buff. **Immatures** resemble adults but somewhat paler and more mottled.

► Nuthatches have greyish blue backs and straight, or slightly upturned, bills. Woodpeckers have straight bills and lack brown, streaky plumage on backs. Wrens stumpy with soft, rounded tails frequently held cocked over back; manner of foraging entirely different.

**VOICE:** Song given primarily in spring, a faint, high-pitched *trees-trees-trees see the trees.* Similar to call of Winter Wren. Call note high *see* that resembles call of Golden-crowned Kinglet.

**HABITAT AND BEHAVIOUR:** Mature deciduous and mixed forest. Flight hasty and usually only from top of one tree to the base of another one. Forages for insects located in crevices in bark. Spirals upward on tree trunk with jerky movements. Uses stiff tail feathers as props.

**STATUS:** Fairly common breeder. Common spring and fall migrant. Rare winter visitor.

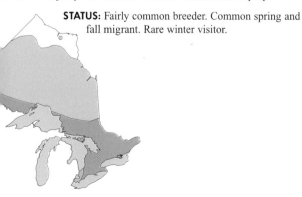

# CAROLINA WREN *Thryothorus ludovicianus* ⨍

L 13–15 cm / 5.5–6.0" Wt 19–22 g / 0.7–0.8 oz

This active and curious species is the largest eastern wren. It responds readily to an observer's "pishing" or hooting calls by cocking its tail and bobbing back and forth.

**APPEARANCE:** Stubby body. Upperparts bright rusty brown. Conspicuous white stripe above eye extends to nape bordered below by dark line and buffy to dusky cheeks. Throat white. Wings rusty brown with faint brown bars; outermost primaries also barred with white. Rump rusty brown. Long tail rusty brown narrowly barred with dusky brown. Two outer feathers spotted with white. Breast, belly, and flanks pale cinnamon. Undertail coverts white with dusky brown bars. **Immatures** resemble adults.

► Distinguished from most other wrens by rusty brown unstreaked upperparts and pale cinnamon breast and belly. Bewick's Wren similar to Carolina Wren in summer and early fall, but former somewhat browner with whiter underparts and tail broadly tipped with white. Marsh Wren smaller with white stripes on back.

**VOICE:** Only male sings. Gives loud, clear, ringing, tri-syllabic song repeated several times: *tea-kettle tea-kettle tea-kettle tea.* Calls include *cheer, ti-dink,* and *pi-zeet.*

**HABITAT AND BEHAVIOUR:** Thickets and tangles in open deciduous woodlands. Nests in residential areas if cover is sufficient. Flies weakly for short distances. Dodges in and out of cover. Hops and flits about near, or ground. Also climbs up tree trunks like nuthatch or creeper.

**STATUS:** Rare to uncommon year round resident.

# EWICK'S WREN *Thryomanes bewickii*

2.5–14.0 cm / 5.0–5.5" Wt 8.5–11.0 g / 0.3–0.4 oz

eeding of Bewick's Wren in Ontario was confirmed during the 50s. However, despite the regular appearance of this western species Point Pelee National Park in spring, evidence of its continued eeding in the province remains elusive.

**PPEARANCE:** Upper-
rts brown. Conspicuous
ite eyebrow bordered
low with dark brown
e-line. Bill blackish
ove, pale brown below.
eeks streaked with
own and white. Wings
ffy brown barred with
rker brown. Relatively
ng, brownish black tail;
ntral feathers barred
th brown, outside
athers barred with
ack and broadly tipped
th white. Throat and underparts white. Sides of breast shaded with
ownish grey. Flanks washed with buff. **Immatures** similar except
ottled above and below with black and grey. Buffy wash on sides and
nks more pronounced.

► Carolina Wren larger and stouter with shorter tail and buffier
derparts; lacks white tail spots. House, Winter, and Sedge wrens lack
ite eyebrow. Marsh Wren has conspicuous white stripes on back and
cks white tail spots. Rock Wren has streaked throat and breast.

**OICE:** Male utters clear, variable song of three to five phrases and
lls: *seee-teu-whee-teu-eeee.* Reminiscent of Song Sparrow. Call note
rsh, scratchy *weed-it weed-it.*

**ABITAT AND BEHAVIOUR:** Thickets, underbrush, and gardens. Flight
quick and direct; usually short distances only. Keeps to
cover. Moves between perches with short, quick
hops. Wags tail from side to side.

**STATUS:** Extremely rare breeder. Rare spring
and fall migrant.

# HOUSE WREN *Troglodytes aedon*

L 11–13 cm / 4.3–5.1" Wt 9–12 g / 0.3–0.4 oz

Male House Wrens are persistent singers from the time of arrival on breeding grounds through the incubation period. Studies indicate that during morning singing bouts, they may deliver more than 600 songs per hour.

**APPEARANCE:** Head, nape, and back greyish brown. Indistinct pale brown eyebrow and eye-ring. Cheeks brownish white finely streaked with buff. Bill dark brown above and yellowish below. Wings and tail brown barred with dark brown. Tail lacks spots. Underparts greyish white, lightest on throat and breast. Sides and flanks tinged with

buff and faintly streaked with brown. **Immatures** similar but have darker mottling on underparts. Flanks and undertail coverts rufous.

▶ Smaller, darker Winter Wren has shorter tail and heavily barred flanks and belly; usually perches with tail cocked. Sedge Wren has streaked crown and back. Other wrens have prominent white eyebrows. Bewick's Wren and accidental Rock Wren also have white buff tail tips.

**VOICE:** Male sings complex series of rapid, bubbling notes that rise in pitch and volume, then fall toward end. Calls include chatters, rattles, and harsh, scolding notes. Incubating female produces short, low whine.

**HABITAT AND BEHAVIOUR:** Open woodland and deciduous forest edges, wooded swamps, and treed residential areas. Flight direct and steady; usually about 1 m (3') from ground when crossing clearings. Cocks tail straight down when singing.

**STATUS:** Common breeder. Common migrant. Rare winter resident.

# WINTER WREN *Troglodytes troglodytes*
10.0–11.5 cm / 3.9–4.5" Wt 8.5–9.5 g / 0.3–0.35 oz

This small, inconspicuous bird is known to many only by its tinkling, musical song as it issues forth from brush piles and dead trees. The Winter Wren also breeds in the gardens of Europe and Asia.

**APPEARANCE:** Very short and stubby with tail held cocked up over back. Thin, slightly decurved bill. Dark reddish brown above. Pale buffy eyebrow. Very short tail reddish brown, barred with dark brown. Underparts pale brown, heavily barred with dusky brown on belly, flanks, and undertail coverts. **Immatures** resemble adults but somewhat darker and less

reddish above. Pale eyebrow indistinct. Underparts less heavily barred.
► House Wren paler overall, particularly below, with much longer tail; dark barring on underparts much less conspicuous. Sedge Wren has white streaking on back and crown, longer tail, and paler underparts that lack dark barring. Marsh, Carolina, and Bewick's wrens paler below and have bright white eyebrows contrasting with reddish brown crowns. In addition, Marsh Wren has bright white stripes on back.

**VOICE:** Male gives melodious series of warbling and trilling notes that lasts nine seconds or more. Rarely sings in winter. Call notes include sharp *kip-kip* and low *churr*.

**HABITAT AND BEHAVIOUR:** Moist coniferous forest, bogs, and swamps with thick underbrush. Active and quick but seldom flies far. Shy. Nervously flits about while foraging. Bobs up and down on tree limbs or logs.

**STATUS:** Common breeder. Spring and fall migrant. Rare winter visitor.

## SEDGE WREN *Cistothorus platensis*

L 10–11 cm / 3.9–4.3" Wt 8.0–8.5 g / 0.3 oz

The distribution of Sedge Wrens, known formerly as Short-billed Marsh Wrens, has become highly localized during the last century because of agricultural intensification. Since colonies of these shy wrens move frequently from year to year, they may be absent from areas where they were observed in previous breeding seasons.

**APPEARANCE:** Crown streaked with tan and dark brown. Thin, pale buff eyebrow on plain, brownish face. Slender, slightly decurved bill. Upperparts brown with indistinct white streaks on back. Wing coverts brown with darker barring. Short tail barred with dark brown. Often held cocked up. Underparts mostly whitish with buffy wash on flanks and undertail coverts. **Immatures** resemble adults but somewhat paler with less streaking.

► Marsh Wren has bright white eyebrow and more conspicuous white streaks on back; crown unstreaked brown; bill and tail longer. Winter Wren smaller with shorter tail; darker overall with plain, unstreaked crown. House Wren larger with longer tail and plain brown upperparts.

**VOICE:** Male gives sharp, metallic *tsip tsip tsip trrrrrrrrrupp,* with first notes given slowly followed by rapid, chattering trill. Frequently sings at night. Call note a sharp *tick.*

**HABITAT AND BEHAVIOUR:** Wet grassy and shrubby fields, marshes, bogs, and beaver ponds. Flight weak and fluttery with rapid wingbeats. Shy; more frequently heard than seen. Clings to vertical stems with feet and moves up and down with dexterity.

**STATUS:** Locally rare breeder.

# MARSH WREN *Cistothorus palustris*
10–14 cm / 4.0–5.5"  Wt 11–14 g / 0.4–0.5 oz

Each spring, a male Marsh Wren will build ten or more nests within his breeding territory. Extra nests may serve as decoys to predators, outline territory boundaries, provide shelter for fledged young, or merely demonstrate his nest-building prowess to prospective mates.

**APPEARANCE:** Crown unstreaked blackish brown. Prominent white eyebrow. Cheeks streaked buff and brown. Long bill. White chin. Upper back blackish with conspicuous white stripes. Lower back and scapulars rusty brown. Wings and tail cinnamon-brown barred with black. Underparts white with buff sides and cinnamon flanks. **Immatures** duller and less-clearly marked. White back streaks and eyebrow may be indistinct.

▶ Sedge Wren has shorter bill and streaked crown; lacks white eyebrow and contrasting back stripes; immatures distinguished by crown markings. Carolina Wren and Bewick's Wren have plain brown backs and brownish crowns. Carolina Wren buffy below. Bewick's Wren has white corners on tail. House Wren and Winter Wren smaller, and lack facial and back striping. Accidental Rock Wren has streaked breast.

**VOICE:** Male utters reedy, gurgling song followed by squeak and raspy trill: *cut-cut-turrrrrrrrrr-ur.* Often given at night. Calls include low *'suck,* or *chuk-chuk,* and rapid, trilling *turr turr turr.*

**HABITAT AND BEHAVIOUR:** Cattail marshes. Flights short with rapid wingbeats. Climbs among emergent vegetation.

**STATUS:** Locally common breeder. Common spring and fall migrant.

# GOLDEN–CROWNED KINGLET *Regulus satrapa*

L 9–11 cm / 3.5–4.0" Wt 5.0–7.5 g / 0.2–0.3 oz

When intruders approach a Golden-crowned Kinglet nest, the attending adults nervously flick their wings and call incessantly. In spite of this display, the small, cup-shaped nest, constructed from twigs, moss, and spiderwebs, is often difficult to locate.

♀

**APPEARANCE:** Crown has orange patch (yellowish in female) bordered on sides and forehead by black stripe. White eyebrow and black eye-line. Indistinct blackish malar stripe. Otherwise, upperparts greenish olive. Wings dark grey with two white wing bars. Notched tail dark grey. Flight feathers of wings and tail edged with greenish olive and greyish white. Underparts pale grey tinged with greenish olive on breast and flanks. **Immatures** resemble adults but lack orange (or yellow) crown-patch.

▶ Kinglets distinguished by small size and short tails. Ruby-crowned Kinglet has conspicuous, white eye-ring; lacks white eyebrow and black-and-gold crown. Warblers larger with longer tails.

**VOICE:** Primary song up to fourteen high-pitched, ascending notes, *tsee-tsee-tsee-tsee-tseetee-leetle,* followed by a long musical warble. Call notes include thin *ti ti,* high *tsee-tsee-tsee,* and drawn-out single *tsee* that resembles call of Brown Creeper.

**HABITAT AND BEHAVIOUR:** Coniferous and mixed woodlands often near edges and clearings. Local flights quick and erratic. Long-distance flight high but not direct. Hops on ground with continuous flicking of wings. Often hangs upside down from twigs while feeding.

**STATUS:** Common breeder. Abundant spring and fall migrant. Uncommon winter resident.

# RUBY-CROWNED KINGLET *Regulus calendula* F
L 9–11 cm / 3.5–4.0" Wt 5–9 g / 0.2–0.3 oz

During courtship, the spritely male Ruby-crowned Kinglet impresses prospective mates by exposing his brilliant red crown and giving his very loud, rolling song.

**APPEARANCE:** Upperparts greyish olive-green. Incomplete, bold, white eye-ring. Adult male has red (rarely orange) crown-patch that is usually obscured. Adult **female** lacks patch. Wings dark olive with two prominent white bars. Underparts dusky white. Tail blackish olive. Spring birds duller than fall birds. **Immatures** greyish brown with dusky mottling on crown and back. Eye-ring dull white. Wing bars buffy brown.

▶ Distinguished from Golden-crowned Kinglet by red crown, white eye-ring, and more greenish plumage. Warblers and vireos larger with longer bills and tails, and do not flick wings. *Empidonax* flycatchers larger with flat, two-toned bill.

**VOICE:** Surprisingly loud, variable song has two to three high-pitched *tee* notes followed by five to six lower *turr* notes, ending with higher-pitched galloping notes: *tee-da-leet tee-da-leet tee-da-leet.* Call notes include husky *che-dit* and prolonged *chirrup.*

**HABITAT AND BEHAVIOUR:** Boreal and mixed forest. Prefers to nest in spruce trees. Flight quick with short bursts of rapid wingbeats. Moves horizontally among foliage with short hops, constantly flicking wings.

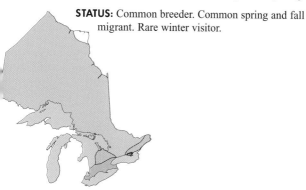

**STATUS:** Common breeder. Common spring and fall migrant. Rare winter visitor.

# BLUE-GRAY GNATCATCHER *Polioptila caerulea*

L 11.5–12.5 cm / 4.5–5.0" Wt 5–7 g / 0.2–0.25 oz

The Blue-gray Gnatcatcher is a curious little bird that is rarely seen in sustained flight. It is more commonly observed hopping along branches and peeking out from behind leaves as it forages for small insects and spiders.

**APPEARANCE:** Tiny, slender bird with slim black bill and narrow tail. Upperparts bluish grey. Prominent white eye-ring. Adult male has narrow black area on forehead that extends as stripe above eye. Wings darker grey with whitish edging. Uppertail coverts and central tail feathers black. Outer tail feathers white. Underparts pale grey to white. Underside of tail white. Legs black. **Female** and **immatures** similar but generally greyer, and lack black stripe over eye.

▶ Kinglets predominantly olive-green with short tails and white wing bars.

**VOICE:** Trilled series of high, insect-like notes, at least ten seconds in duration, but difficult to hear at distances over 50 m (162'). Also high, thin, buzzy call notes that vary in duration and frequency: *psee, tsee,* or *tsseeeit.*

**HABITAT AND BEHAVIOUR:** Deciduous woodlands and oak savannahs, orchards, and shrubby thickets. Flight fluttering and moth-like, or direct with occasional glides with closed wings. Commonly carries tail cocked at an angle to body, or held straight down and slightly fanned. Also frequently flicks tail showing flashes of black and white.

**STATUS:** Uncommon breeder. Uncommon spring and fall migrant.

# NORTHERN WHEATEAR *Oenanthe oenanthe*
14.5–15.5 cm / 5.7–6.1" Wt 20–30 g / 0.7–1.1 oz

The Northern Wheatear is native to Eurasia but breeds in the rocky tundra of Alaska and northern Canada. On rare occasions, this thrush passes through Ontario during migration.

**APPEARANCE: Breeding male** has grey crown, nape, and back. Black mask bordered distinctly with white. Wings black. Rump and uppertail coverts white. Central tail feathers black; outside feathers white at base with broad black tips. Throat and sides of breast buffy cinnamon; paler on belly. Undertail coverts whitish. **Female** pale olive-brown above with white rump. Buffy white eyebrow. Indistinct blackish eyering. Cheeks and sides of neck buffy cinnamon. Chin buff becoming cinnamon on throat and sides of breast. Flanks greyish buff. Belly whitish buff. Wings and tail like breeding male but somewhat duller. **Non-breeding male** greyish brown above with darker buffy underparts. Wings tipped in buff. Tail as in breeding plumage. **Immatures** resemble female but are brighter buff below.

▶ T-shaped black-and-white tail pattern diagnostic in all plumages.

**VOICE:** Musical, rambling song that includes repeated *eu twirra, ewirru, zeeu widdlu yu.* Also utters loud, harsh *chak-chak,* vibrant *ree,* and agitated *weet-tuc-tuc.*

**HABITAT AND BEHAVIOUR:** Rocky tundra in summer. Migrates through open habitats. Flight undulating. Beats wings slowly and fans tail in presence of intruders. Hops on ground.

**STATUS:** Very rare spring and fall migrant.

# EASTERN BLUEBIRD *Sialia sialis*

L 16.0–19.5 cm / 6.0–7.5" Wt 28–32 g / 1.0–1.1 oz

The beautiful male Eastern Bluebird delivers his warbling song from a conspicuous high perch. As he sings, he frequently pivots his body to address listeners in all directions. A delicately fanned tail completes the performance.

**APPEARANCE:** Adult male bright blue above including wings and tail. Throat, breast, sides, and flanks chestnut. Chin, belly, and undertail coverts white. **Female** has greyish blue upperparts with brownish tinge on back. Some females have faint, white eye-ring. Wings and tail dull blue. Throat, belly, and undertail coverts white. Breast and flanks dull reddish brown. **Juveniles** have brown upperparts streaked with white. White eye-ring. Underparts buffy white heavily spotted with dusky brown. Male has bluish wash on wings and tail.

▶ Male Western Bluebird deeper blue above with variable chestnut patch on back; throat blue; belly greyish blue; female has greyish throat and belly. Male Mountain Bluebird entirely blue; female greyish with blue wings and tail; lacks reddish brown on underparts.

**VOICE:** Male sings rich, low-pitched, warbling *tury cherwee cheye-ley.* Both sexes give loud, low-pitched *tu-a-wee.* Alarm calls include chattering *chit-chit-chit* and high-pitched *turr.*

**HABITAT AND BEHAVIOUR:** Agricultural lands, forest clearings, old fields, golf courses, and large lawns. Flight generally low in open areas. Hops sideways. Perches with hunched vertical posture.

**STATUS:** Uncommon breeder. Uncommon spring and fall migrant. Rare winter visitor.

# MOUNTAIN BLUEBIRD *Sialia currucoides*

16.5–20.5 cm / 6.5–8.0"  Wt 26–32 g / 0.9–1.1 oz

The striking Mountain Bluebird differs from other bluebirds in its tendency to hover while foraging. It winters in large flocks in south-central and southwestern North America.

**APPEARANCE:** Breeding male sky-blue overall; darker on upperparts, wings, and tail, lightest on belly. After-second-year male brighter. **Winter male** duller brownish blue with whitish belly and dusky wing tips. **Female** has greyish brown head, back, and underparts. Wings, rump, and tail bright sky-blue. Conspicuous white eye-ring. **Juveniles** similar to female but somewhat darker with breast and sides spotted with greyish brown.

▶ Eastern Bluebird distinguished by presence of rusty brown on underparts; upperparts of male somewhat deeper purplish blue. Male Blue Grosbeak not thrush-like, and has deeper blue plumage with tan wing bars. Townsend's Solitaire resembles female Mountain Bluebird but lacks blue on wings, rump, and tail.

**VOICE:** Short, loud, emphatic song, *chow chow poly-chow poly-chow,* heard before dawn. Resembles song of American Robin. Also utters soft, repetitious warble, *eee-ee-e,* at any time of day. Flocking birds in winter give unmusical *terrr* note.

**HABITAT AND BEHAVIOUR:** Open country with some trees. Also woodland openings and edges. Somewhat fluttery in flight, but agile. Usually flies 3–10 m (10–33') above ground. Capable of high, fast flight when travelling. Walks on ground.

**STATUS:** Rare visitor.

275

# TOWNSEND'S SOLITAIRE *Myadestes townsendi*

L 19–22 cm / 7.5–8.7" Wt 30–36 g / 1.1–1.3 oz

This casual winter visitor more closely resembles a flycatcher in profile and habits. However, its melodious, fluty song proclaims its affinities to other North American thrushes.

**APPEARANCE:** Slender and long-tailed. Dark grey upperparts; somewhat lighter underparts. Narrow white eye-ring. Wings dark grey with wide buff band, prominent in flight. Tertiaries edged in white. Tail dark grey with white corners formed by outer white tail feathers and broad white tip on adjacent feathers. Central feathers have buffy tips. **Juveniles** heavily spotted overall with black, buff, and white. Eye-ring buffy white. Wings and tail like adults.

▶ Superficially resembles Northern Mockingbird but distinguished by white eye-ring, darker breast, and buff wing-patches. Female Mountain Bluebird has blue on wings and tail. Other female bluebirds patterned with blue and rufous.

**VOICE:** Elaborate, variable, clear warbled song that rises and falls in both volume and pitch. Calls include squeaking *cr-eek,* ringing *eeek,* and harsh *waa.*

**HABITAT AND BEHAVIOUR:** Open woodlands. Also open hillsides and shrublands in winter. Flight usually leisurely with slow wingbeats. Generally flies short distances. Eats berries and small fruits in winter. Hops on ground rarely. Upright posture when perched.

**STATUS:** Rare visitor from fall to spring.

# VEERY *Catharus fuscescens*

L 16.5–19.0 cm / 6.5–7.5" Wt 36–45 g / 1.3–1.6 oz

The Veery's ethereal and fluting song is heard most frequently at dawn and twilight. Unlike many other thrushes, the Veery often nests on the ground.

**APPEARANCE:** Upperparts uniformly warm, tawny brown. Pale, thin eye-ring indistinct. Upper mandible blackish; lower pinkish at base with dark tip. Wings and tail unmarked. Cheek, throat, and breast pale buff with wedged-shaped, pale reddish brown spots. Flanks pale grey. Belly white. **Juveniles** dark brown above with olive-green spots on head and back. Underparts white washed with olive. Foreneck, throat, and breast variably spotted with brownish olive. Pink bill.

▶ Other *Catharus* thrushes and Wood Thrush have heavily spotted breasts. Also Veery lacks obvious eye-ring.

**VOICE:** Male sings beautiful, haunting *da-vee-ur vee-ur veer veer* that resonates as if produced by a metal flute. Tips bill up in pauses between songs. Most common call notes soft, down-slurred *wheeu* or *veer.* Utters mournful alarm call, *whee-you-whee-you,* if threatened at nest.

**HABITAT AND BEHAVIOUR:** Cool, damp, deciduous and mixed forests with brushy undergrowth and ferns. While foraging, moves rapidly along ground using long hops. Flips over dead leaves and other ground litter with bill. Sometimes perches on rocks and logs to survey for prey. Occasionally fly-catches for food.

**STATUS:** Common breeder. Common spring and fall migrant.

# GRAY-CHEEKED THRUSH *Catharus minimus*

L 18.0–20.5 cm / 7.1–8.1" Wt 30–36 g / 1.1–1.3 oz

The Gray-cheeked Thrush is Ontario's most northern breeding thrush. Each spring and fall it migrates through southern Ontario en route between wintering grounds in South America and breeding grounds in the Hudson Bay Lowlands.

**APPEARANCE:** Greyish brown above with grey-ish cheeks and pale, incomplete eye-ring. Underparts white with heavy brown spotting on breast and greyish wash on sides and flanks. **Juveniles** somewhat more olive above with buffy streaks on back.

▶ Swainson's Thrush has complete buffy eye-ring and buffy wash on face and upper breast. Hermit Thrush has prominent reddish tail that is frequently cocked up then lowered slowly; also upperparts olive-brown, not greyish. Veery reddish brown above with indistinct brownish spotting on buffy breast. Accidental Bicknell's Thrush best distinguished by more obvious yellow base to lower mandible.

**VOICE:** Thin, nasal song that rises abruptly at end: *whee-wheeoo-titi-whee.* Given by male primarily at dawn and dusk. Suggests song of Veery, which has descending final note. Also gives down-slurred *quee-a.* Call note a sharp *pheu,* higher pitched than that of Veery.

**HABITAT AND BEHAVIOUR:** Boreal forest and scrubby tundra. Other forest during migration. Highly secretive throughout breeding season. Generally forages on the ground for insects.

**STATUS:** Rare breeder. Rare to uncommon spring and fall migrant.

# SWAINSON'S THRUSH *Catharus ustulatus*

L 16.5–19.5 cm / 6.5–7.8" Wt 28–40 g / 1.0–1.4 oz

During migration, Swainson's Thrushes form loose, scattered flocks with other thrushes, such as the Gray-cheeked Thrush and the Veery. Early Ontario ornithologists knew it only as a migrant; however, in 1915 a nest with eggs was reported in Barrie.

**APPEARANCE:**

Upperparts greyish brown. Conspicuous buffy eye-ring. Buff wash on face and upper breast. Otherwise, underparts whitish with dark brown, rounded spots arranged in streaks on throat and breast. Spots become wedge-shaped at sides of throat. Sides and flanks tinged with grey. Underwing has pinkish buff stripe visible from below. **Juveniles** resemble adults but darker olive above with buffy streaks on back.

▶ Hermit Thrush has reddish rump and tail. Raises and lowers tail when perched. Breast somewhat whiter with darker spots. Veery lacks bold eye-ring; spots on underparts less distinct. Wood Thrush has reddish crown and bold black spotting on white underparts. Gray-cheeked and Bicknell's thrushes have grey cheeks; lack buffy wash on breast; conspicuous eye-ring.

**VOICE:** Song a series of rolling, fluting phrases that rises in inflection: *wip-poor-wil-wil-eez-zee-zee.* Call note a sharp *wick.* Night-flying migrants utter *heep* note.

**HABITAT AND BEHAVIOUR:** Edges and clearings of moist coniferous and mixed forest. Flight swift and sustained. Shy but quite tame when approached. Generally forages by hopping on ground, but also fly-catches and gleans while hovering.

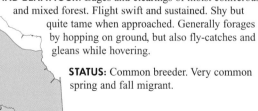

**STATUS:** Common breeder. Very common spring and fall migrant.

# HERMIT THRUSH *Catharus guttatus*

L 18–19 cm / 7.0–7.5" Wt 28–34 g / 1.0–1.2 oz

Those who have heard the beautiful song of the Hermit Thrush will not soon forget it. For that reason, this gifted songster has been revered in both poetry and prose.

**APPEARANCE:** Olive-brown above with distinctive rufous tail. Face greyish brown with white eye-ring and indistinct pale line over lores. Pale buff breast; otherwise, underparts whitish spotted with olive-brown. Spots round on breast, and form long streaks on throat. **Juveniles** olive-brown mottled with buff and black. Underparts buffy white with black spots. Tail rufous.

▶ Only thrush with reddish tail. Gray-cheeked Thrush has greyish upperparts and less conspicuous eye-ring. Upperparts of Veery tawny; lacks eye-ring; also breast spots often indistinct. Swainson's Thrush has more buffy eye-ring, cheeks, and upper breast. Wood Thrush has rusty cap and large, round black spots on breast. Fox Sparrow has rufous tail but can be distinguished by heavy, rusty streaking on breast, greyish streaks on back, and conical bill.

**VOICE:** Male gives haunting, flute-like warble which begins with a long introductory note and rises in frequency. Calls include scolding *tchup-chup-chup,* soft *chuck,* and whinnying *wee.*

**HABITAT AND BEHAVIOUR:** Coniferous and mixed woodland. Flight strong and direct. Runs short distances, then stands. Flicks wings; cocks tail rapidly upward then slowly lowers it.

**STATUS:** Common breeder. Very common spring and fall migrant. Rare winter resident.

# WOOD THRUSH *Hylocichla mustelina*

19–21 cm / 7.5–8.3" Wt 40–50 g / 1.4–1.8 oz

The Wood Thrush is representative of the widespread decline in neotropical migrant birds. Although still considered common in Ontario, populations on wintering grounds are now less than thirty per cent of their 1960 levels.

**APPEARANCE:** Upperparts cinnamon rufous; brightest on crown and nape, somewhat more olive on tail coverts and tail. Narrow, white eye-ring. Cheek and ear coverts greyish, streaked with white and dark brown. Throat whitish buff with black streaks. Breast, sides, and flanks white with large, round black spots. **Juveniles** similar but with tawny streaks and spots on neck, back, and wing coverts.

► Distinguished by large black spots on breast. Hermit, Swainson's, and Gray-cheeked thrushes have smaller, brownish spots on underparts, and lack rufous on head and nape. Hermit Thrush has reddish tail. Veery has buffy breast with pale, wedged-shaped spots.

**VOICE:** Male primarily sings ethereal, flute-like song that begins with two to six quiet, low-pitched *bub bub* notes followed by louder, clear *ee-o-lay* phrase terminating with rapid trill. Most frequently given at dawn and dusk. Call notes include sharp *pit pit pit* and low *quirt.*

**HABITAT AND BEHAVIOUR:** Mature deciduous or mixed forest, preferably undisturbed. Flight powerful and manoeuvrable at low speeds. Hops on ground while foraging. Cocks tail up and slowly lowers it, particularly after landing.

**STATUS:** Common breeder. Common spring and fall migrant.

# AMERICAN ROBIN *Turdus migratorius*
L 23–28 cm / 9–11" Wt 76–86 g / 2.7–3.1 oz

These harbingers of spring are a welcome sight throughout Ontario.
Although generally associated with suburban lawns, the American
Robin occurs in any habitat that provides open areas for ground
foraging and an adequate soil layer to support invertebrate populations.

**APPEARANCE:** Adult
male dark grey above
with blackish head.
White crescents above
and below eye. Yellow
bill has black tip. Outer
tail feathers tipped with
white. Chin and throat
streaked with black and
white. Breast and belly
brick-red. Undertail
coverts white. Adult
**female** resembles male
but paler overall,
particularly greyish
brown head. **Juveniles** similar to adult female but somewhat paler
above with buffy eye markings and feather edges. Throat white.
Remaining underparts heavily spotted with brownish black.

▶ Juveniles distinguished from other thrushes by rusty wash on
spotted underparts and buffy markings around eye. Casual Varied
Thrush has black mask with prominent orange eyebrow; orange
underparts have black breast band.

**VOICE:** Clear, loud, liquid carolling *cheerily cheer-up cheer-up cheerily
cheer-up* typically given from high perch before sunrise and after
sunset. Alarm call is spirited *chirp*. Other calls include repeated *chirr*
that rises in pitch and high-pitched, whining whistle.

**HABITAT AND BEHAVIOUR:** Woodlands, lawns, gardens, bogs, and
lakeshores. Flight generally short and low. Runs well
with rapid steps interspersed with frequent, brief
pauses to scan surroundings.

**STATUS:** Abundant breeder. Abundant spring
and fall migrant. Rare winter resident.

# VARIED THRUSH *Ixoreus naevius*

L 24–26 cm / 9.4–10.2"  Wt 75–80 g / 2.7–2.9 oz

Each year, several Varied Thrushes are reported in Ontario. Most are observed at backyard feeders where dense coniferous trees provide adequate shelter. Berries, nuts, and suet are among the most relished offerings, although one backyard birder sustained a few individuals for two winters on a diet of peanut butter sandwiches.

**APPEARANCE:** Adult male has bluish black upperparts. Orange eyebrow. Blackish wings have two orange wing bars. Underparts deep orange fading to pale orange at undertail coverts. Black breast band. Underwing has prominent, buffy orange bar. **Female** similar but somewhat browner and duller with less distinct brownish breast band. **Juveniles** resemble female but with more scaly appearance on throat and breast and whitish belly.

▶ American Robin lacks orange eyebrow, throat, and wing bars, and black breast band.

**VOICE:** Male utters a series of whistled notes given at different pitches and separated by pauses. Call notes include quiet *tuck* and twangy *zeeee*.

**HABITAT AND BEHAVIOUR:** Active bird feeders with adjacent coniferous trees. Flight robin-like but not as sustained. Usually makes brief flights within understorey. Stays on or near ground; generally sings from low perch.

**STATUS:** Rare visitor from October to April.

# GRAY CATBIRD *Dumetella carolinensis*
L 21.5–24.0 cm / 8.5–9.5"  Wt 28–40 g / 1.0–1.4 oz

The Gray Catbird acquired its vernacular name from its apparently cat-like mewing call. This skilled mimic has been known to incorporate the calls of at least forty-four other avian species into its repertoire.

**APPEARANCE:** Slim, dark grey bird with long, rounded tail. Black forehead and crown. Tail black. Underparts somewhat lighter grey. Deep chestnut undertail coverts not always noticeable. **Juveniles** brownish grey above, lighter on crown. Wings and tail blackish grey. Throat, sides, and undertail coverts pale rufous. Otherwise, underparts mottled grey and brown.

► Northern Mockingbird, Gray Jay, and Townsend's Solitaire lack black cap and chestnut undertail coverts. Brown Thrasher has brown upperparts and streaked underparts.

**VOICE:** Distinctive, scolding cat-like call. Song a soft, disjointed series of notes and phrases in five or six pitches up to ten minutes in length. Often interspersed with whines, mews, and whistles. Also utters loud, harsh, chattering *chek-chek-chek* and soft, low-pitched *whurt.*

**HABITAT AND BEHAVIOUR:** Scrubby vegetation, successional forest, abandoned farmland, plantations, streamsides, and residential areas. Flights usually short and relatively low in vegetation. Rarely flies across large, open spaces. Travels through shrubs by hopping and flying. Frequently flicks tail, particularly while calling. Vigorously defends nest.

**STATUS:** Common breeder. Common migrant. Rare winter resident.

# NORTHERN MOCKINGBIRD *Mimus polyglottos* ꓥF
21–25 cm / 8–10" Wt 47–51 g / 1.7–1.8 oz

The mockingbird's scientific name means "many-tongued mimic." This aptly describes its talent for imitating other birds' calls, as well as the vocalizations of non-avian species and some mechanical sounds.

**APPEARANCE:** Upperparts grey. Rounded wings black with two white wing bars; large white patch on upper wing visible, diagnostic in flight. Tail long, rounded, and mostly black except several white outside feathers. Underparts white to light grey. Bill black. **Juveniles** similar but with faint spotting on breast.
► Loggerhead and Northern shrikes have black mask and strongly hooked bill. Townsend's solitaire darker grey with white eye-ring and buff wing bars.

**VOICE:** Varied and diverse musical medley. Repertoire of individual male may include more than 150 distinct song types. Song typically a prolonged succession of notes, each repeated several times before changing. Call notes include loud *tchak* and *chair*. Sings incessantly throughout summer, often at night.

**HABITAT AND BEHAVIOUR:** Suburban gardens, orchard and woodland edges, hedges, and thickets. Flight varies from rapid and direct to slow with shallow wingbeats. May "parachute" rapidly from perches with wings folded. Acrobatic flights during courtship. When perched, often fans tail and flicks it from side to side, and flashes white wing-patches.

**STATUS:** Rare to locally uncommon breeder. Rare winter resident.

# BROWN THRASHER *Toxostoma rufum*

L 29–30 cm / 11.5–12.0"  Wt 65–70 g / 2.3–2.5 oz

When establishing a breeding territory, the male Brown Thrasher delivers his loud, melodious song from a high, exposed perch. Once nesting begins, he is more difficult to observe as he moves secretively through thick tangles of vegetation.

**APPEARANCE:** Slender and long-tailed. Upperparts rufous brown. Face dull greyish brown. Eyes orangish yellow. Long, decurved bill blackish brown with paler lower mandible. Short, rounded wings have two dull white wing bars. Underparts whitish, tinged with buff on breast and sides, and heavily streaked with dark brown. **Immatures** resemble adults but somewhat duller with greyish eyes.

▶ Accidental Sage Thrasher smaller with greyish brown upperparts and white spots at tip of tail. Hermit Thrush olive-brown above with shorter bill and tail; lacks wing bars.

**VOICE:** Male gives a series of rich, musical phrases, often repeated in pairs: *teeahwee teeahwee* or *chay chay.* Resembles Northern Mockingbird and Gray Catbird. Call notes include harsh *chack* and whistled *pitcheree.*

**HABITAT AND BEHAVIOUR:** Brushy hillsides, hawthorn thickets, and woodland edges. Flight direct and low to ground. Tail often held cocked above back. Aggressive and vigilant defender of nest. Forages on or near ground. Sometimes tosses leaves aside with bill while foraging.

**STATUS:** Common breeder. Common spring and fall migrant.

# ROPEAN STARLING *Sturnus vulgaris* ✓ + F

9.0–21.5 cm / 7.5–8.5" Wt 80–90 g / 2.9–3.2 oz

s aggressive and gregarious Old World starling was introduced to
rth America during the 1890s in a misguided attempt to bring the
ds of Shakespeare to the New World. Its phenomenal success on
continent has had a detrimental effect on many native cavity-
ting species.

**PEARANCE:** Stocky and
rt-tailed bird with
nted wings and long bill.
ing and summer adults
e glossy black plumage
t shows purple and green
escence, particularly on
d and breast. Bill yellow.
lt **fall and winter**
mage black speckled with
te and buff. Bill brownish.
**enile** uniformly brown,
newhat resembling female
wn-headed Cowbird.
► Easily distinguished
m native blackbirds in
ing and summer by
low bill. Also, blackbirds
e shorter bills, longer
s, and more rounded
g tips.

**ICE:** Varied whistles, warbles, clicks, clucks, rattles, and gurgles.
g sometimes melodic, but often not. Wolf whistle, *sweeeuu,*
mmon. Calls include harsh *chackerchackerchacker* and metallic *chip.*
o mimics songs of other bird species such as Eastern Wood-Pewee
Wood Thrush.

**HABITAT AND BEHAVIOUR:** Deciduous and mixed
forest, swamps and marshes, and urban and rural
populated areas. In winter, forage and roost in
large flocks that may comprise many thousands
of individuals. Roosting birds produce
jumbled cacophony of harsh calls that can be
annoying at close range.

**STATUS:** Abundant year-round resident.
Introduced; native to Eurasia.

# AMERICAN PIPIT *Anthus rubescens*

L 15–18 cm / 5.9–7.1" Wt 19–25 g / 0.7–0.9 oz

Long known as the Water Pipit, this species is now considered distinc[t] from pipits occurring from Europe to central Asia.

**APPEARANCE:** Slender body and bill; long tail. In breeding plumage, upperparts pale grey with faint dark streaks on crown and back. Buff eyebrow. Wings and tail brownish grey. Two buff wing bars. Tail has white outer feathers. Underparts buff. Breast has necklace of blackish streaks on some individuals. Flanks lightly streaked. Wing linings buff. Bill dusky brown, yellowish at base. Legs brownish. **Fall plumage** similar, but has brown ground colour above and paler buff below. Breast and flanks heavily streaked with black. Pale legs on some birds. **Immatures** resemble winter adults but darker above and lighter below.

▶ Accidental Sprague's Pipit lighter in colour with heavier streaking on upperparts. Horned Lark has black on head and tail. Longspurs and sparrows have thick, conical bills.

**VOICE:** Loud, continuous, repeated *tjwee* given by male on breeding grounds. During flight display, repeated *tsoo* given on ascent and *chwee* upon descent. Loud *peep* given by both male and female in presence of predator.

**HABITAT AND BEHAVIOUR:** Tundra, bare field[s] sandy and rocky coasts. Primarily ground-dwelling; however, flight strong and undulating[.] Wades in shallow water to feed. Habitually pumps tail up and down, often when callin[g]

**STATUS:** Fairly common breeder. Rare spring migrant. Common fall migrant.

# BOHEMIAN WAXWING *Bombycilla garrulus*

L 19–22 cm / 7.5–8.7" Wt 60–65 g / 2.1–2.3 oz

Gregarious Bohemian Waxwings search for mountain ash, crabapple, and other fruit trees in large, nomadic flocks. Hundreds of individuals may appear overnight, then depart once trees have been stripped of fruit.

**APPEARANCE:** Brownish grey head with pointed crest. Crest may be raised and lowered. Black mask bordered below by white line. Forehead rusty. Chin black. Back and wings greyish brown. Wings have dark grey primaries with white and yellow spots. Secondaries have waxy red tips. Tail brownish grey with yellow tip. Breast greyish brown. Belly grey. Undertail coverts rusty. **Juveniles** greyish brown above with heavily streaked underparts. Small black mask. Pale rust undertail coverts. Wings have white spots and tail tipped with yellow.

▶ Cedar Waxwing smaller and browner with yellowish belly; lacks rusty undertail coverts and distinct white-and-yellow markings on wings.

**VOICE:** Continuous trilled *zzrr zzrr zzrr* that is similar to call of Cedar Waxwing but lower pitched and rougher. Audible only at short distances.

**HABITAT AND BEHAVIOUR:** Breeds in coniferous forest, birch groves, and muskeg; often near water. Widespread in towns and residential areas during winter. Flight active and agile. Hawks for flying insects. Perches in conspicuous locations.

**STATUS:** Rare breeder. Rare to fairly common winter visitor.

# CEDAR WAXWING *Bombycilla cedrorum*

L 15–20 cm / 6–8" Wt 30–36 g / 1.1–1.3 oz

This elegant songbird is named for the distinctive waxy tips on its wings. The function of these structures remains obscure; some ornithologists suggest that they demonstrate social status for mate selection.

**APPEARANCE:** Sleek, brown crest that can be raised or lowered. Sharp, black mask edged with white. Black chin in male; brownish in **female.** Upperparts and breast cinnamon-brown. Pointed dark olive-brown wings have whitish edges and red, waxy tips on secondaries. Rump and uppertail coverts grey. Tail darker grey with yellow tip. Belly yellowish. Undertail coverts white. **Juveniles** greyish brown overall with diffuse streaking, particularly on underparts. Yellow tips on tail feathers. Small black mask.

▶ Bohemian Waxwing larger and greyer above with prominent white, and yellow markings on wings; undertail coverts rusty.

**VOICE:** High-pitched, buzzy lisping *ssse-sssee-seee;* notes sometimes trilled. Calls include blurred, rattling *bzeee* and sharp *chip.*

**HABITAT AND BEHAVIOUR:** Open woodland, old shrubby fields, and brushy riparian areas. Short flights have steady wingbeats. Flaps and glides during longer flight. May briefly hover to pluck fruit. Sometimes fly-catches for insects. Hops quickly along branches. Rarely goes to ground. Feeds in gregarious flocks.

**STATUS:** Common breeder. Common spring and fall migrant. Rare winter visitor.

# BLUE-WINGED WARBLER *Vermivora pinus*

11.0–12.5 cm / 4.4–4.9" Wt 8.5–11.0 g / 0.3–0.4 oz

The Blue-winged Warbler has exhibited dramatic range expansions in the last century. Much of this success has been at the expense of the Golden-winged Warbler, which is more specialized in its habitat requirements.

**APPEARANCE:** Upperparts greenish yellow. Prominent black eye-line. Thin black bill. Bright yellow face and underparts except for white undertail coverts. Crown somewhat greenish in **female.** Wings and tail bluish grey with white wing bars. Tail has white spots on underside. Duller **juveniles** have greenish head with yellow eyebrow.

► Prothonotary Warbler has bright yellow head; lacks black eye-line and white wing bars. Pine and Prairie warblers darker above and lack bright yellow crown and bluish grey wings and tail. Sides and breast streaked. Yellow Warbler has yellow wings and lacks black eye-line; male streaked with chestnut below.

**VOICE:** Song a buzzy *beee-bzzz* that sounds as if inhaled and exhaled. May also sing primary song of Golden-winged Warbler. Calls are variable *chip*s.

**HABITAT AND BEHAVIOUR:** Second-growth forest, swamps, and overgrown fields and pastures. Flight quick and erratic and not prolonged. Often forages head-down in foliage. Frequently observed near the ground.

**STATUS:** Rare to locally uncommon breeder. Rare spring and fall migrant.

# GOLDEN-WINGED WARBLER
*Vermivora chrysoptera*
L 13–14 cm / 5.0–5.5" Wt 8.5–10.0 g / 0.3–0.4 oz

Golden-winged and Blue-winged warblers hybridize to form Lawrence's and Brewster's warblers. Despite plumage differences, there is little genetic distance between the two species. Furthermore, the Golden-winged Warbler occasionally sings the Blue-winged Warbler's primary song.

**APPEARANCE:** Adult male has bright yellow crown and black mask. Conspicuous white eyebrow and moustache. Back and rump unmarked grey. Wings grey with bright yellow wing-patch. Tail grey with white spots usually concealed. Throat and upper breast black. Otherwise, underparts white. **Female** similar but has yellowish olive
crown, grey (not black) facial markings, grey throat, and greyish underparts. **Immatures** resemble female with yellowish green tinge on upperparts and underparts washed with pale yellow.

▶ Blue-winged Warbler has yellow face and underparts. Black eye-line; greyish blue wings have two white wing bars; identification complicated by hybrids intermediate in plumage. Lawrence's Warbler resembles Blue-winged Warbler with black facial pattern of Golden-winged Warbler. Brewster's Warbler grey above and below like Golden-winged Warbler, with yellow crown but black on face restricted to prominent eye-line.

**VOICE:** Unmusical, buzzy *zeee bee bee bee*. Also utters stuttering trill. Call notes include *chip* and *zeee*.

**HABITAT AND BEHAVIOUR:** Damp abandoned fields, wooded swamps, and alder bogs. Raises crown and spreads tail during agonistic encounters.

**STATUS:** Rare to uncommon breeder. Rare spring and fall migrant.

# TENNESSEE WARBLER *Vermivora peregrina*

11.5–12.5 cm / 4.5–4.9" Wt 9.0–10.5 g / 0.3–0.4 oz

Although relatively common, breeding populations of Tennessee Warblers vary considerably from year to year. This species relies heavily on spruce budworm for food when raising young and will migrate to locations where this prey is readily available.

**APPEARANCE:** Breeding male has bluish grey crown, cheeks, and nape. White eyebrow and black eye-line. Thin, black bill. Back, rump, wings, and tail olive-green. Underparts white. Breeding **female** similar but with olive-green cap, yellowish olive upperparts, and yellowish throat and breast. **Winter adults** have greenish yellow upper-parts with yellow eyebrow. Underparts  yellowish except for white undertail coverts. **Immatures** resemble female but with two faint yellowish wing bars.

▶ Male in breeding plumage may be confused with vireos, which are stouter with thicker, hooked bills. Warbling Vireo also has much less green on upperparts. Philadelphia Vireo has yellow breast and sides. Orange-crowned Warbler lacks white eyebrow and bluish grey head; also may have incomplete whitish eye-ring and dusky streaking on breast.

**VOICE:** Male gives accelerating, loud *ticka-ticka-ticka swit-swit-swit-swit chew-chew-chew-chew-chew.* Call notes include high, thin *seet* and rich *chip.*

**HABITAT AND BEHAVIOUR:** Coniferous and mixed woodland. Quick and jerky in flight and while feeding. Usually sings and forages high in forest canopy. Heard more frequently than seen.

**STATUS:** Uncommon to common breeder. Common spring and fall migrant.

# ORANGE-CROWNED WARBLER *Vermivora celata*

L 11–14 cm / 4.3–5.5" Wt 8–11 g / 0.3–0.4 oz

Primarily a western species, this drab little wood-warbler can be found breeding in the boreal forest and on the Hudson Bay Lowlands. It is occasionally recorded as a migrant in southern Ontario en route to wintering grounds in Central America.

**APPEARANCE:** Breeding adults dingy olive-green above; somewhat brighter on rump and uppertail coverts. Greyish olive crown has dark orange-patch that is usually concealed. Crown-patch may be duller or absent in **female.** Thin, pale, broken eye-ring separated by dusky eye-line. No wing bars. Underparts greenish yellow with faint olive streaking. Bill and feet dusky brown. **Winter adults** duller. **Immatures** similar but somewhat greyish overall with yellow undertail coverts.

► Non-breeding and immature Tennessee Warblers similar but can be distinguished by white (not yellow) undertail coverts and lack of streaking on breast. Philadelphia Vireo more contrasting above and below, and has prominent white eyebrow and black eye-line.

**VOICE:** Male gives high-pitched, trilling *chee chee chee chew chew.* End of phrase rises or falls in pitch; highly variable. Call note a sharp *chip.*

**HABITAT AND BEHAVIOUR:** Thickets and woodland groves often associated with watercourses. Flight direct with rapid wingbeats. Hovers briefly when gleaning insects from vegetation. Hops among foliage. Only goes to ground rarely to forage or search for nesting material.

**STATUS:** Uncommon breeder. Rare spring migrant. Uncommon fall migrant.

# NASHVILLE WARBLER *Vermivora ruficapilla* ✓

11.5–12.5 cm / 4.5–5.0" Wt 9–11 g / 0.3–0.4 oz

The female Nashville Warbler constructs her compact nest from mosses, leaves, and grasses. It is usually located on the ground, frequently along streams or near the edges of ponds and marshes.

**APPEARANCE:** Breeding male has bluish grey head with prominent white eye-ring and dull rufous crown-patch (not always visible). Throat yellow. Back, wings, rump, and tail olive-green. Underparts yellow. May be some white on lower belly. **Female** and **winter male** paler with brownish grey heads, light yellow underparts, and buffy eye-rings. **Immatures** duller still with brownish tinge to upperparts and whitish throat. No wing bars or tail spots in any plumage.

▶ Orange-crowned Warbler duller overall with olive-green underparts; lacks conspicuous eye-ring. Tennessee Warbler has white belly and prominent white eye stripe. Connecticut and Mourning Warblers much larger with greyish or brownish hoods that include throat and upper breast. Female Wilson's Warbler has yellow eyebrow but lacks pale eye-ring.

**VOICE:** Male gives two-part song. First part is high-pitched, repeated bi-syllabic phrases, *see-bit see-bit see-bit see-bit,* followed by lower-pitched rapid trill: *ti-ti-ti-ti-ti-ti.* Musical calls include dry *chip,* loud, metallic *tink,* and clear *see* given in flight. Female gives bright *chinck* while foraging.

**HABITAT AND BEHAVIOUR:** Open deciduous and mixed woodlands. Second-growth forest. Flicks and wags tail somewhat while foraging. Sings from within canopy. Often feeds near tips of branches.

**STATUS:** Common breeder. Very common spring and fall migrant.

# NORTHERN PARULA *Parula americana*

L 10.5–12.5 cm / 4.1–4.9" Wt 6–9 g / 0.2–0.3 oz

The dainty Northern Parula occurs from northwestern Ontario south to Florida. However, breeding is rarely observed because this species prefers undisturbed forest, where hanging moss and tendrils obscure the nest.

**APPEARANCE:** Adult male bluish grey above with greenish-patch on back. Incomplete white eye-ring. Blackish wings, with bluish edgings, have two white wing bars. Yellow throat and breast separated by black-and-rufous band. Belly and undertail coverts white. **Female** similar but somewhat duller and lacking breast band. **Immatures** paler with much less distinct markings.

▶ Nashville and immature Mourning Warbler larger with greener upperparts and more extensive yellow on underparts; also lack wing bars.

**VOICE:** Male gives upwardly winding, buzzy song that ends abruptly: *zeeeeeeeee-up.* Also gives series of buzzy notes on one pitch terminated by a trill. Call notes include Yellow Warbler–like *chip* and wispy *seet.*

**HABITAT AND BEHAVIOUR:** Humid deciduous, coniferous, or mixed forest. Flight quick and erratic. Flies high above ground when travelling, but, otherwise, from tree to tree. Hops among vegetation. Forages by gleaning twigs and branches. Sometimes hawks insects in flight.

**STATUS:** Rare to uncommon breeder. Uncommon spring and fall migrant.

Ceska

# YELLOW WARBLER *Dendroica petechia*

12–13 cm / 4.7–5.1" Wt 9–11 g / 0.3–0.4 oz

The Yellow Warbler is a common host of the brood parasitic Brown-headed Cowbird. Rather than abandoning an affected nest, this warbler buries the cowbird's eggs under additional nest linings.

**APPEARANCE:** Adult male has yellowish green upperparts. Indistinct yellow eye-ring surrounds beady black eye. Somewhat darker wing and tail feathers have yellow edges. Two yellow wing bars. Yellow patches on inner webs of tail. Underparts bright yellow with thin chestnut streaks on breast. Adult **female** duller yellowish green. Chestnut streaks

on underparts indistinct or lacking. **Fall and winter adults** somewhat duller. **Immature** male resembles female. Immature female drab olive-green with yellow tail spots restricted to outer feathers.

► Only warbler with yellow patches on inner webs of tail. Female and immature Wilson's Warblers more olive-green above; tail feathers lack yellow spots; all plumages lack yellow wing bars and yellow edges on flight feathers. Orange-crowned Warbler has dusky streaking on breast; also lacks beady-eyed look and yellow on tail and wings.

**VOICE:** Male sings lively, cheerful *tseet-tseet-tseet-sitta-sitta see*. Call notes include short, high-pitched *chip* and *seet*.

**HABITAT AND BEHAVIOUR:** Wet deciduous thickets, overgrown pastures, and gardens. Gleans insects from undersides of leaves. Also fly-catches and hovers to pick prey from surfaces. Hops among vegetation.

**STATUS:** Common breeder. Common spring and fall migrant.

# CHESTNUT-SIDED WARBLER  Cotra
## *Dendroica pensylvanica*
L 11.5–13.5 cm / 4.5–5.3" Wt 10–13 g / 0.4–0.5 oz

The Chestnut-sided Warbler is one of the few neotropical migrants to have benefited from human modifications in central North America. A habitué of scrubby habitats, it has thrived in the successional vegetation that has followed the removal of primordial forest.

**APPEARANCE:** Breeding male has yellow crown, white cheeks and throat, and black lores, eye-line, and malar stripe. Nape, back, and rump black with yellowish stripes. Black wings and tail edged with yellowish green and grey. Two yellow wing bars. Tail has white spots on outer feathers. Underparts whitish with broad chestnut streak on sides and flanks. Breeding **female** similar but duller with less black on face and smaller chestnut stripes. **Fall and winter adults** yellowish green above with pale grey face and bold white eye-ring. Chestnut streak on sides. Two yellow wing bars. Underparts whitish. **Immatures** similar but lack chestnut sides.

▶ Easily identified in all plumages except immature. Bay-breasted Warbler also has chestnut on sides but can be distinguished by dark cheek and crown. Immature Chestnut-sided Warbler more easily confused. Ruby-crowned Kinglet smaller and more energetic; white wing bars. Immature Bay-breasted Warbler has white wing bars and buffy underparts, and lacks grey cheeks.

**VOICE:** Male sings loud, clear *pleased pleased pleased to meet-cha* with descending last note. Call note a rich *chip*.

**HABITAT AND BEHAVIOUR:** Early successional deciduous pastures and forests. Hops on ground and in foliage. Forages by searching undersides of leaves. Climbs inclined branches aided by fluttering wings. Often holds tail above level of back.

**STATUS:** Common breeder. Common spring and fall migrant.

# MAGNOLIA WARBLER *Dendroica magnolia*

L 11–13 cm / 4.3–5.1" Wt 9–14 g / 0.3–0.5 oz

This handsome and conspicuous wood-warbler is better described by its original common name, the "Black-and-yellow Warbler," because it does not frequent magnolia trees but prefers young stands of spruce and hemlock.

**APPEARANCE:** Adult male has grey crown, black mask, and white eyebrow. White crescent below eye. Throat yellow. Back and scapulars blackish. Black wings edged in grey, have conspicuous white-patch. Rump bright yellow. Tail black with large white patch in middle of outer feathers. Breast and belly bright yellow with bold black streaks. Undertail coverts white. Adult **female** similar but duller and more olive than male. Two white wing bars (no patch). **Immatures** and **non-breeding adults** resemble breeding female but with greyish olive unmarked head and upperparts (sometimes spotted), thin, pale eye-ring, faintly streaked sides, and narrow, greyish olive breast band.

▶ Yellow-rumped Warbler lacks yellow underparts in all plumages. Breeding male Cape May Warbler has prominent chestnut cheeks and yellowish neck-patches. Immature Prairie Warbler has dusky jaw stripe and lacks yellow rump; also wags tail.

**VOICE:** Male sings accented *weechy weechy-weechip* with ascending final note. Both male and female give high, buzzy *zee* in flight, and long, nasal *clenk.*

**HABITAT AND BEHAVIOUR:** Second-growth coniferous and mixed forest. Flight direct, usually with tail spread to display white patches. Also droops wings to flash white-patch. Hops among vegetation while foraging.

**STATUS:** Very common breeder. Very common spring and fall migrant.

# CAPE MAY WARBLER *Dendroica tigrina*

L 12–14 cm / 4.7–5.5" Wt 9–11 g / 0.3–0.4 oz

The Cape May Warbler is a spruce budworm specialist. Its population density frequently expands during outbreaks, then declines sharply in subsequent years as its favoured prey species becomes less numerous.

**APPEARANCE:** Breeding male yellowish green above streaked with black; somewhat darker on crown. Chestnut cheek-patch bordered above by yellow eyebrow. Black eye-line. Chin and neck-patch yellow. Blackish wings have prominent white patches. Rump yellow. Short blackish tail. Underparts yellow heavily streaked with black. Breeding **female** similar but lacks chestnut cheek-patch. Underparts paler and less heavily streaked. Adults and **immatures** in fall resemble breeding female but duller olive-grey with brownish spots. Rump greenish yellow. Underparts whitish washed with yellow and streaked with dusky brown. Yellow neck-patch present in all plumages.

▶ Immature Yellow-rumped Warbler larger and lacks yellow neck-patch. Immature Palm Warbler has indistinct streaking on underparts and buffy yellow undertail coverts; usually observed near ground.

**VOICE:** Male sings three to five high-pitched, rising *seet* notes. Notes may be given as couplets: *seetee seetee seetee.* Calls include high, sharp *seet* and descending *tzee tzee.*

**HABITAT AND BEHAVIOUR:** Coniferous forest, particularly spruce. Flight direct with rapid wingbeats. Occasionally hovers while gleaning. Walks rapidly along branches. Hops within foliage.

**STATUS:** Rare to fairly common breeder. Uncommon spring and fall migrant.

# BLACK-THROATED BLUE WARBLER

*Dendroica caerulescens*

12–14 cm / 4.7–5.5" Wt 9–11 g / 0.3–0.4 oz

Male Black-throated Blue Warblers are aggressive defenders of their breeding territories. Boundary disputes, characterized by rapid calling and chasing, may last for hours or days.

♂

**APPEARANCE:** Adult male has dark greyish blue crown and upperparts. Face, throat, and flanks black. Bill black. Wings and tail black with blue edgings. Conspicuous white wing-patch. Also, white patches on outer tail feathers. Lower underparts white. Adult **female** unstreaked olive-green above with somewhat darker and greyer tail and wings. Whitish yellow eyebrow and lower eyelid, black eye-line, and dark brownish cheek-patch. White wing spot at base of primaries sometimes concealed. Underparts buffy yellow. **Immatures** resemble female; however, male may have bluish edging on flight feathers. White spot on wing may be absent.
► Male Cerulean Warbler lacks black face, throat, and flanks; female has bluish grey crown, two white wing bars, and lacks dark cheek-patch.

♀

Philadelphia Vireo and fall Tennessee Warbler distinguished from female and immature Black-throated Blue Warbler by darker green upperparts; also, lack white-patch and dark cheeks.

**VOICE:** Male sings husky, whistling *zur zur zur zreee.* Also utters fast twittering series of trilled notes. Both sexes give flat *ctuk* call note.

**HABITAT AND BEHAVIOUR:** Undergrowth of mature deciduous and mixed forest. Flashes wing spot in flight. Hops on ground and among foliage.

**STATUS:** Fairly common breeder. Fairly common spring and fall migrant.

# YELLOW-RUMPED WARBLER *Dendroica coronata*

L 13–15 cm / 5.1–5.9" Wt 12–14 g / 0.4–0.5 oz

The eastern Myrtle and western Audubon's warblers, collectively called the Yellow-rumped Warbler, were once considered separate species. Studies have demonstrated that they frequently interbreed where their ranges overlap in western Canada.

**APPEARANCE:** Breeding male bluish grey above with bright yellow crown and rump. Black cheeks. Thin white eyebrow and broken eye-ring. Back streaked with black. Greyish wings have two white wing bars. Tail grey with white spots on inner webs of outer feathers. Throat white. Large black breast-patch like inverted "U" extends in streaks to flanks. Conspicuous yellow patch on sides. Belly and undertail coverts white. Breeding **female** similar but brown above with brown or grey cheeks and brownish streaking on underparts. **Winter male** resembles breeding female. **Winter female** and **immatures** duller with somewhat less yellow on crown and sides. Streaking on underparts may be diffuse.

▶ Magnolia and Cape May warblers extensively yellow below in all plumages. Yellow-throated Warbler has yellow throat, prominent white eyebrow, and lacks yellow crown and rump. "Audubon's Warbler" distinguished by yellow throat.

**VOICE:** Male gives somewhat erratic, flat trilling song, *tuwee-tuwee-tuwee,* usually rising in pitch at end. May lack distinctive pattern. Also gives emphatic *chek* and soft, clear *tsee.*

**HABITAT AND BEHAVIOUR:** Mature coniferous and mixed forests. Most flight between and among trees. Climbs vertical tree trunks while foraging.

**STATUS:** Very common breeder. Common to abundant spring and fall migrant.

# BLACK-THROATED GREEN WARBLER F
## *Dendroica virens*
L 11–12 cm / 4.3–4.7" Wt 8.5–11.0 g / 0.3–0.4 oz

Male Black-throated Green Warblers may deliver more than 450 songs per hour. Their active, noisy foraging and aggressive defence behaviour makes them easy to observe.

**APPEARANCE:** Breeding male has yellowish green upperparts. Sides of head and neck lemon yellow. Olive-green streak behind eye. Wings and tail dusky with grey edges. Two white wing bars. Outer tail feathers have white spots. Chin, throat, and breast black. Underparts yellowish white. Sides heavily streaked with black. Breeding **female** similar but with pale yellow chin and throat. Blackish necklace on breast. **Fall and winter adults** have whitish feather tips on underparts that veil black plumage. **Immatures** resemble fall female but somewhat more olive. Sides indistinctly streaked with dusky brown. Black on throat lacking.

► Combination of black throat, yellow face, and white wing bars distinctive. Pine Warbler, Cape May Warbler, and female Blackburnian Warbler yellowish below.

**VOICE:** Male sings husky *zee zee zee zoo zee* or *zoo zee zoo zoo zee. Zoo* notes lower pitched than *zee* notes. Calls include high, thin *seet* and flat *tsip.*

**HABITAT AND BEHAVIOUR:** Coniferous and mixed forest. Flight generally within or between trees. Occasionally flies across open spaces or over water between islands. Hops on ground and within vegetation.

**STATUS:** Common breeder. Very common spring and fall migrant.

# BLACKBURNIAN WARBLER *Dendroica fusca*

L 11.5–14.0 cm / 4.5–5.5" Wt 9.5–11.0 g / 0.3–0.4 oz

The brilliantly coloured Blackburnian Warbler prefers mature forest for nesting. During the breeding season, this insectivorous species relies primarily on caterpillars, such as spruce budworm.

**APPEARANCE:** Breeding male has boldly striped orange and black head. Throat orange. Back black with white streaks. Wings blackish, narrowly edged with grey, with large white wing-patch. Rump black edged with white. Tail black with white spots on outer feathers. Underparts whitish with black streaks on sides and flanks. **Female** and **non-breeding male** similar but with yellow (not orange) head stripes and throat, and brownish olive (not black) face patches and side streaks. Crown-patch obscured. **Immatures** somewhat duller with less yellow on throat.

► Orange-and-black head pattern of breeding male distinctive. Yellow-throated Warbler distinguished from other plumages by grey unstreaked back and prominent white eyebrow. Female and immature Townsend's Warbler lacks whitish streaks on back and median crown stripe.

♂

♀

**VOICE:** Male utters thin, high-pitched songs: *zip zip zip zip zip zip zip zip titittiti tseeeee* and *teetsa teetsa teetsa teetsa.* Calls include various single and double *chip* notes.

**HABITAT AND BEHAVIOUR:** Coniferous and mixed forest, particularly where hemlock present. Generally flies within or between trees, and rarely across small forest clearings. Hops in arboreal vegetation; seldom goes to ground.

**STATUS:** Common breeder. Common spring and fall migrant.

# YELLOW-THROATED WARBLER *Dendroica dominica*

✓ + F

12–14 cm / 4.7–5.5" Wt 9–11 g / 0.3–0.4 oz

The Yellow-throated Warbler forages within the canopy along tree trunks and horizontal branches. It uses its thin bill to probe bark crevices in a manner similar to that of the Brown Creeper.

**APPEARANCE:** Upper-parts grey. Black face has prominent white eyebrow and white crescent beneath eye. Bright yellow chin and throat. White patch on side of neck. Wings and tail greyish black. Two white wing bars. Outer tail feathers have white spots. Lower breast to undertail coverts white. Sides and flanks have bold black streaks. **Female** and **immatures** some-what duller and browner than male.

► Yellow-rumped and Magnolia warblers have conspicuous yellow rumps and lack white neck-patch. Magnolia Warbler more extensively yellow below. Yellow-rumped Warbler has white chin and throat. First-year Blackburnian Warbler lacks white neck-patch and unmarked grey back.

**VOICE:** Male sings loud, clear, slurred series of notes that drop somewhat in pitch, then rise abruptly with last note: *tee-ew tew tew tew tew tew tew wi.* Call notes include sharp, sweet *chip* and loud, high *see.*

**HABITAT AND BEHAVIOUR:** Open deciduous woodlands and groves. Flies from branch to branch with quivering wingbeats. Climbs tree trunks and large limbs like Brown Creeper but moves along horizontal branches by hopping.

**STATUS:** Very rare visitor.

# PINE WARBLER *Dendroica pinus*

L 12.5–14.5 cm / 4.9–5.7" Wt 10–15 g / 0.4–0.5 oz

Pine Warbler populations declined during the 1800s with the removal of pine forests through logging. However, the recent implementation of pine plantations in southwestern counties may be aiding this species' recovery.

**APPEARANCE:** Adult male unstreaked olive above. Indistinct yellowish eyebrow and eye-ring. Ear coverts olive. Blackish wings have two whitish wing bars. Tail black with white spots on outer tips. Chin, throat, and breast yellow. Breast streaked with greenish olive. Belly and undertail coverts white. Black legs. Adult **female** resembles male but greyer above with pale yellow underparts; belly washed with buff. **Immatures** similar but greyish brown above (brown in female) with faint wing bars and dull underparts. Breast and sides may be tinged with yellow.

▶ Yellow-throated Vireo larger with heavier bill, prominent spectacles, grey rump, and unstreaked underparts. Blue-winged Warbler has black eye-line and lacks streaked underparts. Immature Blackburnian, Bay-breasted, and Blackpoll warblers have streaked upperparts. Immature Cape May Warbler has yellow neck spot, pale rump, and heavier streaking below.

**VOICE:** Soft, somewhat leisurely, musical trill on one pitch: *zit zit ziz-ziz-ziz-ziz-ziz-ziz-ziz-ziz.* Call notes soft *chip* and thin, high-pitched *seet.*

**HABITAT AND BEHAVIOUR:** Open pine woodland or deciduous forest with pine groves. Flight direct with several rapid wingbeats followed by brief glide. Hops on ground, through foliage, and up and down tree trunks, sometimes aided with flapping wings. Pumps tail.

**STATUS:** Uncommon to locally common breeder. Rare to uncommon spring and fall migrant.

# KIRTLAND'S WARBLER *Dendroica kirtlandii*

14–15 cm / 5.5–6.0" Wt 12–14 g / 0.4–0.5 oz

Historically a rare species, the endangered Kirtland's Warbler has not bred in Ontario for several decades. Although protected on its remaining nesting grounds in central Michigan, surviving populations likely total fewer than 1000 pairs.

**APPEARANCE:** Adult male has dark bluish grey upperparts (brownish in fall) streaked with black. Face black with white crescents above and below eye. Greyish wings, edged in dull white, have two dull whitish wing bars. Greyish rump and tail. Bright yellow underparts with black streaks at sides of breast. Undertail coverts whitish. **Female** similarly marked but has paler underparts and greyish, not black, face. **Immatures** resemble female but somewhat browner above with less distinct wing bars.

▶ Prairie and Palm warblers more olive above with yellowish faces in all plumages and conspicuous yellow eyebrows. Fall Magnolia Warbler has yellow rump, and prominent white bars and tail spots. Also has white eyebrow during breeding season.

**VOICE:** Clear, emphatic *chip-chip-che-way-o.* Resembles songs of Northern Waterthrush and House Wren. Also utters brief, rapid chattering notes: *chu-chu-chu-chu.* Call note a faint *chip.*

**HABITAT AND BEHAVIOUR:** Extensive stands of young jack pine. Fast, agile flyer through dense foliage. Usually moves along ground or twigs by hopping, but can also run. Bobs tail persistently.

**STATUS:** Very rare spring and fall migrant. Endangered in Ontario and Canada due to loss of habitat.

# PRAIRIE WARBLER *Dendroica discolor*

L 11–13 cm / 4.3–5.1" Wt 7–9 g / 0.25–0.3 oz

Throughout the early 1900s, the Prairie Warbler's range expanded with the regeneration of abandoned agricultural land. More recent redevelopment of this habitat for cottage and recreational uses has caused serious population declines.

**APPEARANCE:** Adult male yellowish green above and bright yellow below. Black eye-line and malar stripe. Indistinct chestnut spots on back. Wings and tail blackish edged with greyish olive. Two yellow wing bars may be difficult to observe. White tail spots visible in flight. Sides and flanks heavily streaked with black. **Female** similar but duller ♀ with less distinct olive (not black) markings. **Immatures** resemble female but are duller still with greyish face.

▶ Palm Warbler has brownish cap; upperparts browner and underparts more extensively streaked with chestnut; also bobs tail. Pine Warbler has white lower belly and undertail coverts; facial markings and streaks on sides much duller. Immature Palm Warbler distinguished by whitish underparts. Immature Magnolia Warbler has yellow rump and dull breast band.

**VOICE:** Thin, buzzy, ascending series of five to sixteen notes: *zee zee zee zee zee zee.* Speed of delivery varies. Call notes include sweet, emphatic *chip* and alert *chek.*

**HABITAT AND BEHAVIOUR:** Brushy pastures, dunes, and regenerating forest. Rapid wingbeats alternate with pauses during which wings folded. May fly-catch while flying from perch to perch. Hops only; does not walk. Bobs tail less frequently than Palm Warbler.

**STATUS:** Rare breeder. Rare spring and fall migrant.

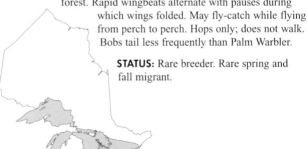

# PALM WARBLER *Dendroica palmarum* F
11.5–14.5 cm / 4.5–5.7" Wt 8–12 g / 0.3–0.4 oz

The Palm Warbler is broadly distributed throughout northern Ontario, primarily in bogs with scattered black spruce. Field identification of this species is facilitated by its habitual tail-wagging behaviour.

**APPEARANCE:** Breeding adults have chestnut crown. Eyebrow and throat yellow. Lores black. Back brown. Wings have two indistinct buffy wing bars. Rump greenish yellow. Blackish brown tail. Throat and undertail coverts bright yellow. Breast and belly white (rarely yellow) streaked with brown. **Immatures** and **winter adults** have streaked brownish crown and whitish eyebrow stripe. Underparts buffy white streaked with dusky brown. Blackish brown wings and tail have paler feather edges. Retain buffy wing bars and yellow undertail coverts.

► Prairie Warbler also wags tail but can be distinguished by bold black moustache and black stripes on sides; lacks chestnut crown. Fall and immature Yellow-rumped Warbler distinguished by bright yellow rump and white undertail coverts.

**VOICE:** Continuous buzzy trill, *tsee tsee tsee tsee tsee tsee tsee tsee,* of four to fourteen syllables given in one pitch. Resembles song of Chipping Sparrow but less energetic. Also utters thin *tsip* and sharper *hick* notes.

**HABITAT AND BEHAVIOUR:** Open coniferous forest usually near water. On breeding grounds, flies generally between elevated song posts. Walks along ground continually wagging tail like a pipit.

**STATUS:** Common breeder. Common spring and fall migrant.

# BAY-BREASTED WARBLER *Dendroica castanea*

L 12.5–15.0 cm / 5–6" Wt 12–15 g / 0.4–0.5 oz

The Bay-breasted Warbler relies heavily on spruce budworm for food during the breeding season. Consequently, its population densities are correlated with the cyclical outbreaks of this insect pest.

**APPEARANCE:** Breeding male has chestnut crown, throat, upper breast, sides, and flanks. Black face. Large buff neck-patches. Otherwise, upperparts greenish grey streaked with black. Two white wing bars. Tail has small white spots. Underparts buffy white. **Female** similar but much paler. Throat white. Buff neck-patch inconspicuous. **Immatures** and **non-breeding adults** have greenish grey upperparts and buff, unstreaked underparts. Two white wing bars. Flanks washed with pale chestnut. Undertail coverts buff. Dark legs and feet.

♂

► Breeding Chestnut-sided Warbler has yellow crown and large white cheek-patch. Non-breeding Blackpoll Warbler distinguished by streaked underparts, pinkish legs, and white undertail coverts; also lacks chestnut flanks.

♀

**VOICE:** Male gives very high-pitched, lispy *seetzy-seetzy-seetzy-see* uttered rapidly. Resembles song of Black-and-white Warbler. Call notes include loud, buzzy *sip* or *seee* and sharp, metallic *chip*.

**HABITAT AND BEHAVIOUR:** Coniferous forest. Mixed forest during migration. Hops rapidly among branches while foraging. Stops to peer in all directions. Occasionally wags or flicks tail in shallow up-down movement.

**STATUS:** Fairly common breeder. Common spring and fall migrant.

# BLACKPOLL WARBLER *Dendroica striata*

12.5–15.0 cm / 5–6" Wt 12–14 g / 0.4–0.5 oz

Blackpoll Warblers migrate over 8000 km (5000 miles) from arctic and subarctic breeding grounds to winter in Brazil. Some individuals breeding in northeastern Canada travel over the Atlantic Ocean with a brief stopover in Bermuda.

**APPEARANCE:** Breeding male has black cap and malar stripe. White cheeks. Olive-grey upperparts streaked with black. Wings black with two white bars. Black tail has white spots near tip. Underparts white with black stripes on sides and flanks. Legs pinkish. Adult **female** olive-grey above. Blackish streaks on crown and back. Pale eyebrow. Dark malar streaking. Whitish wing bars and tail spots. Underparts whitish with buffy wash and narrow black streaking. **Non-breeding male** resembles female but with yellowish wash on underparts and face. Less prominent streaks on crown. Dark eye-line. **Immatures** duller overall with reduced streaking and, occasionally, dark legs.

♂

♀

▶ Black-and-white Warbler has a black-and-white striped crown. Accidental Black-throated Gray Warbler has black cheek-patch. Non-breeding and immature Bay-breasted Warbler yellowish green above with buffy sides and undertail coverts; dark legs. Immature Pine Warbler has unstreaked greyish brown back, and dark legs and ear coverts.

**VOICE:** Very high-pitched, staccato *tsit tsit tsit tsit tsit tsit.* Call notes include loud *smack,* high *see,* and sharp *chip.*

**HABITAT AND BEHAVIOUR:** Coniferous forest. Flight speed during migration 38–43 km/h (23–26 mph) at altitudes of 400–6000 m (1300–19,500'). Moves slowly along branches while foraging.

**STATUS:** Fairly common breeder. Common spring and fall migrant.

# CERULEAN WARBLER *Dendroica cerulea*

L 10.0–12.5 cm / 3.9–4.9" Wt 8.5–10.5 g / 0.3–0.4 oz

During the 1800s, the Cerulean Warbler was considered a "regular summer resident" in southern Ontario. Extensive clearing of mature deciduous forest for agricultural purposes undoubtedly caused the decline in population densities.

**APPEARANCE:** Adult male light blue above, brightest on crown. Blackish streaks on back. Wings and tail blackish, edged with blue. Two white wing bars. Underparts white with narrow blackish band across upper breast. Sides and flanks streaked with black. Adult **female** has dull bluish green crown blending to olive-green on remainder of upperparts. Dull white eyebrow. Wings and tail blackish, edged with olive. Two white wing bars. Underparts dull white, tinged with yellow, with diffuse olive streaking on sides. **Immatures** resemble female but somewhat more greenish above and yellowish below. Immature male slightly more blue above with indistinct breast band.

♂

♀

▶ Male Black-throated Blue Warbler has black mask and throat. Female Black-throated Blue and Tennessee warblers lack wing bars. Non-breeding Blackpoll Warbler resembles female Cerulean Warbler but has greener, streaked upperparts.

**VOICE:** Song a rapid, enthusiastic series of three to five short notes on same pitch followed by higher, drawn-out note: *zray zray zray zray zray zreeee.* Resembles songs of Northern Parula and Black-throated Blue Warbler.

**HABITAT AND BEHAVIOUR:** Mature deciduous forest, particularly in river valleys. Nests and forages high in the forest canopy. Gleans and hawks for insects.

**STATUS:** Rare to uncommon breeder. Rare to uncommon spring and fall migrant. Vulnerable in Ontario and Canada due to habitat loss.

# BLACK-AND-WHITE WARBLER *Mniotilta varia* ✓+F

11–13 cm / 4.3–5.1" Wt 9–14 g / 0.3–0.5 oz

The Black-and-white Warbler's scientific name, which means "variegated moss-plucker," accurately describes its distinctive foraging strategy. This species creeps along tree trunks and limbs in nuthatch-like fashion using its decurved bill to probe the bark.

**APPEARANCE:** Adult male has black crown with central white stripe. Eyebrow, malar stripe, and eye-ring white. Black cheeks and throat. Neck and back striped black and white. Two white wing bars on black wings. Tail black with white spots. Underparts white with bold black streaks on breast and sides. Adult **female** resembles male, but with pale grey cheeks, white throat, and dull black neck and back. Underparts white with diffuse greyish streaking on sides. **Immatures** somewhat browner above and buffier below with more heavily streaked sides.

♂

► Male Blackpoll Warbler has solid black crown, white cheeks and throat, and lacks white eye-stripe; dull olive female lacks bold streaking. Male Black-throated Gray

♀

Warbler has solid black cap, broad black cheek-patch, and grey back; female and immatures duller overall with white throat.

**VOICE:** High-pitched, thin, repetitive *weesee weesee weesee* resembles sound of wet rag cleaning glass. Call notes include sharp *chip* and weak *tsit*.

**HABITAT AND BEHAVIOUR:** Mature and second-growth deciduous and mixed forest. Moves upward, downward, and sideways on trunks and limbs. Also gleans from foliage but rarely hovers.

**STATUS:** Common breeder. Common spring and fall migrant.

Castle

# AMERICAN REDSTART *Setophaga ruticilla* F

L 11–13 cm / 4.3–5.1" Wt 6–9 g / 0.2–0.3 oz

Noted ornithologist Frank M. Chapman once described the American Redstart as the "village belle with coquettishly held skirts tripping the mazes of a country dance," a quaint but apt image of the pretty wing-and-tail fanning behaviour of this colourful bird as it forages.

**APPEARANCE:** Adult male black with bright orange patches on wings and base of tail. Two central tail feathers black. Sides and flanks bright orange. Lower belly white. **Female** has grey head. Back and rump olive-grey. Sides and flanks yellow. Underparts dull white. Wing and tail pattern like male's except with yellow spots on olive-grey ground. **Immatures** resemble female but somewhat browner and paler. **First-year male** similar to female but with orangish markings and some black feathers on body.
▶ Distinctive in all plumages.

♂

♀

**VOICE:** Loud, clear, high-pitched *zweet zweet* repeated several times in one pitch. Male utters sweet, canary-like song in flight: *che-wee-che-wee-chee-chee*. Call notes include metallic *chip*.

**HABITAT AND BEHAVIOUR:** Deciduous woodlands and shrubby second-growth forest, frequently associated with water. Hops and flies rapidly between perches. Fans wings and tail, apparently flushing insects from vegetation. Also makes acrobatic flycatcher-like aerial sallies.

**STATUS:** Common breeder. Common spring and fall migrant.

# PROTHONOTARY WARBLER *Protonotaria citrea*

14 cm / 5.5" Wt 14–16 g / 0.5–0.6 oz

This delightful wood-warbler was named for its striking plumage, which resembles robes worn by papal clerks, or prothonotaries. It is listed as endangered in Canada owing to loss of both breeding and wintering habitat.

**APPEARANCE:** Adult male has bright orangish yellow head, breast, and belly. Conspicuous black eyes. Back greenish olive. Wings and rump grey. Tail black, edged with grey. Tail feathers, except central pair, have large white patches. Lower belly and undertail coverts white with yellowish wash. **Female** resembles male but with greenish olive wash on

head, nape, and neck, and smaller tail-patches. **Immatures** resemble adults of their sex but somewhat duller. Wings have two olive wing bars.

► Male Yellow Warbler more extensively yellowish, particularly on upperparts; also has chestnut streaks on breast and belly; female has greenish yellow back, wings, and tail; flight feathers edged with yellow; tail has yellow spots. Blue-winged Warbler has greenish nape, black eye-line, and bold, white wing bars.

**VOICE:** Simple series of loud, clear *zweet* notes repeated many times in one pitch. Resembles call of Solitary Sandpiper. Male sings *chwee-chwee-chwee-chwee teer teer teer* during display flight. Call note a loud *tschip.*

**HABITAT AND BEHAVIOUR:** Wooded swamps. Flight somewhat undulating. Usually flies within or below canopy, occasionally above during display. Climbs up tree trunks.

**STATUS:** Very rare breeder and spring and fall migrant in Ontario. Endangered in Canada.

# WORM-EATING WARBLER *Helmitheros vermivorus*

L 12–14 cm / 4.7–5.5" Wt 18–22 g / 0.6–0.8 oz

The Worm-eating Warbler gleans insects and spiders from both suspended clusters of dead leaves and ground leaf litter. Its heavy reliance on caterpillars (once known as "worms") during spring and summer accounts for its vernacular name.

**APPEARANCE:** Buffy head with two black stripes and black line through each eye. Back, wings, and tail dull greyish olive. No wing bars or tail spots. Underparts buff. Legs yellowish pink. **Immatures** similar but somewhat browner overall with dusky brown head stripes.

► Swainson's Warbler has plain rufous brown crown, pale eyebrow, and thin, dark eye-line; also has somewhat browner upperparts.

**VOICE:** Male gives sweet, high, insect-like trills about two seconds in duration. Resembles song of Chipping Sparrow. Call notes include sharp, loud *chip* and buzzy *tseet.*

**HABITAT AND BEHAVIOUR:** Large tracts of mature deciduous and mixed forest, particularly on hillsides and ravines. Flight direct, usually within the canopy. Hops and flits from branch to branch and along the ground. Nests on the ground under dense, low vegetation.

**STATUS:** Very rare visitor from April to October.

## OVENBIRD *Seiurus aurocapillus*  F

14.0–16.5 cm / 5.5–6.6" Wt 18–22 g / 0.6–0.8 oz

...s oven-shaped domed nest of leaves and grasses gives this species its ommon name. The well-camouflaged structure is often built under a re-existing tent of vegetation.

**APPEARANCE:** Upper-arts unmarked olive-reen. Crown has orange tripe delimited by broad, ark brown stripes. Prominent white eye-ing. White throat ordered with thin, dark rown lines. Breast and elly whitish heavily marked with elongated ark brown spots. Flanks ale olive-green. Undertail coverts white. ong, slender, dark bill.

**Immatures** much browner with less distinct markings.

▶ Plumage similar to that of Wood and Hermit thrushes, but Ovenbird much smaller. Northern and Louisiana waterthrushes have rownish upperparts, broad white eyebrows, and lack orange crown.

**VOICE:** Loud, emphatic, ringing *teach-er teach-er teach-er* is highly variable among males. Flight song given as part of aerial courtship isplay, commonly at twilight, is rapid jumble of warbling notes (*ple-leep ple-bleep*), usually ending in *teach-er teach-er.* Call notes at nest sharp *cheep* or *chock*.

**HABITAT AND BEHAVIOUR:** Dense woodlands with little understorey. Flight low and steady; manoeuvres quickly among trees. Walks on forest loor to forage among leaf litter. Does not hop. Pumps tail up and down n a wave-like fashion. Sometimes holds tail high and droops wings.

**STATUS:** Common breeder. Common spring and fall migrant.

# NORTHERN WATERTHRUSH *Seiurus noveboracensis*

*[handwritten: νοῦἐο-]*

L 12.5–15.0 cm / 5–6" Wt 15–18 g / 0.5–0.6 oz

The Northern Waterthrush is not a thrush but a large wood-warbler. It common name accurately suggests its propensity for water.

**APPEARANCE:** Upperparts unmarked olive-brown. Narrow eyebrow stripe yellowish or buff bordered below with dusky olive streak. Throat yellowish or off-white and finely spotted. Underparts generally yellowish (rarely white) with sharp, dark brown spots and streaks. Spots may form brown necklace on throat. Bill and legs brown. Tail olive-brown with white tips on outer feathers. **Immatures** similar but with more mottled upperparts. Buffy tips on tertiaries. Underparts yellowish with less defined streaks. Lack white tips on outer tail feathers.

▶ Similar to Louisiana Waterthrush, which is whiter above with brighter eye-line; underparts have lighter, less defined streaks; also ha pinkish, not brown, legs. Northern Waterthrush lacks pinkish buff was on flanks and breast. Ovenbird more olive with orange-and-brown crown; walks with tail held up.

**VOICE:** Primary song of male loud, ringing, rapid *sweet sweet sweet swee wee wee chew chew chew chew.* Only last notes are audible from distance. In flight, gives loud, sharp *chip*s of increasing frequency.

**HABITAT AND BEHAVIOUR:** Cool forested wetlands, brushy bogs, an streamside thickets. Bounding flight generally between canopy and understorey. May hover to glean insects from twigs and leaves. Continually bobs and wags tail down-up-down while walking.

**STATUS:** Common breeder. Common spring an fall migrant.

costa

# OUISIANA WATERTHRUSH *Seiurus motacilla*
15 cm / 6"  Wt 20–22 g / 0.7–0.8 oz

he drab plumage of this wood-warbler contrasts remarkably with its
ear, ringing song, which is often loud enough to be heard above the
shing streams of its preferred woodland habitat.

**PPEARANCE:** Upper-
rts plain greyish olive.
/ide, white eyebrow
ripe extending to nape.
alar region white,
ecked with olive.
hroat white, sometimes
nely spotted. Bill dark
own near base with
ack tip. Underparts
hitish and washed with
uff on flanks. Breast
d belly streaked with
reyish olive. Legs
nkish. **Immatures**
milar but have buffier eye-stripe and flanks, and more distinct
reaking on underparts.

► Distinguished from Northern Waterthrush by larger bill, whiter
ot yellowish) eye-stripe, and less streaking on throat and underparts.
venbird has olive-green plumage and white eye-ring. Thrushes much
rger and lack white eye-stripe.

**OICE:** Loud, whistled *see-you see-you see-you chew chew to-wee.*
hree slurred introductory notes distinctive. Somewhat higher pitched
nd given more emphatically than song of Northern Waterthrush. Call
otes sharp, metallic *chip,* soft *zizz,* and sputtering *churr-churr-churr.*

**ABITAT AND BEHAVIOUR:** Deep forested ravines with running
treams. Flight direct and bounding. Territorial encounters involve
uick, veering chases through vegetation. Teeters and bobs when
walking; constantly wags tail up and down.

**STATUS:** Rare breeder. Rare spring and fall
migrant. Vulnerable in Ontario and Canada due
to loss of habitat.

# KENTUCKY WARBLER *Oporornis formosus*

L 12.5–14.5 cm / 4.9–5.7" Wt 12–15 g / 0.4–0.5 oz

The Kentucky Warbler is a persistent vocalist that usually delivers its song from shrubbery. Consequently, this commonly heard but infrequently seen species is best identified by its vocalizations.

**APPEARANCE:** Upperparts unmarked olive-green. Blackish crown. Yellow spectacles and broad black sideburns extending down from eyes. No wing bars or tail spots. Underparts yellow. **Female** has somewhat greyer crown and smaller sideburns. **Immatures** similar but slightly more brownish above with reduced or absent sideburns.

► Male Common Yellowthroat has black mask that covers eyes; both sexes have white or buffy (not yellow) bellies; female lacks yellow spectacles. Female Hooded Warbler has entirely yellow face framed with blackish feathering, and white tail spots. Canada Warbler grey above with necklace of black streaks on throat and breast.

**VOICE:** Male sings series of bi-syllabic chanting notes repeated five to ten times: *tor-ry tor-ry tor-ry tor-ry tor-ry tor-ry.* Similar to Carolina Wren but quieter and somewhat less musical. Call notes include low-pitched *chuck* and metallic *chip.*

**HABITAT AND BEHAVIOUR:** Woodland undergrowth. Flight straight, not undulating. Most often observed on the ground. Walks and hops. Moves with short hops or flights within vegetation.

**STATUS:** Very rare spring visitor. Extremely rare fall visitor.

# CONNECTICUT WARBLER *Oporornis agilis*

13.5–15.0 cm / 5.3–5.9" Wt 14–16 g / 0.5–0.6 oz

The common name of the Connecticut Warbler is a misnomer as it is neither a breeder nor a common migrant in the state. However, like many North American birds, this species was named after the location where it was first discovered by scientists.

**APPEARANCE:** Complete white or buffy white eye-ring and very long undertail coverts. Breeding male has slate-grey hood (greyish olive in non-breeding male). Otherwise, upperparts olive with somewhat darker wings and tail. Lower breast through undertail coverts yellow. Long, pinkish legs. **Female** like male but duller and paler. Hood brownish grey with

brownish olive throat. **Immatures** have less distinct brownish hood that blends with brownish olive upperparts. Underparts dull yellow with brownish buff throat.

► Mourning Warbler has greyish hood but lacks conspicuous, complete eye-ring; male has blackish throat; immatures have incomplete eye-ring and yellowish throat. Much smaller Nashville Warbler has eye-ring but lacks hood; underparts yellowish from chin to undertail coverts. Accidental MacGillivray's Warbler has bold, incomplete eye-ring and short undertail coverts. Male has dark grey hood; female and immatures have grey throats.

**VOICE:** Loud, ringing song: *tu-chibee-too chibee-too chibee-too.* Call notes include sharp *peek,* metallic *plink,* and soft *poit.*

**HABITAT AND BEHAVIOUR:** Spruce bogs and other open forests with well-developed understorey. Flies nimbly through vegetation. Walks on ground or branches with bouncy gait (Mourning Warbler hops). Raises and lowers tail rapidly.

**STATUS:** Rare to uncommon breeder. Rare spring and fall migrant.

# MOURNING WARBLER *Oporornis philadelphia*

L 10–15 cm / 3.9–5.9" Wt 11–14 g / 0.4–0.5 oz

Nesting Mourning Warblers are often difficult to observe. Rather than flying from the nest when disturbed, these skulky birds walk stealthily away.

**APPEARANCE:** Adult male has slate-grey hood on head and throat. Some individuals have incomplete white eye-ring. Otherwise, upperparts olive-green. Underparts yellow except for black "bib" on breast. Bib less distinct in winter. **Female** resembles male but somewhat duller with lighter grey hood. Also, lack black patch on breast. Faint, pale eye-ring may be present. **Immatures** olive-green above and yellowish below. Dull greyish olive hood often difficult to observe. Incomplete pale yellow eye-ring.

▶ Connecticut and accidental MacGillivray's warblers similar but have prominent white eye-rings. Connecticut Warbler also larger and lacks black bib. Female Common Yellowthroat resembles immature Mourning Warbler but is somewhat smaller with whitish belly.

**VOICE:** Male sings rhythmic *churry churry churry churry chorry chorry. Chorry* notes lower in pitch. Calls include loud, harsh *tshrip* and higher *tsip*. Calls rougher than those of Connecticut Warbler but less rough than MacGillivray's Warbler.

**HABITAT AND BEHAVIOUR:** Clearings, open woodland, and forest edges. Generally short, rapid flights among and between foliage. Hops on ground and along branches in undergrowth. Flips wings and tail during agonistic encounters.

**STATUS:** Common breeder. Common spring and fall migrant.

# COMMON YELLOWTHROAT *Geothlypis trichas*

11–13 cm 4.3–5.1" Wt 9–11 g 0.3–0.4 oz

The Common Yellowthroat delivers a loud song that is easily identifiable at a distance. During breeding season, the male sings from prominent song posts, including cattails and tall shrubs.

**APPEARANCE:** Adult male plain brownish olive above. Broad black mark bordered above by pale bluish grey band. Bright yellow throat and breast. Flanks buffy brown. Belly white. Undertail coverts yellow. **Female** resembles male but lacks black mask. Face brownish olive with dingy whitish eye-ring. **Immatures** duller and browner overall. Immature male may have hint of black mask. Immature female may have only pale yellow tinge to throat.

♂

► Adult male distinctive. Kentucky Warbler resembles immature male but has conspicuous yellow spectacles and entirely yellow underparts. Female Nashville Warbler has bluish crown and prominent white eye-ring. Connecticut and Mourning warblers have greyish hoods.

♀

**VOICE:** Male sings bright, quick series of twenty-five or more *witchity-witchity-witchity* notes. May be considerable individual variation. Call note a sharp, husky *tcheck.*

**HABITAT AND BEHAVIOUR:** Marshes, streams, wet thickets, and brushy pastures. Flights usually short and direct. Hops along branches or shuffles sideways to reach food. Usually hops on ground; occasionally walks.

**STATUS:** Very common breeder. Very common spring and fall migrant.

# HOODED WARBLER *Wilsonia citrina*

L 12.5–14.5 cm / 5.0–5.7" Wt 9.5–12.0 g / 0.3–0.4 oz

The Hooded Warbler is an "area-sensitive" species that breeds only in larger tracts of mature forest. Its numbers have declined considerably because of forest fragmentation due to agriculture and urbanization.

**APPEARANCE:** Adult male olive-green above with contrasting black hood enclosing bright yellow forehead and cheeks. Breast, belly, and undertail coverts bright yellow. Tail has large white spots on outer feathers, visible when tail fanned. Adult **female** similar but lacks hood, although yellow face may be sharply outlined in black in some females. **Immatures** resemble female but duller.

♂

► Male distinctive. Female similar to female Wilson's Warbler, but latter is smaller and lacks white tail spots. Other olive-and-yellow female warblers have white eye-rings.

**VOICE:** Clear, ringing song, *weeta weeta wee-tee-o,* with *tee* much higher pitched. Similar to Magnolia Warbler's song but louder and more

♀

emphatic. Hooded Warbler also gives fast, repeated *chippity-chup* followed by low, harsh *zrrr.*

**HABITAT AND BEHAVIOUR:** Shrubby clearings in mature deciduous or mixed woodland. Flight direct; can hover and fly in downward spiral while foraging. Frequently fans tail to reveal large white tail spots.

**STATUS:** Rare breeder. Rare spring and fall migrant. Threatened in Canada due to loss of habitat.

# WILSON'S WARBLER *Wilsonia pusilla* *Costa*

10–12 cm / 3.9–4.7" Wt 5.5–8.5 g / 0.2–0.3 oz

his "busy" little wood-warbler exhibits many characteristic behaviours, ncluding lateral tail-flicking, tail-waving, and wing-flashing. In flight, : demonstrates great agility with aerial cartwheels and fluttering sallies o capture flying insects.

**APPEARANCE:** Breeding nale has glossy black crown. Forehead, yebrow, lores, and nderparts bright yellow. Conspicuous black eyes. Jpperparts and ear overts unmarked ellowish olive-green. Adult **female** similar but uller overall. Crown-atch usually olive or lack heavily mottled vith olive. **Winter male** esembles female.

**immatures** similar to adults of same gender but duller. Crown-patch maller and more olive in coloration.

▶ Black crown of male distinctive. Yellow Warbler distinguished rom female and immatures by two yellow wing bars, yellow spots on ail, and absence of tail-waving. Female and immature Hooded Warblers have larger bill, dusky lores, darkish border between ear overts and nape, and white in tail. Orange-crowned Warbler much uller overall with finely streaked underparts, shorter tail, and longer, more pointed bill.

**VOICE:** Loud, rapid chattering that drops in pitch: *chi chi chi chi chet het.* Call note a soft, nasal ringing *chip.*

**HABITAT AND BEHAVIOUR:** Boggy areas or clearings in wet woodlands. Flight direct with rapid wingbeats. Hops restlessly between perches.

**STATUS:** Fairly common breeder. Fairly common spring and fall migrant.

# CANADA WARBLER *Wilsonia canadensis*

L 12–15 cm / 4.7–5.9" Wt 9.5–12.5 g / 0.3–0.4 oz

Archaic vernacular names for this species include the Canadian Flycatcher and Canadian Flycatching Warbler. These reflect only one of the many ways that this active wood-warbler procures its food.

**APPEARANCE:** Adult male has bluish grey upperparts. Forehead, lores, and sides of face black. Yellow stripe above lores. Yellowish white eye-ring. Wings and tail greyish black narrowly edged with bluish grey. Underparts bright yellow, except white undertail coverts. Necklace of short, black stripes on upper breast. Adult **female** similar to  male but duller overall with greyish facial markings and fainter greyish olive necklace. **Immatures** resemble adults of respective genders but somewhat duller with less distinct facial pattern and necklace.

▶ Kentucky Warbler distinguished by olive upperparts, yellow undertail coverts, and lack of necklace. Immature Canada Warbler resembles immature Wilson's Warbler but latter is more olive above and lacks necklace.

**VOICE:** Variable, staccato song, *chip chupety swee-ditchety,* given persistently by male. Call notes include subdued *chip,* loud, sharp *check,* and high-pitched *zzee.* Wings *whirr* when fly-catching.

**HABITAT AND BEHAVIOUR:** Undergrowth of mature woodlands. Flight direct. Hops and climbs along branches. Holds tail cocked and flicks wings while gleaning foliage or foraging on ground for insects and spiders.

**STATUS:** Fairly common breeder. Common spring and fall migrant.

# YELLOW-BREASTED CHAT *Icteria virens*

17–20 cm / 6.7–7.9" Wt 24–30 g / 0.9–1.1 oz

The Yellow-breasted Chat combines the curious, flitting behaviour typical of wood-warblers with a somewhat unwarbler-like size. In Ontario, the breeding range of this species is restricted to the deciduous forests of the extreme south.

**APPEARANCE:** Chunky wood-warbler with heavy dark bill and long tail. Upperparts olive-green. White spectacles and black lores (greyish in **female**). Chin, throat, and breast bright yellow. No wing bars. Belly and undertail coverts white. **Immatures** resemble adults.

► Large size distinctive among warblers. Other olive green-and-yellow warbler species, such as Common Yellowthroat, Kentucky Warbler, and Wilson's Warbler, much smaller.

**VOICE:** Varied song consists of jumbled rattles, whistles, and squawks usually given from within thick brambles or shrubs. Sometimes uttered during hovering display flight. Suggests Gray Catbird or Northern Mockingbird with limited repertoire; single *whoit* or *chack* notes distinctive.

**HABITAT AND BEHAVIOUR:** Thickets, briars, and tangled vegetation. Rarely seen away from cover. Typically thrashes noisily in underbrush. Gleans insects from low vegetation.

**STATUS:** Very rare breeder. Rare spring and fall migrant. Vulnerable in Ontario and Canada.

# SUMMER TANAGER *Piranga rubra*

L 18–19 cm / 7.0–7.7" Wt 23–25 g / 0.8–0.9 oz

The Summer Tanager is considered a rare visitor to southern Ontario. However, a few observations of singing males and courting pairs suggest that this species may have nested in the province.

♂

**APPEARANCE:** Adult male bright red with slightly duller wings and tail. Bill yellowish. **Female** has yellowish green upperparts. Somewhat more yellow on crown and rump. Pale yellow bill. Back sometimes greyish. Underparts dull yellow tinged with olive-green on sides. **Immature** male similar to female with variable pinkish orange wash on foreparts and tail coverts. **Second-year male** resembles adult male but duller, paler, and more yellowish.

▶ Scarlet Tanager male distinguished by black wings and tail. Female Scarlet Tanager greener above with blackish brown wings. Male Western Tanager predominantly yellow with red face; female has dark grey wings with two prominent wing bars and dark grey tail. Female orioles have wing bars.

**VOICE:** Musical, rolling song with sweet, clear phrases, *hee para vee-er chewit terwee hee para vee-er.* Also gives rattling, dry *pit-a-chuck,* occasionally extended to *pik-i-tuck-i-tuck.*

♀

**HABITAT AND BEHAVIOUR:** Deciduous forest, often near gaps or along edges. Flight swift and direct; bursts of wingbeats alternate with brief pauses.

**STATUS:** Very rare spring and fall visitor. Occasional summer visitor.

# SCARLET TANAGER *Piranga olivacea*

16–17 cm / 6.3–6.7" Wt 23–36 g / 0.8–1.3 oz

This species is highly sensitive to forest fragmentation and the corresponding increase in nest predation and brood parasitism. Woodlots smaller than 3 hectares (7.4 acres) generally will not support breeding Scarlet Tanagers.

**APPEARANCE:** Breeding male bright red with black wings and tail. Bill pale grey. Adult **female** olive-green above. Bill pale olive-grey. Wings and tail brownish olive edged with green. Underparts olive-yellow; undertail coverts somewhat brighter. Underwing coverts white. **Non-breeding male** resembles female but with brighter green back and richer yellow underparts. Plumage mottled red and green during moults. **Immatures** similar to female; however, **first-year male** may be somewhat orangish with dark brown wings and tail.

♂

► Male Summer Tanager has reddish wings and tail; female and immatures browner above with less-contrasting wings and tail; underwing coverts yellow. Female Western Tanager has white-and-yellow wing bars. Male Northern Cardinal has crest, red wings and tail, and black mask.

♀

**VOICE:** Song a series of four to five short, nasal syllables, *querit queer queery querit,* which resembles hoarse American Robin. Call a variable, high-pitched *chip-churr* accompanied by dipping of tail.

**HABITAT AND BEHAVIOUR:** Dense mature forest. Flight strong, swift, and direct. Wingbeats alternate with brief pauses. Wings held close to body during glides. Hops and walks between perches and on ground. Climbs vertically on tree trunks.

**STATUS:** Fairly common breeder. Fairly common spring and fall migrant.

# WESTERN TANAGER *Piranga ludoviciana*

L 16.5–19.5 cm / 6.5–7.7" Wt 24–36 g / 0.9–1.3 oz

A casual visitor to Ontario, the Western Tanager breeds as far east as Manitoba. Despite showy plumage and strong song, its sluggish nature and tendency to remain among foliage make it difficult to observe.

**APPEARANCE:** Breeding male has yellow nape, rump, and underparts. Face bright red. Bill dull yellow. Back, wings, and tail black. Wings have yellow upper and white lower wing bars. **Winter male** washed with olive and dusky brown. Usually lacks red face. **Female** dull olive green above with greyer back and yellowish rump. Underparts variable from bright to greyish yellow. Wings and tail dusky olive. Wings have two yellowish white wing bars. **Immatures** resemble female but male is brighter overall.

♂

▶ Adult male distinctive. Female and immature distinguished from other tanagers by presence of wing bars. Few immature Scarlet Tanagers have two yellowish wing bars but can be distinguished by "saddle-backed" look of Western

♀

Tanager's grey back and paler head and rump. Female orioles have pale faces and tails, and long, pointed bills.

**VOICE:** Deliberate *pir-ri pir-ri pee-wi pir-ri pee-wi* resembles song of American Robin but hoarser and lower pitched. Also utters soft, whistling *fu-weet* and purring *tu-weep.* Call an explosive, slurred *pit-ick.*

**HABITAT AND BEHAVIOUR:** Open coniferous and mixed woodlands. Flight strong and swift with rapid, powerful wingbeats. Hops on ground and in vegetation.

**STATUS:** Rare visitor fall to spring

# EASTERN TOWHEE *Pipilo erythrophthalmus*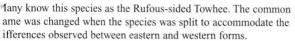
18–21 cm / 7.0–8.5" Wt 36–43 g / 1.3–1.5 oz

Many know this species as the Rufous-sided Towhee. The common name was changed when the species was split to accommodate the differences observed between eastern and western forms.

**APPEARANCE:** Red eyes. Male has black hood, upper breast, and upperparts. Sides and flanks rufous. Wings have small white patch at base of primaries and edging on inner wing feathers. Tail black with large white spots at corners visible from below or in flight. Lower breast and belly white. Undertail coverts buff. **Female** brown where male is black and has smaller tail spots. **Juveniles** sparrow-like with heavily streaked cinnamon brown upperparts and buffy underparts. Eyes brown. Tail blackish in male, brownish in female. **First-winter** and **second-summer males** have black-and-brown wing coverts.

▶ Scapulars and wings of accidental Spotted Towhee more extensively spotted; adult female somewhat darker than female Eastern Towhee with greyish black or brownish black upperparts.

**VOICE:** Primary song of male a distinctive, musical *drink-your-teeeeeee.* Female utters prolonged whinny, *tititititetetecteetectectee,* and husky, flat *shreeeee* trills. Alarm calls include scratchy *tow-hee* and screaming *chewink.*

**HABITAT AND BEHAVIOUR:** Deciduous thickets, woodland edges and openings. Flight variable, both direct and undulating. Hops deliberately on ground. Scratches leaf litter with both feet with backward hop.

**STATUS:** Uncommon breeder. Uncommon spring and fall migrant.

# AMERICAN TREE SPARROW *Spizella arborea*

L 14.5–16.5 cm / 5.5–6.5" Wt 15–20 g / 0.5–0.7 oz

Cool October weather brings these handsome sparrows south from their Hudson Bay and James Bay breeding grounds. They remain in southern Ontario long enough to greet spring with their beautiful songs, then return to their northern home in April or May to breed.

**APPEARANCE:** Crown and eye-stripe chestnut. Remainder of head, neck, and throat grey. Back and shoulders streaked with black, buff, and brown. Wings tinged with chestnut and have two conspicuous white wing bars. Rump brown. Tail dusky with outer tail feathers edged in white. Breast and belly greyish white to buff with dusky central breast spot. Also, small chestnut patch on each side of breast. Upper mandible dusky to black. Lower mandible yellow. **Juveniles** similar but with streaked breast, flanks, and crown.

▶ Distinguishable from other sparrows by breast spot, chestnut cap, and yellow lower bill. Chipping Sparrow has black eye-line. Field Sparrow has white eye-ring and pinkish bill.

**VOICE:** Only male sings. Variable song clear and sweet; first two note usually higher: *tsi-tsi-tsweeee-tswee-tswee-tswee-tswit-tswit-sut.* Both sexes utter excited, musical triple call note, *tseedle-eet,* and soft *tseeep*

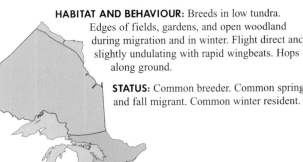

**HABITAT AND BEHAVIOUR:** Breeds in low tundra. Edges of fields, gardens, and open woodland during migration and in winter. Flight direct and slightly undulating with rapid wingbeats. Hops along ground.

**STATUS:** Common breeder. Common spring and fall migrant. Common winter resident.

# CHIPPING SPARROW *Spizella passerina*

12.5–14.5 cm / 5.0–5.7" Wt 11–14 g / 0.4–0.5 oz

"Chippies" are named for their frequently heard, chipping call note. They typically deliver their trilled song from an elevated perch.

**APPEARANCE:** Breeding adults have bright rufous cap, prominent whitish eyebrow, and black eye-line. Bill black. Cheeks, neck, rump, and underparts grey. Back brown with black streaks. Wings and tail dusky brown edged in pale cinnamon. **Non-breeding adults** have duller crown streaked with black, and brownish cheeks. Eyebrow and underparts tinged with buff. **Juveniles** similar but duller and browner. Heavily streaked crown lacks rufous entirely. Brown cheek-patch outlined with dark brown. Buff eyebrow and median crown stripe. Dark lores and indistinct whisker mark. Underparts may be finely streaked.

▶ Breeding plumage distinguished from other rufous-capped sparrows by white eyebrow and black eye-line. In winter, Tree and Field sparrows retain unstreaked rufous crowns. Smaller Clay-colored Sparrow has brownish, not greyish, rump in winter.

**VOICE:** Male sings rapid series of short *tssips* arranged unmusically into a single-pitched trill. Female utters soft, rapid *see-see-see-see.* Call notes include sharp *chip,* high, sweet *tseep,* and harsh *zee-zee-zee.*

**HABITAT AND BEHAVIOUR:** Open, grassy areas bordered by woodland or thickets; parks and gardens. Flights short and direct; somewhat undulating. Short bursts of flapping followed by pauses.

**STATUS:** Common to abundant breeder. Common to abundant spring and fall migrant.

# CLAY-COLORED SPARROW *Spizella pallida*

L 12.5–14.0 cm / 5.0–5.5" Wt 9–13 g / 0.3–0.5 oz

Once considered rare and sporadic east of Lake Superior, the Clay-colored Sparrow is now a widespread summer inhabitant throughout the Great Lakes region. This expansion is due to an increase in suitable open habitat created by logging and agricultural activities.

**APPEARANCE:** Breeding adults have dark brown crown with white median stripe. Also prominent white eyebrow and malar stripe, and dark whisker mark. Brownish cheek-patch outlined above and below with thin, dark brown lines. Nape and sides of neck grey. Buffy brown back has sharp blackish streaking. Rump brown. Wings and tail brown margined with buff. Underparts unmarked white or buffy white. Bill light brown with dark tip. **Non-breeding adults** somewhat duller and buffier. **Immatures** similar to adults but very buff-coloured, with less defined median crown stripe and paler finely streaked crown.

▶ Distinguished from many other sparrows by contrasting grey on neck and nape. Distinguished from Chipping Sparrow by brown rump and head. Other striped-headed sparrows larger and darker brown

**VOICE:** Series of two to eight low-pitched, insect-like buzzes. Most common call note a soft, thin *tsip*.

**HABITAT AND BEHAVIOUR:** Open shrubland, second-growth abandoned fields, and young evergreen plantations. Flies short distance when disturbed. Frequently lands on ground when flushed from perch. Hops along ground.

**STATUS:** Rare to locally common breeder. Rare spring and fall migrant.

# FIELD SPARROW *Spizella pusilla*
L 12.5–15.0 cm / 5–6" Wt 11.5–15.5 g / 0.4–0.6 oz

The Field Sparrow's range and abundance in Ontario increased during the twentieth century due to clearing of forest for agriculture and the subsequent abandonment of farms.

**APPEARANCE:** Grey head with rusty brown crown and streak behind eye. White eye-ring. Bill bright pink. Back rusty brown streaked with dark brown. Rump brown. Wings and tail brown streaked with buff and black. Two white wing bars. Underparts greyish brown with buff wash on breast and flanks. No central breast spot, but sides of breast pale rust. Undertail coverts pale grey. **Juveniles** duller with thin streaks on breast and flanks.

▶ American Tree Sparrow larger, and has dark breast spot and yellow lower mandible. Chipping Sparrow has black bill, black eye-line, and white stripe above eye. Field Sparrow distinguished from other brownish sparrows by pink bill and white eye-ring.

**VOICE:** Sweet song begins with deliberate, slurring notes that accelerate into a trill: *seeeea-seeeea-seeee-seee-wee-wee-we-we-we-we.* Call note *tsip* or *tsee.*

**HABITAT AND BEHAVIOUR:** Successional brushy pastures, woodland openings, and scrubby roadsides. Flight direct. Hops on ground or branches. Does not scratch ground with both feet simultaneously. Sings from conspicuous perches in open habitat.

**STATUS:** Common breeder. Common spring and fall migrant. Rare to uncommon winter visitor

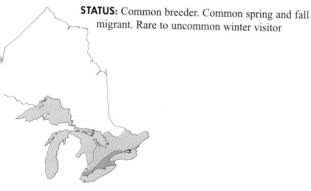

## VESPER SPARROW *Pooecetes gramineus*

L 14.0–16.5 cm / 5.5–6.5" Wt 22–27 g / 0.8–1.0 oz

The Vesper Sparrow was formerly more common across southern Ontario. It has been suggested that changes in agricultural practices in recent decades have favoured the Savannah Sparrow at the Vesper Sparrow's expense.

**APPEARANCE:** Upperparts pale greyish brown with dark brown streaks. White eye-ring. Upper mandible dusky brown, lower pinkish. Underparts dull greyish white with dark brown streaks on throat, breast, sides, and flanks. Sometimes tinged with buff. No central breast spot. Wings have diagnostic chestnut shoulder-patch and two indistinct, buffy wing bars. Outer tail feathers mostly white. **Immatures** resemble adults.

▶ Most other sparrows lack white outer tail feathers and chestnut shoulder-patch. Immature Lark Sparrow has streaking on breast. Savannah Sparrow has yellow stripe above eye. American Pipit has thinner bill, greyer, unstreaked upperparts, and lacks shoulder-patch. Female Lark Bunting larger with obvious white wing-patch and larger, silvery bill.

**VOICE:** Song has two sweet, musical opening notes followed by two higher-pitched notes and descending, rapid trills: *here-here where-where all-together-down-the-hill*. Call note a sharp *chirp*. Sings from low perches or in flight.

**HABITAT AND BEHAVIOUR:** Open fields and shrublands, and coniferous plantations. Flashes white outer tail feathers as it flies. Generally forages while hopping on ground. Frequently takes dust baths.

**STATUS:** Uncommon to fairly common migrant and breeder.

# LARK SPARROW *Chondestes grammacus*

L 14–16 cm / 5.5–6.3" Wt 25–28 g / 0.9–1.0 oz

There are few breeding records of this species in Ontario, which represents the extreme northern limits of its primary range in central and western United States. Males are easy to identify in open country both by plumage and by their melodious song.

**APPEARANCE:** Adults have striking quail-like head pattern of chestnut, white, and black stripes. Upperparts brown streaked with black. Wings have indistinct, whitish wing bars. Breast white with central black spot. Black tail has white outer feathers. **Immatures** resemble adults but somewhat duller overall with streaked brown crown, brownish cheeks, and finely streaked breast. Lack central breast spot. Adult head pattern present but much less evident.

▶ Adult head plumage unmistakable. Immature may be confused with Vesper Sparrow, but latter more heavily streaked and lacks distinct head pattern.

**VOICE:** Song comprises clear notes, trill, and buzzes punctuated with pauses. Sings from ground or in flight. Call note a metallic *tink*.

**HABITAT AND BEHAVIOUR:** Open country with scattered bushes and trees, and roadsides. Flight strong with alternating bouts of wingbeats and glides. Walks or hops on ground. Small flocks commonly seen on roadsides.

**STATUS:** Rare breeder. Rare spring and fall migrant.

# LARK BUNTING *Calamospiza melanocorys*

L 16.5–19.0 cm / 6.5–7.5"  Wt 34–39 g / 1.2–1.4 oz

Large flocks of Lark Buntings gather in migration and in winter sporting their brown, sparrow-like plumage. Individual Lark Buntings have been recorded in northwestern Ontario in most months of the year.

**APPEARANCE:** Breeding male black with white wing-patch. **Female** has brownish upperparts with light brownish streaking. Brown cheeks bordered above and below by whitish line. Indistinct whitish wing-patch. Brown tail rounded with white corners. Underparts whitish with brown streaks. **Winter** and **immature male** resemble female but somewhat darker and may have blackish primaries and chin.

▶ Breeding male Bobolink has white patches on back, buff nape, and whitish rump. Female, winter male, and immature Lark Bunting resemble sparrows but can be distinguished by larger size, brown cheek-patch, larger bill, whitish wing-patch, and rounded tail with white corners; also similar to female Purple Finch, which species lacks wing-patches and whitish tail corners, and occurs in different habitat.

**VOICE:** Song cardinal-like with long slurs and unmusical chat-like *chugs*. Also gives two-note whistle.

**HABITAT AND BEHAVIOUR:** Plains and prairies. Looks round-winged in flight with shallow wingbeats. Gregarious but quite cautious and easily frightened. Feeds largely on ground.

**STATUS:** Rare visitor.

# SAVANNAH SPARROW *Passerculus sandwichensis*

L 12.5–16.5 cm / 5.0–6.6" Wt 17–22 g / 0.6–0.8 oz

The Savannah Sparrow is the most common breeding bird of Ontario's fields and meadows. Forest clearing for agriculture during the nineteenth century, and subsequent planting of large tracts of alfalfa, has greatly favoured this species.

**APPEARANCE:** Brown striped head has yellow eyebrow. Nape, back, and rump light brown streaked with dark brown. Wings and short, slightly forked tail brown with pale edges. No wing bars. Underparts white to pale beige. Breast streaked with brown, often has small central spot. Short, conical bill dusky with upper mandible somewhat darker than lower. Legs pink. **Immatures** similar but with less distinct stripes on head and heavier streaking on body.

▶ Distinguishable from other sparrows by yellow over eye. Vesper Sparrow has chestnut shoulder-patches. Adult Grasshopper Sparrow has unstreaked breast. Lincoln's Sparrow has buffy jawline and breast, and grey eyebrow.

**VOICE:** Usually only male sings. High-pitched, buzzy song, preceded by short series of high *chip*s and ends with a few lower notes. Sings throughout daylight hours while foraging. Utters many calls including slow, pure *dyoo-dyoo-dyoo-dyoo,* high-pitched *tsip,* and *buzt-buzt-buzt* alarm call.

**HABITAT AND BEHAVIOUR:** Grassy meadows, grain fields, grazed pastures, roadsides, and tundra. Generally walks on ground while foraging for seeds and small insects. Runs or hops to cover. Flights usually short, rapid, and low; alternates between wingbeating and gliding on longer flights.

**STATUS:** Very common breeder. Very common spring and fall migrant.

# GRASSHOPPER SPARROW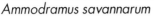
## *Ammodramus savannarum*
L 12.0–13.7 cm / 4.8–5.8" Wt 14.5–20.0 g / 0.5–0.7 oz

Some ornithologists have suggested that the Grasshopper Sparrow's common name derives from its dietary preferences; others profess that the name describes this sparrow's insect-like song.

**APPEARANCE:** Dark brown crown, narrowly streaked with buff, has whitish median stripe. Orangish yellow lores. Beady black eyes. Face unmarked yellowish buff. Chestnut streaks on greyish nape. Back streaked with buff, rust, and black. Wings and tail brown, edged with yellowish buff. Underparts buff; lighter on throat and belly, darker on breast and sides. Sides have obscure brown streaks. **Juveniles** browner with a little buff on underparts and diffuse brown streaking across breast.

▶ Immature Henslow's Sparrow darker and less buffy overall, with distinct facial pattern. Adult Henslow's Sparrow resembles immature Grasshopper Sparrow but darker with brown facial marks, olive head, and rusty wings. Le Conte's Sparrow more extensively yellowish buff on face with dark triangular patch on cheek, and prominent brown streaking on sides. Baird's Sparrow resembles immature Grasshopper Sparrow but has black-and-yellow stripes on crown and more distinct facial pattern.

**VOICE:** Male gives thin, squeaky introductory notes followed by buzzy trill: *tic-zzzzzz-zeeur-zeer-zeer-zrr.* Both sexes utter descending trill: *ti-ti-i-i-i-i-i.* Alarm call: *tik.*

**HABITAT AND BEHAVIOUR:** Short treeless grasslands. Walks and runs while foraging. Holds head down, occasionally flicks wings and tail.

**STATUS:** Rare to uncommon breeder. Rare to uncommon spring and fall migrant.

# HENSLOW'S SPARROW *Ammodramus henslowii*

L 12–13 cm / 4.7–5.1" Wt 11–14 g / 0.4–0.5 oz

Henslow's Sparrow was first recorded as breeding in Ontario in the 1890s. By the 1930s, it was considered fairly common. Unfortunately, it is now absent or very rare throughout much of its former Ontario range with agricultural intensification being the purported cause of its demise.

**APPEARANCE:** Large pale bill and flat head profile. Dull olive head has brown crown and whisker stripes, and brown smudge near ear coverts. Nape and hind-neck olive. Wings dark chestnut. Back and tail brown, tinged with rust. Tail deeply notched. Underparts whitish with brown stripes on buff breast; buff sides and flanks. **Juveniles** resemble adults but extensively unstreaked buff below.

▶ Other sparrows lack olive-green head and nape. Adult Grasshopper Sparrow also lacks dark whisker marks and prominent streaking on underparts. Juvenile Grasshopper Sparrow has breast streaks but lacks olive-green head. Savannah Sparrow lacks buff breast. Le Conte's Sparrow has yellowish buff face and grey cheeks.

**VOICE:** Male throws head back and sings persistently from exposed perches. Utters loud, Dickcissel-like *si-chi-lick* with merging last notes. Call note a thin *sip*.

**HABITAT AND BEHAVIOUR:** Weedy fields. Flight usually low and jerky, often with swivelling motion of tail. Spends much of time on ground. Flushes reluctantly when disturbed.

**STATUS:** Very rare breeder. Very rare migrant. Endangered in Ontario and Canada due to loss of habitat.

# LE CONTE'S SPARROW *Ammodramus leconteii*

L 11.5–13.5 cm / 4.5–5.3" Wt 12.5–15.0 g / 0.4–0.5 oz

One of Ontario's most elusive sparrows, Le Conte's Sparrow rarely perches above low vegetation. When disturbed, it prefers to run along the ground rather than fly.

**APPEARANCE:** Crown has whitish median stripe flanked by wide dark brown stripes. Buffy yellow face and upper breast. Greyish tan lores and cheek bordered behind with dark brown triangular patch. Bill bluish. Chestnut-streaked nape. Back dark grey patterned with black, brown, buff, and white. Wings brown. Rump grey. Tail brown edged with buff. Sides and flanks dull cinnamon buff with distinct black streaks. Belly white. Wing linings pinkish buff. **Juveniles** are paler overall with light streaking on breast and rusty tinge on wings.

▶ Similar Nelson's Sharp-tailed Sparrow distinguished by unstreaked grey nape, well-defined cheek patch, white back stripes, and no pale median crown stripe. Grasshopper Sparrow has yellow restricted to lores; dull buff on face extends to belly. Henslow's and Baird's sparrows have generally duller buff plumage and dark streaking across breast.

**VOICE:** Only male sings thin, grasshopper-like *tzeek-tzzzzzzz*. Often given in evening and at night. Flight song includes several *chip* and *buzz* notes. Female utters *chit-chit-t-t-t-ti* at nest.

**HABITAT AND BEHAVIOUR:** Grassy marshes and moist grassland. Flight slow and somewhat weak. Walks and hops on ground.

**STATUS:** Common breeder. Uncommon spring and fall migrant.

# NELSON'S SHARP-TAILED SPARROW
*Ammodramus nelsoni*
L 11–13 cm / 4.5–5.5" Wt 12–17 g / 0.4–0.6 oz

This northern summer resident is known in southern counties as a shy and obscure migrant. However, during the breeding season, unpaired males advertise their status by singing from an exposed perch.

**APPEARANCE:** Crown has grey stripe bordered with brown lateral stripes. Broad orangish buff eyebrow and malar stripe. Ear coverts and sides of neck grey. Dark brown upper mandible; lower paler. Dark brown upperparts with greyish stripes on back. Wings and tail brown. No wing bars. Breast, sides, and flanks bright, buffy orange. Flanks indistinctly streaked with brown. Belly white. **Juveniles** similar but with brown crown and less distinct face markings. Back feathers have large, dark centres and less obvious pale streaking.

▶ Most easily confused with Le Conte's Sparrow, which has white stripe through dark crown, chestnut streaks on nape, and straw-coloured back streaking. Other sparrows generally lack extensive buffy orange plumage.

**VOICE:** Short, raspy song with quiet introductory notes, *tuptup-sheeeeeeeeeee,* resembles sound of hot metal dropped into water. Some males sing during the night. Call notes include soft *chick* and harsh *zhree-zhree.*

**HABITAT AND BEHAVIOUR:** Marshes. Long-distance flight direct, relatively fast, and slightly undulating. Short flights buzzy and slow, with rapid wingbeats. Runs like a mouse; often stops at intervals and climbs atop vegetation to survey surroundings.

**STATUS:** Locally common breeder. Rare spring and fall migrant.

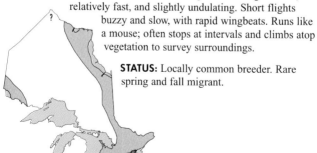

# FOX SPARROW *Passerella iliaca*

L 17–19 cm / 6.7–7.5" Wt 28–35 g / 1.0–1.3 oz

Almost equal in size to the European Starling, the Fox Sparrow is the behemoth of little brown birds. Despite its girth, this species remains inconspicuous in dense undergrowth until the breeding male springs forth with his loud, whistled courtship songs.

**APPEARANCE:** Large, plump sparrow with rufous-red tail. Grey crown, eyebrow, and nape. Stubby, conical bill. Upperparts rusty streaked with grey and brown. Wings and rump reddish brown. Underparts whitish with heavy, reddish brown streaks that nearly converge into central breast spot. Pinkish legs. **Juveniles** resemble adults but somewhat browner with less grey on head.

▶ Other sparrows much smaller and less rusty. Hermit Thrush more olive-brown and has spots, not stripes, on underparts; lacks grey on head and upperparts; bill much thinner.

**VOICE:** Variable long series of melodious notes. Begins with introductory whistle followed by several sliding notes, whistles, and slurs. Clearer than song of Song Sparrow. Calls are various *clicks* and *chips*.

**HABITAT AND BEHAVIOUR:** Wooded undergrowth and brush. Flies from bush to bush with quick, jerky movements and fanned tail. Rustles among leaf litter like a towhee, using feet to scratch ground vigorously.

**STATUS:** Uncommon to fairly common breeder. Uncommon spring and fall migrant.

# SONG SPARROW *Melospiza melodia* ✓

14–18 cm / 5.5–7.1" Wt 18–23 g / 0.6–0.8 oz

The male Song Sparrow's musical performance is well known throughout Ontario. At dawn in early spring, he delivers six to eight songs per minute. As summer progresses, he sings more slowly and less frequently.

**APPEARANCE:** Upperparts and tail brown, streaked with black and grey. Crown brown with narrow grey stripe. Broad, grey eyebrow and ear coverts. Two indistinct whitish wing bars. Underparts whitish with dark brown streaks on breast, sides, and flanks. Breast streaks form a dark central spot. Heavy dark brown moustache. **Winter adults** buffier on head and underparts. Streaking more diffuse. **Juveniles** have yellowish white underparts. Usually no central breast spot.
► Fox Sparrow reddish with heavier markings below; lacks grey central crown stripe. Savannah Sparrow has white crown stripe, yellow lores, and notched tail, and lacks dark moustache; lightly streaked breast with no central spot. Lincoln's Sparrow has buff on head and breast; underparts have less streaking. Swamp Sparrow greyish below with finer streaking. Cheeks, collar, and eyebrow greyer; broad black streaks on back.

**VOICE:** Highly variable song begins with clear *sweet sweet sweet,* then continues with buzzy *towee* and ends with descending trill. Call notes include nasal *tchuk* and hissing *tsip.*

**HABITAT AND BEHAVIOUR:** Shrubby areas, thickets, and pastures; often near water. Flight usually short, jerky movements through thickets on rapid wingbeats. Slinks through understorey when frightened. Scratches ground with both feet simultaneously.

**STATUS:** Common to abundant breeder. Uncommon winter visitor.

# LINCOLN'S SPARROW *Melospiza lincolnii*

L 13–15 cm / 5–6" Wt 17–20 g / 0.6–0.7 oz

Lincoln's Sparrow is a secretive species that stops singing and skulks away when an observer is detected. It will not resume its vocalizing until the intruder has retreated to a respectable distance.

**APPEARANCE:** Crown has narrow median grey stripe bordered by brown stripes. Conspicuous grey stripe over eye. Brown eye-line and inconspicuous buffy eye-ring. Brownish cheeks outlined by dark brown stripe. Bill brown above and yellowish below. Buffy malar stripe. Sides of neck and nape grey. Back and rump brown with black streaks. Wings and tail rusty brown. Central tail feathers have dusky median stripe. Throat white with fine black streaks. Breast and flanks buff, streaked with black. Breast streaks sometimes form central spot. Belly whitish. **Juveniles** similar but more olive-grey.

▶ Juvenile Swamp Sparrow similar but has duller breast, unspotted throat, chestnut wings, and blacker crown. Song Sparrow is larger, has broader streaks on breast, and lacks buffy chest.

**VOICE:** Sweet, gurgling, wren-like song given by male: *kee kee kee see see see-dle see-dle see-dle see-see-see-see.* Starts at low pitch, ascends, then drops. Alarm calls high-pitched, insect-like *zeet* and aggressive *chip*.

**HABITAT AND BEHAVIOUR:** Boreal forest edge, muskeg, brushy meadows, and bogs. Usually short flights between shrubs, always staying near cover. Holds tail up when landing. Makes quick, leaping hops into vegetation when ground foraging.

**STATUS:** Common breeder. Common spring and fall migrant.

# SWAMP SPARROW *Melospiza georgiana*

L 12.5–14.5 cm / 5.0–5.7" Wt 16.5–22.5 g / 0.6–0.8 oz

The Swamp Sparrow's song exemplifies Ontario's wetlands. Males call persistently from exposed perches in cattails, alders, and willows.

**APPEARANCE:** Chestnut crown. Eyebrow, sides of face and neck, and nape greyish. Brown eye-line and malar stripe. Bill dark brown above and yellowish below. Back brown, broadly streaked with black and buff. Wings black, edged with chestnut. Rump rusty, streaked with dark brown. Tail rusty brown. Throat, belly, and undertail coverts whitish. Breast grey. Flanks rusty brown. Underparts finely streaked with brown. **Female** paler with less complete chestnut cap. **Immatures** have blackish crown and pale brown facial markings. Back and wings black, edged with chestnut. Wing coverts paler and rustier. Underparts brownish, sometimes streaked with darker brown.

▶ Most similar to Lincoln's Sparrow, which can be distinguished by prominent streaking on throat and flanks, and lack of rusty wings. Chipping Sparrow has white eyebrow. Tree and Field sparrows have conspicuous wing bars. Immature Song Sparrow buffier below, and browner on head, with longer tail and heavier bill.

**VOICE:** Male gives loud, metallic *weet-weet-weet-weet-weet* repeated on same pitch. Male also utters buzzy *zhrew.* Call note a sweet, metallic *chip* that resembles White-throated Sparrow's.

**HABITAT AND BEHAVIOUR:** Marshes with open water and brushy wet meadows. Rarely flies long distances, except during migration. Walks on ground while foraging. Wades in shallow water.

**STATUS:** Common breeder. Common spring and fall migrant. Rare winter resident.

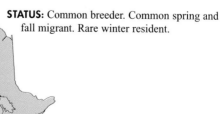

# WHITE-THROATED SPARROW
*Zonotrichia albicollis*

L 15–18 cm / 6–7" Wt 22–32 g / 0.8–1.1 oz

The plaintive, whistled song of the White-throated Sparrow is inherently associated with the northern wilderness. This species occurs in two different head-stripe colour morphs that are independent of gender, age, or geographic distribution.

**APPEARANCE:** Crown black with white median and above eye-stripes. Some individuals have black and tan head-stripes. Lores yellow. White throat-patch edged in black. Cheeks grey. Bill dark brown. Back chestnut, streaked with black, feathers edged with beige. Wings brown, edged with buff; two narrow white wing bars. Rump greyish brown.

Tail brown. Breast grey, sometimes finely streaked with brown. Flanks light brown, streaked with dark brown. Belly white. **Juveniles** generally have tan stripes on crown, greyish throat-patch, more heavily streaked breast, and lacks yellow lores. Some adults with black-and-tan striped crowns can be distinguished from immatures by bright yellow lores.

▶ Frequently confused with White-crowned Sparrow, which has bold black and white stripes on crown (light and dark brown in immatures), unmarked light grey throat and neck, and pink or yellowish bill; lacks yellow lores.

**VOICE:** Distinctive pure, whistled series of two clear notes followed by three-note phrase repeated three times. Often paraphrased *oh sweet Canada Canada Canada.* Call notes loud, hard *chink* and thin, slurred *tseet.*

**HABITAT AND BEHAVIOUR:** Semi-open coniferous or mixed forest. Flight direct. Hops on ground while foraging. Clears leaf litter by rapid kicking with both legs.

**STATUS:** Very common breeder. Very common spring and fall migrant. Rare winter resident.

# HARRIS'S SPARROW *Zonotrichia querula*

L 17–20 cm / 6.7–7.9" Wt 30–40 g / 1.1–1.4 oz

This large sparrow breeds along Hudson Bay in the northern tip of Ontario but can be observed on migration south through Lake of the Woods.

**APPEARANCE:** Breeding adult has black crown, throat, and central upper breast. Sides of head grey. Bill pink. Remainder of upperparts generally brown with black streaking on back and scapulars. Wings have two narrow white wing bars. Tail greyish brown with outer feathers tipped with white. Underparts generally whitish. Buffy sides have

blackish streaks. **Winter adults** browner with less glossy black hood. **Immatures** resemble winter adult but have buffier head with traces of black on crown. Throat and upper breast whitish with scattered black feathers. Wing bars beige. **Second-year** birds have black chins.

▶ Black hood of adult distinctive. Lapland Longspur distinguished by more extensive black on sides of head margined by bold white stripe and conspicuous chestnut nape; immature longspurs distinguished by shorter tail with white outer feathers and sharply defined brownish ear-patch.

**VOICE:** Only male sings. Song consists of one to three clear, plaintive whistles in same pitch in minor key. Also gives hoarse, buzzy *zhee zhee zhee*. Alarm note: *weenk.*

**HABITAT AND BEHAVIOUR:** Breeds in scrubby tundra. Winters in brushy, open woodland and successional pastures. Flight direct with rapid wingbeats. Flies into trees when alarmed. Hops along branches and on ground. Forages by probing and scratching.

**STATUS:** Rare breeder. Rare to uncommon spring and fall migrant.

# WHITE-CROWNED SPARROW
## *Zonotrichia leucophrys*
L 14–18 cm / 5.5–7.0" Wt 25–28 g / 0.9–1.0 oz

The primary song of the White-crowned Sparrow is highly variable geographically. Consequently, the vocalizations of this elegant species are among the more well studied.

**APPEARANCE:** Crown boldly patterned with black and white stripes. Remainder of head, sides of neck, and breast grey grading to white on belly. Bill pinkish. Back and scapulars light grey, streaked with brown. Wings brown with two white wing bars. Rump and undertail coverts pale brown. Tail dark brown. **Immatures** browner with lighter streaks on back. Crown stripes cinnamon and buff.

▶ White-throated Sparrow is browner overall with well-defined white throat-patch, yellow spot in front of eye, and dark bill. Accidental Golden-crowned Sparrow larger and browner with dull gold crown-patch bordered with black.

**VOICE:** Generally only male sings. Variable, clear, plaintive whistles followed by husky, trilled notes. Call notes include high, thin *seet* and harsh *rasp*.

**HABITAT AND BEHAVIOUR:** Woodland and stream edges, forest burns, and willows clumps on tundra. Hops along ground while foraging. Kicks leaf litter with two feet simultaneously. Runs mouse-like into cover when disturbed.

**STATUS:** Common breeder. Common spring and fall migrant.

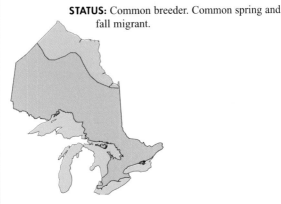

# DARK-EYED JUNCO *Junco hyemalis*
14–17 cm / 5.5–6.7" Wt 25–28 g / 0.9–1.0 oz

Dark-eyed or "Slate-colored" Juncos can be observed foraging in woodlots or beneath backyard feeders throughout Ontario at some time during the year. When alarmed, they flash their distinctive white outer tail feathers as they dash for cover.

**APPEARANCE:** Adult male has dark grey upperparts, head, and breast. Pink bill. Dark grey tail with white outer tail feathers. Belly white. Adult **female** similar but somewhat duller greyish brown, rather than dark grey. **Juveniles** resemble female but with buffy brown streaking on head, back, and breast.

► Eastern Towhee larger with prominent rufous sides, red eyes, and blackish bill. White on tail restricted to corners. Vesper Sparrow may be confused with immature Dark-eyed Junco because of striped plumage and white outer tail feathers; latter has somewhat darker plumage and lacks white eye-ring and malar stripe.

**VOICE:** Simple, dry trill in one pitch resembles song of Chipping Sparrow but somewhat more musical. Call notes include light *smack* and *ti-ti-tic*.

**HABITAT AND BEHAVIOUR:** Coniferous and mixed forest, shrubby clearings, and gardens. Male often sings from tops of tall trees. Forages on ground but does not scratch for food like many other sparrows.

**STATUS:** Very common breeder.
Very common spring and fall migrant.

# LAPLAND LONGSPUR *Calcarius lapponicus*

L 15–17 cm / 5.9–6.7" Wt 28–50 g / 1.0–1.8 oz

The Lapland Longspur has the most northerly breeding distribution of Ontario's two longspur species. These gregarious birds are often found among flocks of Snow Buntings and Horned Larks in winter.

**APPEARANCE:** Breeding male has black crown, face, throat, and upper breast. White stripe behind eye extends down behind ear coverts. Nape chestnut. Back and wings streaked buff and black. Forked black tail has only two white outer feathers. Underparts white with black streaking on sides and flanks. Breeding **female** has buff-and-black streaked crown,

WINTER

buff eyebrow, brownish ear-patch outlined with black, and rufous nape. Variable black on neck and throat. Otherwise, resembles breeding male. **Winter male** similar to female in summer. **Winter female** and **immatures** lack rufous on nape and black on neck. Breast buff with fine dark streaking. Many winter birds of both genders have conspicuous rufous tinge on wings.

▶ Less white on tail than other longspurs; distinctive in all plumages. Smith's Longspur has buffy orange underparts; male has black-and-white face pattern. Snow Bunting has black-and-white wings. Horned Lark and pipits have white in tail, but other plumage different.

**VOICE:** Male gives slurring warble with rich, organ-like quality during display flight. Other flight calls, rattling *trididit* and descending *teew,* often given in sequence.

**HABITAT AND BEHAVIOUR:** Breeds on tundra. Pastures and cropland during migration. Flocks flash white outer tail feathers when flushed.

**STATUS:** Locally common breeder. Uncommon spring and fall migrant and winter visitor.

# SMITH'S LONGSPUR *Calcarius pictus*

15–17 cm / 5.9–6.7" Wt 20–32 g / 0.7–1.1 oz

The polygynandrous mating system of Smith's Longspur results in some clutches of mixed paternity. At these nests, two or more males assist the female in caring for young.

♂ SUMMER

**APPEARANCE:** Breeding male has black crown and triangular ear-patch with white centre. Eyebrow and lores white. Back and wings blackish brown with paler edging. Small white patch on shoulder. Tail blackish brown with two outer pairs of white feathers. Throat, collar, and underparts warm buff. Flanks finely streaked. **Female** streaked with dull buff and dark brown above. Brown triangular patch on male face. Pale buff below, faintly streaked with brown on breast. **Immatures** and **winter male** resemble female, but male may be buffier below with some white on shoulder.

▶ Distinguished from other longspurs by buffy underparts, distinctive facial pattern, and longer bill. Vesper Sparrow distinguished from female- and female-like plumage by heavily streaked breast and whitish underparts. Thinner-billed Sprague's Pipit lacks facial markings. Immature Horned Lark has different tail pattern and indistinct brownish collar on foreneck.

**VOICE:** Wheezy *ta ta tee twe twe twee werr-tee* suggests Chestnut-sided Warbler. Utters rattling *tic-tic-tic-tic* call and short, sneezy *syu*.

**HABITAT AND BEHAVIOUR:** Prairies, fields, and tundra. Short flights direct. Walks and runs on ground. Hunches head down when observed.

**STATUS:** Uncommon breeder. Uncommon spring and fall migrant.

GB

# SNOW BUNTING *Plectrophenax nivalis*

L 15–18 cm / 5.9–7.0" Wt 32–36 g / 1.1–1.3 oz

The Snow Bunting breeds in the far north but winters throughout central North America. Wintering flocks may comprise 1000 or more continuously bickering birds.

**APPEARANCE:** Summer male white with black back. Bill black. Wings largely white with black tips and wrist-patches. Central tail feathers black. **Summer female** similar but duller with dark brown, not black, markings. Also has mottled grey on back, buffy crown and ear coverts, and pale rufous wash on flanks and breast band. **Winter adults**

WINTER

have buffy brown crown, ear coverts, and nape. Bill straw-coloured. Back and scapulars streaked black and beige. Rump bright buff. Wing tips and central tail feathers brownish black. Large white wing-patch. Outer tail feathers white. Underparts white with buffy sides. **Immatures** similar but somewhat greyer.

▶ Distinguishable in summer by predominantly white plumage. Some individuals quite brown in winter but can be easily identified by large, flashing white wing-patches.

**VOICE:** Male sings warbling *tee-sip-purr-tee-tee-sip-purr-twee-twit* tha recalls Lapland Longspur or Horned Lark. Numerous calls, including rippling *pirr-rrit tirr-rrip,* whistled *teer,* and hissing *sis-sis-sis.*

**HABITAT AND BEHAVIOUR:** Breeds on rocky tundra. Open weedy an grassy fields in winter. Runs between plant stalks while foraging.

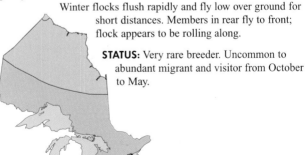

Winter flocks flush rapidly and fly low over ground for short distances. Members in rear fly to front; flock appears to be rolling along.

**STATUS:** Very rare breeder. Uncommon to abundant migrant and visitor from October to May.

# NORTHERN CARDINAL *Cardinalis cardinalis* ✓ †F

20.5–23.5 cm / 8.0–9.3" Wt 42–48 g / 1.5–1.7 oz

The Northern Cardinal's bright coloration results from the ingestion of foods that contain carotenoid pigments. Studies have demonstrated that the colour intensity of the male's breast and the female's underwing coverts is correlated with higher reproductive success and better-quality territories.

**APPEARANCE:** Adult male red with pointed head crest. Black mask surrounds heavy, triangular red bill. Adult **female** olive-brown above and buffy brown below with some red on crest, face, breast, wings, and tail. Red areas more prominent on older females. Grey to blackish mask and orangish red bill. **Juveniles** similar to female but somewhat more brownish grey, particularly flight feathers. Mask less well defined. Bill greyish black.

► Male Summer Tanager also all red but lacks crest and black mask, and has whitish bill.

♂

♀

**VOICE:** Loud, clear, whistled *what-cheer cheer cheer cheer cheer.* Some variation between individuals. Call notes include short, thin *chip.* Alarm call *shriek* and *chitter.*

**HABITAT AND BEHAVIOUR:** Woodland edges, thickets, and suburban gardens. Flight undulating through open areas. Hops on ground and in vegetation.

**STATUS:** Common year-round resident.

# ROSE-BREASTED GROSBEAK

*Pheucticus ludovicianus*

L 18.0–21.5 cm / 7.1–8.5" Wt 40–50 g / 1.4–1.8 oz

Male Rose-breasted Grosbeaks are accomplished songsters that frequently sing from the nest as they incubate eggs or as they fly between trees while foraging. Unlike most songbirds, the female is equally capable of singing.

♂

**APPEARANCE:** Heavy, conical pale bill. Breeding male has black hood and upperparts. Red breast and wing linings. Boldly patterned black-and-white wings. Tail black with white spots on outer feathers. Rump, belly, and undertail coverts white. **Female** has dark brown head and upperparts. Greyish eyebrow and malar stripe. Brown wings have two white wing bars. Yellowish wing linings. Underparts buffy white with dark brown streaks on breast and sides. **Winter male** resembles female but retains red wing linings, traces of red on breast, and bold wing pattern. **Immature** female like adult female with buffy wash on breast. Immature male resembles winter male but brownish with less red on breast. **First-spring male** like breeding male but duller with brown flight feathers.

♀

▶ Breeding male distinctive. Female accidental Black-headed Grosbeak has buffy orange breast with finely striped sides and flanks. Purple Finch female much smaller with plain crown and wings but heavier streaking on underparts. Sparrows much smaller and lack heavy, conical bills.

**VOICE:** Male gives mellow series of rising and falling warbles that end with *eek* notes. Female gives softer, shorter rendition. *Eek* call also given singly.

**HABITAT AND BEHAVIOUR:** Deciduous and mixed forest. Stiff, deliberate mannerisms almost parrot-like.

**STATUS:** Common breeder. Common migrant.

# BLUE GROSBEAK *Guiraca caerulea*

15–19 cm / 5.9–7.5" Wt 25–30 g / 0.9–1.1 oz

After breeding, the handsome male Blue Grosbeak moults into a new coat of brownish feathers. On the wintering grounds in Central America, the tips of these feathers wear off to reveal the beautiful deep blue nuptial plumage.

**APPEARANCE:** Heavy, conical, black bill. Breeding male deep blue with black around base of bill. Wings have two rusty wing bars. Blue plumage of **winter male** obscured beneath cinnamon-and-buff feather tips. **Female** warm brown, somewhat darker above, with whitish throat. Two dull rust or buff wing bars. Shoulder and rump tinged with blue. **Immatures** resemble female; some are richer brown above. **First-spring male** patchy blue and brown.

♂

♀

► Indigo Bunting has smaller bill and body; male lacks wing bars; female and immatures have dark brown streaking on breast, wing bars much less conspicuous. Female and immature Brown-headed Cowbird paler brown and lack wing bars. Eastern Bluebird has thinner bill and rusty breast.

**VOICE:** Male sings a series of sweet, warbled phrases that rise and fall. Resembles song of Purple Finch but somewhat slower and more guttural. May sing persistently from open perch. Call a distinctive, loud *chink*.

**HABITAT AND BEHAVIOUR:** Thick brush, thickets, and shrubby fields near water. Flight swift, low, and undulating. Frequently perches on utility wires and fences. Flicks and spreads tail.

**STATUS:** Very rare visitor April to August.

# INDIGO BUNTING *Passerina cyanea*

L 13.5–14.5 cm / 5.3–5.7" Wt 12–18 g / 0.4–0.6 oz

The Indigo Bunting is frequently observed singing from a high perch during spring. The breeding male's spectacular blue plumage is best seen in bright light; otherwise, he will appear uniformly dark.

**APPEARANCE:** Breeding male deep, brilliant blue with purplish head and black lores. Darker wing and tail feathers have blue edges. Bill black with curved upper mandible. **Fall male** unstreaked brown, above and below, with blue on wings, tail, and rump. **First-year** males variable. Some mottled blue and olive-brown; others resemble full adults, but less intensely blue. All retain buff-brown wing bars and obvious breast streaking, which may be used to distinguish them from fall male. Adult **female** uniformly brown with paler, sometimes faintly streaked, breast. May be tinged with blue on shoulder, wing coverts, tail, and rump. Upper mandible black, lower pinkish brown.

♂

► Male Indigo Bunting distinguishable from Eastern Bluebird by smaller size and lack of ruddy breast. Blue Grosbeak larger with more robust bill.

♀

**VOICE:** Only male sings. High-pitched, strident series of couplets; eac pair of notes at different pitch, second pair particularly harsh: *swee-swee zreet-zreet swee-swee zay-zay seeit-seeit.* Considerable variation among individuals. Both male and female give sharp, thin call note, *tsic*

**HABITAT AND BEHAVIOUR:** Open deciduou and mixed woodlands, shrubby fields, fen rows, orchards; rarely, residential gardens. Flight direct. Male glides and uses "butter flight" during territorial encounters with other males. Hops along ground and branches while foraging.

**STATUS:** Common breeder. Common spring and fall migrant.

# DICKCISSEL *Spiza americana*

15–18 cm / 5.9–7.1" Wt 25–30 g / 0.9–1.1 oz

Dickcissels nest sporadically in Ontario. This is compounded by a general decline in population densities across the northern boundaries of their breeding distribution. Some populations exhibit almost complete nesting failure and an overabundance of unmated males.

**APPEARANCE:** Adult male has grey head with yellow eyebrow. Bluish grey bill. Whitish eye crescent, chin, and moustache. Black V-shaped patch on throat and upper breast outlined broadly with yellow. Back greyish, striped with black. Rufous patch on shoulder. Sides buffy and belly greyish white. **Autumn and winter male** muted with indistinct black breast-patch. **Female** patterned like male but duller and more brownish. Breast only somewhat yellowish and lacks black patch. Underparts finely streaked with brown. **Immatures** plainer; breast and sides

♂ SUMMER

finely streaked with brown, and may lack yellow. Face pattern like female but buff and brown. May have some rufous on shoulder.

▶ Female and immatures resemble House Sparrow but have more contrasting face pattern, bluish grey bill, and streaked underparts; may have some yellow below and rufous shoulder-patch. Female Bobolink has striped crown and dark eye-line.

**VOICE:** Song one to three sharp notes followed by a trill: *dick dick dick-cissel.* Male calls incessantly from exposed perches in spring. Flight call a low *bzzt.*

**HABITAT AND BEHAVIOUR:** Abandoned fields, croplands, and grassy roadsides. Occasionally individuals observed among flocks of House Sparrow at feeders during winter.

**STATUS:** Rare breeder. Very rare spring and fall visitor. Rare winter visitor.

# BOBOLINK *Dolichonyx oryzivorus*

L 15.0–20.5 cm / 6–8"  Wt 30–55 g / 1.1–2.0 oz

The breeding range of the Bobolink expanded eastward with the removal of primordial forests by early settlers. Populations have since declined considerably because of changes in agricultural practices.

**APPEARANCE:** Breeding male has black head and underparts. Prominent buffy yellow patch on nape. Wings black. Scapulars, lower back, and rump white. Stiff black tail has sharp, pointed tips. **Female** has buffy yellow upperparts heavily streaked with dark brown. Crown dark brown with broad, buff central stripe. Face yellowish olive with prominent dark brown eye-line. Nape pale buff with thin brown stripes. Dusky wings and tail edged in buff. Underparts dull buffy white, somewhat more yellow on breast. Sides, flanks, and undertail coverts streaked with brown. **Winter male** resembles female with darker back and more yellow on face. **Immatures** also resemble female but generally more yellowish.

♂

♀

▶ Male in breeding plumage distinctive. Female resembles female Red-winged Blackbird but lighter and buffier. Savannah Sparrow has streaked breast.

**VOICE:** Songs given only by male. Bubbling flight song, *bobolink-bobolink-bobolink-bobolink-bobolink,* has banjo-like quality. First notes low and reedy, then ascending. Call note a clear *pink* heard during migration.

**HABITAT AND BEHAVIOUR:** Grasslands and pastures. Flapping flight alternates with short glides. Wings much above and below horizontal when flapping. Walks, and occasionally runs.

**STATUS:** Common breeder. Common spring and fall migrant.

# RED-WINGED BLACKBIRD *Agelaius phoeniceus*

19–24 cm / 7.5–9.5" Wt 50–70 g / 1.8–2.5 oz

Male Red-winged Blackbirds return to the breeding grounds earlier in spring than do the females. Their well-known call, given from exposed perches, serves to establish breeding territories in anticipation of the females' arrival.

**APPEARANCE:** Adult male entirely glossy black except for bright red shoulder-patch with buff lower border. Patch sometimes hidden when bird at rest. **Female** has dark brown upperparts tinged with black and grey. Prominent buffy white eyebrow and dark streak through eye. Buffy white underparts heavily streaked with blackish brown. **Second-year female** has brownish to salmon-coloured shoulders. **Third-year** and older females may have pinkish throat and dull orange shoulders. **Immatures** to second-year males have very dark brown upperparts. Orangish red shoulder-patch spotted with brown or black. White eyebrow. Underparts heavily streaked.

♂

♀

► Adult male distinctive. Female and immatures distinguished from other blackbirds by heavily streaked underparts.

**VOICE:** Male sings distinctive, liquid *conk-ka-ree* from exposed, prominent perches. Given most frequently during breeding season. Female utters three- to five-element song that includes *chit, teer, check, hee,* and *ti* notes. Call notes include low *chuck,* high-pitched *tee-ay,* and metallic *kink.*

**HABITAT AND BEHAVIOUR:** Marshes, grassy roadsides, and suburban gardens. Flight agile and somewhat undulating. May fly long distances daily between foraging and roosting areas. Walks well; frequently forages on the ground.

**STATUS:** Abundant breeder. Abundant spring and fall migrant. Fairly common winter visitor.

# EASTERN MEADOWLARK *Sturnella magna*

L 18.0–25.5 cm / 7–10" Wt 80–100 g / 2.9–3.6 oz

Despite its name, the Eastern Meadowlark is not a lark. It is most closely related to New World blackbirds.

**APPEARANCE:** Crown dark brown with buff median stripe and yellow and white line over eye. Cheeks and sides of neck greyish white. Straight, pointed greyish bill about as long as head. Upperparts cryptically patterned with buff, brown, and black. Sides and flanks whitish, broadly streaked, and spotted with black. Underparts bright yellow with conspicuous black U-shaped crest on breast. Short tail barred with black and brown; white outer tail feathers. **Immatures** similar, but head markings less sharply defined and yellow underparts much paler.

▶ Western Meadowlark almost identical, but can be distinguished by yellow on lower cheeks, somewhat paler plumage, and less heavily barred tail.

**VOICE:** Male primarily gives series of two to eight loud, plaintive, whistled notes, *tee-yah tee-yair,* usually descending in pitch. Call notes include harsh, explosive *dzert* and buzzy *zeree.*

**HABITAT AND BEHAVIOUR:** Grassy pastures and meadows, old orchards, and weedy areas with trees. Primarily terrestrial; forages for insects and seeds by walking or running. Flicks tail when walking. In flight, alternates periods of gliding with rapid, stiff wingbeats.

**STATUS:** Common breeder. Common spring and fall migrant. Rare winter visitor.

# WESTERN MEADOWLARK *Sturnella neglecta*

22.5–25.5 cm / 8.9–10.0" Wt 90–120 g / 3.2–4.3 oz

Ontario's two meadowlarks are exceedingly difficult to tell apart by appearance. Furthermore, they tend to occupy similar habitats and occasionally to interbreed. Where the two species overlap in southwestern Ontario, an observer is well advised to use their different songs and calls to distinguish them.

**APPEARANCE:** Upperparts mottled with buff, brown, and black. Brown, striped crown, yellow-and-buff eyebrow, and dark brown eye-line. Yellow on throat extends to cheeks. Long, sharp bill. Wings and tail barred with brown. Short, broad tail has white outer feathers. Underparts yellow with broad, black U-shaped breast band. Sides and flanks whitish with dark streaking. Long, pinkish legs. **Immatures** similar but somewhat paler with less distinct markings.

► Eastern Meadowlark slightly darker with blacker crown and eye-line; yellow on throat does not extend to cheek; more heavily barred tail; best distinguished by song.

**VOICE:** Begins with one to six flute-like whistles followed by rolling, melodic notes. Richer and more lower pitched than song of Eastern Meadowlark. Call note a loud, sharp *chupp*. Male frequently sings from fenceposts.

**HABITAT AND BEHAVIOUR:** Meadows and pastures, croplands, and grassy roadsides. Flight generally low with bouts of energetic flapping alternating with glides on stiff, downward bowed wings. Walks briskly when foraging. Uses long bill to dig food from soil.

**STATUS:** Rare to locally common breeder. Rare spring and fall migrant.

# YELLOW-HEADED BLACKBIRD
## *Xanthocephalus xanthocephalus*
L 20–28 cm / 8–11"  Wt 60–100 g / 2.1–3.6 oz

This gregarious blackbird nests in loud, riotous colonies. Males occupy conspicuous perches, fluff their feathers out, and deliver their cacophonous song with considerable effort.

**APPEARANCE:** Adult male has bright yellow head, neck, and breast. Small black mask over eyes. Black bill. Body black. Prominent white wing-patches best observed in flight. Adult **female** much smaller than male with dusky brown upperparts and belly. Face and upper breast yellow, with poorly defined brownish patch on cheeks. Lower breast variably streaked with white. Older females more brightly coloured than younger ones. **Immatures** resemble adult female with somewhat lighter and more restricted yellow areas, particularly in immature female.

♂

▶ Adult male distinctive. Female Rusty, Brewer's, and Red-winged blackbirds lack yellow on head.

**VOICE:** Male gives hoarse, raspy song, usually preceded by several fluid introductory notes:

♀

*kuk koh-koh-koh waaaaaaaaaaa.* Resembles sound of rusty hinges. Female utters rapid, harsh, nasal chatter: *cheee-cheee-cheee.* Call notes include low *kack* and *tscheck.*

**HABITAT AND BEHAVIOUR:** Deep marshes and marsh zones of lakes with cattails. Flight slightly undulating. Walks or hops on ground in wetland vegetation while foraging. Climbs up or slides down plant stalks to attain perch.

**STATUS:** Rare breeder. Rare spring and fall migrant.

# RUSTY BLACKBIRD *Euphagus carolinus*
L 21–25 cm / 8.3–9.8" Wt 54–65 g / 1.9–2.3 oz

The Rusty Blackbird is the most northerly breeding North American blackbird species. Its sturdy nests are frequently reused by Solitary Sandpipers.

**APPEARANCE:** Breeding male black faintly glossed with green. Eyes yellow. Slightly decurved, acutely pointed black bill. Breeding **female** slate-grey to greyish brown. Upperparts somewhat darker than lower with faint bluish green gloss. Eyes yellow. **Fall and winter adults** have rusty crown, back, and breast. Conspicuous buffy eyebrow and throat. Dark patch around eyes. Wings edged with brown. Rump and lower underparts dark grey. **Immatures** dark grey with olive-brown wash on throat and back. Wing coverts edged with brown. Eyes dark brown, turning light yellow during first fall.

▶ Common Grackle larger with more iridescent plumage and long, wedge-shaped tail. Male Brewer's Blackbird in breeding plumage has whitish eyes and obvious purple gloss on head; appears longer-tailed and smaller-headed with straight, conical bill; female greyish brown with dark eyes.

**VOICE:** Male sings creaking *tk-tseeeik* that resembles rusty hinges. Song often interspersed with harsh, metallic *chek* notes. Droops wings and fans tail while singing. Flicks tail up and down while calling. Also utters down-slurred whistle.

**HABITAT AND BEHAVIOUR:** Wet coniferous and deciduous forests, and wooded swamps. Walks or runs while foraging on ground. Also wades in shallow water to belly like sandpiper.

**STATUS:** Uncommon breeder. Common spring and fall migrant. Rare winter visitor.

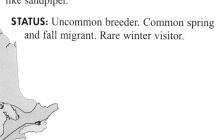

## BREWER'S BLACKBIRD *Euphagus cyanocephalus*

L 20.5–25.5 cm / 8.1–10.0"  Wt 56–67 g / 2.0–2.4 oz

The Brewer's Blackbird—resembling a hybrid between a Brown-headed Cowbird and a Common Grackle—is a comparatively recent addition to Ontario's avifauna. This western native was first recorded near Thunder Bay in 1945.

**APPEARANCE:** Breeding male has green-glossed black body. Head glossed with purple. Sharply pointed black bill. Whitish eye. **Female** brownish grey with blackish lower back, wings, and tail, which is sometimes glossed with green. Eyebrow and throat somewhat paler grey. Eyes dark brown. **Immatures** resemble adult female. **First-winter male** may be blackish with greyish eyebrows and barring on breast.

▶ Common Grackle larger with keeled tail. Rusty Blackbird bulkier with longer, more slender bill and shorter tail; less glossy; both male and female have yellowish eyes. Male Brown-headed Cowbird has brown head; female much paler below and has thick, conical bill. European Starling has short tail, long bill, dark eyes, and speckled plumage in winter.

**VOICE:** Song is creaky *ksheeik*. Resembles song of Rusty Blackbird but hoarser. Metallic *check* and other call notes heard in flocks.

**HABITAT AND BEHAVIOUR:** Moist meadows, roadsides near wetlands and groves. Jerks head back and forth when walking. Usually nests in colonies comprising up to fourteen pairs.

**STATUS:** Rare to uncommon breeder. Rare spring and fall migrant.

# COMMON GRACKLE *Quiscalus quiscula*

L 28.0–34.5 cm / 11.0–13.5" Wt 90–125 g / 3.2–4.5 oz

Anyone who has watched Common Grackles in the backyard during spring are familiar with their many demonstrative courtship and territorial displays, including sky-pointing, V-tail flight, and "ruffed-out squeak."

**APPEARANCE:** Body blackish overall with yellow eyes and long, dark bill. Adult male has head, neck, and upper breast glossed with metallic greenish blue. Back and lower breast have brassy iridescent sheen. Long, keel-shaped black tail. **Female** similar but somewhat smaller and less glossy. **Immatures** greyish brown without gloss. Brown eyes.

▶ Blackbirds and cowbirds smaller and stockier with shorter tails and bills. Male Rusty and Brewer's blackbirds have dull purplish gloss; female more greyish or brownish. Female Brewer's Blackbird has brown eyes. Male Brown-headed Cowbird black with brown head. European Starling has yellow bill in summer and white spots in winter; tail much shorter. Accidental Great-tailed Grackle much larger than Common Grackle with longer tail; male has glossy purple plumage; female brownish with buffy olive breast.

**VOICE:** Highly variable *readle-eak* sounds like rusty gate. Frequently utters harsh, sharp *chack*. Female also gives prolonged *chitip*.

**HABITAT AND BEHAVIOUR:** Agricultural land, residential areas, groves, and marshes. Flight level without undulation. Occasionally hovers over water and dives in to capture prey. Walks along ground.

**STATUS:** Abundant breeder. Abundant spring and fall migrant. Rare to locally common winter visitor.

# BROWN-HEADED COWBIRD *Molothrus ater*

L 15–18 cm / 6–8" Wt 40–50 g / 1.4–1.8 oz

The Brown-headed Cowbird is native to the Great Plains, but its expansion into eastern North America was facilitated by the removal of primordial forest. It is an obligate brood parasite that lays its eggs in the nests of more than 220 reported host species, thereby relinquishing its parental duties.

**APPEARANCE:** Adult male glossy, iridescent black with rich brown head. Short tail. Short, conical, black bill. Adult **female** uniform brownish grey. **Juveniles** similar to adult female but paler greyish brown plumage is variably streaked with darker grey.

► Brown head on black body distinctive among male blackbirds. Female Brewer's and Rusty blackbirds larger with longer bill and much darker plumage. Female grackles much larger and have yellow eyes. Immature European Starling has longer bill and very short tail.

♂

♀

**VOICE:** Song of male high-pitched, squeaky, and bubbly *glug-glo-lum-tseeee* usually associated with courtship display; frequently ends with loud *squeek* note. Also gives two- to five-note squeaky whistle in flight: *whssss-pseee.* Chatter call *ch-ch-ch-ch-ch* uttered primarily by female.

**HABITAT AND BEHAVIOUR:** Woodland edges, brushy thickets, pastures, orchards, and residential areas. Swift, continuous wingbeats distinguish this cowbird from other blackbirds in flight. Walks on ground, rarely on branches. Courtship displays by male include bowing and sky-pointing with bill; also puffs feathers, swells body, and fans wings and tail while giving bubbling song.

**STATUS:** Very common breeder. Very common spring and fall migrant. Rare winter visitor.

# ORCHARD ORIOLE *Icterus spurius*
L 15–18 cm / 6–7" Wt 16–25 g / 0.6–0.9 oz

Orchard Orioles seldom return to their Ontario breeding grounds before mid-May. Following a brief nesting period, they often depart for wintering grounds in Central America by mid-July.

**APPEARANCE:** Adult male has black head, throat, back, and tail. Wings black with narrow white wing bar and white feather edging. Breast, belly, shoulder, and rump deep chestnut. **Female** olive-green above and bright greenish yellow below. Brownish wings have two white wing bars. **Immatures** resemble female. **First-year male** similar to female except with black chin and throat.

♂

▶ Chestnut on male distinctive. Baltimore and accidental Bullock's and Hooded orioles black and bright orange. Accidental Scott's Oriole black with yellow belly. Female Orchard Oriole more difficult to distinguish. Baltimore and Bullock's orioles greyer above with more patterned face; larger, longer bill; whitish belly and flanks. Scott's Oriole darker overall with dusky streaks on

♀

back. Hooded Oriole brighter yellow below with longer tail. Female tanagers have heavy bills and lack wing bars.

**VOICE:** Male sings seven to nineteen rapid, variable, musical notes with downward slur at end. Resembles Purple Finch. Slightly higher in pitch and harsher than Baltimore Oriole. Calls include soft, diagnostic *chuk* and rapid *chatter*.

**HABITAT AND BEHAVIOUR:** Orchards, fields with scattered trees, and residential areas. Flight light and buoyant; more like flight of small sparrow. Makes short, wing-assisted hops through vegetation when foraging.

**STATUS:** Rare to uncommon breeder. Rare to uncommon spring and fall migrant.

# BALTIMORE ORIOLE *Icterus galbula*

L 20–23 cm / 8–9" Wt 30–40 g / 1.1–1.4 oz

This species frequently hybridizes with the Bullock's Oriole. Consequently, both orioles were once considered a single species, the Northern Oriole, despite differences in plumage, song, and behaviour.

**APPEARANCE:** Adult male has black hood and back. Rump, breast, and undertail coverts bright orange. Wings black with orange shoulder bar and white wing bar. Central tail feathers black, outside feathers yellowish orange with black base. Adult **female** greyish brown above with variable spotting. Crown, nape, and neck golden brown. Dark brownish grey wings have two white bars. Tail dark brownish olive. Underparts variable yellowish orange; somewhat paler on belly and chin. Greyish wash on flanks. **Immatures** and **first-winter male** resemble adult female. **First-spring male** dull orange with splotchy black hood and golden brown back.

♂

♀

▶ Male accidental Bullock's Oriole has orange cheek and eyebrow, and broad, white wing-patch; female much paler and greyer than female Baltimore Oriole with yellow restricted to face, breast, and undertail coverts. Male Orchard Oriole dark chestnut below. Female Orchard and accidental Hooded and Scott's orioles greyish green to olive above with yellowish underparts. Female tanagers have pale, heavy bills.

**VOICE:** Flute-like, whistled, and somewhat disjointed, song. Call note a low, whistled *hew-li*.

**HABITAT AND BEHAVIOUR:** Open woodland and shade trees. Flight strong and agile. Rarely on ground. Hops through vegetation. Often hangs upside down.

**STATUS:** Common breeder. Common spring and fall migrant.

# PINE GROSBEAK *Pinicola enucleator*

L 20–25 cm / 7.9–9.8" Wt 53–78 g / 1.9–2.8 oz

The Pine Grosbeak breeds north of the Great Lakes. It is frequently, but erratically, observed in small feeding flocks in southern Ontario during winter.

**APPEARANCE:** Adult male has pinkish red body; greyish under eyes and on throat, sides, flanks, and undertail coverts. Conical, black bill. Wings blackish with two white wing bars. Long, notched blackish tail. **Female** has greyish back and underparts. Head and rump yellowish bronze. Black bill. Wings and tail like male. **Immatures** resemble female but browner, particularly on crown. Wings edged with buff. Head and rump of male immatures may be tinged with pink.

♂

▶ White-winged Crossbill similarly coloured but has distinctively crossed mandibles. Red Crossbill lacks wing bars. Female crossbills variably streaked below. Male Purple Finch much smaller; brownish wings edged with pink, lack white wing bars.

**VOICE:** Song a clear, flute-like variable warble that resembles song of Purple Finch but shorter and weaker. Flight call a whistling *tee-tee-tew*. Utters quiet, chattering notes while feeding in flocks.

♀

**HABITAT AND BEHAVIOUR:** Coniferous and mixed forest. Flight powerful and undulating. Capable of hovering for short periods to catch slow-flying insects. Walks or hops on ground while feeding.

**STATUS:** Uncommon year-round resident. Rare winter visitor outside breeding range.

# ✓ PURPLE FINCH *Carpodacus purpureus*

L 12.5–15.5 cm / 5–6" Wt 19–23 g / 0.7–0.8 oz

The Purple Finch has been described as a sparrow dipped in raspberry juice. Its distinctive call note usually signals its presence it as it flies overhead.

♂

♀

**APPEARANCE:** Adult male has red crown, nape, neck, throat, breast, and sides. Cheeks reddish brown. Dark-brown-streaked back washed with red. Rump unmarked bright red. Wings and notched tail dusky brown edged in pink. Lower belly whitish. **Female** has dark brown upperparts indistinctly streaked with white. Whitish eyebrow and malar area. Dark brown tail. Underparts whitish, heavily streaked with dark brown. **Immatures** resemble female, but **first-year male** sings like adult.

▶ Frequently confused with House Finch. Adult male House Finch has red only on crown, eyebrow, throat, and rump; underparts heavily streaked with dark brown; female and immatures most easily distinguished by plain head that lacks distinct eyebrow and malar stripe, and more uniformly brown back. Accidental Cassin's Finch male also has less red on foreparts; female and immatures have less distinct facial pattern. Male Pine Grosbeak much larger with black wings and tail.

**VOICE:** Rich, bubbly, rapid, warbling notes delivered in various pitches. Lower pitched and less strident than song of House Finch. Gives soft *pick* in flight.

**HABITAT AND BEHAVIOUR:** Coniferous or mixed open forest, orchards, and gardens. Flight undulating. Usually hops on ground. Walks sideways for short distances in trees.

**STATUS:** Common breeder. Common spring and fall migrant. Rare winter visitor.

# HOUSE FINCH *Carpodacus mexicanus*

L 12.5–14.0 cm / 5.0–5.5" Wt 19–23 g / 0.7–0.8 oz

Eastern populations of this western native are derived from a few individuals introduced to New York in 1940. Males obtain their brightly coloured plumage from carotenoid pigments in their food, and the colour intensity reflects their access to specific items when moulting.

**APPEARANCE:** Forehead, eyebrow, throat, breast, and rump of adult male deep red (rarely orange). Body drab greyish brown with pale-buff-and-brown-streaked underparts. Wings dull brown with two indistinct wing bars. Squarish tail brown. Adult **female** and **immatures** lack red on foreparts and rump, and have somewhat stronger streaking on underparts. Head lacks conspicuous pattern.

♂

► Male Purple Finch distinguished by deep raspberry coloration that extends down back and belly, lack of streaking on breast, and deeply notched tail. Female Purple Finch more heavily streaked than female House Finch, and has contrasting face markings.

**VOICE:** Scrambled, hoarse warbling series of notes that often ends in downward-slurring note. Flight call a sweet *cheeet,* often repeated. Song slower, less fluid, and higher in pitch than that of Purple Finch.

♀

**HABITAT AND BEHAVIOUR:** Residential lawns and gardens, usually near dwellings. Nests in conifers. Flight undulating, usually above trees.

**STATUS:** Very common breeder. Locally common spring and fall migrant. Uncommon winter resident.

# RED CROSSBILL *Loxia curvirostra*    UK

L 14.0–20.5 cm / 5.5–8.0"  Wt 26–40 g / 0.9–1.4 oz

Crossbills use their unique bill to pry open the seed cones of spruce, pine, and fir trees. Variation in bill and body size among individuals allows for the exploitation of different cone sizes.

**APPEARANCE:** Distinctive crossed mandibles. Adult male dull red, brighter on rump. Wings and tail blackish. **Female** greyish olive, more yellowish on rump and underparts. Back and breast sometimes diffusely streaked. **Juveniles** have buffy edging on wing coverts and heavily streaked underparts. Plumage coloration of immature male variable. May resemble adult male or adult female, or exhibit intermediate condition.

♂

► White-winged Crossbill distinguished in all plumages by presence of two white wing bars; male more pinkish orange. Pine Grosbeak larger with white wing bars. Purple Finch more raspberry-coloured with pinkish brown wings. Both lack crossed mandibles.

♀

**VOICE:** Finch-like song of warbles, trills, and chips: *pit-pit tor-r-ree tor-r-ree.* Gives *chip-chip-chip* in flight. Alarms calls, *tuck tuck tuck,* and harsh screams.

**HABITAT AND BEHAVIOUR:** Coniferous forest. Flight rapid and powerful; undulating on short flights. Long-distance flights high above canopy. Uses bill to grab branches, cones, and needles in parrot-like fashion. Hops on ground. Breeds opportunistically like White-winged Crossbill.

**STATUS:** Uncommon and irruptive year-round resident.

# WHITE-WINGED CROSSBILL *Loxia leucoptera*

L 15–18 cm / 6–7" Wt 24–26 g / 8.5–9.0 oz

Unlike most temperate bird species, the White-winged Crossbill breeds opportunistically throughout the year whenever food is sufficient for the female to produce eggs and feed her young.

**APPEARANCE:** Distinctive crossed mandibles. Adult male mostly bright pink above with black wings and tail. Two conspicuous large white wing bars visible in flight and when perched. Underparts lighter pink, particularly in fall and winter. Undertail coverts black with white tips. Adult **female** dull olive-grey with yellowish underparts and rump. Also has prominent white wing bars. Flight feathers dark brown. **Juveniles** similar to female with variable brown streaking on body.

♂

▶ Red Crossbill similar but lacks white wing bars. Pine Grosbeak much larger and lacks crossed mandibles.

♀

**VOICE:** Series of loud trills in different pitches interspersed with chirps and warbles: *trrr-tweet-tweet-tweet-trrr-tchet-tchet-tweet-tweet-tweet-trrrrr-tweet-tweet.* Sings vigorously while perched in treetop or in flight. Call notes nasal, liquid *cheit-cheit-cheit* and dry, rapid *chut-chut-chut-chut* given in flight.

**HABITAT AND BEHAVIOUR:** Coniferous forest. Flight rapid and powerful. Hops along ground. Uses bill to grab branches and needles when climbing among cones. Also cracks cones open with bill.

**STATUS:** Uncommon year-round resident. Uncommon to locally abundant winter visitor.

# COMMON REDPOLL *Carduelis flammea* \M/

L 12.5–14.0 cm / 4.9–5.5" Wt 11–16 g / 0.4–0.6 oz

Redpolls are most readily observed throughout southern Ontario in winter. Local occurrences of this "winter finch" may be erratic because flocks search nomadically for heavy seed crops on birch and alder.

**APPEARANCE:** Bright red cap on forehead. Black chin. Upperparts, rump, sides, and under-tail coverts streaked with brown and greyish buff. Wings and notched tail dark brown. Belly whitish. Adult male has distinctive pink wash on breast that may extend down flanks to rump. Breast of **female** white or pale grey. **Juveniles** resemble adults but have somewhat heavier streaking. Also lack red cap and black chin.

▶ Hoary Redpoll paler with plain white or pale pink, not streaked, rump and lighter streaking on sides; undertail coverts unstreaked. Male House and Purple finches are larger and redder, particularly on rump, and lack black chin; female lacks red cap and black chin. Pine Siskin heavily streaked overall with yellow on flight feathers.

**VOICE:** Gives rattling *chet-chet-chet-chet* in flight. Song a twittering trill followed by flight call. Call note a soft *swe-eet* that resembles call of American Goldfinch. Indistinguishable from Hoary Redpoll by song.

**HABITAT AND BEHAVIOUR:** Breeds in scrubby tundra. Open fields, forest edges, and backyards in winter. Feeding flocks constantly in motion with individuals flitting continually between plants. Often comes to bird feeders in winter. Quite tame when approached.

**STATUS:** Common year-round resident in north. Uncommon to locally abundant migrant and winter visitor elsewhere.

# HOARY REDPOLL *Carduelis hornemanni* uvc

_ 12.5–15.0 cm / 4.9–5.9" Wt 15–19 g / 0.5–0.7 oz

Hoary Redpolls are occasional summer residents on the coastal tundra of Hudson Bay. In winter, they may occur farther south with Common Redpolls in mixed feeding flocks.

**APPEARANCE:** Similar to Common Redpoll but somewhat "frostier" overall. Red cap and black chin. Upperparts greyish with diffuse streaking from nape to lower back. Unstreaked rump whitish or pale pink. Wings and notched tail dark brown. Underparts whitish. Flanks may have pale brown streaks. Breast of adult male slightly tinged with pale pink.

**Juveniles** resemble adult but lack red cap and black chin.
► Common Redpoll usually darker with heavier brown streaking, particularly on rump and sides; pink wash on breast of adult male more extensive. Coloration variation present in both species; some darker Hoary Redpolls may be confused with lighter Common Redpolls. Lack of streaking on rump of Hoary Redpoll may be best field mark.

**VOICE:** Gives rattling *chet-chet-chet-chet* in flight. Song a twittering trill followed by flight call. Call note a soft *swe-eet* that resembles call of American Goldfinch. Indistinguishable from Common Redpoll by song.

**HABITAT AND BEHAVIOUR:** Coastal tundra. Open fields, forest edges, and backyards in winter. Gleans from snow, ground, and low vegetation. Occasionally seen at bird feeders.

**STATUS:** Rare migrant and winter visitor. Possible breeder.

## PINE SISKIN *Carduelis pinus*

L 11.5–13.0 cm / 4.5–5.0" Wt 12–18 g / 0.4–0.6 oz

These little finches are renowned for their noisy and aggressive antics at backyard bird feeders. They occur in nomadic flocks in winter.

**APPEARANCE:** Upperparts brown with heavy dusky brown streaking. Long, thin, dusky bill. Wings have diagnostic yellow patches at base of flight feathers. Tail has yellow patches at base of outer feathers; best observed in flight. Underparts whitish, heavily streaked with dark brown. Plumage some-what variable; some have yellowish olive wash on upperparts or less heavily streaked underparts. **Juveniles** similar to adult but somewhat browner above and yellowish buff below. Wing bars yellowish buff. Bill pinkish brown.

▶ Female House Finch similar; distinguished by thicker, conical bill and lack of yellow tail-patches. Redpolls have red spot on crown and black on throat. Juvenile redpolls lack yellowish buff markings. Winter American Goldfinch similar in size and shape but lacks extensive brown streaking.

**VOICE:** Low, husky, trilling song, *che-che-che chew zzzhreeee to ta chew,* has downward-slurring notes that end with *brrrrr.* Gives vicious, raspy notes during disputes.

**HABITAT AND BEHAVIOUR:** Coniferous and mixed woodlands, and residential areas. Flight undulating with rapid wingbeats during ascent and closed wings on descent. Moves in trees with short steps. Challenges flock members at feeders by lowering head and spreading wings and tail.

**STATUS:** Common year-round resident. Uncommon to common migrant and winter visitor.

# AMERICAN GOLDFINCH *Carduelis tristis* ✓

L 11.5–13.0 cm / 4.5–5.1" Wt 11–14 g / 0.4–0.5 oz

This lively little finch is also known as the "wild canary." Gregarious throughout most of the year, the American Goldfinch is often observed in large feeding flocks in winter.

**APPEARANCE:** Breeding male yellow above and below with black forehead, crown, and lores. Wings black with two white wing bars. Black tail has large white spots on tips of inner webs. Rump and undertail coverts white. Breeding **female** yellowish olive above. Throat to belly yellow. Sides and flanks buff. Rump and undertail coverts white. Wings and tail brownish. **Winter** adults olive-brown above and olive-yellow below with buffy sides and flanks. Male retains black on wings and tail only. Female somewhat duller than male with less yellow on throat and head. **Juveniles** resemble female except with rich buffy upperparts and wing bars.

SUMMER

WINTER

▶ Male Lesser Goldfinch has prominent white wing-patch; female greenish yellow with yellow undertail coverts (not white), and greenish yellow rump. Juvenile Indigo Bunting browner with heavily streaked underparts. Yellow Warbler entirely yellow, including wings and tail.

**VOICE:** Male gives sweet and clear, sometimes jumbled, canary-like song. In flight, *per-chik-o-ree* often uttered between wingbeats. Call notes include whining *chi-ee.*

**HABITAT AND BEHAVIOUR:** Open woods, lawns, roadsides, and weedy fields. Characteristic deeply undulating flight with few rapid wingbeats on ascent, followed by brief descent with wings closed.

**STATUS:** Common breeder. Common spring and fall migrant. Fairly common winter visitor.

# EVENING GROSBEAK *Coccothraustes vespertinus*

L 18.0–21.5 cm / 7.1–8.5" Wt 55–70 g / 2.0–2.5 oz

Nomadic flocks of these large, colourful finches will eat enormous quantities of sunflower seeds from backyard feeders in winter, then leave as rapidly as they appeared. They also congregate along roadsides to feed on rock salt.

**APPEARANCE:** Large, conical, yellowish green bill. Adult male has yellow forehead and eyebrow. Head, nape, back, and throat rich brown blending to bright yellow on lower back, rump, and belly. Wings black with large, white wing-patch. Tail black. **Female** greyish above. Underparts somewhat paler and tinged with yellow. Thin black malar stripe. Wings like male's. Black tail has white spots on inner webs. Undertail coverts white. **Juvenile** female resembles adult female. Juvenile male more yellowish overall but has wings and tail like that of adult male.

♂

► American Goldfinch much smaller with tiny bill and white wing bars (not patches); breeding male bright yellow with black cap.

♀

**VOICE:** Song a short, jerky, wandering warble. Loud, ringing, finch-like *clee-ip* resembles call of House Sparrow.

**HABITAT AND BEHAVIOUR:** Coniferous and mixed forest. Also deciduous trees, fruiting shrubs, and bird feeders in winter. Flight undulating. Winter flocks noisy and quarrelsome. Mated pairs much more secretive when breeding. Males feed females during courtship.

**STATUS:** Fairly common breeder. Fairly common migrant and winter visitor.

# HOUSE SPARROW *Passer domesticus* ✓

L 14–16 cm / 5.5–6.5" Wt 28–31 g / 1.0–1.1 oz

The familiar House Sparrow, native to Eurasia and Northern Africa, was introduced to North America in the 1850s in an effort to control cankerworm outbreaks. However, like many non-native floral and faunal introductions, it has rapidly become a nuisance species and an agricultural pest.

**APPEARANCE:** Somewhat stouter and shorter-legged than native sparrows. Breeding male has grey crown; otherwise, upperparts brown with black streaking. Bold white wing bar. Cheeks white. Throat and breast black; belly grey. Bill black. **Winter male** has black confined to chin. Bill yellowish. **Female** and **juveniles** plainer. Upperparts brown with streaked back and wings. Pale buff line through eye. Underparts dingy light brown. Bill pinkish brown.

▶ Male distinctive. Female not unlike many plain native sparrows but can easily be distinguished by habits, habitat, and voice.

♂

**VOICE:** Various garbled, nervous, non musical chirps. Most frequently heard *chirrup chirrup chirrup*. Calls also include *cher cher* and *tchee*.

♀

**HABITAT AND BEHAVIOUR:** Generally associated with human-modified environments. Usually absent from extensive forest. Flight direct. Extremely aggressive among themselves and to other bird species.

**STATUS:** Abundant year-round resident. Introduced.

# Accidentals

### Gaviidae / Loons
**YELLOW-BILLED LOON** *Gavia adamsii*
L 76–89 cm / 30–35" Wt 4.5–7.0 kg / 10.0–15.5 lb
Resembles Common Loon with yellow, uptilted bill. Breeding adults have black head with white necklace of vertical stripes. Red eyes. Breast whitish. Black back checkered with white. Sides and flanks black with small white dots. Brownish in winter but paler than Common Loon on sides of head, foreneck, and breast. Diagnostic brownish ear-patch. Retains yellow bill in winter. Immatures similar to wintering adults.

### Podicipedidae / Grebes
**WESTERN GREBE** *Aechmophorus occidentalis*
L 56–74 cm / 22–29" Wt 1.0–1.8 kg / 2.2–4.0 lb
Black forehead and crown. Red eyes. Dagger-like bill dull greenish yellow with dark ridge. Chin, cheeks, and throat white. Long, swan-like neck white on front and blackish behind. Back, wings, and flanks greyish black. Wings have prominent white patch visible in flight. Underparts white.

### Procellariidae / Shearwaters and Petrels
**BLACK-CAPPED PETREL** *Pterodroma hasitata*
L 35.5–46.0 cm / 14–18" Wt 260–280 g / 9–10 oz
White head with black cap. Broad white collar. Black, hooked, tube-nosed bill. Mantle dark grey. Wings have darker trailing edge. Rump black. Long black tail with wide white base. Underparts white. Wing linings white with black margins and tips, and distinctive diagonal black bar.

**GREATER SHEARWATER** *Puffinus gravis*
L 45–50 cm / 17.7–19.7" Wt 750–900 g / 1.7–2.0 lb
Dark greyish brown cap. White collar. Long, slim, blackish, hooked, tube-nosed bill. Upperparts variably brown and black giving somewhat scaly appearance. Flight feathers black. Narrow, white U-shaped band at base of tail. Underparts white with dark smudge on belly. Undertail coverts dark greyish brown. Wing linings white outlined with black.

**AUDUBON'S SHEARWATER** *Puffinus lherminieri*
L 30.5 cm / 12" Wt 125–195 g / 4.5–7.0 oz
Dark blackish brown above and whitish below. No white collar. Black, hooked, tube-nosed bill. Often has dark smudges at side of breast. Underwing white with dark primaries and front and back edges. Pinkish legs contrast with dark brown undertail coverts.

### Hydrobatidae / Storm-petrels
**WILSON'S STORM-PETREL** *Oceanites oceanicus*
L 18 cm / 7" Wt 35 g / 1.3 oz
Black, tube-nosed bill. Brownish black above and below except white rump and undertail coverts. Rump patch broader at centre. Rounded wings. Blackish tail square or slightly rounded. Long, dark legs with yellow webbed feet that extend beyond tail in flight. Flies with almost continuous flapping.

**LEACH'S STORM-PETREL** *Oceanodroma leucorhoa*
L 20.5 cm / 8" Wt 42–55 g / 1.5–2.0 oz
Dark brown above and below. Black, tube-nosed bill. Wings long and pointed, held at an angle in flight. Dusky line divides conspicuous V-shaped

rump patch. No white undertail coverts. Blackish forked tail. Long, dark legs and feet extend beyond tail in flight. Flight resembles that of nighthawk.

### BAND-RUMPED STORM-PETREL *Oceanodroma castro*
L 21.5–24.0 cm / 8.5–9.5" Wt 30–50 g / 1.1–1.8 oz

Blackish above and below. Blackish, tube-nosed bill. Crescent-shaped whitish rump patch. Long, dark brown, slightly forked tail and rounded wings. Narrow white patch across undertail coverts. Dark legs and feet do not extend beyond the tail in flight. Feeds with wings held horizontally.

*Pelecanidae / Pelicans*

### BROWN PELICAN *Pelecanus occidentalis*
L 106.5–137.0 cm / 42–54" Wt 2.4–3.6 kg / 5.3–8.0 lb

Long, flat, greyish bill with large, blackish throat pouch. Head whitish; somewhat yellow on crown. Eyes yellow. White line extends down sides of neck; otherwise, neck brown in summer and white in winter. Body and wings silvery brown with dark greyish brown flight feathers. Underparts blackish. Immatures brownish above and dusky white below. Like herons, folds neck in flight.

*Phalacrocoracidae / Cormorants*

### GREAT CORMORANT *Phalacrocorax carbo*
L 86.5–101.5 cm / 34–40" Wt 2.5–5.0 g / 5.5–11.0 lb

Black with white on chin and sides of face. White on crown, nape, neck, and flanks during breeding. Heavy bill. Small gular pouch yellow, not orange. Immatures typically blackish brown above with pale throat, light brown neck and breast, and white belly. Gular pouch pale yellow.

*Anhingidae / Anhingas*

### ANHINGA *Anhinga anhinga*
L 81.5–91.5 cm / 32–36" Wt 1.1–1.5 kg / 2.4–3.3 lb

Slim, long-tailed bird resembles cormorant with snaky neck. Adult male black with white plumes on upperparts. Dagger-like bill yellow. Tail tipped with white. Female resembles male but with buffy head, neck, and breast. Immatures similar to female but browner. Swims with only head and neck above surface. Often perches with wings half spread to dry feathers.

*Fregatidae / Frigatebirds*

### MAGNIFICENT FRIGATEBIRD *Fregata magnificens*
L 94.0–114.5 cm / 37–45" Wt 1.1–1.6 kg / 2.4–3.5 lb

Large, black seabird. Long, narrow wings with bend at wrist. Long, greyish bill has hook at tip. Long, deeply forked tail (often folded in flight). Male has orange throat pouch that becomes red and can be inflated during breeding season. Female lacks pouch but has whitish breast. Immature has whitish head, neck, and breast.

*Threskiornithidae / Ibises*

### WHITE IBIS *Eudocimus albus*
L 56–71 cm / 22–28" Wt 800–980 g / 1.8–2.2 lb

White with black-tipped primaries. Long, red, decurved bill. Bare facial skin red. Legs red during breeding; otherwise, slate-coloured. Immature has brown upperparts with mottled brown head and neck; bill pinkish brown; wings dark brown; rump and belly white; legs brown. Flies with neck and legs extended.

### WHITE-FACED IBIS *Plegadis chihi*
L 48.5–66.0 cm / 19.1–26.0" Wt 700–810 g / 1.6–1.8 lb

Breeding adults dark chestnut with metallic purple gloss on foreparts and underparts. Gloss on crown, wings, and tail somewhat greenish. Bare facial skin maroon during breeding season and pale pink in winter. Bare skin and eye surrounded by thin white line of feathers. Greyish legs, feet, and long, decurved bill somewhat reddish when breeding. Wintering adults similar but with pale streaks on head and neck; lack white line on face. Immatures resemble adults in winter.

## Ciconiidae / Storks

### WOOD STORK *Mycteria americana*
L 89–114.5 cm / 35–45" Wt 2.0–2.8 kg / 4.4–6.2 lb

Body white. Black flight feathers of wings and tail contrast with white underwing coverts. Blackish, scaly, unfeathered head and neck. Heavy blackish bill decurved at tip. Wings long and rounded. Juveniles similar but with yellowish bill and dull greyish brown feathering on head and neck. In flight, long, blackish legs extend well beyond short tail.

## ANSERIFORMES

### Anatidae / Ducks, Geese, and Swans

### BLACK-BELLIED WHISTLING-DUCK *Dendrocygna autumnalis*
L 51–56 cm / 20–22" Wt 780–900 g / 1.8–2.0 lb

Large and long-necked. Crown, nape, back, lower neck, and breast chestnut. Face and throat grey. Bright red bill. Belly, wing linings, rump, tail, and trailing edge of wings black. Large white wing-patch visible in flight and at rest. Long, pinkish legs. Immatures much duller with dark grey bill and legs.

### FULVOUS WHISTLING-DUCK *Dendrocygna bicolor*
L 45–53 cm / 18–21" Wt 675–780 g / 1.5–1.8 lb

Goose-like duck with buffy head, neck, and underparts. Centre of crown and hindneck somewhat darker. Whitish streaking on foreneck. White stripe on flanks borders dark brown back with conspicuous rusty feather tips. Wings blackish above and below. Narrow white crescent on rump. Blackish tail. Bill and legs dark grey. Immatures somewhat duller.

### GARGANEY *Anas querquedula*
L 35.5–40.5 cm / 14–16" Wt 365–410 g / 13.0–14.5 oz

Breeding male has dark brownish purple head with prominent white eyebrow curving back to nape. Long black-and-white scapulars overlap grey upper back. Lower back and tail coverts mottled brown and buff. Breast blackish. Sides and flanks silver. Female has contrasting dark-brown-and-whitish mottling. Prominent lighter lines on face, including distinct whitish eyebrow and dark eye-line. Circular light spot on cheeks at base of bill.

### TUFTED DUCK *Aythya fuligula*
L 40.5–45.5 cm / 16–18" Wt 1.0–1.4 kg / 2.2–3.1 lb

Yellow eyes. Breeding male has blackish upperparts and breast. Plumed head has purplish gloss. Broad grey bill has black tip. Wings black with broad white stripe on trailing edge. White flanks. Tail black. Female has dark brown upperparts and breast with paler flanks and sides. Head rounded with short crown plume. Bluish bill with black tip. Brownish wings patterned similarly to male's.

### SMEW *Mergellus albellus*
L 35.5–40.5 cm / 14–16" Wt 520–800 g / 1.2–1.8 lb

Breeding male white with black spot near base of bill, which encloses eye. Tapered black bill. White crest has black stripe. Black V-shaped blaze on nape. Back black. Flanks marked with close wavy lines. Two vertical black bars on sides of breast. Female has bright cinnamon head with white lower cheek and neck. Body dark grey above, paler below. Male in eclipse resembles female but has whitish upper wing coverts.

## FALCONIFORMES

Accipitridae / Hawks, Kites, and Eagles

### SWALLOW-TAILED KITE *Elanoides forficatus*

L 51.0-63.5 cm / 20-25" Wt 445-500 g / 1.0-1.1 lb

Head, neck, underparts, and wing linings white. Black wings and back. Deeply forked black tail. Skims water's surface like a swallow. Snatches insect prey on the wing. Immatures similar but duller with fine white streaks on head and breast.

### FERRUGINOUS HAWK *Buteo regalis*

L 56.0-68.5 cm / 22-27" Wt 1.1-1.7 kg / 2.5-3.7 lb

Very large hawk. Adults brownish above with paler head. Feather edgings rufous, particularly on back and shoulders. Thighs brown with heavy black barring. Legs are feathered to toes. Whitish tail often has cinnamon near tip. Underparts white with few dusky or rufous bars on flanks. Wing linings white. Immatures dark brown above with some spotting on mantle. Belly and flanks pale cinnamon with scattered dark spots. Tail whitish with brownish grey near tip. White-feathered legs.

Falconidae / Caracaras and Falcons

### CRESTED CARACARA *Caracara cheriway*

L 50-63 cm / 20-25" Wt 615-900 g / 1.4-2.0 lb

White head with black crest. Base of bill and bare facial skin red. Tip of bill pale grey. Neck white. Breast and upper back barred whitish and black. Lower back and upper wing black. Long white tail with fine black barring and broad, black subterminal band. Wing linings black with large white patches. Immatures similar but somewhat browner with streaked breast.

### PRAIRIE FALCON *Falco mexicanus*

L 35.5-45.5 cm / 14-18" Wt 800-1000 g / 1.8-2.2 lb

Pale brown above with buffy feather edges. Sides of head whitish with darkish eyebrow and thin moustache. Whitish underparts have brown spotting and streaking on breast and belly. Thighs barred with brown. Wing linings and upper flanks dark brown spotted with white. Immatures resemble adults except upperparts are darker and underparts are darker buff with heavy streaking.

## GRUIFORMES

Rallidae / Rails, Gallinules, and Coots

### BLACK RAIL *Laterallus jamaicensis*

L 13-15 cm / 5-6" Wt 28-35 g / 1.0-1.2 oz

Tiny blackish rail with short blackish bill and red eyes. Head black. Nape chestnut. Black back speckled profusely with white. Very short, dark tail. Underparts generally dark grey with black-and-white barring on flanks. Legs greenish. Immatures similar but paler.

### PURPLE GALLINULE *Porphyrula martinica*

L 30.5-35.5 cm / 12-14" Wt 210-280 g / 7.5-10.0 oz

Deep bluish purple head and underparts. Red bill has yellow tip. Shield on forehead pale blue. Back and wings bronzy green. Undertail coverts white. Bright yellow legs. Immatures have greenish brown back and wings. Head and underparts buff. White undertail coverts. Bill dark yellowish brown.

Gruidae/Cranes

### WHOOPING CRANE *Grus americana*

L 127-151 cm / 50-60" Wt 4.0-5.5 kg / 8.7-12.0 lb

Large, long-necked wading bird. Plumage entirely white except black primaries. Bare red skin on crown and cheeks. Eyes yellow. Bill greenish yellow. Legs and feet black. Neck and legs fully extended in flight.

Immatures washed with cinnamon, particularly on head. Belly and secondaries white.

## CHARADRIIFORMES

### Charadriidae / Plovers

#### MONGOLIAN PLOVER *Charadrius mongolus*
L 19.0–20.5 cm / 7.5–8.0" Wt 50–70 g / 1.8–2.5 oz

Breeding male warm brown above with rufous crown, collar, and breast band. Black mask and bill. White forecrown bordered above with black. White throat bordered below with black. Belly and undertail coverts white. Female similar but generally duller with less distinct black-and-rufous markings. Adults in winter and immatures have warm brown upperparts. Lores and ear coverts buff. Underparts white.

#### SNOWY PLOVER *Charadrius alexandrinus*
L 15–17 cm / 5.9–6.7" Wt 37–48 g / 1.3–1.7 oz

Small plover with light greyish brown upperparts. Breeding adults have incomplete blackish breast band. Face white with black forecrown and ear coverts. White eyebrow. Underparts white. Bill and legs blackish. Winter plumage has black patches replaced by greyish brown. Immatures resemble winter adults but paler with buff edges on back and wing coverts.

#### WILSON'S PLOVER *Charadrius wilsonia*
L 18–20 cm / 7–8" Wt 56–64 g / 2.0–2.3 oz

Heavy black bill. Breeding male greyish brown above with white collar, forehead, and eyebrow, and wide, black breast band. Forecrown and lores blackish. Underparts whitish. Legs pinkish grey. Adult female resembles male with brown, rather than black, markings. Immatures similar to female but often have incomplete brownish breast band.

### Haematopodidae / Oystercatchers

#### AMERICAN OYSTERCATCHER *Haematopus palliatus*
L 43.0–53.5 cm / 17–21" Wt 495–625 g / 1.1–1.4 lb

Black hood. Long, chisel-tipped orangish red bill. Yellowish eyes surrounded with reddish skin. Mantle and wings brown. Wings have bold white stripe. White uppertail coverts contrast with blackish tail. Underparts white. Legs pink.

### Recurvirostridae / Stilts and Avocets

#### BLACK-NECKED STILT *Himantopus mexicanus*
L 34.5–39.5 cm / 13.5–15.5" Wt 150–175 g / 5.4–6.3 oz

Male has black upperparts and wings. White spot above dark red eyes. Needle-like black bill. Rump and tail white. Underparts, including sides of face and neck, white. Very long, pinkish red legs. Immatures and female resemble male but somewhat brownish black above.

### Scolopacidae / Sandpipers and Phalaropes

#### SPOTTED REDSHANK *Tringa erythropus*
L 30.5 cm / 12" Wt 155–165 g / 5.5–6.0 oz

Breeding adults sooty black with small white speckles on back and wings. Straight, dark bill has orangish red base. White wedge-shape on back visible in flight. Trailing edge of wing white. Rump and tail narrowly barred black and white. Long red legs. Wintering adults dull grey above with white underparts. Legs deep red. Immatures similar but browner with warm brownish grey barring on underparts.

#### WANDERING TATTLER *Heteroscelus incanus*
L 26–29 cm / 10.5–11.5" Wt 130–160 g / 4.6–5.7 oz

Straight, medium-length, grey bill. Uniform grey upperparts and whitish eyebrow. Dark eye-line. In breeding plumage, underparts and face heavily barred with dark grey. Lower belly white. Winter adults and immatures lack barring. Breast and flanks washed with grey. Legs greenish yellow. Lack pattern on upper wing in flight. Bobs and teeters like Spotted Sandpiper.

### ESKIMO CURLEW *Numenius borealis*
L 30–36 cm / 12–14" Wt 405–505 g / 14.5–18.0 oz

Upperparts rich brown with buff spots and narrow buff feather edges. Dark brown crown bordered below with buff eyebrow. Slender, dark brownish bill slightly decurved. Unbarred blackish grey primaries. Throat and breast warm buff streaked with brown. Otherwise underparts whitish with dark brown chevrons on sides and flanks. Wing linings cinnamon. Legs slate-grey. Endangered or extinct.

### SLENDER-BILLED CURLEW *Numenius tenuirostris*
L 40.5 cm / 16" Wt 330–370 g / 11.8–13.2 oz

Brownish crown finely streaked with white. White eyebrow. Otherwise, upperparts uniformly checkered with brown and white. Long, thin decurved dark bill. Wings have dark brown primaries and paler secondaries barred with white. Lower back and rump white. Underparts white with brown heart-shaped spots on breast and flanks.

### LONG-BILLED CURLEW *Numenius americanus*
L 51–66 cm / 20–26" Wt 810–1000 g / 1.8–2.2 lb

Very large shorebird with very long, decurved bill (12.5–17.5 cm; 5–7"). Long neck. Plumage generally warm, buffy brown with darker mottling on wings and back. Lacks bold crown stripes of Whimbrel. Chin whitish. Tail barred with buff and brown. Underparts pale buff finely streaked with brown on breast, sides, and flanks. Wing linings cinnamon.

### BLACK-TAILED GODWIT *Limosa limosa*
L 36–44 cm / 14–17" Wt 250–330 g / 8.9–11.8 oz

Breeding adults have chestnut head, neck, and breast. Long, straight bill pinkish at base with black tip. Upperparts brownish. Broad white wing bars visible in flight. White rump; black tail. Belly and flanks white with blackish bars. White wing linings. Wintering adults grey. Immatures similar but with buffy neck and breast.

### LITTLE STINT *Calidris minuta*
L 14.7–15.2 cm / 5.8–6.0" Wt 20–28 g / 0.7–1.0 oz

Breeding adults mottled rufous and dark brown above with buffy feather edges. Throat and underparts white. Short, thin black bill. Whitish eyebrow. Breast bright buff with dark spots on sides. Legs and feet dark. Immatures similar but somewhat browner on upperparts and breast. Lacks bold, dark spotting on sides of breast.

### SHARP-TAILED SANDPIPER *Calidris acuminata*
L 20.5–23.0 cm / 8–9" Wt 62–78 g / 2.2–2.8 oz

Breeding adults rusty brown above with chestnut-and-buff feather edges. Rusty crown, buffy white eyebrow, and black bill. Buffy breast finely streaked with dark brown. Otherwise, underparts whitish. Flanks have dark, chevron-shaped spots. Wintering aduls greyish brown above and buff to white below. Immatures similar but with somewhat brighter rufous crown and orangish buff breast.

## Laridae / Gulls, Terns, and Allies

### HEERMANN'S GULL *Larus heermanni*
L 42–47 cm / 16.5–18.5" Wt 350–500 g / 12.5–18.0 oz

Breeding adults have white head and dark grey mantle. Neck and underparts grey. Dark wings have white trailing edge. Black tail tipped with white. Bill red with black tip. Wintering adults have dusky head. Immatures chocolate-brown. Bill pinkish with black tip. First- and second-winter birds increasingly lighter brownish grey white tail band and dull reddish bill.

### SLATY-BACKED GULL *Larus schistisagus*
L 64.0–68.5 cm / 24–28" Wt 1.2–1.6 kg / 2.6–3.5 lb

Dark slate-grey wings and back. Head and body white. Pale yellow eyes. Yellow bill with red spot on lower mandible. Black wing tips spotted with white resemble "string of pearls." Wings have wide white trailing edge. Underwing grey. Legs and feet pink. Wintering adults have dusky head. First-year birds dark dusky brown with black bill and pale pink legs. Second year birds have dark back and whitish wings. Yellow bill has black tip.

### ROSS'S GULL *Rhodostethia rosea*
L 32–35.5 cm / 12.5–14" Wt 170–210 g / 6.1–7.5 oz

White body and grey mantle. Very short black bill. Distinctive thin black collar extends from hind crown to chin; may be absent in winter. White, wedged-shaped tail visible in flight. Underparts washed with pink. Underwing pale to dark grey. Legs red. First-winter birds have dark spot behind eye, grey crown, black tip on tail, and dark M-shaped pattern on open wings.

### ROYAL TERN *Sterna maxima*
L 45.5–53.5 cm / 18–21" Wt 450–490 g / 1.0–1.1 lb

Large, slim tern with white body and pearly grey mantle. Early in breeding season, adult has black cap with shaggy black crest at nape. Remainder of year forehead and crown white. Large, orangish yellow bill. Underside of primaries pale grey. Deeply forked tail. Black legs. Juveniles have yellowish bill and dusky wash on flight feathers.

### SANDWICH TERN *Sterna sandvicensis*
L 35.5–40.5 cm / 14–16" Wt 195–238 g / 7.0–8.5 oz

Pearl-grey mantle and white body. Black cap and shaggy black crest at back of head. Forehead black during early breeding but white during nesting and wintering. Slender black bill has yellow tip. Deeply forked tail. Black feet. Immatures have white forehead, mottled brown-and-grey mantle, and greyish tail.

### LEAST TERN *Sterna antillarum*
L 21.5–24.0 cm / 8.5–9.5" Wt 28–32 g / 1.0–1.1 oz

Small whitish tern with pale grey mantle. Forehead white. Crown and nape black in breeding plumage; whitish flecked with black in winter. Broad, black eye-line. Wedge of black on leading edge of wing diagnostic in flight. Bill yellow with black tip. Feet yellow. Juveniles have forehead and mantle mottled with greyish brown. Eye-line and nape blackish. Bill blackish.

### SOOTY TERN *Sterna fuscata*
L 38–43 cm / 15–17" Wt 165–225 g / 6–8 oz

Adults black above with white forehead and cheeks. Broad black line through eye. Bill and feet black. Underparts white. Deeply forked tail black with white outer feathers. Juveniles brownish black above and below with fine white spots on mantle. Undertail coverts white.

### WHITE-WINGED TERN
*Chlidonias leucopterus*
L 22–24 cm / 8.7–9.5" Wt 60–75 g / 2.1–2.7 oz

Breeding adults have black head, body, and wing linings. Upperwing coverts, rump, tail, and undertail coverts white. Primaries and secondaries grey. Short bill red. Feet red. Tail slightly forked. In winter, head white with black ear coverts and greyish hind crown. Otherwise, upperparts greyish. Bill black. Legs reddish brown. Underparts white.

### BLACK SKIMMER *Rynchops niger*
L 40.5–51.0 cm / 16–20" Wt 260–335 g / 9.3–12.0 oz

Upperparts black with white forehead, cheeks, and trailing edge of wings. Diagnostic, long bright red bill has black tip; lower mandible much longer than upper. Short, slightly notched, black tail has white outer tail feathers. Underparts white. Immatures similar to adult but with brownish speckled upperparts and somewhat shorter bill.

## Alcidae / Auks, Murres, and Puffins

### DOVEKIE *Alle alle*
L 19–23 cm / 7.5–9.0" Wt 100–150 g / 3.6–5.4 oz

Small and short-necked. Black hood and back in breeding plumage. Stubby black bill. White scapulars. Blackish wing linings. Otherwise, underparts white. Cheeks, chin, and neck white in winter. Incomplete black collar extends from nape to sides of neck. Immatures resemble winter adults.

### THICK-BILLED MURRE *Uria lomvia*
L 43.0–48.5 cm / 17–19" Wt 840–1000 g / 1.9–2.2 lb

Black hood and back in breeding plumage. Thick, black bill has white line at base of upper mandible. White underparts form inverted "V" at foreneck. White trailing edge on wings. In winter, foreneck, chin, and lower cheek white. Black crown extends from below eyes to nape with no white at ear coverts. Immatures and first-summer birds resemble adults but somewhat browner.

### RAZORBILL *Alca torda*
L 35.5–44.5 cm / 15.0–17.5" Wt 500–600 g / 1.1–1.3 lb

Notably big-headed with thick neck and distinctive heavy, black, blade-like bill. Black head and upperparts in breeding plumage. White line on bill, lores, and trailing edge of wings. Underparts white. Wintering birds have white throat, chin, and cheeks. White ear crescent. Immatures resemble adults in winter but with smaller bill that lacks white line.

### LONG-BILLED MURRELET *Brachyramphus perdix*
L 28.0–30.5 cm / 11–12" Wt 200–240 g / 7.1–8.6 oz

Breeding adults mottled brown with whitish throat. Somewhat darker above. Long, thin, black bill. Winter plumage greyish above with white chin, cheeks, foreneck, and underparts. Small pale oval patches on nape. All plumages show large, whitish patch under wing in flight. Immatures resemble winter adults but with brownish grey, mottled underparts.

### ANCIENT MURRELET *Synthliboramphus antiquus*
L 24–26 cm / 9.5–10.2" Wt 210–240 g / 7.5–8.5 oz

Breeding adults have black face and crown with white plumes behind eyes. Back grey with short, whitish plumes on shoulders. Chin, throat, sides, flanks, and flight feathers blackish brown. Bill yellowish. Underparts white. Wintering adults lack white plumes. Immatures resemble winter adults but have white, not black, throat.

### ATLANTIC PUFFIN *Fratercula arctica*
L 30.5–33.0 cm / 12–13" Wt 450–560 g / 1.0–1.3 lb

Breeding adults best identified by massive, laterally compressed red, yellow, and blue bill. Crown, neck, and upperparts black. Face and underparts white. Legs and feet orangish red. Wintering adults have smaller, duller bill and greyish face. Immatures and first-winter birds resemble adults in winter but with darker faces and smaller bills.

## COLUMBIFORMES
## Columbidae / Pigeons and Doves

### BAND-TAILED PIGEON *Columba fasciata*
L 35–38 cm / 13–15" Wt 250–420 g / 9.0–15.0 oz

Resembles Rock Dove. Dark bluish grey mantle with conspicuous iridescent nape, border above with white crescent. Head and upper breast purplish grey in adult male, greyish brown in female. Yellow bill has black tip. Wings dark. Long, squarish tail black at base, with broad, pale grey band at tip. Immatures greyish with brown or russet edging on wing feathers.

### EURASIAN COLLARED-DOVE *Streptopelia decaocto*
L 30–32 cm / 12.0–12.5" Wt 130–190 g / 4.6–6.8 oz

Head pale grey. Conspicuous black half-collar on back of neck bordered with white. White skin surrounding eye. Bill black. Otherwise, upperparts generally sandy brown to grey and underparts pale grey. Primaries dusky brown. Tail greyish brown at base with broad pale grey tips. Immatures lack collar and are somewhat sandier overall. Feathers of upperparts have narrow, buff edges.

### WHITE-WINGED DOVE *Zenaida asiatica*
L 25–32 cm / 10.0–12.5" Wt 125–180 g / 4.5–6.5 oz

Generally greyish brown with paler underparts. Pinkish tinge to head. Small, black dot beneath eye bordered with bronzy iridescent patch. Blue skin surrounding eye. Iris red. Blackish wings with white coverts form conspicuous white band on closed wing. Broad, long, fan-shaped tail grey with rectangular white patches at ends of outer feathers. Immatures paler and greyer.

### INCA DOVE *Columbina inca*
L 19–22 cm / 7.5–8.5" Wt 39–58 g / 1.4–2.0 oz

Small, greyish dove with scaled plumage most evident on upperparts. Adult male has pinkish forehead. Underparts light grey. Chestnut primaries and wing linings visible as large patch on spread wing. Long, narrow tail brown and black centrally with white outer edges widening toward tip. Immatures similar to adult female but with buff bars near edges of back and wing feathers.

### COMMON GROUND-DOVE *Columbina passerina*
L 16.5–18.0 cm / 6.5–7" Wt 28–42 g / 1.0–1.5 oz

Very small dove. Adult male greyish brown overall with scaly appearance on foreparts. Pinkish tinge to head and breast. Black spots on wing coverts. Large rufous patch on wing visible in flight. Short, rounded tail. Central tail feathers brown or grey; outer feathers black with white tips. Adult female and immatures similar but somewhat duller in coloration.

## CUCULIFORMES
### Cuculidae / Cuckoos

### GROOVE-BILLED ANI *Crotophaga sulcirostris*
L 30.5–33.0 cm / 12–13" Wt 70–85 g / 2.5–3.0 oz

Long-tailed cuckoo with black, puffin-shaped bill. Plumage black with purplish gloss on wings and tail. Feathers of head have greenish edging. Distinctive parallel grooves on sides of upper mandible in most adults. Feet have two toes pointing forward, two toes reversed. Immatures similar but somewhat browner, and often lack grooves on bill.

## STRIGIFORMES
### Strigidae / Owls

### BURROWING OWL *Athene cunicularia*
L 23–28 cm / 9–11" Wt 150–170 g / 5.3–6.0 oz

Long, sparsely feathered legs. Head, back, and wings sandy brown mottled with white and buff. Large yellow eyes. Conspicuous white eyebrows, chin, and throat. Facial discs tawny brown. Short tail barred with brown and buffy white. Breast and belly buffy white barred with brown. Juveniles resemble adults, but lack barring below.

## CAPRIMULGIFORMES
### Caprimulgidae / Nightjars

### LESSER NIGHTHAWK *Chordeiles acutipennis*
L 20.5–23.0 cm / 8–9" Wt 50–60 g / 1.8–2.1 oz

Large, flattened head with small bill. Long wings and long notched tail. Mottled above and below with buff, brown, grey, and white. Underparts somewhat paler. Throat white or buff. Undertail coverts buff. Wings have conspicuous buff patch between bend of wing and wing tip. Underside of tail barred with several buffy and one wider white band and black tip.

### COMMON POORWILL *Phalaenoptilus nuttallii*

L 18.0–21.5 cm / 7.0–8.5" Wt 45–55 g / 1.6–2.0 oz

Smallest nightjar with rounded wings and short tail. Upperparts brown and grey with fine black markings. Face blackish. White band on throat bordered below by black upper breast. Otherwise, underparts subtly barred with black and grey. Tail has black-and-brown barred outer feathers broadly tipped with white. Central feathers greyish. Lacks white patch on wings.

## APODIFORMES
### Trochilidae / Hummingbirds

### GREEN VIOLET-EAR *Colibri thalassinus*

L 11.5 cm / 4.5" Wt 4–5 g / 0.15 oz

Bronzy green above and below with purple patches on lores, ear coverts, and breast. Bill relatively short and decurved. Undertail coverts dark grey. Tail has dark band. Female slightly duller than male. Immatures similar but have grey edging on feathers.

### BROAD-BILLED HUMMINGBIRD *Cynanthus latirostris*

L 9–10 cm / 3.5–4.0" Wt 3–4 g / 0.1 oz

Red bill with black tip. Thin white line behind eye. Adult male dark green above and below with iridescent blue throat. Forked tail deep indigo. Undertail coverts whitish. Upperparts of female dark green, somewhat duller than male. Underparts mostly grey with green wash on flanks. Undertail coverts whitish. Tail of female rounded with whitish tips on outside feathers. Immatures similar but with buffy feather edging.

### BLACK-CHINNED HUMMINGBIRD *Archilochus alexandri*

L 7.5–9 cm / 3.0–3.5" Wt 3.0–3.5 g / 0.1 oz

Adult males dark green above. Black chin bordered by iridescent purple band. Lower throat white. Underparts whitish tinged with olive. Shallowly notched tail. Female has greenish upperparts. Whitish below with buffy flanks. Both sexes have small white spot behind eye. Female indistinguishable from female Ruby-throated Hummingbirds. Immatures similar but with buffy feather edges.

### RUFOUS HUMMINGBIRD *Selasphorus rufus*

L 7.5–9.0 cm / 3.0–3.5" Wt 3.0–3.5 g / 0.1 oz

Adult males orangish rufous above, with iridescent, orangish red throat bordered below with white. Belly and flanks rufous. Females greenish with rufous rump and tail. Throat white with small red or gold spots. Underparts white with rufous wash on sides. Immatures resemble female; however, some young males have some red on throat.

## PICIFORMES
### Picidae / Woodpeckers

### LEWIS'S WOODPECKER *Melanerpes lewis*

L 25.5–28.0 cm / 10–11" Wt 100–110 g / 3.5–4.0 oz

Upperparts greenish black with dark red face. Bill black. Collar and upper breast grey. Lower breast and belly pinkish red. Immatures somewhat browner above and lack red face and grey collar. Underparts paler red, sometimes with diffuse streaking or barring.

## PASSERIFORMES
### Tyrannidae / Flycatchers

### WESTERN WOOD-PEWEE *Contopus sordidulus*

L 15–17 cm / 6.0–6.7" Wt 11–14 g / 0.4–0.5 oz

Dark olive-grey above. Two whitish wing bars; buff in first-winter birds.

Underparts whitish, washed with olive-grey on breast and sides. Tail uniformly dark. Blackish upper mandible darker than lower mandible. Reliably distinguished from Eastern Wood-Pewee only by song.

### GRAY FLYCATCHER *Empidonax wrightii*
L 13.5–15.0 cm / 5.3–5.9" Wt 11–14 g / 0.4–0.5 oz

Upperparts grey with blackish wings and tail. Whitish eye-ring, wing bars, and outer edge of outer tail feathers. Lower mandible buffy at base with black tip. Underparts pale grey. Plumage tinged slightly with olive in fall and winter. Immatures resemble adults but with buffy white wing bars and somewhat shorter bill.

### DUSKY FLYCATCHER *Empidonax oberholseri*
L 12.5–14.5 cm / 4.9–5.7" Wt 13–16 g / 0.5–0.6 oz

Greyish olive above and yellowish below. White throat. Breast tinged with olive. White eye-ring. Lower mandible orangish with dusky tip. Wings blackish with white wing bars. Black tail has greyish white outer edge of outer tail feathers. Immatures resemble adults but paler below with buffy wing bars.

### SAY'S PHOEBE *Sayornis saya*
L 19.0–20.5 cm / 7.5–8.0" Wt 16–23 g / 0.6–0.8 oz

Brownish grey above with darker wings and tail. Very faint, narrow, grey wing bars. Black bill. Throat pale grey. Belly cinnamon. Immatures resemble adults but browner with two cinnamon wing bars.

### VERMILION FLYCATCHER *Pyrocephalus rubinus*
L 14.0–16.5 cm / 5.5–6.5" Wt 18–22 g / 0.6–0.8 oz

Adult male has bright scarlet crown and underparts. Bill, eye, eye-line, and upperparts black. Female greyish brown above with blackish tail. Whitish eyebrow and forehead. White throat and breast streaked with dusky brown. Belly and undertail coverts peach. Immatures resemble female but with white belly tinged with yellow, and heavier spotting on breast. First-winter male has red belly and some red feathering on head.

### ASH-THROATED FLYCATCHER *Myiarchus cinerascens*
L 18–22 cm / 7.1–8.7" Wt 27–30 g / 1.0–1.1 oz

Upperparts greyish brown. Wings tinged with rufous and have two white wing bars. Tail cinnamon brown with dusky tip. Throat whitish. Bill black. Breast pale grey. Belly pale yellowish white. Immatures similar but with somewhat more reddish brown in tail.

### SULPHUR-BELLIED FLYCATCHER *Myiodynastes luteiventris*
L 20.5–23.0 cm / 8.1–9.0" Wt 40–50 g / 1.4–1.8 oz

Large, stocky flycatcher heavily streaked above and below with olive, brown, and buff. Face boldly striped with dark grey and white. Throat whitish with fine, dark speckling. Heavy, black bill. Rump and tail bright rufous. Lower belly and undertail coverts unmarked pale yellow.

### VARIEGATED FLYCATCHER *Empidonomus varius*
L 17–19 cm / 6.7–7.5" Wt 30–35 g / 1.1–1.3 oz

Upperparts olive-brown diffusely mottled with dark brown. Broad, dark eye-line. Prominent white eyebrow and malar stripe. Concealed yellow crown-patch. Whitish throat. Black bill has pale base. Uppertail coverts and tail edged with rufous. Underparts buffy yellow streaked with dusky brown.

### TROPICAL/COUCH'S KINGBIRD *Tyrannus melancholicus/couchii*
L 20.5–24.0 cm / 8.1–9.5" Wt 40–50 g / 1.4–1.8 oz

Crown and nape grey. Broad, grey eye-line and dark ear-patch. Throat white. Back greyish green. Wings and notched tail dark brown. No white markings on tail. Upper breast pale grey tinged with olive at sides. Lower breast, belly, and undertail coverts bright yellow. Immatures resemble adults but have pale buff edgings on wing coverts. Tropical and Couch's kingbirds distinguished only by song. Identity of this accidental record undetermined.

### CASSIN'S KINGBIRD *Tyrannus vociferans*
L 20.5-23.0 cm / 8-9" Wt 43-48 g / 1.5-1.7 oz

Dark grey upperparts and breast. Back tinged with olive. Chin and upper throat whitish. Orangish red crown-patch usually concealed. Wings dark brown. Unforked, dark brown tail has narrow buffy tips but lacks white on outer feathers. Belly and undertail coverts yellow. Immatures somewhat browner above and paler below with buffy edges on wing coverts.

### GRAY KINGBIRD *Tyrannus dominicensis*
L 20.5-23.0 cm / 8-9" Wt 40-48 g / 1.4-1.7 oz

Upperparts grey with blackish mask. Long, heavy, black bill. Red crown-patch generally concealed. Wings and forked tail black. No white tip on tail. Underparts white with greyish wash on breast and sides, and pale yellow wash on belly and undertail coverts. Immatures similar but somewhat browner.

### FORK-TAILED FLYCATCHER *Tyrannus savana*
L 33-40.5 cm / 13-16" Wt 24-30 g / 0.9-1.1 oz

Black head. Bright yellow crown-patch usually concealed. Back grey. Wings dark greyish brown. Very long, forked tail black narrowly edged with white on upper half. Underparts white. Immatures similar but with sooty brown cap, no crown-patch, dull grey back, and short tail.

## Vireonidae / Vireos

### BELL'S VIREO *Vireo bellii*
L 11.5-12.5 cm / 4.5-5.0" Wt 9.5-11.0 g / 0.3-0.4 oz

Upperparts grey washed in olive-green. Whitish eyebrow and eye-ring. One white wing bar. Some have second, less distinct, wing bar. Underparts whitish, with pale yellow tinge to sides.

### BLACK-CAPPED VIREO *Vireo atricapillus*
L 11.5 cm / 4.5" Wt 9.5-10.5 g / 0.3-0.4 oz

Adult male has black crown, nape, and face. Bold white spectacles around eye. Eyes red. Throat white. Back yellowish olive. Wings and tail blackish, edged in yellowish green. Two pale yellow wing bars. Underparts whitish with grey or yellow wash on sides and flanks. Female similar but with slaty grey head.

### PLUMBEOUS VIREO *Vireo plumbeus*
L 13-15 cm / 5-6" Wt 14-18 g / 0.5-0.6 oz

Crown, nape, and sides of neck grey to greyish olive. Back and rump greyish olive. Black wings have two wide, whitish wing bars. Conspicuous wide, white eye-ring and white lores confer spectacled appearance. Underparts white. Flanks washed with yellow. Sides grey.

## Corvidae / Crows and Jays

### CLARK'S NUTCRACKER *Nucifraga columbiana*
L 30-33 cm / 11.8-13.0" Wt 130-140 g / 4.6-5.0 oz

Stout, grey body. Forehead, throat, and undertail coverts whitish. Long, heavy, black bill. Wings and central tail feathers black. Large white patch on inner wing, and white outer tail feathers conspicuous in flight. Legs black. Immatures similar but browner with brownish tips on wing coverts.

### EURASIAN JACKDAW *Corvus monedula*
L 30.5-33.0 cm / 12-13" Wt 230-250 g / 8.2-8.9 oz

Small, compact crow. Upperparts black except grey nape and ear coverts. Pale grey eyes. Stubby black bill. Underparts dark grey. May have some whitish feathers at base of neck. Immatures resemble adults but somewhat duller.

**FISH CROW** *Corvus ossifragus*

L 37–44 cm / 14.5–17.5" Wt 390–435 g / 14.0–15.5 oz

Entirely glossy black with purplish sheen visible in bright light. Strong bill and feet. Squarish tail. Distinguishable from American Crow only by two-toned nasal *ca-hah* call, or short, nasal, repeated *ca* note.

## Hirundinidae / Swallows

**VIOLET-GREEN SWALLOW** *Tachycineta thalassina*

L 14 cm / 5.5" Wt 12–15 g / 0.4–0.5 oz

Adult male bright green above with purple on wing coverts and centre of rump. Wings and notched tail blackish purple. Face, underparts, and sides of rump white. Female somewhat browner, particularly on head. Immatures grey above and pale sooty brown below. Brownish mottling on face.

**CAVE SWALLOW** *Petrochelidon fulva*

L 12.5–15.0 cm / 5–6" Wt 14–17 g / 0.5–0.6 oz

Crown and back bluish black. Back has narrow white stripes. Forehead rufous. Cheeks and rump buff. Wings and square-tipped tail dark brown. Pale buff throat often forms collar around nape. Underparts whitish with buffy grey wash on sides. Immatures duller with small dark spots on nape.

## Paridae / Chickadee and Titmice

**CAROLINA CHICKADEE** *Poecile carolinensis*

L 11.0–11.5 cm / 4.3–4.5" Wt 9.5–12.0 g / 0.3–0.4 oz

Nearly identical to Black-capped Chickadee. Cap and bib black. Bib has sharply defined lower edge. Cheeks white. Upperparts grey. Underparts white with buffy sides and flanks. Whitish patch formed by grey feather edging on wing, less defined than in Black-capped Chickadee. Calls higher pitched and more rapidly uttered.

## Troglodytidae / Wrens

**ROCK WREN** *Salpinctes obsoletus*

L 12.5–15.0 cm / 5–6" Wt 15.0–17.5 g / 0.5–0.6 oz

Long, thin bill. Whitish eyebrow. Upperparts greyish brown, finely speckled with black and white. Rump cinnamon. Rounded tail brown above, barred with black and tipped with buff. Underparts dull white blending to buff and cinnamon on flanks, lower belly, and undertail coverts. Fine, brownish streaking on breast. Immatures similar to adults but lack streaking on breast.

## Turdidae / Thrushes

**SIBERIAN RUBYTHROAT** *Luscinia calliope*

L 15.0–16.5 cm / 6.0–6.5" Wt 22–25 g / 0.8–0.9 oz

Male has scarlet throat, and white eyebrow and moustache outlined with black. Lores black. Upperparts and flanks warm brown. Buffy white breast and belly bordered above by grey band. Female resembles male but has white throat and greyish brown breast. Belly and undertail coverts buffy white.

**BICKNELL'S THRUSH** *Catharus bicknelli*

L 16–17 cm / 6.3–6.7" Wt 25–30 g / 0.9–1.1 oz

Brown above with greyish brown cheeks and faint, incomplete, greyish eye-ring. Lower mandible yellowish. Tail warm brown. Whitish below with heavy dark spotting on breast. Sides olive-grey. Juveniles resemble adults but somewhat darker above with buffy streaking on back.

**EURASIAN BLACKBIRD** *Turdus merula*

L 24–26 cm / 9.5–10.2" Wt 90–120 g / 3.2–4.3 oz

Male black with orangish yellow bill and eye-ring. Female dark brown above with paler underparts. Chin brown speckled with white. Bill brown. Juveniles mottled with rufous and brown. Bill black.

### FIELDFARE *Turdus pilaris*
L 24–27 cm / 9.5–10.5" Wt 85–90 g / 3.0–3.2 oz

Head and rump grey. Bill yellowish. Short white eyebrow. Back and wing coverts reddish brown. Tail black. Throat, breast, and flanks buff with black chevron-shaped spots. Belly and undertail coverts whitish. Legs black. Wing linings silvery white.

## Mimidae / Mockingbirds and Thrashers

### SAGE THRASHER *Oreoscoptes montanus*
L 20–23 cm / 8–9" Wt 40–45 g / 1.4–1.6 oz

Greyish brown above; somewhat darker on wings and tail. Eyes yellow. Bill short and slender. Two white wing bars. Tail tipped with white. Underparts whitish with brown streaks, heaviest on breast. Belly and undertail coverts often washed with buff. Juveniles browner above with more diffuse streaking below. Eyes brown.

## Motacillidae / Pipits

### SPRAGUE'S PIPIT *Anthus spragueii*
L 15.0–17.5 cm / 5.9–6.9" Wt 24–29 g / 0.9–1.0 oz

Upperparts heavily streaked with black, brown, and buff. Conspicuous dark brown eyes on buffy face. Two buffy wing bars. Outer tail feathers white. Underparts buff with thin necklace of brown streaks on breast. White wing linings. Legs and lower mandible yellow. Immatures resemble adults but darker above with narrow buff-and-white streaks.

## Ptilogonatidae / Silky-Flycatchers

### PHAINOPEPLA *Phainopepla nitens*
L 18.0–19.5 cm / 7.1–7.7" Wt 22–28 g / 0.8–1.0 oz

Adult male glossy black with shaggy crest and long tail. Eyes red. Two white wing-patches visible in flight. Adult female resembles male but greyish brown. Juveniles similar to female but browner and paler below. Wings have conspicuous pale feather edgings.

## Parulidae / Wood-Warblers

### VIRGINIA'S WARBLER *Vermivora virginiae*
L 11–12 cm / 4.3–4.7" Wt 7.0–8.5 g / 0.25–0.3 oz

Resembles Nashville Warbler but paler. Upperparts grey except yellow rump. Reddish crown-patch usually concealed. Conspicuous white eye-ring. No wing bars. Throat and belly whitish. Breast and undertail coverts yellow. Sides washed with grey. Immatures similar but somewhat browner above with less yellow on rump and breast.

### BLACK-THROATED GRAY WARBLER *Dendroica nigrescens*
L 11.5–12.5 cm / 4.5–5.0" Wt 8–9 g / 0.3 oz

Adult male has black crown, lores, cheeks, and throat. Broad white eyebrow bordered in front by yellow spot. Bold, white malar stripe. Grey upperparts faintly streaked with black. Two white wing bars. White outer tail feathers. Underparts white. Sides and flanks streaked with black. Female resembles male but has greyish crown and white throat. Immatures paler with grey (not black) markings.

### TOWNSEND'S WARBLER *Dendroica townsendi*
L 11.5–13.0 cm / 4.5–5.0" Wt 8.5–10 g / 0.3–0.4 oz

Adult male has black crown, cheeks, and throat. Cheeks bordered above and below by broad yellow stripes. Back olive-green streaked with black. Two white wing bars. White outer tail feathers. Breast yellow. Belly white. Yellow sides and flanks heavily streaked with black. Adult female similar but has olive crown, brownish cheeks, and yellow throat. Immatures similar to female but somewhat duller.

### HERMIT WARBLER *Dendroica occidentalis*

L 11.5–14 cm / 4.5–5.5" Wt 8.5–10 g / 0.3–0.4 oz

Adult male has bright yellow face and forehead, and black throat. Hind crown, nape, and back dusky grey with black streaks. Grey wings have two white wing bars. Outer tail feathers white. Underparts white, sometimes faintly streaked with grey on sides. Female similar but with greyer back and less black on throat. Immatures paler with greenish tinge on upperparts. Black throat-patch lacking.

### SWAINSON'S WARBLER *Limnothlypis swainsonii*

L 13–14 cm / 5.1–5.5" Wt 12.5–14.0 g / 0.4–0.5 oz

Olive-brown above with reddish brown crown. Buffy eyebrow and dark brown eye-line. Long, pointed bill thick at base. Underparts plain buffy white. Immatures resemble adults. Legs and feet pinkish.

### MACGILLIVRAY'S WARBLER *Oporornis tolmiei*

L 12.5–14.5 cm / 4.9–5.7" Wt 9–11 g / 0.3–0.4 oz

Resembles Mourning Warbler. Breeding male has slate-grey hood bordered below by blackish upper breast. White crescents above and below eye. Back, wings, and tail olive-green. Underparts yellow. Female, non-breeding males, and immatures similar but duller. Hood olive or brown with paler greyish or brownish throat.

### PAINTED REDSTART *Myioborus pictus*

L 12.5–14.5 cm / 4.9–5.7" Wt 7–9 g / 0.2–0.3 oz

Adult has glossy black upperparts, throat, and upper sides. White crescent beneath eye. Broad white patches on wing coverts and outer tail feathers. Breast and upper belly brilliant scarlet. Belly and undertail coverts whitish. Immatures similar but somewhat sooty black above and greyish below. Lack scarlet on underparts.

## Emberizidae / Sparrows and Allies

### GREEN-TAILED TOWHEE *Pipilo chlorurus*

L 16.5–18.0 cm / 6.5–7.1" Wt 24–34 g / 0.9–1.2 oz

Reddish brown crown. White throat bordered by black and white lines. Face and breast grey. Upperparts greyish green. Wings and tail greenish. Flanks greyish brown. Belly and undertail coverts dull white. Underwing coverts bright yellow. Juveniles lack reddish crown and are streaked above and below. Two narrow, buffy wing bars.

### SPOTTED TOWHEE *Pipilo maculatus*

L 18–21 cm / 7.0–8.5" Wt 34–45 g / 1.2–1.6 oz

Red eyes. Hood and upperparts of adult male black. Wings and back heavily spotted with white. Wide rufous sides. Black tail has large white patches on corners, best seen in flight. Lower breast and belly white. Undertail coverts buff. Female similar but with greyish brown hood and upperparts. Juveniles heavily streaked with adult-like tail pattern.

### CASSIN'S SPARROW *Aimophila cassinii*

L 13–15 cm / 5.2–5.8" Wt 17–22 g / 0.6–0.8 oz

Upperparts greyish, streaked with brown. Buff eyebrow and pale eye-ring. Long, conical bill. Two indistinct greyish wing bars. Long, rounded, dark grey tail has crosswise brown streaks and white tips on outer feathers. Underparts pale buff or whitish with some brown streaking on flanks. Juveniles similar but with more streaking on underparts.

### BACHMAN'S SPARROW *Aimophila aestivalis*

L 14–15 cm / 5.1–5.5" Wt 18–22 g / 0.6–0.8 oz

Grey above heavily streaked with chestnut brown. Sides of head buffy grey. Buff eyebrow and thin, dark brown eye-line. Wings and long, rounded tail brownish, tinged with rust. Breast and sides buffy grey. Belly white.

Juveniles resemble adults with pale eye-ring, and streaked throat, breast, and sides.

### BLACK-THROATED SPARROW *Amphispiza bilineata*
L 12.0-13.5 cm / 4.7-5.3" Wt 12-15 g / 0.4-0.5 oz

Upperparts dark grey. Prominent white eyebrow and malar streak. Lores and triangular throat-patch black. Bill dark grey. Wings greyish brown. Tail blackish brown with white outer feathers. Sides pale grey; otherwise, underparts white. Juveniles similar but much browner with buffy wings and brown-streaked underparts; lack black throat.

### BAIRD'S SPARROW *Ammodramus bairdii*
L 12.5-14.0 cm / 4.9-5.5" Wt 16.0-18.5 g / 0.6-0.7 oz

Crown and nape dark orange streaked with dark brown. Two brown spots behind ear. Dark brown whisker marks. Wings and tail dark brown edged with lighter brown and buff. Throat whitish. Breast pale buff sometimes streaked with dark brown. Belly white. Juveniles similar but with darker upperparts, more streaking on underparts, and less obvious orange coloration on head.

### GOLDEN-CROWNED SPARROW *Zonotrichia atricapilla*
L 15-18 cm / 6-7" Wt 25-30 g / 0.9-1.1 oz

Crown has dull gold patch bordered at sides and forehead by black. Inconspicuous white eye-ring. Otherwise, head and breast dark grey. Breeding adults have dark bill. Back and shoulders dusky brown heavily streaked with dark brown. Wings brown with two white wing bars. Long tail brown.

### CHESTNUT-COLLARED LONGSPUR *Calcarius ornatus*
L 14.0-16.5 cm / 5.5-6.5" Wt 17.5-19.5 g / 0.6-0.7 oz

Breeding male has black-and-white striped crown, buff face, and broad chestnut collar on nape. Upperparts brown with black streaks. White tail has blackish central triangle. Underparts black except white undertail coverts. Plumage patterns somewhat obscured by buff feather tips in winter. Female buff with fine dark streaks on crown and heavy blackish streaking on back. Indistinct chestnut nape. Immatures resemble female but somewhat plainer buff.

## Cardinalidae / Grosbeaks and Buntings

### BLACK-HEADED GROSBEAK *Pheucticus melanocephalus*
L 18.0-21.5 cm / 7.1-8.5" Wt 40-48 g / 1.4-1.7 oz

Heavy, conical bill black above, pale below. Adult male has black head and orangish brown breast, collar, flanks, and rump. Back black with tawny stripes. Wings and tail boldly patterned black and white. Lower belly yellowish. Female has buff-and-dark-brown-striped head. Underparts buffy yellow streaked with brown. Wings and tail dark brown. Immatures resemble female but with white head stripes and paler underparts.

### LAZULI BUNTING *Passerina amoena*
L 12.5-15.0 cm / 5-6" Wt 14-17 g / 0.5-0.6 oz

Adult male has bright blue head, back, and rump. Wings black with one bold, white wing bar. Breast and flanks orangish brown. Belly white. Tail black, edged in blue. Adult female and immatures greyish brown upperparts with light blue on wings and tail. Buff breast and white belly.

### VARIED BUNTING *Passerina versicolor*
L 11.5-14.0 cm / 4.5-5.5" Wt 12-15 g / 0.4-0.5 oz

Adult male iridescent purplish blue with bright red on nape, neck, and breast. Wings and tail bluish black. Colours visible in bright light, otherwise will appear uniformly dark. Adult female and immatures dark brownish grey with darker wings and tail. Lack conspicuous wing bars.

**PAINTED BUNTING** *Passerina ciris*

L 12.5–14.0 cm / 5.0–5.5" Wt 12–15 g / 0.4–0.5 oz

Adult male has bright blue head, green back, and red rump. Wings and tail brownish. Underparts bright red. Adult female green with darker back, wings, and tail. Underparts greenish yellow. Immatures resemble female but somewhat greyer.

## Icteridae / Blackbirds and Allies

**GREAT-TAILED GRACKLE** *Quiscalus mexicanus*

L 35.5–45.5 cm / 14.0–17.9" Wt 165–225 g / 6–8 oz

Adult male shiny black glossed with purple on head, neck, and back. Eyes yellow. Blue gloss on breast. Very long, scoop-shaped tail. First-year male dull black with brown eyes. Adult female warm olive-brown with slight metallic sheen. Pale yellow eyes. First-year female paler and greyer with pale eyebrow, brown eyes, and dark eye-line. Immatures resemble female but less glossy with streaked underparts.

**HOODED ORIOLE** *Icterus cucullatus*

L 18–20 cm / 7.0–7.8" Wt 30–40 g / 1.1–1.4 oz

Adult male has orangish yellow head with black face and throat. Back, wings, and tail black. Two white wing bars. Underparts and rump orangish yellow. Female greenish yellow; darker on upperparts. Wings greenish grey with two white wing bars. Immature male similar to female but somewhat more richly coloured with small black bib.

**BULLOCK'S ORIOLE** *Icterus bullockii*

L 18.0–21.5 cm / 7.0–8.5" Wt 30–45 g / 1.1–1.6 oz

Adult male has black crown, nape, chin, and back. Thin black eye-line. Eyebrow, cheek, and underparts bright orange. Wings mostly black with broad white patch. Rump orange. Tail black with orange outer feathers. Female pale grey with yellow foreparts, rump, and undertail coverts. Wings darker grey with two white wing bars. Immature male similar to female but more orangish yellow in coloration, with black chin and eye-line.

**SCOTT'S ORIOLE** *Icterus parisorum*

L 18.5–21.5 cm / 7.3–8.5" Wt 32–40 g / 1.1–1.4 oz

Adult male has black head, back, and breast. Wings black with yellow patch and white wing bars. Underparts and rump bright yellow. Tail yellow at base with broad black band at tip. Female and immature male greenish yellow with streaking on back. Wings have two whitish wing bars. Variable amounts of black on throat, except in younger females.

## Fringillidae / Finches

**BRAMBLING** *Fringilla montifringilla*

L 14–15 cm / 5.5–5.9" Wt 21–26 g / 0.8–0.9 oz

Breeding male has black head, upper back, and tail. Greyish bill. Wings black, boldly marked with orange and white. Rump white. Throat and breast orange. Belly and undertail coverts white. Flanks orangish spotted with black. Female and autumn male similarly marked in dull orange, buff, and grey. Black feathers edged in buffy orange. Bill pale yellow with dark tip.

**GRAY-CROWNED ROSY-FINCH** *Leucosticte tephrocotis*

L 14.0–16.5 cm / 5.5–6.5" Wt 22–28 g / 0.8–1.0 oz

Male has cinnamon-brown body with pinkish red on rump, shoulder, belly, and flanks. Grey crown. Black forehead and forecrown. White feathers cover nostrils. Cinnamon-brown cheeks. Wings and tail dark brown. Bill yellowish in winter, blackish in summer. Female similar but somewhat duller, particularly on head.

### CASSIN'S FINCH *Carpodacus cassinii*
L 14–15 cm / 5.5–6.0" Wt 20–23 g / 0.7–0.8 oz

Adult male has bright red crown and throat, with somewhat duller upper breast and rump. Nape and back brown with darker streaks. Wings and tail brown. Female and immatures have dark brown upperparts lightly streaked with white. Face brown with indistinct white streaking. Underparts whitish, heavily streaked with dark brown.

### LESSER GOLDFINCH *Carduelis psaltria*
L 10.0–11.5 cm / 4.0–4.5" Wt 8.0–11.5 g / 0.3–0.4 oz

Adult male has black crown, black to greenish upperparts. Crown, wings, and tail black. Wings have white patch at base of primaries and white edging on inner wing feathers. Tail black, white on inner webs. Underparts yellow. Female yellowish green overall, somewhat darker above. Throat and undertail coverts yellowish. Wings and tail like male's except duller. Immatures resemble female.

Passeridae / Old World Sparrows

### EURASIAN TREE SPARROW *Passer montanus*
L 12.5–14.0 cm / 5.0–5.5" Wt 20–24 g / 0.7–0.9 oz

Chocolate-brown crown. White cheek-patch and collar. Black ear coverts, lores, and chin. Bill blackish. Back brown with black streaks. Rump brown. Wings and tail brown edged with greyish buff. Wings have two narrow white wing bars. Underparts pale greyish brown, somewhat lighter on belly. Juveniles resemble adults but duller.

# Extirpated

## GALLIFORMES

Phasianidae / Partridges, Grouse, and Turkeys

### GREATER PRAIRIE-CHICKEN *Tympanuchus cupido*
L 43–46 cm / 17–18" Wt 900–1000 g / 2.0–2.2 lb

Head and neck mottled with brown, cinnamon, and buff. Buffy eyebrow and chin. Elongated dark feathers on neck (longer in male). Bold brown-and-buff bars on mantle, flanks, and underparts. Short, rounded brownish tail inconspicuously barred with buff in female. Displaying male erects neck feathers to form tall "horns." Immatures resemble female but somewhat buffier above and lacking elongated neck feathers.

# Extinct

## COLUMBIFORMES

Columbidae / Pigeons and Doves

### PASSENGER PIGEON *Ectopistes migratorius*
L 38–43 cm / 15–17" Wt 280–390 g / 10–14 oz

Extinct. Upperparts of adult male slaty blue with iridescent patch on nape. Wings greyish brown with white-tipped secondaries. Throat and breast pale cinnamon blending to white on abdomen. Central feathers of long tail brownish grey; outer feathers white. Adult female similar with duller plumage and shorter tail. Immatures resemble female, but white-tipped feathers on foreparts confer scaly appearance.

# GLOSSARY

**accidental**—a species that has been reported only a few times in a given area, and is well out of its normal range.

**agonistic**—aggressive or threatening, of interaction between individuals.

**caruncles**—fleshy, wrinkled bumps or knobs, usually on the head or neck; often brightly coloured.

**casual**—a species that does not occur annually, but demonstrates some pattern of occurrence over decades.

**cere**—soft covering at the base of the upper mandible.

**congener** (**congeneric**)—member of the same genus.

**conspecific**—member of the same species.

**coverts**—small feathers that usually overlie the bases of the flight feathers (*see also* **ear coverts**).

**crespuscular**—active at dawn or dusk.

**dabbling**—method of foraging in which the head and neck are submerged, but the body and tail protrude from the water.

**decurved**—turned downward.

**dihedral**—V-shaped.

**dimorphic**—having two different appearances.

**diurnal**—active during the day.

**drake**—male duck.

**ear coverts**—feathers overlying region of ears.

**eclipse plumage**—dull plumage worn by male ducks while growing new flight feathers.

**extirpation**—localized extinction in part of a species' range.

**eye crescents**—curved patches above and below eyes (usually) that form incomplete pale eye-ring.

**eye-ring**—feathers encircling the eye; often distinctively coloured (*see also* **orbital ring**).

**flight feathers**—long, characteristically shaped feathers of the wings and tail.

**gape**—mouth opening.

**genus** (pl. **genera**)—taxonomic group that includes a number of species.

**gular pouch**—bare patch of skin on throat.

**immature**—any young bird from the time it acquires juvenal plumage until it achieves full adult plumage. Some immatures are capable of breeding.

**juvenal plumage**—first coat of true feathers acquired before bird leaves nest.

**juvenile**—bird that has not reached sexual maturity.

**lek**—communal display ground.

**lores**—space between the eyes and bill.

**malar**—side of head between base of the bill, lores, eyes, and ear region.

**mandibles**—upper and lower parts of the bill.

**mantle**—upper back. Also includes scapulars and upperwing coverts when they are the same colour as the upper back.

**mirrors**—small white spots at or near the tips of dark primary wing feathers.

**monomorphic**—having the same appearance.

**morphs**—two or more distinct colour types that occur within a species.

**nail**—*see* **terminal nail.**

**nares**—*see* **perforate nares.**

**nape**—back of head above hindneck.

**nocturnal**—active at night.

**obligate brood parasite**—bird that does not build a nest or care for its young, but lays its eggs in the nest of another bird species.

**orbital ring**—bare skin encircling eye; often brightly coloured (*see also* **eye-ring**).

**patagium**—membrane that extends along front edge of wing from shoulder to wrist.

**pelagic**—over the open seas.

**perforate nares**—pierced nostrils that lack nasal septum.

**phases**—*see* **morphs.**

**polygynandrous**—mating system in which both males and females mate with two or more members of the opposite sex.

**primaries**—flight feathers on outermost part of wing.

**recurved**—turned upward.

**scapulars**—feathers over the shoulders.

**secondaries**—flight feathers adjacent to primaries at mid-wing.

**snood**—pendulous skin over the beak of a turkey.

**speculum**—brightly coloured patch on the trailing edge of the wings of ducks.

**stern**—back end.

**subadult**—generally individuals that are two to three years old and have not yet achieved full adult plumage.

**subterminal**—near, but not at, tip of wing or tail.

**syllable**—a repeated unit of a song.

**syrinx**—the "voice box" in birds.

**terminal nail**—horny tip on the upper mandible of waterfowl.

**tertiaries** (*also* **tertials**)—flight feathers adjacent to secondaries at inner wing.

**underparts**—lower surface from chin to tail.

**underprimary coverts**—feathers covering base of primaries on underside of wing.

**upperparts**—upper surface from forehead to tail.

**ventral**—lower (under-) side of the body.

**webs**—fleshy membrane joining toes in some aquatic birds.

**wettable**—not resistant to becoming soaked with water.

**wing lining**—underside of wing.

# TOPOGRAPHY OF A BIRD

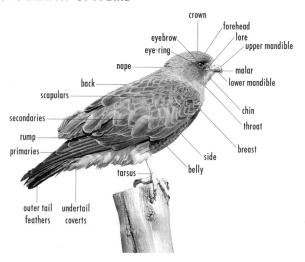

crown
forehead
eyebrow
lore
eye-ring
upper mandible
nape
malar
back
lower mandible
scapulars
chin
secondaries
throat
rump
primaries
breast
side
belly
tarsus
outer tail feathers
undertail coverts

# CHECKLIST OF ONTARIO BIRDS

This list contains 473 species of birds that have been recorded officially in Ontario. Species marked with an asterisk (*) are known to have bred in the province. Accidental species are indicated with an (A), and extinct or extirpated species by an (E).

**LOONS**
- ☐ Red-throated Loon *
- ☐ Pacific Loon *
- ☑ Common Loon *
- ☐ Yellow-billed Loon (A)

**GREBES**
- ☑ Pied-billed Grebe *
- ☐ Horned Grebe *
- ☑ Red-necked Grebe *
- ☐ Eared Grebe *
- ☐ Western Grebe (A)

**SHEARWATERS AND PETRELS**
- ☐ Northern Fulmar
- ☐ Black-capped Petrel (A)
- ☐ Greater Shearwater (A)
- ☐ Audubon's Shearwater (A)

**STORM-PETRELS**
- ☐ Wilson's Storm-Petrel (A)
- ☐ Leach's Storm-Petrel (A)
- ☐ Band-rumped Storm-Petrel (A)

**GANNETS**
- ☐ Northern Gannet

**PELICANS**
- ☐ American White Pelican *
- ☐ Brown Pelican (A)

**CORMORANTS**
- ☑ Double-crested Cormorant *
- ☐ Great Cormorant (A)

**ANHINGA**
- ☐ Anhinga (A)

**FRIGATEBIRDS**
- ☐ Magnificent Frigatebird (A)

**HERONS AND BITTERNS**
- ☑ American Bittern *
- ☐ Least Bittern *
- ☑ Great Blue Heron *
- ☑ Great Egret *
- ☐ Snowy Egret *
- ☑ Little Blue Heron

- ☐ Tricolored Heron
- ☐ Cattle Egret *
- ☑ Green Heron *
- ☑ Black-crowned Night-Heron *
- ☐ Yellow-crowned Night-Heron

**IBISES**
- ☐ White Ibis (A)
- ☐ Glossy Ibis
- ☐ White-faced Ibis (A)

**STORKS**
- ☐ Wood Stork

**VULTURES**
- ☐ Black Vulture
- ☑ Turkey Vulture *

**DUCKS, GEESE, AND SWANS**
- ☐ Black-bellied Whistling-Duck (A)
- ☐ Fulvous Whistling-Duck (A)
- ☐ Greater White-fronted Goose
- ☐ Snow Goose *
- ☐ Ross's Goose *
- ☑ Canada Goose *
- ☐ Brant
- ☑ Mute Swan *
- ☐ Trumpeter Swan
- ☐ Tundra Swan *
- ☐ Wood Duck *
- ☑ Gadwall *
- ☐ Eurasian Wigeon
- ☐ American Wigeon *
- ☐ American Black Duck *
- ☑ Mallard *
- ☐ Blue-winged Teal *
- ☐ Cinnamon Teal *
- ☐ Northern Shoveler *
- ☐ Northern Pintail *
- ☐ Garganey (A)
- ☐ Green-winged Teal *
- ☐ Canvasback *
- ☐ Redhead *
- ☐ Ring-necked Duck *
- ☐ Tufted Duck

- ❏ Greater Scaup *
- ❏ Lesser Scaup *
- ❏ King Eider *
- ❏ Common Eider *
- ❏ Harlequin Duck
- ❏ Surf Scoter *
- ❏ White-winged Scoter *
- ❏ Black Scoter
- ❏ Long-tailed Duck (Oldsquaw) *
- ❏ Bufflehead *
- ❏ Common Goldeneye *
- ❏ Barrow's Goldeneye
- ❏ Smew (A)
- ☑ Hooded Merganser *
- ☑ Common Merganser *
- ☑ Red-breasted Merganser *
- ❏ Ruddy Duck *

## HAWKS, KITES, AND EAGLES
- ☑ Osprey *
- ❏ Swallow-tailed Kite (A)
- ❏ Mississippi Kite
- ☑ Bald Eagle *
- ❏ Northern Harrier *
- ☑ Sharp-shinned Hawk *
- ❏ Cooper's Hawk *
- ☑ Northern Goshawk *
- ❏ Red-shouldered Hawk *
- ❏ Broad-winged Hawk *
- ☑ Swainson's Hawk
- ☑ Red-tailed Hawk *
- ❏ Ferruginous Hawk (A)
- ☑ Rough-legged Hawk *
- ❏ Golden Eagle *

## CARACARAS AND FALCONS
- ❏ Crested Caracara (A)
- ☑ American Kestrel *
- ❏ Merlin *
- ❏ Gyrfalcon
- ❏ Peregrine Falcon *
- ❏ Prairie Falcon (A)

## PARTRIDGES, GROUSE, AND TURKEYS
- ❏ Gray Partridge *
- ❏ Ring-necked Pheasant *
- ❏ Ruffed Grouse *
- ❏ Spruce Grouse *

- ❏ Willow Ptarmigan *
- ❏ Rock Ptarmigan
- ❏ Sharp-tailed Grouse *
- ❏ Greater Prairie-Chicken * (E)
- ☑ Wild Turkey *

## NEW WORLD QUAIL
- ❏ Northern Bobwhite *

## RAILS, GALLINULES, AND COOTS
- ❏ Yellow Rail *
- ❏ Black Rail *
- ❏ King Rail *
- ❏ Virginia Rail *
- ❏ Sora *
- ❏ Purple Gallinule (A)
- ☑ Common Moorhen *
- ❏ American Coot *

## CRANES
- ❏ Sandhill Crane *
- ❏ Whooping Crane (A)

## PLOVERS
- ❏ Black-bellied Plover
- ❏ American Golden-Plover *
- ❏ Mongolian Plover (A)
- ❏ Snowy Plover (A)
- ❏ Wilson's Plover (A)
- ❏ Semipalmated Plover *
- ❏ Piping Plover *
- ❏ Killdeer *

## OYSTERCATCHERS
- ❏ American Oystercatcher (A)

## STILTS AND AVOCETS
- ❏ Black-necked Stilt (A)
- ❏ American Avocet *

## SANDPIPERS AND PHALAROPES
- ❏ Greater Yellowlegs *
- ❏ Lesser Yellowlegs *
- ☑ Spotted Redshank (A)
- ❏ Solitary Sandpiper *
- ❏ Willet
- ❏ Wandering Tattler (A)
- ☑ Spotted Sandpiper *
- ❏ Upland Sandpiper *
- ❏ Eskimo Curlew (A)
- ❏ Whimbrel *
- ❏ Slender-billed Curlew (A)

- ❏ Long-billed Curlew (A)
- ❏ Black-tailed Godwit (A)
- ❏ Hudsonian Godwit *
- ❏ Marbled Godwit *
- ❏ Ruddy Turnstone
- ❏ Red Knot
- ❏ Sanderling
- ❏ Semipalmated Sandpiper *
- ❏ Western Sandpiper
- ❏ Little Stint (A)
- ❏ Least Sandpiper *
- ❏ White-rumped Sandpiper
- ❏ Baird's Sandpiper
- ❏ Pectoral Sandpiper *
- ❏ Sharp-tailed Sandpiper (A)
- ❏ Purple Sandpiper
- ❏ Dunlin *
- ❏ Curlew Sandpiper
- ❏ Stilt Sandpiper *
- ❏ Buff-breasted Sandpiper
- ❏ Ruff
- ❏ Short-billed Dowitcher *
- ❏ Long-billed Dowitcher
- ☑ Common Snipe *
- ☑ American Woodcock *
- ❏ Wilson's Phalarope *
- ❏ Red-necked Phalarope *
- ❏ Red Phalarope

### GULLS, TERNS, AND ALLIES
- ❏ Pomarine Jaeger
- ❏ Parasitic Jaeger *
- ❏ Long-tailed Jaeger
- ❏ Laughing Gull
- ❏ Franklin's Gull
- ❏ Little Gull *
- ☑ Black-headed Gull
- ❏ Bonaparte's Gull *
- ❏ Heerman's Gull (A)
- ❏ Mew Gull
- ☑ Ring-billed Gull *
- ❏ California Gull *
- ☑ Herring Gull *
- ❏ Thayer's Gull
- ❏ Iceland Gull
- ❏ Lesser Black-backed Gull
- ❏ Slaty-backed Gull (A)
- ❏ Glaucous Gull

- ☑ Great Black-backed Gull *
- ❏ Sabine's Gull
- ❏ Black-legged Kittiwake
- ❏ Ross's Gull (A)
- ❏ Ivory Gull
- ☑ Caspian Tern *
- ❏ Royal Tern (A)
- ❏ Sandwich Tern (A)
- ☑ Common Tern *
- ❏ Arctic Tern *
- ❏ Forster's Tern *
- ❏ Least Tern *
- ❏ Sooty Tern (A)
- ❏ White-winged Tern (A)
- ❏ Black Tern *
- ❏ Black Skimmer (A)

### AUKS, MURRES, AND PUFFINS
- ❏ Dovekie (A)
- ❏ Thick-billed Murre (A)
- ❏ Razorbill (A)
- ❏ Black Guillemot *
- ❏ Long-billed Murrelet (A)
- ❏ Ancient Murrelet (A)
- ❏ Atlantic Puffin (A)

### PIGEONS AND DOVES
- ☑ Rock Dove *
- ❏ Band-tailed Pigeon (A)
- ❏ Eurasian Collared-Dove (A)
- ❏ White-winged Dove (A)
- ☑ Mourning Dove *
- ❏ Passenger Pigeon * (E)
- ❏ Inca Dove (A)
- ❏ Common Ground-Dove (A)

### CUCKOOS
- ❏ Black-billed Cuckoo *
- ❏ Yellow-billed Cuckoo *
- ❏ Groove-billed Ani (A)

### BARN OWLS
- ❏ Barn Owl *

### TYPICAL OWLS
- ❏ Eastern Screech-Owl *
- ❏ Great Horned Owl *
- ❏ Snowy Owl
- ❏ Northern Hawk Owl *
- ❏ Burrowing Owl (A)

- ❏ Barred Owl *
- ❏ Great Gray Owl *
- ❏ Long-eared Owl *
- ❏ Short-eared Owl *
- ❏ Boreal Owl *
- ❏ Northern Saw-whet Owl *

## NIGHTJARS
- ❏ Lesser Nighthawk (A)
- ❏ Common Nighthawk *
- ❏ Common Poorwill (A)
- ❏ Chuck-will's-widow *
- ❏ Whip-poor-will *

## SWIFTS
- ❏ Chimney Swift *

## HUMMINGBIRDS
- ❏ Green Violet-ear (A)
- ❏ Broad-billed Hummingbird (A)
- ☑ Ruby-throated Hummingbird *
- ❏ Black-chinned Hummingbird (A)
- ❏ Rufous Hummingbird (A)

## KINGFISHERS
- ☑ Belted Kingfisher *

## WOODPECKERS
- ❏ Lewis's Woodpecker (A)
- ❏ Red-headed Woodpecker *
- ❏ Red-bellied Woodpecker *
- ❏ Yellow-bellied Sapsucker *
- ☑ Downy Woodpecker *
- ☑ Hairy Woodpecker *
- ❏ Three-toed Woodpecker *
- ❏ Black-backed Woodpecker *
- ☑ Northern Flicker *
- ❏ Pileated Woodpecker *

## FLYCATCHERS
- ❏ Olive-sided Flycatcher *
- ❏ Western Wood-Pewee (A)
- ☑ Eastern Wood-Pewee * h.
- ☑ Yellow-bellied Flycatcher *
- ❏ Acadian Flycatcher *
- ☑ Alder Flycatcher *
- ❏ Willow Flycatcher *
- ☑ Least Flycatcher *
- ❏ Gray Flycatcher (A)
- ❏ Dusky Flycatcher (A)

- ☑ Eastern Phoebe *
- ❏ Say's Phoebe (A)
- ❏ Vermilion Flycatcher (A)
- ❏ Ash-throated Flycatcher (A)
- ❏ Great Crested Flycatcher *
- ❏ Sulphur-bellied Flycatcher (A)
- ❏ Variegated Flycatcher (A)
- ❏ Tropical/Couch's Kingbird (A)
- ❏ Cassin's Kingbird (A)
- ❏ Western Kingbird *
- ☑ Eastern Kingbird *
- ❏ Gray Kingbird (A)
- ❏ Scissor-tailed Flycatcher
- ❏ Fork-tailed Flycatcher (A)

## SHRIKES
- ❏ Loggerhead Shrike *
- ❏ Northern Shrike *

## VIREOS
- ❏ White-eyed Vireo *
- ❏ Bell's Vireo (A)
- ❏ Black-capped Vireo (A)
- ❏ Yellow-throated Vireo *
- ❏ Plumbeous Vireo (A)
- ❏ Blue-headed Vireo *
- ❏ Warbling Vireo *
- ❏ Philadelphia Vireo *
- ❏ Red-eyed Vireo *

## CROWS AND JAYS
- ❏ Gray Jay *
- ☑ Blue Jay *
- ❏ Clark's Nutcracker (A)
- ❏ Black-billed Magpie *
- ❏ Eurasian Jackdaw (A)
- ☑ American Crow *
- ❏ Fish Crow (A)
- ☑ Common Raven *

## LARKS
- ❏ Horned Lark *

## SWALLOWS
- ☑ Purple Martin *
- ☑ Tree Swallow *
- ❏ Violet-green Swallow (A)
- ☑ Northern Rough-winged Swallow *
- ☑ Bank Swallow *

☐ Cliff Swallow *
☐ Cave Swallow (A)
☐ Barn Swallow *

## CHICKADEES AND TITMICE
☐ Carolina Chickadee (A)
☑ Black-capped Chickadee *
☐ Boreal Chickadee *
☐ Tufted Titmouse *

## NUTHATCHES
☑ Red-breasted Nuthatch *
☑ White-breasted Nuthatch *

## CREEPERS
☑ Brown Creeper *

## WRENS
☐ Rock Wren (A)
☐ Carolina Wren *
☐ Bewick's Wren *
☑ House Wren *
☐ Winter Wren *
☐ Sedge Wren *
☐ Marsh Wren *

## KINGLETS
☐ Golden-crowned Kinglet *
☐ Ruby-crowned Kinglet *

## GNATCATCHERS
☐ Blue-gray Gnatcatcher *

## THRUSHES
☐ Siberian Rubythroat (A)
☐ Northern Wheatear
☐ Eastern Bluebird *
☐ Mountain Bluebird
☐ Townsend's Solitaire
☐ Veery *
☐ Gray-cheeked Thrush *
☐ Bicknell's Thrush (A)
☐ Swainson's Thrush *
☑ Hermit Thrush *
☐ Wood Thrush *
☐ Eurasian Blackbird (A)
☐ Fieldfare (A)
☑ American Robin *
☐ Varied Thrush

## MOCKINGBIRDS AND THRASHERS
☑ Gray Catbird *

☑ Northern Mockingbird *
☐ Sage Thrasher (A)
☐ Brown Thrasher *

## STARLINGS
☑ European Starling *

## PIPITS
☐ American Pipit *
☐ Sprague's Pipit (A)

## WAXWINGS
☐ Bohemian Waxwing *
☑ Cedar Waxwing *

## SILKY-FLYCATCHERS
☐ Phainopepla (A)

## WOOD-WARBLERS
☐ Blue-winged Warbler *
☐ Golden-winged Warbler *
☐ Tennessee Warbler *
☐ Orange-crowned Warbler *
☑ Nashville Warbler *
☐ Virginia's Warbler (A)
☐ Northern Parula *
☐ Yellow Warbler *
☐ Chestnut-sided Warbler *
☑ Magnolia Warbler *
☐ Cape May Warbler *
☑ Black-throated Blue Warbler *
☐ Yellow-rumped Warbler *
☐ Black-throated Gray Warbler (A)
☐ Black-throated Green Warbler *
☐ Townsend's Warbler (A)
☐ Hermit Warbler (A)
☐ Blackburnian Warbler *
☐ Yellow-throated Warbler
☐ Pine Warbler *
☐ Kirtland's Warbler *
☐ Prairie Warbler *
☐ Palm Warbler *
☐ Bay-breasted Warbler *
☐ Blackpoll Warbler *
☐ Cerulean Warbler *
☑ Black-and-white Warbler *
☐ American Redstart *
☐ Prothonotary Warbler *
☐ Worm-eating Warbler
☐ Swainson's Warbler (A)
☐ Ovenbird *

- ❏ Northern Waterthrush *
- ❏ Louisiana Waterthrush *
- ❏ Kentucky Warbler
- ❏ Connecticut Warbler *
- ❏ Mourning Warbler *
- ❏ MacGillivray's Warbler (A)
- ☑ Common Yellowthroat *
- ❏ Hooded Warbler *
- ❏ Wilson's Warbler *
- ☑ Canada Warbler *
- ❏ Painted Redstart (A)
- ❏ Yellow-breasted Chat *

## TANAGERS
- ❏ Summer Tanager
- ❏ Scarlet Tanager *
- ❏ Western Tanager

## SPARROWS AND ALLIES
- ❏ Green-tailed Towhee (A)
- ❏ Spotted Towhee (A)
- ❏ Eastern Towhee *
- ❏ Cassin's Sparrow (A)
- ❏ Bachman's Sparrow (A)
- ❏ American Tree Sparrow *
- ❏ Chipping Sparrow *
- ☑ Clay-colored Sparrow *
- ❏ Field Sparrow *
- ❏ Vesper Sparrow *
- ❏ Lark Sparrow *
- ❏ Black-throated Sparrow (A)
- ❏ Lark Bunting
- ❏ Savannah Sparrow *
- ❏ Grasshopper Sparrow *
- ❏ Baird's Sparrow (A)
- ❏ Henslow's Sparrow *
- ❏ Le Conte's Sparrow *
- ❏ Nelson's Sharp-tailed Sparrow *
- ❏ Fox Sparrow *
- ☑ Song Sparrow *
- ❏ Lincoln's Sparrow *
- ❏ Swamp Sparrow *
- ❏ White-throated Sparrow *
- ❏ Harris's Sparrow *
- ❏ White-crowned Sparrow *
- ❏ Golden-crowned Sparrow (A)
- ❏ Dark-eyed Junco *
- ❏ Lapland Longspur *
- ❏ Smith's Longspur *

- ❏ Chestnut-collared Longspur (A)
- ❏ Snow Bunting *

## CARDINALS AND ALLIES
- ☑ Northern Cardinal *
- ❏ Rose-breasted Grosbeak *
- ❏ Black-headed Grosbeak (A)
- ❏ Blue Grosbeak
- ❏ Lazuli Bunting (A)
- ❏ Indigo Bunting *
- ❏ Varied Bunting (A)
- ❏ Painted Bunting (A)
- ❏ Dickcissel *

## BLACKBIRDS
- ❏ Bobolink *
- ☑ Red-winged Blackbird *
- ❏ Eastern Meadowlark *
- ❏ Western Meadowlark *
- ❏ Yellow-headed Blackbird *
- ❏ Rusty Blackbird *
- ❏ Brewer's Blackbird *
- ☑ Common Grackle *
- ❏ Great-tailed Grackle (A)
- ❏ Brown-headed Cowbird *
- ❏ Orchard Oriole *
- ❏ Hooded Oriole (A)
- ❏ Bullock's Oriole (A)
- ❏ Baltimore Oriole *
- ❏ Scott's Oriole (A)

## FINCHES
- ❏ Brambling (A)
- ❏ Gray-crowned Rosy-Finch (A)
- ❏ Pine Grosbeak *
- ☑ Purple Finch *
- ❏ Cassin's Finch (A)
- ☑ House Finch *
- ❏ Red Crossbill *
- ❏ White-winged Crossbill *
- ❏ Common Redpoll *
- ❏ Hoary Redpoll
- ☑ Pine Siskin *
- ❏ Lesser Goldfinch (A)
- ☑ American Goldfinch *
- ❏ Evening Grosbeak *

## OLD WORLD SPARROWS
- ☑ House Sparrow *
- ❏ Eurasian Tree Sparrow (A)

# INDEX

# PHOTOGRAPHERS

Sam Barone, 52, 54, 56, 57, 61A, 62A, 110A, 119, 182, 223, 268, 346, 363, 379A

Barry Cherriere, 31B, 68A, 80A, 115, 122, 174A, 176, 330B

Scott Fairbairn, 26, 35, 37, 38, 39, 42, 89A, 121, 123, 130, 186, 209, 241, 244, 257, 272 282, 284, 297, 309, 310A, 311A, 313A, 314 A, 318, 323A, 325, 326, 329B, 367, 375A, 380A, 380B

Kim Flynn, 22, 43, 44, 45, 46, 47, 65A, 66A, 67A, 69A, 69B, 70A, 70B, 71A, 74B, 75B, 76A, 76B, 78A, 78B, 79A, 79B, 81A, 82A, 83A, 84A, 85B, 86A, 87A, 95, 98, 102, 114, 118, 131, 136, 142, 151, 156, 159, 167, 171, 178, 180, 181, 190, 193, 195, 197, 201, 217, 229, 231, 232, 233, 234, 237, 238, 248, 261, 263, 269, 270, 276, 277, 283, 290, 294, 295, 296, 299, 306, 307, 311B, 312A, 312B, 314B, 315, 323B, 324B, 327, 328B, 331, 332, 335, 336, 337, 339, 341, 342, 344, 349, 352, 354, 355B, 356B, 357A, 361A, 362, 365, 378, 381B

Albert Kuhnigk, 29, 41, 100, 112, 125, 199, 200, 202, 246

John P. Marechal, 91, 355A

Robert McCaw, 24, 48, 58, 71B, 73, 80B, 96, 99, 109, 110B, 111A, 111B, 113, 126, 132, 133, 137, 139, 140, 145, 155, 157, 158, 173, 189, 203, 205, 212, 214, 218, 220, 224, 227, 245, 250, 251, 254, 258, 262, 266, 274, 275, 281, 291, 292, 298, 322, 329A, 334, 338, 340, 345, 347, 351, 356A, 358A, 359, 360A, 360B, 361B, 364A, 364B, 366, 368B, 369A, 370A, 370B, 371A, 371B, 372A, 372B, 373B, 374B, 375B, 376

George K. Peck, 27, 31A, 164, 185, 192, 239, 240, 264, 265, 319, 369B, 379B

Mark K. Peck, 20B, 21, 25, 51, 53, 59A, 59B, 86B, 92, 103, 127, 128, 141, 143, 147, 150, 152, 153, 162R, 177, 183, 184, 221, 222, 247, 253, 256, 259, 350, 373A

John Reaume, 32, 33, 40, 134, 236, 242, 243, 285, 289, 293, 300, 301A, 302, 304A, 313B, 317, 320, 333, 348, 374A

James R. Richards, 50, 55, 63A, 63B, 68B, 74A, 120, 129, 138, 160, 161, 162L, 163, 169A, 179, 198, 204, 207, 211, 216, 219, 226, 228, 230, 280, 324A, 330A, 358B, 381A

A. H. Rider, 60, 67B, 72, 94, 168A, 328A, 377

Royal Ontario Museum, 75A

Michael D. Stubblefield, 20, 62B, 84B, 87B, 108A, 135, 144, 146, 148, 149, 165, 168B, 169B, 170, 172, 179, 208, 235, 252B, 260, 267, 271, 279, 286, 287, 288, 301B, 303

VALAN: Anthony J. Bond, 154; Ken Cole, 101; John Eastcott & Yva Momatiuk, 104; Jeff Foott, 108B; E. Kootenays, 249; Wayne Lankinen, 36; B. Lyon, 175; John Mitchell, 97; Wilf Schurig, 255; Robert C. Simpson, 308, 343; Y. R. Tymstra, 166

VIREO: G. Bailey, 278; R. Behrstock, 174B; R. & N. Bowers, 81B; J. Cancalosi, 105; R. Curtis, 316, 321; Bob De Lange, 107; J. Dunning, 304B; J. Heidecker, 82B; A. & E. Morris, 61B, 64, 65B, 66B, 77A, 77B, 83B, 353, 368A; R. Saldino, 252A; C. R. Sams II & J. F. Stoick, 117; B. Schorre, 310B, 357B; R. & A. Simpson, 85A; Michael D. Stubblefield, 305; F. Truslow, 89B; T. J. Ulrich, 187; T. Vezo, 273; B. K. Wheeler, 90, 93; J. R. Woodward, 196

# ACKNOWLEDGEMENTS

I would like to thank the many individuals whose expertise and dedication contributed so much to this work. They are as follows— project director, Glen Ellis, for his vision, optimism, and enthusiasm; senior consultants (ornithology) Dr. Ross James, Mark Peck, and Dr. James Rising, for their valuable comments and advice; the many photographers whose quest for the perfect image took them into field, meadow, stream, marsh, and swamp; photo researchers Dora Nudelman and Pamela Vega, who looked at literally thousands of photographs, in search of those same perfect images; editors Andrea Gallagher, Alexander Schultz, and Donna Williams, for their meticulous attention to the text; designers Virginia Morin and Tara Winterhalt, who did so much to make this a beautiful book; and production managers Victoria Black and Krystyna Ross, who supervised the printing. Thanks also to Douglas Gibson, Brian Porter, and Jonathan Webb, for their encouragement, and to Mark Lockhart and the Faculty of Forestry and the Forest Environment, Lakehead University, who assisted with the distribution maps. I am grateful to my family for their consideration through the course of this work, and especially to my husband, Ron, whose devotion inspires and sustains me.

*Janice M. Hughes*

The Royal Ontario Museum gratefully acknowledges the Louise Hawley Stone Charitable Trust for its generous support of this publication.

McClelland & Stewart acknowledges the financial support of the Government of Canada through the Book Publishing Industry Development Program and that of the Government of Ontario through the Ontario Media Development Corporation's Ontario Book Initiative. We further acknowledge the support of the Canada Council for the Arts and the Ontario Arts Council for our publishing program.

Film, colour separations, and scans by Quadratone Graphics Ltd., Toronto, Ontario.

Printed and bound in Canada

**Front Cover**: *Little Blue Heron*, John Reaume

This guide includes all of the birds observed and observable in Ontario, both rare and common species. One of the joys of birding is the thrill of spotting a rare and beautiful specimen. The elegant Little Blue Heron, a rare to occasional visitor from March to December, ranges in Ontario from Pelee Island to Ottawa, and as far north as Thunder Bay.

**Back Cover** (clockwise from top left): *Pectoral Sandpiper*, Michael D. Stubblefield; *Hooded Merganser*, Jim Flynn; *Great Gray Owl*, Jim Flynn; *Indigo Bunting*, Robert McCaw; *Canada Warbler*, Scott Fairbairn; *King Eider*, James R. Richards; *Scarlet Tanager*, Robert McCaw; *Snowy Egret*, Scott Fairbairn; *Gyrfalcon*, John Eastcott & Yva Momatiuk / VALAN.